THE LITERATURE OF ABSOLUTE WAR

This book explores for the first time the literature of absolute war in connection to World War II. From a transnational and comparative standpoint, it addresses a set of theoretical, historical, and literary questions, shedding new light on the nature of absolute war, the literature on the world war of 1939–45, and modern war writing in general. It determines the main features of the language of absolute war, and how it gravitates around fundamental semantic clusters. *The Literature of Absolute War* studies the variegated responses given by literary authors to the extreme and seemingly unsolvable challenges posed by absolute war to epistemology, ethics, and language. It also delves into the different poetics that articulate the writing on absolute war, placing special emphasis on four literary practices: traditional realism, traumatic realism, the fantastic, and catastrophic modernism.

NIL SANTIÁÑEZ is Professor of Spanish and International Studies at Saint Louis University. He has authored *Wittgenstein's Ethics and Modern Warfare* (2018); *Topographies of Fascism: Habitus, Space, and Writing in Twentieth-Century Spain* (2013); *Goya/Clausewitz: Paradigmas de la guerra absoluta* (2009); *Investigaciones literarias: Modernidad, historia de la literatura y modernismos* (2002); *Ángel Ganivet: Una bibliografía anotada, 1892–1995* (1996); *De la Luna a Mecanópolis: Antología de la ciencia ficción española 1832–1913* (1995); and *Ángel Ganivet, escritor modernista: Teoría y novela en el fin de siglo español* (1994).

THE LITERATURE
OF ABSOLUTE WAR

Transnationalism and World War II

NIL SANTIÁÑEZ

Saint Louis University

CAMBRIDGE
UNIVERSITY PRESS

CAMBRIDGE
UNIVERSITY PRESS

University Printing House, Cambridge CB2 8BS, United Kingdom

One Liberty Plaza, 20th Floor, New York, NY 10006, USA

477 Williamstown Road, Port Melbourne, VIC 3207, Australia

314-321, 3rd Floor, Plot 3, Splendor Forum, Jasola District Centre, New Delhi - 110025, India

103 Penang Road, #05-06/07, Visioncrest Commercial, Singapore 238467

Cambridge University Press is part of the University of Cambridge.

It furthers the University's mission by disseminating knowledge in the pursuit of
education, learning and research at the highest international levels of excellence.

www.cambridge.org
Information on this title: www.cambridge.org/9781108817035
DOI: 10.1017/9781108861144

First published 2020
First paperback edition 2022

A catalogue record for this publication is available from the British Library

Library of Congress Cataloging in Publication data
Names: Santiáñez-Tió, Nil, author.
TITLE: The literature of absolute war : transnationalism and World War II / Nil Santiáñez.
DESCRIPTION: New York : Cambridge University Press, 2020. | Includes bibliographical
references and index.
IDENTIFIERS: LCCN 2019052907 (print) | LCCN 2019052908 (ebook) | ISBN 9781108495127
(hardback) | ISBN 9781108817035 (paperback) | ISBN 9781108861144 (epub)
SUBJECTS: LCSH: War in literature. | World War, 1939–1945–Literature and the war.
CLASSIFICATION: LCC PN56.W3 S314 2020 (print) | LCC PN56.W3 (ebook) |
DDC 809/.933582824–DC23
LC record available at https://lccn.loc.gov/2019052907
LC ebook record available at https://lccn.loc.gov/2019052908

ISBN 978-1-108-49512-7 Hardback
ISBN 978-1-108-81703-5 Paperback

Cambridge University Press has no responsibility for the persistence or
accuracy of URLs for external or third-party internet websites referred to in
this publication, and does not guarantee that any content on such websites is,
or will remain, accurate or appropriate.

Contents

Acknowledgements

I owe a debt of gratitude to several loyal friends and admired colleagues who have assisted me in various ways. First of all, I am most thankful to Vincent Casaregola and Justin Crumbaugh. In spite of their many projects and professional engagements, they found the time to meticulously read the entire manuscript of *The Literature of Absolute War*, and made shrewd remarks as well as valuable suggestions. Edward Baker, Albert Freixa, Roberto Ludovico, Michael Papio, Gonzalo Pontón Gijón, Silvia Sesé, and Noël M. Valis kindly read and commented on parts of this book. With John Wade I spent countless hours talking about the Second World War, trauma theory, and the Nazi destruction of the European Jews. With António Horta Fernandes I have had the privilege to exchange stimulating emails on all sorts of matters related to the history and philosophy of war. I am also grateful to Jim Hicks for his many and excellent recommendations, and to Jean-Louis Pautrot for our conversations on French war literature. The two anonymous readers of this monograph engaged with my study on its own terms; their enthusiasm and praising comments reassured me, while their critical remarks helped me to improve my work. I cannot forget here my tireless and thorough research assistant, Richard Leo Gamp. I also would like to express my profound gratitude to the late José Antonio Barbón Rodríguez, who several years ago played a determining role in fostering my investigations in comparative literature by providing me with the means and an idyllic setting (his house with *hortus conclusus* in Königswinter) for refining my knowledge of German literature and culture. In more than one sense, without him and his wife Diana Auad this book probably would have never been written. As always, María Soledad Barbón read early drafts of the book, and she gave me invaluable advice in addition to her unconditional support.

I have included in this book revised versions of passages from previously published pieces: "Representations of the Void, or, The Language of Silence in the Fiction on the Strategic Bombing of Germany," *Neophilologus* 102.3

(2018), 403–20; "Aerial Bombing and Catastrophic Modernism," *Neohelicon* 45.1 (2018), 229–48; and "Kempowski's War," *The German Quarterly* 89.4 (2016), 447–62. I thank their editors-in-chief for kindly granting me permission to use these articles.

The Literature of Absolute War was written at Meshuggah Café (St. Louis, Missouri) and Cushman Market & Café (Amherst, Massachusetts). I truly enjoyed putting together the pieces of this jigsaw on one of their tables while drinking tea, and can hardly imagine places more conducive for writing than those two public establishments.

Note on the Text

Unless otherwise indicated, all translations from German, French, Italian, and Portuguese are mine. Except for works written in Russian or Japanese, whose titles appear in English only, the titles of primary sources are given in the original, followed by an English translation the first time that they are quoted in each chapter.

All italics within quotations throughout the text appear in the original; when the emphasis is mine, I point it out in parenthesis.

Preface
Targets

At 8:15 local time on the sunny morning of August 6, 1945, a Boeing B-29 Superfortress piloted by Colonel Paul W. Tibbets dropped an atomic bomb on the Japanese city of Hiroshima. Code-named "Little Boy," the bomb slowly descended on a parachute towards its target until it went off at the height of 580 meters above sea level, its blast wiping out 90 percent of the city and killing 80,000 people. Three days later, on August 9, another B-29, flown by Major Charles W. Sweeney, dropped an atomic weapon on Nagasaki. It was 11:02 a.m. Nagasaki time when "Fat Man" (the bomb's code name) detonated, completely razing to the ground 63 percent of the city, destroying 90 percent of its buildings and constructions, and causing the instant death of approximately 45,000 men and women. By November 1945, the combined death toll of those killed outright by the bombs and those who died days, weeks, or months after the blasts as a result of their wounds or the radiation delivered by the atomic weapons surpassed the figure of 200,000. Although scholars have recently argued that the Japanese did not capitulate because of the atomic attacks on their homeland (the Japanese government decided to surrender to the Americans only after learning about the Soviet invasion of Manchuria),[1] the truth is that dropping two atomic weapons on civilian targets put a murderous closure to a war that was, and still is, the deadliest one on record. The world war of 1939–45 is the military conflict in which absolute war reached extremes never attained before.[2] Between 21 and

---

[1] See Tsuyoshi Hasegawa, "Were the Atomic Bombings of Hiroshima and Nagasaki Justified?," *Bombing Civilians: A Twentieth-Century History*, ed. Yuki Tanaka and Marilyn B. Young (New York: New Press, 2009), 97–134.

[2] A term coined by Carl von Clausewitz, "absolute war" is at once a theoretical concept and a type of war. As a theoretical concept, it refers to war in itself, considered as an independent and unconditioned reality that impels real military conflicts to an escalation of hostilities as well as the performance of its intrinsic extremes of violence and animus. Usually, external factors such as policy control and halt the enormous destructive power that is at the core of the nature of war. In most

25 million troops were killed during the war, and at least 50 million civilians died either as a direct consequence of the conflict or because of catastrophes triggered by the war. Leaving aside the Nazi destruction of the European Jews (a war-related event that has its own specificity), the use of the atomic bombs devised by the scientists of the Manhattan Project brought to the highest possible pitch the merciless violence displayed in many battles (particularly those that took place on the eastern front and the Pacific theater of war) for almost six years, as well as the immense destruction of lives, cultural memory, and human habitation caused by the round-the-clock aerial bombing of British, German, and Japanese urban centers.

To be sure, in addition to being – as this book shows – an absolute war, the Second World War was a total war (in several belligerent countries, many civilians were mobilized in support of the war effort) and a global war (on account of the many nations that participated in the war, of the fact that the war was fought on several continents, and also because of the decisive consequences that it would have for the future history of the entire world). Given the terrible, annihilating violence performed in 1939–45, the absolute animosity between the warring sides, and the gruesome, barbaric quality of the violence carried out by combatants, it may be argued that, of all those three structural constituents of the Second World War, absolute war is the most defining and dominant. After all, the world had already witnessed, in 1914–18, a total war (according to many parameters, the first total war in history) and a global war (the First World War was fought mostly in Europe, but combats also developed in the Middle East, Africa, South America, North America, Asia, and Oceania). If something fundamental differentiates the Second World War from the First World War, this is essentially the fact that the former was an absolute war in certain fronts, whereas in the latter, instances of absolute war were exceptional. In the Second World War, absolute war manifested itself through the unrestrained and in many cases barbarian violence perpetrated

cases, real wars do not actualize their inherent full destructiveness. In very special circumstances, however, war may develop practically unhindered by policy. When war approaches or reaches its absolute degree, the term "absolute war" names a type of real war. Some of the main traits of an absolute war are the performance of an unbracketed, unrestrained, extreme violence; an absolute enmity between the belligerent armies; the drive to exterminate the opponent or force him to an unconditional surrender; the almost complete predominance of military criteria over political decision-making; the consideration of combat as a merciless struggle for life or death; the use of any possible means to annihilate the opponent; and the view of enemy civilians as a legitimate target. For a thorough and nuanced description of absolute war, see the first section of the Introduction.

by the armies of the main countries involved, whose combatants usually perceived and dealt with the enemy as someone who must be annihilated.

This monograph explores for the first time the literature of absolute war in connection with the world war of 1939–45.[3] From a transnational standpoint, I address a set of theoretical, historical, and literary questions whose answers shed new light on the nature of absolute war, the literature on the world war of 1939–45, modern war writing in general, and the symbiotic relation between combat and linguistic expression. In order to achieve these objectives, I follow four intertwined analytical paths. First, I determine the main features of the language of absolute war, which gravitate around three fundamental semantic clusters: the horror, terror, and spectrality. I pay particular attention to the thematic, rhetorical, and tropological characteristics of the writing produced to express war in its absolute degree. It is important to bear in mind the fact that, like any other type of war, absolute war consists not only of the activities performed in the nonlinguistic world; it is also made up of a series of linguistic strategies. War is always permeated by language and it always permeates speech. As James Dawes has remarked, military conflicts begin and are carried on and remembered through a proliferation of linguistic discourse.[4] This is never a neutral activity, for the narration and remembrance of war through language have an inevitable distorting effect. Referring to the discursive expression of fighting, Joanna Bourke has noted that the act of narrating modifies and reformulates the experience of combat; the event enters "into imagination and language, to be interpreted, elaborated, structured and restructured."[5] Furthermore, in warfare language may be used as a weapon,[6] while language itself can be the field of fierce struggles for power.[7] The centrality of writing in any study of war – absolute or otherwise – is, therefore, indisputable. Second, I study the variegated responses given by literary authors to the difficult, seemingly unsolvable

[3] For general authoritative histories of the Second World War, see Alya Aglan and Robert Frank, eds., *1937–1947: La guerre-monde*, 2 vols. (Paris: Gallimard, 2015); Antony Beevor, *The Second World War* (New York: Back Bay Books, 2012); John R. Ferris et al., eds., *The Cambridge History of the Second World War*, 3 vols. (Cambridge University Press, 2015); Max Hastings, *Inferno: The World at War, 1939–1945* (New York: Alfred A. Knopf, 2011); Victor Davis Hanson, *The Second World Wars: How the First Global Conflict Was Fought and Won* (New York: Basic Books, 2017); and John Keegan, *The Second World War* (New York: Penguin, 1989).
[4] James Dawes, *The Language of War: Literature and Culture in the U.S. from the Civil War through World War II* (Cambridge, MA: Harvard University Press, 2002), 15.
[5] Joanna Bourke, *Fear: A Cultural History* (Emeryville, CA: Shoemaker & Hoard, 2006), 288.
[6] On this score, see Marie Louise Pratt, "Harm's Way: Language and the Contemporary Arts of War," *PMLA* 124.5 (2009), 1515–31.
[7] See Robin Tolmach Lakoff, *The Language War* (Berkeley, CA: University of California Press, 2000).

challenges posed by absolute war to epistemology, ethics, language, and representation. Its multiple dimensions, its breakup of all boundaries, its extreme violence, and its enormity hinder the cognitive mastering of absolute war, undermine the ethical values held by the warring sides, place military conflict at the boundaries of significant language, and make the cultural representation of absolute warfare extremely difficult. Certainly, all these consequences are not exclusive of absolute war, but it is in absolute war that they find their most extreme expression. Third, I analyze the interplay between absolute war and representation. Whereas it is true that absolute war partly determined the literary choices made by authors, it is equally unquestionable that literature, alongside other cultural expressions (most particularly cinema), has decisively shaped our view of absolute war as it was fought in 1939–45. Accordingly, I examine in detail the literary account of absolute war within a historical and theoretical framework, paying attention to the different perspectives of absolute war offered by literary works devoted to the Second World War. I focus, therefore, on the overlapping or the discrepancies among images of absolute war – images that help us to understand the language and nature of that kind of war – as well as the violent experiences endured by those who underwent it. Finally, I delve into the different poetics that articulate the writing on absolute war, placing special emphasis on four literary practices or modes: traditional realism, traumatic realism, what I call "catastrophic modernism" (a concept defined in the Introduction), and to a lesser extent, the fantastic.

The Literature of Absolute War vindicates the notion of "absolute war" as a legitimate category for historical, theoretical, and cultural analysis. This vindication is openly expressed in the Introduction only. However, my close readings of a corpus of literary artifacts on absolute war ultimately aim at demonstrating the validity of that concept, even if the immediate goal of such readings is of an analytic and hermeneutic nature. I strongly believe that "absolute war" is a term that ought to be incorporated into our critical vocabulary. At present, with few exceptions it has practically vanished from historical and theoretical discourse,[8] while its meaning has been problematically subsumed under the category of "total war." In contrast to that common practice, the main presupposition of this monograph emphatically states that "absolute war" and "total war" represent two different phenomena. As we will see in the Introduction, the former refers

---

[8] Exceptions to the norm are Chris Bellamy, *Absolute War: Soviet Russia in the Second World War* (New York: Alfred A. Knopf, 2007); and António Horta Fernandes, *Livro dos contrastes: Guerra & política* (Porto: Fronteira do Caos Editores, 2017).

basically to the *intension* of warfare (i.e., its extreme, unbracketed degree of animosity and violence, as well as the unusual levels of cruelty and barbarism usually performed in the pursuit of the extermination or the unconditional surrender of the enemy), while the latter alludes to the *extension* of a military conflict (i.e., the total mobilization of an entire society in support of the war effort). After the Second World War, a number of historians have conflated those two phenomena under the same category. Remarkably, despite the widespread use of the term "total war" there is no complete consensus as to what it really means. Equally significant, oftentimes scholars do not furnish a working definition of "total war," taking its meaning for granted, as if it were self-evident. I would like to encourage the inclusion of "absolute war" in historical, theoretical, and cultural accounts of warfare. Provided that we differentiate it from "total war," the incorporation of "absolute war" into our critical vocabulary will greatly enrich our understanding of the history and theory of war, as well as the culture produced to represent and understand it.

As mentioned earlier, my approach to war literature is transnational. Written artifacts on absolute war are grouped not by their belonging to a national tradition, as has been the norm in specialized scholarship, but rather by their points of overlap or contrast. Most books on Second World War literature center on one single national literary field.[9] To be sure, there is no lack of international approaches, but not a few of the monographs written with a comparative spirit treat literary artifacts by national

---

[9] A few examples drawn from three different scholarly traditions will suffice. For Germany: Dagmar Barnouw, *Germany 1945: Views of War and Violence* (Bloomington, IN: Indiana University Press, 1996), and her *The War in the Empty Air: Victims, Perpetrators, and Postwar Germans* (Bloomington, IN: Indiana University Press, 2005); Elisabeth Krimmer, *The Representation of War in German Literature* (Cambridge University Press, 2010), 107–49; and Judith Ryan, *The Uncompleted Past: Postwar German Novels and the Third Reich* (Detroit, MI: Wayne State University Press, 1983). For Great Britain: Patrick Deer, *Culture in Camouflage: War, Empire, and Modern British Literature* (Oxford University Press, 2009); Marina MacKay, *Modernism and World War II* (Cambridge University Press, 2007); Alan Munton, *English Fiction of the Second World War* (London: Faber and Faber, 1989); Adam Piette, *Imagination at War: British Fiction and Poetry, 1939–1945* (London: Papermac, 1995); Mark Rawlinson, *British Writing of the Second World War* (New York University Press, 2000); Victoria Stewart, *Narratives of Memory: British Writing of the 1940s* (New York: Palgrave Macmillan, 2006); and Lyndsey Stonebridge, *The Writing of Anxiety: Imagining Wartime in Mid-Century British Culture* (New York: Palgrave Macmillan, 2007). For the United States: Dawes, *The Language of War*, 157–91; George Hutchinson, *Facing the Abyss: American Literature and Culture in the 1940s* (New York: Columbia University Press, 2018); John Limon, *Writing after War: American War Fiction from Realism to Postmodernism* (Oxford University Press, 1994), 128–53; Ichiro Takayoshi, *American Writers and the Approach of World War II, 1935–1941: A Literary History* (Cambridge University Press, 2015); Joseph J. Waldmeir, *American Novels of the Second World War* (The Hague: Mouton & Co., 1969); and Jeffrey Walsh, *American War Literature, 1914 to Vietnam* (New York: St. Martin's Press, 1982), 112–84.

traditions (e.g., a chapter on German literature, a chapter on French literature, another one on American literature, and so on), thereby eschewing a truly transnational and comparative view.[10] These are perfectly legitimate choices. The problem lies, however, in the fact that by analyzing one national literature only, or several of them separately, such monographs do not reflect the constitutive international dimension of the war under scrutiny, and consequently the transnational nature of the cultural objects produced to represent it is neglected. Furthermore, by taking as a point of reference single national literary fields, scholars tacitly reproduce the confrontational nature of the war. By contrast, a transnational approach respects not only the global, multinational dimension of the Second World War; in addition, by placing works from different national traditions into dialogue, a transnational methodology creates sites for a common understanding, for a shared humanity beyond the military confrontation of the countries in which they have been written. I believe that specialized scholarship ought to approach the two world wars transnationally. My monograph attempts to overcome self-imposed limitations. I will analyze *together* works created within different national traditions, mostly German, British, Italian, American, French, Russian, and Japanese. A transnational methodology reveals the existence of a robust global tradition of literature on absolute war, as well as similarities and differences that have never been analyzed before due to the national standpoint taken by many specialists. The practice of transnationalism opens up, therefore, new avenues for literary and historical investigations on war writing.

   Due to my interest in exploring the literary representation of absolute war, I concentrate my analysis on works of fiction, and on occasion, on plays, diaries, and memoirs. The division of the book into three chapters aims to convey the different dimensions of absolute war. In 1939–45,

---

[10] For international approaches to the literature produced on the Second World War, see William Cloonan, *The Writing of War: French and German Fiction and World War II* (Gainesville, FL: University Press of Florida, 1999); Paul Crosthwaite, *Trauma, Postmodernism and the Aftermath of World War II* (Basingstoke: Palgrave Macmillan, 2009); Jörg Echternkamp and Stefan Martens, eds., *Experience and Memory: The Second World War in Europe* (New York: Berghahn Books, 2010); Frederick Harris, *Encounters with Darkness: French and German Writers on World War II* (New York: Oxford University Press, 1983); Ian Higgins, ed., *The Second World War in Literature: Eight Essays* (Edinburgh: Scottish Academic Press, 1986); Holger Klein, with John Flower and Eric Homberger, eds., *The Second World War in Fiction* (London: Macmillan Press, 1984); Elena Lamberti and Vita Fortunati, eds., *Memories and Representations of War: The Case of World War I and World War II* (Amsterdam: Rodopi, 2009); Marina MacKay, ed., *The Cambridge Companion to the Literature of World War II* (Cambridge University Press, 2009); and Reiko Tachibana, *Narrative as Counter-Memory: A Half-Century of Postwar Writing in Germany and Japan* (Albany, NY: State University of New York Press, 1998).

absolute war was fought by regular armies and guerrillas, but armies also targeted enemy civilians. Furthermore, fighting in absolute war affected in important ways those who were involved in them; this makes it necessary to explore the literature written on veterans and war survivors. In my transnational reading of absolute war literature I cover, therefore, three situations (battles between armies, the aerial bombing of civilians, the veteran's homecoming), three spaces (the battlefield, the city under aerial attack, the homeland where the veteran returns), and three subjects (combatants, victims, survivors) of absolute war. As regards the historical period studied here, I center on absolute war in a – to borrow the terminology developed by Fernand Braudel to explain historical time – short time span (i.e., 1939–45). My study of the literature produced to represent it covers, however, a conjunctural time span that encompasses the war itself, the Cold War, and the transitional historical period known as globalization, in which we are still immersed.

In the Introduction, I define the main concepts of *The Literature of Absolute War* (i.e., "absolute war," "absolute enmity," "total war," "traumatic realism," "catastrophic modernism," and "spectrum of possibilities") and comment on some of the extreme challenges posed by absolute war to modern war writing.

Chapter 1, "The Horror," starts with a summary of the two main absolute wars in 1939–45: the Pacific War and the war between Nazi Germany and the Soviet Union. The remaining four sections of this chapter examine several family resemblances of the literature written on the eastern front. I begin with three traits that are quite common in fiction on absolute war: kaput, the abject, and the writing of cruelty. These three constituents are studied as deployed by Curzio Malaparte in *Kaputt* (1944) and Theodor Plievier in *Stalingrad* (1945). Useless suffering and the absurd are the next family resemblances of absolute war writing. Drawing my ideas from the philosophy of Emmanuel Levinas, I relate the useless suffering of civilians and soldiers to the senselessness of absolute war in my analysis of Gert Ledig's *Die Stalinorgel* (Stalin's Organ) (1955) and Vasily Grossman's *Life and Fate* (1980, finished 1960). The examination of the suffering of the victim is followed by the study of radical evil in Jonathan Littell's *Les Bienveillantes* (The Kindly Ones) (2006). A reading of Walter Kempowski's ten-volume *Das Echolot. Ein kollektives Tagebuch* (The Sonar: A Collective Diary) (1993–2005) closes Chapter 1. In this last section of the chapter I concentrate on one "extreme" of catastrophic modernism, namely the practice of a "total representation" by means of a massive collage of thousands of texts and dozens of photographs, and also on what I consider as an antidote to the notion of absolute enmity: the ethics of otherness that underpins *Das Echolot*. All these family resemblances of absolute war writing are studied against the backdrop of the horror unleashed by war in its absolute degree, a horror that is understood in two different, if complementary, senses. On the one hand, horror is a quality of the absolute destruction wrought by absolute war, that is, the quality of exciting extreme repugnance and dread. On the other, it is an emotion compounded of shock, loathing, and great fear; this second meaning of horror refers to the potential readerly reaction to the literary representation of absolute war. Naturally, all wars contain a horrific dimension, but – and this is crucial – it is usually more moderate, in relative terms, than the unbearable horror experienced in absolute war and depicted in literature.

Chapter 2, "Terror," shifts the attention from the combatant to the civilian under fire. I use the word "terror" in two different ways: as the state of being terrified and as the act of causing terror. If the practice of absolute war as waged between armies is closely connected to horror, the deliberate targeting of civilians by bombing urban centers during the Second World War needs to be considered in terms of the terror that it causes. After an introductory section in which I summarize the theory of strategic bombing and the milestones of the air war in Europe and Japan in 1940–45, I move on to analyze the catastrophic modernism deployed to narrate the aerial bombing of Germany, France, and Britain. Basically, I concentrate on Gert Ledig's *Vergeltung* (Payback) (1956), Alexander Kluge's *Der Luftangriff auf Halberstadt am 8. April 1945* (The Air Raid against Halberstadt on April 8, 1945) (1977), Louis-Ferdinand Céline's *Féerie pour une autre fois* (Fable for Another Time) (1952–54), and James Hanley's *No Directions* (1943). Following my discussion of the catastrophic modernism of these works, there comes a section on realist works on the aerial bombing of Britain and Germany; in this section I include, too, modernist texts endowed with a strong representational drive. I analyze novels by Graham Greene, Elizabeth Bowen, Henry Green, and Otto Erich Kiesel. In Chapter 2 I also explore in detail the narrative voiding of aerial bombing in Kurt Vonnegut's *Slaughterhouse-Five* (1969) and Hubert Fichte's *Detlevs Imitationen "Grünspan"* (Detlev's Imitations) (1971). This chapter ends with an analysis of the representation of the atomic bombing of Hiroshima and Nagasaki in works by Yōko Ōta, Tamiki Hara, Masuji Ibuse, Takashi Nagai, and John Hersey, among others.

Chapter 3, "Specters," applies spectral theory as developed by Jacques Derrida, Avery F. Gordon, and other theorists, to the study of literature on veterans and survivors of absolute war. I claim that veterans are haunted by memories of the horror they have seen or performed, while at the same time they constitute haunting entities for those who surround them back home. In the introductory pages I suggest the deployment of a *hauntology of war* and delve with the issues affecting homecoming veterans. Then my attention falls, first, on the return of the specter as treated in Wolfgang Borchert's *Draußen vor der Tür* (The Man Outside) (1947) and Heinrich Böll's *Der Engel schwieg* (The Silent Angel) (1992, written 1949–50), as well as the trauma of prisoners of war and veterans as depicted in novels by Josef Martin Bauer, Henry Green, and Rose Macaulay. The spectrality of bombed-out cities and their inhabitants is my next focus. I concentrate particularly, if not only, on testimonials written by Japanese survivors of the atomic bombing of Hiroshima and Nagasaki, Hans Erich Nossack's *Nekyia. Bericht eines Überlebenden* (Nekyia: A Report by a Survivor) (1947), and Hermann Kasack's *Die Stadt hinter dem Strom* (The City beyond the River) (1947). This chapter ends with a spectral analysis of the exorcism of the ghosts of war as performed in Sloan Wilson's *The Man in the Gray Flannel Suit* (1955) and Walter Kolbenhoff's *Heimkehr in die Fremde* (Return to a Foreign Land) (1949).

A Coda titled "Remains" closes *The Literature of Absolute War*. Taking as a point of reference Alain Resnais's motion picture *Hiroshima mon amour* (1959), I contend there that narratives on absolute war may be considered as textual remains of warfare. As such, they are endowed with a haunting power that impels readers to reflect on literary choices, historical accounts, and ethical claims made in connection with absolute war.

Introduction
Concepts

Absolute War

The term "absolute war" was coined and developed by the Prussian general and philosopher of war Carl von Clausewitz in his unfinished book *Vom Kriege* (On War), posthumously published by his widow in 1832–34.[1] Clausewitz lays out in *Vom Kriege* the most significant philosophical account of war ever written in the Western world. Time is unforgiving, and some arguments made by Clausewitz, particularly those of a more technical nature, may sound somewhat quaint to contemporary ears, while others are simply outdated. However, and regardless of whether one agrees or not with the idealist philosophy that underpins *Vom Kriege*, Clausewitz's considerations on the nature of war, his treatment of the moral and psychological factors involved in warfare, his pivotal ideas about the determining role played by policy in conventional military conflicts, and the development of his important notion of the "friction" of war are still relevant today for a better understanding and assessment of military conflicts.

Absolute war constitutes one of the mainstays of *Vom Kriege*.[2] In a "Note" signed on July 10, 1827, which functions as a prologue to *Vom*

---

[1] For general approaches to Clausewitz and *Vom Kriege*, see Raymond Aron, *Penser la guerre, Clausewitz* (Paris: Gallimard, 1976); Michael I. Handel, ed., *Clausewitz and Modern Strategy* (Totowa, NJ: Frank Cass and Company Limited, 1986); Michael Howard, *Clausewitz* (Oxford University Press, 1983); Peter Paret, *Clausewitz and the State* (Oxford University Press, 1976); Anatol Rapoport, "Introduction," *On War*, by Carl von Clausewitz, ed. Anatol Rapoport (London: Penguin, 1982), 11–80; and Hew Strachan, *Carl von Clausewitz's On War: A Biography* (New York: Atlantic Monthly Press, 2006). Anders Engberg-Pedersen's *Empire of Chance: The Napoleonic Wars and the Disorder of Things* (Cambridge, MA: Harvard University Press, 2015) includes stimulating reflections on Clausewitz.

[2] On the notion of absolute war in Clausewitz's work, see W. B. Gallie, *Philosophers of Peace and War: Kant, Clausewitz, Marx, Engels and Tolstoy* (Cambridge University Press, 1978), 37–65; António Horta Fernandes, *Livro dos contrastes: Guerra & política* (Porto: Fronteira do Caos Editores, 2017), 170–208; Howard, *Clausewitz*, 47–58; Hans Speier, "The Social Types of War," *American Journal of Sociology* 46.4 (1941), 445–54; Strachan, *Carl von Clausewitz's On War*, 147–52, 160–76; and

Kriege, Clausewitz states one of his two main theses: "war," Clausewitz claims, "is nothing but the continuation of policy [*Staatspolitik*] with other means."[3] Further on in *Vom Kriege*, he suggests his second basic thesis in the form of a distinction: he asserts there that war may be considered in "its absolute form or one of the variant forms that it actually takes" (582). It is crucial to understand that the adjective *absolute* is used by Clausewitz in its philosophical sense. Accordingly, with the expression "absolute war" (*absoluter Krieg*) Clausewitz designates war in itself, endowed with its own nature and its own constitutive rules of articulation; absolute war is an independent and unconditioned reality that deploys itself without the interference of extraneous determinants. External factors such as policy, which plays a crucial role in conventional military conflicts, do not have a significant impact on absolute war. Ideology (e.g., anti-communism, anti-fascism, racism, a colonialist drive), and hence politics, may have a pivotal role in absolute war, but policy usually has serious problems in determining the course taken by that kind of military conflict. The diminished agency of policy-makers in situations of absolute war partly accounts for its extremes and its mercilessness.

The nature of war is described early in *Vom Kriege*. Clausewitz writes that war is an "act of force to compel our enemy to do our will" (75). Force, he adds, is the means, the imposition of our will on the enemy is the object, and in order to secure that object, "we must render the enemy powerless" (75). In Clausewitz's view (and this is crucial for understanding his notion of "absolute war"), there is no logical limit to the application of force. The two warring forces will reciprocally apply the maximum strength so as to achieve their objective, a situation that "must lead, in theory, to extremes" (77). This is, in Clausewitz's expression, the first "extreme" of war. The second extreme stems from the fact that in any military conflict there is a clash between two living forces whose interaction leads to the escalation of hostilities (77). Clausewitz formulates the third extreme of war in a section significantly titled "The Maximum Exertion of Strength." Therein, the Prussian philosopher of war argues that the two warring forces evaluate the opponent's power of resistance by assessing the total means at their disposal and the strength of their will.

Hans-Ulrich Wehler, "'Absoluter' und 'totaler' Krieg. Von Clausewitz zu Ludendorff," *Politische Vierteljahresschrift* 19 (1969), 220–48.
3 Carl von Clausewitz, *On War*, trans. and ed. Michael Howard and Peter Paret (Princeton University Press, 1984), 69. Further references in text. On occasion, I slightly modify the translation based on my own reading of the German text: *Vom Kriege*, ed. Werner Hahlweg (Bonn: Ferdinand Dümmlers, 1973).

Each side adjusts its own strength accordingly, "competition will again result and, in pure theory, it must again force you to extremes'" (77). He concludes his explanation of the three extremes of war with an important proposition. War, Clausewitz underscores, is constituted by a "trinity" of elements, namely: (i) "primordial violence, hatred, and enmity, which are to be regarded as a blind natural force"; (ii) "the play of chance and probability"; and (iii) the subordination of war to policy (77). Given that each side must perceive war as an act of force to compel the enemy to comply with its will, logically speaking hostilities could not end until after "one or the other side were finally defeated" (579). The unleashing of those extremes leads to absolute war. In its absolute form, war lacks what Clausewitz calls interchangeably a "nonconducting medium" (579) and an "intervening neutral void" (582), that is to say a barrier that prevents war's full discharge. Absolute war dictates that the only result that counts is the merciless and complete annihilation of the enemy, as well as the devastation of his land (579). Although Clausewitz does not put it like this, from his argument it follows that absolute war implies either the *unconditional* surrender of the enemy, or his *complete* destruction – or both.

In principle, absolute war is a regulative idea required by philosophical argumentation to understand the nature of war, as well as its empirical varieties. In the philosophical context of *Vom Kriege*, without this regulative idea the philosopher of war might fall prey to historicism or, even worse, end up merely stringing together an anecdotal series of war stories. In order to reflect philosophically on war, the theorist must determine first the basic principles of war, and then explore its practical realizations throughout history by taking absolute war as the theoretical standard. In Clausewitz's philosophy of war, "real" (*wirklicher*) war is nothing other than the partial, limited, bracketed actualization of war's essential annihilating force. A real war, he argues, has its own grammar (that is, its specific rules of articulation), but it follows the logic of policy, in the sense that war is one tool, among others, for working out the differences between national or tribal communities. As mentioned earlier, for Clausewitz war is the continuation of policy with other means, or, as he says at some point in a more nuanced language, "with the admixture [*Einmischung*] of other means" (605). This means that political intercourse is not replaced by war; rather, it is supplemented by it. Real wars – as we saw earlier – contain a sort of "nonconducting medium" that obstructs a "total discharge" (579). The external factors added to the war machine can interrupt or modify hostilities (579). As a series of actions framed by the world of experience, real war is a part, in fact, of a whole – political activity (605–7). Consequently, the intrusion of extrinsic forces controls and restrains the impulse to annihilate the enemy and lay waste to his land, preventing the complete fulfillment of the intrinsic elements of war, that is to say its absolute form.

Now, the relation between "absolute war" and "real war" undergoes a decisive transmutation as soon as the first factor of the binomial moves from the abstract realm of philosophical argumentation to the world of experience. According to Clausewitz, this intrusion occurred during the French Revolutionary Wars (1792–1802) and the Napoleonic Wars (1803–15). The observation of this phenomenon (i.e., absolute war's metamorphosis from a pivotal theoretical construct to a category that describes a specific class of real war) constitutes yet another important contribution to the philosophy of war elaborated in *Vom Kriege*, even if we decide – as we must – that Clausewitz was wrong in believing that absolute war did not emerge until the end of the eighteenth century as a result of the French Revolution. Mostly thinking of the so-called cabinet wars waged in Europe in the eighteenth century, Clausewitz states that the history of war demonstrates that the normal condition of armies in a war is immobility and inactivity (217). The wars that immediately followed the French Revolution reverted that constant. In the Revolutionary Wars, "and even more in the campaigns of Bonaparte, warfare attained the unlimited [*unbedingt*] degree of energy that we consider to be its elementary law. We see it is possible to reach this degree of energy"; and he crucially adds: "if it is possible, it is necessary" (217). Elsewhere in *Vom Kriege*, Clausewitz calls this kind of military conflict "war proper" (*eigentlicher Krieg*) and "absolute war" (*absoluter Krieg*), which in this specific passage he seems to consider as interchangeable (488–89). A defining characteristic of absolute war is the way it is fought: absolute war is an unbound military conflict, it is a "struggle of life and death" (488).

Clausewitz elaborates on the concept of "absolute war" in book 8 of *Vom Kriege*, specifically in chapters 2, 3A, and 3B. He acknowledges that "one may wonder whether there is any truth at all in our concept of the absolute character of war were it not for the fact that with our own eyes we have seen warfare achieve this state of absolute perfection" (580), a state that Bonaparte brought about "swiftly and ruthlessly"; in his hands, war "was waged without respite until the enemy succumbed" (580). With the French Revolution, "Suddenly war again became the business of the people – a people of thirty million, all of whom considered themselves to be citizens" (592). In contrast to the limited wars fought in the eighteenth century before 1793, "The people became a participant in

war; instead of governments and armies as heretofore, the full weight of the
nation was thrown into the balance" (592). Clausewitz maintains that
"Since Bonaparte . . . war, first among the French and subsequently among
their enemies, again became the concern of the people as a whole, took on
an entirely different character, or rather closely approached its true character, its absolute perfection [*absolute Vollkommenheit*]" (592–93). In sum:
"The sole aim of war was to overthrow the opponent. Not until he was
prostrate was it considered possible to pause and try to reconcile the
opposing interests" (593).

Absolute war erodes and breaks up all boundaries. Clausewitz had
referred to this very issue earlier in *Vom Kriege*, when he argues that after
the French Revolution the "limits" of military operations had been
expanded so much that a return to the "old narrow limitations can only
occur briefly, sporadically, and under special conditions, the true nature of
war will break through again and again with overwhelming force [*Allge-
walt*], and must, therefore, be the basis of any permanent arrangements"
(313). In the closing chapters of his groundbreaking book, the German
philosopher revisits this idea: by becoming an affair not only of governments or dynasties, but of the entire nation, in the Revolutionary Wars
and the Napoleonic campaigns, "There seemed no end to the resources
mobilized; all limits disappeared in the vigor and enthusiasm shown by
governments and their subjects" (593). As he states, "once barriers . . . are
torn down, they are not so easily set up again. At least when major interests
are at stake, mutual hostility will express itself in the same manner as it has
in our own day" (593). Furthermore, this unbracketing means that in
absolute war the human agency that usually controls it dilutes itself. One
may conclude that absolute war is the subject agent of itself; those who
participate in absolute war are, in truth, *functions* of a grammar and a logic
that control and determine their actions. The same applies to political
activity, which instead of regulating the course of war becomes determined
by war itself. The synonymy established by Clausewitz between "whole
war" (*ganzer Krieg*) and "absolute war" (605) seems to point out the
relative lack of agency of its participants.

One of the distinctive traits of *Vom Kriege* is its historical approach to
war. Clausewitz repeatedly argues that wars cannot be understood in the
abstract, outside of their historical circumstances. In Clausewitz's synopsis
(586–94), the history of warfare comprises three phases, each of them
corresponding to a moment of a dialectical process: the Middle Ages
(armies formed with the kings' and feudal lords' vassals), a long period
that comprises the sixteenth, seventeenth, and eighteenth centuries

(standing mercenary armies), and finally, the era inaugurated by the French Revolution (armies made up by conscripted free citizens called up by the state). This third period meant the empirical actualization of war's essence. Because of the way it was done (i.e., participation of the entire people in the affairs of the nation), it has to be considered as the end of a dialectical process made up with a thesis (personal service to a feudal lord, a prince, or the king), its antithesis (monetary payment to mercenaries), and its synthesis (*obligatory* military *service* – a medieval remainder – *paid* by the state – reminiscent of the economic bond between governments and their standing armies of mercenaries – of all young male citizens of the nation). Since in this third phase, precisely because of its synthesis of service to and remuneration by the state, absolute war appears in the empiric world according to Clausewitz, it is by no means far-fetched to compare this dialectical movement to Hegelian idealism. In Hegel's philosophy the state is the locus where the objective spirit realizes itself. Extrapolating Hegel to Clausewitz, absolute war is not an entity, but the intrinsic constitution of all real wars. In truth, war has always been "absolute"; its history is the dialectical development of that essence until it reaches its self-realization; with the emergence, in the real world, of absolute war, war becomes what it already was. Every single war contains, within itself, the *possibility* of becoming absolute. Absolute war is embedded in the ontological structure of any war. Despite the dialectical evolution of war, Clausewitz does not think that absolute war as carried out by Napoleon is the last stage in the history of warfare. Due precisely to its historical determinants, one has to assume that in certain cases war will be conducted by very specific political objectives that will prevent the discharge of the annihilating brutality of war in its absolute degree. The Korean War (1950–53) and the Gulf War (1990–91) are two cases in point.

Book 8 seems to harmonize the phenomenology of war deployed in book 1 with a historical view of war. A closer inspection, however, reveals that the self-realization of war entails an erosion of the methodological and theoretical rigor of *Vom Kriege*. The amplitude, the almost unlimited deployment of men and resources, the spatial expansion and the multiplication of fronts, the ferocity of combats, and the lack of solid political and ethical breaks in absolute war make it difficult, if not impossible, to place it within the boundaries of a theoretical framework. To explain, in a coherent and consistent fashion, this kind of war is a challenge to reason. Clausewitz finds it difficult to relate absolute war to political activity. Actually, due to its *unconditioned* nature absolute war cannot be

determined by policy. In one passage, he affirms that during the Napoleonic Wars "warfare attained [*erreichte*] the unlimited degree of energy that
we consider to be its elementary law" (217). In other passages, however,
Clausewitz maintains that in the Napoleonic campaigns war "rather closely
approached [*hat … sich sehr genähert*] its true character, its absolute
perfection" (593). In the latter case, war pertains to the logic of politics,
but not in the former. Properly speaking, absolute war is a war without
policy. That inconsistency could be attributed to the fact that *Vom Kriege*
is an unfinished book. But acknowledging this does not eliminate, obviously, the inconsistency. Although in chapter 6B of book 8 he claims that
war has its own grammar, but not its own logic, since logic is determined
by policy, Clausewitz introduces some observations to qualify this thesis, as
if it were not totally clear to him that war lacks a logic of its own. He states
that, for some, war is an activity divorced from political life; "whenever this
occurs … the many links that connect the two elements are destroyed, and
we are left with something pointless and devoid of sense" (605). If we read
that statement carefully, we will see that the problem lies not in the
hypothetical erroneousness of that view of war, but rather in the fact that,
were it to be correct, war would be a human activity lacking in meaning,
placing itself, consequently, beyond policy and philosophy. This situation
would tacitly undermine and question the task undertaken by Clausewitz
in *Vom Kriege*, namely the elaboration of a unified theory of war.

In sum: Clausewitz does not consider, initially, that absolute war could
condition political life, even destroy it. Sometimes, however, he seems to
suggest the opposite: in such cases, war possesses, in addition to its own
grammar or rules of articulation, its own logic, namely its development
towards goals that do not necessarily coincide with those established by
policy. To be sure, one must not forget Clausewitz's historical horizon. The
layout and development of his theses were necessarily conditioned by the
examples available at the time. Even so, Clausewitz intuited the political
and theoretical consequences derived from the self-realization of absolute
war, an issue to which he refers from the very beginning of *Vom Kriege*. In
chapter 1 of book 1, he writes: "The more powerful and inspiring the
motives for war, the more they affect the belligerent nations and the fiercer
the tensions that precede the outbreak, the closer will war approach its
abstract concept, the more important will be the destruction of the enemy,
the more closely will the military aims and the political objects of war
coincide, and the more military and less political will war appear to be"
(87–88). At the end of *Vom Kriege* he stops short of conceding that absolute
war is not subordinated to an extrinsic factor – policy. Clausewitz finds it

inconceivable that political activity could completely disappear in war, "unless pure hatred made all wars a struggle for life and death" (607). But that is precisely what happened, to give two examples from Clausewitz's own time, in the war in the Vendée (it has been calculated that in 1793–94 alone, between 220,000 and 250,000 people lost their lives) and in the Peninsular War (1808–14). The inconsistency in Clausewitz's argument is clear: if absolute war is unconditioned, it cannot stop being unconditioned when it becomes a real war; otherwise it would not be absolute, pure, something "in itself." If we confine ourselves strictly to the unconditioned nature of absolute war, the only thing that the theorist can do is describe the structure and functioning intrinsic to absolute war, without considering external factors. Since in theory absolute war lacks exteriority, in its self-realization it places itself in a twilight zone, in a locus that is alien to the usual political relations, in a space of linguistic, epistemological, and ethical uncertainty. To keep the unconditioned character of absolute war in its self-realization would amount to acknowledging that, in some cases, war imposes its own logic – and not only its grammar – to the belligerent societies, something that Clausewitz is not willing to admit openly. Ultimately, absolute war escapes political control; military events determine the course of policy, and not the other way around. Due to its enormous untrammeled discharge of energy, absolute war challenges ethics, epistemology, language, and representation in ways that no other kind of war does.

Absolute Enmity

"Enmity" is one of the three constituents of the "blind natural instinct" of war's trinity (the other two being, let us remember, primordial violence and hatred). As we saw earlier, the subordination of war to policy deters the constituents of the blind natural instinct of warfare from reaching their respective extremes. However, as soon as war attains its absolute state, the first component of the trinity manifests itself in all its purity, without constraints of any sort, imposing itself over the usual predominance of policy. In absolute war the "unbounded element of enmity" (605) is unleashed. Clausewitz categorically maintains that "The more earnestly a war is waged, the more it is charged with hatred and animosity, and the more it becomes a struggle for mastery on both sides, the more all activity will lead to bloody battles" (259).

Absolute war is, therefore, an activity geared towards the annihilation of what the philosopher of law and politics Carl Schmitt has termed the "absolute enemy" (*absoluter Feind*).[4] Essentially, the notion of "absolute enemy" is predicated on the absolute injustice of the enemy. This kind of enemy is not simply, as Hegel would put it, a "negated otherness," but rather a criminalized otherness. The twin concepts of "absolute enmity" and "absolute enemy" are of the utmost importance for understanding absolute war. To be sure, they may apply to all sorts of military conflicts, including those of a limited, conventional nature (e.g., the Gulf War [1990–91]). But whereas there can be conventional wars in which the enemy is not considered in absolute terms (e.g., the Falklands War [April–June 1982]), there is no absolute war without absolute enmity. Schmitt had already suggested the concept of "absolute enmity," without using the term, in *Der Begriff des Politischen* (The Concept of the Political) (1932) and *Der Nomos der Erde im Völkerrecht des Jus Publicum Europaeum* (The Nomos of the Earth in the International Law of the Jus Publicum Europaeum) (1950). Initially, Schmitt argues that although war is "the existential negation of the enemy," the enemy is, in principle, my equal.[5] War simply serves to settle who is right in a dispute. As he would clearly say in *Theorie des Partisanen* (Theory of the Partisan) (1963), "An enemy is not someone who, for some reason or other, must be eliminated and destroyed because he has no value. The enemy is on the same level as I am. For this reason, I must fight him to the same extent and within the same bounds as he fights me, in order to be consistent with the definition of the real enemy by which he defines me."[6] This was precisely the notion of enemy held by the warring sides in the cabinet wars of the eighteenth century commented on by Clausewitz in *Vom Kriege*. Kant had already reflected philosophically on that state of affairs by claiming that "No war of independent states against each other can be a *punitive war*"; this is so because punishment "occurs only in relation of a superior ... to those subject to him ... and states do not stand in that relation to each other."[7]

Now, sometimes the enemy is not treated as an equal, and instead, he is criminalized. One can discern this state of affairs in the notion of just war as it was conceived of in the twentieth century. Schmitt contends that in present-day just wars, precisely because they designate a just cause, there is

---

[4] Carl Schmitt, *Theory of the Partisan: Intermediate Commentary on the Concept of the Political*, trans. G. L. Ulmen (New York: Telos, 2007), 51–52, 58–59, 85, 89–95.
[5] Carl Schmitt, *The Concept of the Political*, trans. George Schwab, expanded ed. (University of Chicago Press, 2007), 32–33.
[6] Schmitt, *Theory of the Partisan*, 85.
[7] Immanuel Kant, *The Metaphysics of Morals*, trans. and ed. Mary Gregor (Cambridge University Press, 1996), 117 (section 57).

a latent tendency to characterize the opponent as an "unjust enemy."[8] When that is the case, war easily turns into a penal action, thereby acquiring a "punitive character."[9] The enemy who purportedly defends an "unjust cause" becomes ipso facto, in the eyes of his opponent, a criminal, an outlaw, a pirate.[10] The privation of his rights as well as the plundering of his land follow from this specific conceptualization.[11] In the twentieth century (but also, alas, in our twenty-first century), establishing a difference between just and unjust war is used instrumentally, for it serves to treat the enemy not as a *iustus hostis*, that is as an equal with rights, but merely as a criminal delinquent who cannot be considered to be on the same level as a regular combatant.[12] War ceases to be a concept from the *ius gentium*; it metamorphoses into a disciplinary activity.[13] Since the enemy has committed a "crime," forcefully acting against him is not, properly speaking, an act of war; waging war against him is something akin to a "police action against a gangster."[14] This sort of war deploys itself as a measure taken against a "perturbing" element; because of his criminal condition, such kind of enemy needs to be annihilated ruthlessly by using all modern means of destruction.[15] When enemies do not acknowledge each other as being on the same juridical and moral dimension, war is, properly speaking, abolished.[16] Schmitt designates this kind of punitive war as "the discriminating concept of war."[17]

For Carl Schmitt, the dehumanization of the enemy is essential in the construction of the absolute enemy. A warring faction dehumanizes the enemy either by attributing to him certain traits (e.g., he is a threat to humanity), or by justifying war on universal values (e.g., one fights him to restore world peace). Schmitt exemplifies his point by imagining a war fought to abolish war itself. If pacifists, Schmitt speculates, decided to launch a war to abolish all wars then war would be of the uttermost brutality because it would be "considered the absolute last war of humanity."[18] Due to the fact that this kind of war transcends the limits of political intercourse (something that we already saw in Clausewitz's understanding of absolute war), it is "necessarily unusually intense and inhuman";[19] the enemy is degraded into moral categories, he is characterized as

---

[8] Carl Schmitt, *The Nomos of the Earth in the International Law of the Jus Publicum Europaeum*, trans. G. L. Ulmen (New York: Telos, 2003), 123.
[9] Ibid., 123. [10] Ibid., 122. [11] Ibid., 123. [12] Ibid., 123. [13] Ibid., 124.
[14] Ibid., 124. [15] Ibid., 124. [16] Ibid., 124.
[17] On the discriminating concept of war, see Carl Schmitt, *Writings on War*, trans. and ed. Timothy Nunan (Cambridge: Polity, 2011), 30–74.
[18] Schmitt, *The Concept of the Political*, 36. [19] Ibid., 36.

a monster "that must not only be defeated but also utterly destroyed. In other words, he is an enemy who no longer must be compelled to retreat into his borders only."[20] As Schmitt says elsewhere, when a country fights against its enemy on behalf of abstract and universal categories, such as "humanity," war can easily turn into a brutal, merciless affair. In fact, that kind of war is not truly a war for the sake of humanity, but rather a war "wherein a particular state seeks to usurp a universal concept against its military opponent. At the expense of its opponent, it tries to identify itself with humanity in the same way one can misuse peace, justice, progress, and civilization in order to claim these as one's own and to deny the same to the enemy."[21]

In his book on the theory of the partisan, Carl Schmitt would refer to this kind of enemy with the expression "absolute enemy." A war predicated on absolute enmity knows no limits or bracketing: it is (like Clausewitz's absolute war) an unbound military conflict. In the eighteenth century, "with the bracketing of war, European humanity had achieved something extraordinary: renunciation of the criminalization of the opponent, i.e., the relativization of enmity, the negation of absolute enmity."[22] All this changed in the twentieth century with the Russian Revolution and its deployment of the notion of "class enemy." "By comparison with a war of absolute enmity," Schmitt writes, "the bracketed war of classical European international law, recognizing accepted rules, is similar to a duel between cavaliers seeking satisfaction. To a communist like Lenin, inspired by absolute enmity, such a war must have appeared to be mere play, which he might join in if the situation demanded, but which basically he would find contemptible and ludicrous," and he concludes: "The war of absolute enmity knows no bracketing."[23] Schmitt tacitly establishes a connection between absolute enmity and absolute war when he affirms that Lenin, "a professional revolutionary of global civil war," turned the enemy into an absolute one. Clausewitz might have spoken of absolute war, but he always presupposed, according to Schmitt, an existing state, "He could not conceive of a state becoming an instrument of a party"; and he adds: "With the absolutization of the party, the partisan also became absolute and a bearer of absolute enmity."[24] In a war driven by absolute animosity, men "must declare their opponents to be totally criminal and inhuman, to be a total non-value."[25] When such a view of the enemy is taken, the logic of value and non-value "reaches its full

---

[20] Ibid., 36.   [21] Ibid., 54.   [22] Schmitt, *Theory of the Partisan*, 90.   [23] Ibid., 52.
[24] Ibid., 94.   [25] Ibid., 94.

destructive consequence, and creates ever newer, ever deeper discrimina-
tions, criminalizations, and devaluations, until all non-valuable life has
been destroyed."[26]

In modern times, absolute animosity arose in fact not with the Russian
Revolution, as Schmitt claims, but with the French Revolution. Following
a tradition that was born with the Enlightenment, the Girondins and,
years later, Napoleon Bonaparte, conceived of war as a necessary evil to
end all wars and reach universal peace. In his intervention at the National
Convention on October 12, 1792, Charles-François Dumouriez summarized the feeling and speeches of fellow Girondins by declaring that "this
war will be the last one" (on September 20, 1792, General Dumouriez
had defeated the Prussians in the Battle of Valmy, and on November 6 he
would defeat the Austrian army at the Battle of Jemappes). Napoleon
fashioned himself as a man of peace whose ultimate goal was to end all
wars. Such a universal objective, seemingly altruistic, presupposes the
absolute lack of reason of the enemy, for his presumed "opposition" to
universal peace turns him into an unreasonable belligerent. In the same
historical period, Kant would write, in his *Metaphysik der Sitten* (The
Metaphysics of Morals) (1797), that there are no limits to a state's right to
act against an "unjust enemy" (*ungerechter Feind*) as regards the quantity,
although there are limits regarding the quality.[27] In other words: a state
cannot use all possible means to defend itself against an unjust enemy, but
it can take its measures with all the strength it is capable of. For Kant, an
unjust enemy is that whose explicit will reveals a maxim that, were it to
turn into a practical law, would make peace among nations impossible,
thereby perpetuating forever the state of nature, considered by Kant as the
condition of legal injustice. Although Kant does not sufficiently elaborate
his theses on this issue, the consequences of that perception of the enemy
are evident if one reviews the history of warfare. The extermination
campaign in the Vendée (1793–96), for instance, derived in part from
the internalization of that perception of the enemy. As Carl Schmitt put
it, to invoke and monopolize notions such as "humanity," "peace," or any
other universal value to justify a war "has certain incalculable effects, such
as denying the enemy the quality of being human and declaring him to be
an outlaw of humanity; and a war can thereby be driven to the most
extreme inhumanity."[28]

[26] Ibid., 94.   [27] Kant, *The Metaphysics of Morals*, 118–19 (section 60).
[28] Schmitt, *The Concept of the Political*, 54–55.

Total War

"Absolute war" designates at once a theoretical concept required by philosophical argument and a type of war. By contrast, the expression "total war" is a non-theoretical notion that emerged to explain a very specific event: the world war of 1914–18. While absolute war functions as one of the mainstays of a philosophical edifice, there is no solid theory of total war – not even today.[29] Despite the fact that it is common currency among historians, cultural commentators, scholars in literary studies, experts in war studies, and journalists, "total war" is an under-theorized term. Moreover, in spite of its widespread use, the term lacks a stable or consistent meaning, in part because "total war" does not stem from a general theory of war but rather from the urge to understand and describe specific military conflicts. This situation has led to some conceptual confusion.

The expression "*guerre totale*" or "total war" was first used by the French during the First World War. Georges Clemenceau put it in circulation in the political arena in a speech delivered at the French Senate on July 22, 1917. The first book to develop the notion appeared in 1918 before the end of the war: *La guerre totale* (Total War), written by the famed right-wing journalist and novelist Léon Daudet. By "total war," Daudet understands "the expansion of fighting . . . into politics, economics, trade, industry, intellectual life, law, and the world of finance."[30] Not only do the armies fight each other, argues Daudet, but so too do "traditions, institutions, customs, codes, intellects, and especially, the banks."[31] Unfortunately, Daudet does not draw the full consequences of his theory and concentrates most of his attention on German infiltration into French society and institutions. Instead of concluding, as some

---

[29] For general or theoretical considerations on "total war," see, for instance, Roger Chickering, "Are We There Yet? World War II and the Theory of Total War," *A World at Total War: Global Conflict and the Politics of Destruction, 1937–1945*, ed. Roger Chickering and Stig Förster (Cambridge University Press, 2005), 1–18, his "Introduction to Part II," *The Cambridge History of War*, vol. 4: *War and the Modern World*, ed. Roger Chickering, Dennis Showalter, and Hans van de Ven (Cambridge University Press, 2012), 183–91, and his "Total War: The Use and Abuse of a Concept," *Anticipating Total War: The German and American Experiences, 1871–1914*, ed. Manfred F. Boemeke, Roger Chickering, and Stig Förster (Cambridge University Press, 1999), 13–28; Stig Förster, "Introduction," *Great War, Total War: Combat and Mobilization on the Western Front, 1914–1918*, ed. Roger Chickering and Stig Förster (Cambridge University Press, 2000), 1–16; and his "Das Zeitalter des totalen Krieges," *Mittelweg 36* 8 (1999), 19–29; Markus Pöhlman, "Zur Etymologie des totalen Krieges," *An der Schwelle zum totalen Krieg. Die militärische Debatte über den Krieg der Zukunft, 1919–1939*, ed. Stig Förster (Paderborn: Ferdinand Schöningh, 2002), 346–51; and Wehler, "'Absoluter' und 'totaler' Krieg," 220–48.
[30] Léon Daudet, *La guerre totale* (Paris: Nouvelle Librairie Nationale, 1918), 8.   [31] Ibid., 8.

military theorists and historians would do years later, that in 1914–18 the main warring countries carried out a total war, or something close to it, for partisan propagandistic reasons he attributes the practice of total war to Germany alone.

The first significant book on total war would be written by none other than General Erich Ludendorff, the man who, together with Field Marshal Paul von Hindenburg, had total control over German military operations from 1916 until he tendered his resignation from his post to the Kaiser in late October 1918. Published in 1935, Ludendorff's treatise *Der totale Krieg* (Total War) set some of the main guidelines for future understandings of the concept of total war. Deeply immersed in Romantic right-wing nationalism – which means that his description of total war is extremely ideological – , after considering its essential nature, or *Wesen*, Ludendorff elaborates on the spiritual unity of the *Volk* (which he takes as the basic foundation for total war), explains the importance of the economy and the world of finance in total war, spells out the strength of the armed forces needed in conditions of total war, establishes how total war should be conducted, and ends with a description of the main characteristics that a commander-in-chief should possess. Notably, Ludendorff's *Der totale Krieg* was written against the backdrop of Clausewitz's *Vom Kriege*. From the very beginning, the author is keen to differentiate his book from Clausewitz's. The desire to distance himself from the Prussian philosopher of war is extremely significant, for it suggests that total war is by no means the same thing as absolute war. The very first sentence of the book is a declaration of principles: in stark contrast to Clausewitz's theoretical undertaking, "I do not want," Ludendorff states, "to write a theory of war."[32] In Ludendorff's view, war is reality, "the earnest reality in the life of a people" (3). These two statements indicate two characteristics of total war that would pervade in books on that matter published after 1945: (i) total war does not belong to a philosophical system or a theoretical argument, and (ii) total war is a descriptive expression (which does not mean that it is free from ideological considerations and underpinnings).

In *Der totale Krieg* Ludendorff uses the notion of total war atheoretically to characterize the First World War and, particularly, the wars of the future. According to Ludendorff, the Great War exhibited a character that was completely different from the wars waged in the previous 150 years. The war of 1914–18 was not only led, as had been the case hitherto, by the

---

[32] Erich Ludendorff, *Der totale Krieg* (Munich: Ludendorffs Verlag, 1935), 3. Further references in text.

leadership of the armed forces; it also involved the *Volk*, for many people participated in the war in variegated ways (4–5). In Ludendorff's opinion, total war was not born due to a change in the conduct of politics, but rather through "the introduction of general conscription ... and the way of fighting" (5). More specifically, this kind of war takes place when the self-preservation (*Lebenserhaltung*) of the people is threatened, and the people decidedly take it upon themselves to defend it (6). Total war, in sum, is the highest expression of the people's will to live (10). The people are, therefore, the crucial, defining element of total war. The essence of total war calls for the total force of the people (9, 28). Such is the relevance of the people in a total war, that the armed forces depend, according to Ludendorff, on the spiritual unity (*seelische Beschlossenheit*) of the *Volk* (9). Without such unity, the war will be lost. In the chapter on the spiritual unity of the people as the foundation of total war, Ludendorff argues that the armed forces are factually rooted in the *Volk* (11). Spiritual force gives both the armed forces and the *Volk* their unity (11). In a total war, war involves all members of the *Volk*, and everyone must do his or her due to help win it (61). Given the decisive importance of the unity of the *Volk* for winning a total war, keeping and fostering such unity is the most pressing duty of the leaders of what the German general calls "total politics" (16). The mobilization of all financial and economic resources for the war effort is another pillar of total war; this is closely related to the unity of the people, who participate in the war effort (48). In sum: "With the call to total mobilization, financial, economic, and political measures have been executed in our country so as to regulate the life of people and the course of the economy, maintain their unity, and put an end to the law of the 'discontents.' With the application of those measures starts in the father-land the work for the supply of both the people and the army" (102).

Generally speaking, "total war" designates, in the works of Daudet and Ludendorff, the mobilization of entire societies, which are set in motion so as to participate, one way or another, in the war effort. They conceive of total war as the involvement of all adult citizens, social organizations, institutions, the cultural field, the economic system, and political life in the war; the government is in charge of orchestrating this total mobilization – a notion that would be defined by Ernst Jünger in a seminal essay published in 1930 titled "Die totale Mobilmachung" (Total Mobilization). In the same way that absolute enmity is a key element in the configuration of absolute war, total mobilization plays a defining role in total war.

In his essay, Jünger points out that the times are long gone in which it sufficed to muster a 100,000-man army under professional leadership to wage war. What Jünger calls "partial mobilization" belongs to the essence of monarchy.[33] Throughout the nineteenth century the "spirit of progress" penetrated the "genius of war" (123, 125–26). Monarchy "oversteps its bounds" as soon as it has to include the forces of democracy in preparing for war (125–26). This is something that Clausewitz had clearly argued in *Vom Kriege*: after the French Revolution, wars will not be fought for the crown, but for the nation; they will be the affair of all the citizens of a country – a fact that would radically transform the way of waging war.[34] Jünger echoes this idea and concludes that "the image of war as armed conflict merges into the more extended image of a gigantic labor process" (126). Thus, in addition to the armies that clash on the battlefield, there are the "modern armies of commerce and transport, foodstuffs, the manufacture of armaments – the army of labor in general" (126). This phenomenon, which, according to Jünger, was not discernible at the beginning of the war, could be perfectly detected towards its end, when there was "no longer any movement whatsoever – not even that of the homeworker at her sewing machine – without at least some indirect use to the battlefield" (126). Jünger sees "In this unlimited marshaling of potential energies ... the most striking sign of the dawn of the age of labor," which makes the First World War "a historical event superior in significance to the French Revolution" (126). The key factor of this "age of labor" is total mobilization. After recognizing that countries have at their disposal an enormous proportion of energies, Jünger affirms that carrying out the mobilization befitting those energies is the task of total mobilization. This phenomenon is described, symptomatically, as if it were the industrial output of a gigantic machine: total mobilization is "an act which, as if through a single grasp of the control panel, conveys the extensively branched and densely veined power supply of modern life towards the greater current of martial energy" (126–27). Among the elements of total mobilization mentioned by Jünger, the planned management of foodstuffs and raw materials, the national guard duty, the arming of merchant vessels, the transposition of industrial conditions to military circumstances, and the merging of military and political command stand out (127). The technical side of total mobilization is not, however, decisive. Its basis lies in the "readiness for mobilization" (129). Such readiness is far more

---

[33] Ernst Jünger, "Total Mobilization," trans. Joel Golb and Richard Wolin, *The Heidegger Controversy: A Critical Reader*, ed. Richard Wolin (New York: Columbia University Press, 1991), 125. Further references in text.

[34] Clausewitz, *On War*, 579–84, 592–93, 610.

extended in liberal democracies than in monarchies. Progress was, according to Jünger, the source of the Great War's "effective appeal to the great masses ... This appeal alone accounts for the decisive aspect of their total mobilization" (129–30). This explains in part the fact that, in the end, the United States turned out to be the real victorious nation to emerge from the war: "in the United States with its democratic constitution, mobilization could be executed with a rigor that was impossible in Prussia, where the right to vote was based on class" (130). The course of war was decided "not by the degree to which a state was a 'military state,' but by the degree to which it was capable of total mobilization" (130), and thus the liberal democracies had a great advantage over Germany, where "despite all the care with which it undertook partial mobilization, large areas of its strength escaped total mobilization" (130–31).

Léon Daudet, Erich Ludendorff, and Ernst Jünger tacitly describe total war and total mobilization as phenomena essentially different from absolute war. However, the differences between absolute war and total war would be blurred in the approaches to total war developed after the Second World War. In the decades that followed its end, the term "total war" became common currency for describing the specific nature of the two world wars, as well as other modern wars, such as the Napoleonic Wars (1803–15), the American Civil War (1861–65), and the Franco-Prussian War (1870–71). A few examples will suffice to show the lack of clarity and the semantic inconsistencies of the term as it is generally used.

In *The Century of Total War*, Raymond Aron considers total war (which he also denominates "hyperbolic war") in connection with "the relentless mobilization of national resources and the competition over new inventions,"[35] as well as with mass production and mass destruction. For Aron, total war is a phenomenon at once intensive and extensive. After the United States entered the war, "The extent and intensity of the fighting increased without limit. The successive stages of that amplification illustrate the irrepressible dynamism of modern war with its strategic bombing, guerrilla warfare, deportation of civilians, and death camps."[36] He writes elsewhere in the book about the universalization of violence with Hitler, and notes that "Strategic bombing, deportations of workers, guerrilla warfare, terrorism, the police state – this multiplication of violence proceeds logically from an imperialist war conducted with the aid of modern industry."[37] While the book does not contain a clear definition of total

[35] Raymond Aron, *The Century of Total War* (New York: Doubleday & Company, 1954), 19.
[36] Ibid., 39.   [37] Ibid., 43.

war, readers may deduce that for Raymond Aron total war comprises, among other things, what Clausewitz understood by "absolute war." A slightly different notion of total war articulates the book that canonized the use of the term for referring to the Second World War: *The Ordeal of Total War, 1939–1945*, by Gordon Wright.[38] Like Aron, this scholar does not properly define what he means by "total war." Wright believes that in total war there is a widening in the scope of warfare. He analyzes such broadening in scope in chapters 3 (the economic dimension), 4 (the psychological dimension), and 5 (the scientific dimension). This seems to suggest that for Wright "total war" refers to the participation of the social in the war effort. A similar conceptual neglect can be found in *Total War: The Causes and Courses of the Second World War*, by Peter Calvocoressi, Guy Wint, and John Pritchard, and in Michael A. Barnhart's book *Japan Prepares for Total War: The Search for Economic Security, 1919–1941*.[39] In contrast to the aforementioned books, Eric Markusen and David Kopf's monograph *The Holocaust and Strategic Bombing: Genocide and Total War in the Twentieth Century* does provide a working definition of "total war." However, Markusen and Kopf's notion of total war differs in a significant way from the views offered or implied in the previous works. For these two authors, total war is almost synonymous with absolute war. Markusen and Kopf define it as "when two or more governments slaughter each other's civilian citizens, as well as military personnel."[40] The use of the notion of "total war" to describe specific wars of the modern age since the nineteenth century has been consolidated thanks to four important books published by Cambridge University Press between 1997 and 2003.[41] To those books we must add a collection of essays edited by Stig Förster on the debates on total war in the interwar period, Jeremy Black's *The Age of Total War, 1860–1945*, a controversial

[38] Gordon Wright, *The Ordeal of Total War, 1939–1945* (New York: Harper & Row, 1968).

[39] Peter Calvocoressi, Guy Wint, and John Pritchard, *Total War: The Causes and Courses of the Second World War*, 2nd ed. (New York: Pantheon Books, 1989); Michael A. Barnhart, *Japan Prepares for Total War: The Search for Economic Security, 1919–1941* (Ithaca, NY: Cornell University Press, 1987).

[40] Eric Markusen and David Kopf, *The Holocaust and Strategic Bombing: Genocide and Total War in the Twentieth Century* (Boulder, CO: Westview Press, 1995), 4.

[41] Stig Förster and Jörg Nagler, eds., *On the Road to Total War: The American Civil War and the German Wars of Unification, 1861–1871* (Cambridge University Press, 1997); Manfred Boemeke, Roger Chickering, and Stig Förster, eds., *Anticipating Total War: The German and American Experiences, 1871–1914* (Cambridge University Press, 1999); Roger Chickering and Stig Förster, eds., *Great War, Total War: Combat and Mobilization on the Western Front, 1914–1918* (Cambridge University Press, 2000); and Roger Chickering and Stig Förster, eds., *The Shadows of Total War: Europe, East Asia, and the United States, 1919–1939* (Cambridge University Press, 2003).

book by David A. Bell on the Napoleonic Wars, and more recently, Alya Aglan and Robert Frank's edited two-volume history of the Second World War.[42] A common characteristic of all these books on total war lies in the fact that they merge two orders of reality: the total mobilization of a society and the intensity of the struggle. In general terms, scholars tend to subsume absolute war within the notion of total war. Enzo Traverso writes, for instance, that "for Nazi Germany, total war was synonymous with the conquest of Europe, the destruction of the Soviet Union, the colonization of the Slavic world, and the extermination of the Jews," whereas for the Allies total war meant "the unconditional surrender of the enemy."[43] In turn, Jeremy Black summarizes that common move consisting in subsuming absolute war within the semantic field of total war when he defines total war in terms of the intensity of the struggle, the degree of involvement of civil society in the conflict, the geographical and temporal range of the war, and finally, the kind of goals set by the warring sides.[44]

In *The Literature of Absolute War*, "absolute war" refers, as already noted, to the *intension* of the struggle, let us repeat it, to its extreme, unbridled annihilating force, its rupture of all limits, its absolute animosity, its resistance to policy, and the potential barbaric quality of its violence (among other traits laid out and analyzed earlier in this Introduction), while "total war" means the *extension* of the conflict to all social strata, including the cultural field, the economy, and politics, in sum, the total mobilization of civilian society for the war effort. In a total war, industrial output, economic exchanges, political activity, social relations, and cultural production lose their relative autonomy in times of peace, becoming now functions of warfare; governments try to control the main fields of social activity; society becomes a *regimented* society, the economy, a *war* economy, political disputes give way to a provisional unity among antagonistic forces. This situation took place in the two world wars, and the crucial, defining link between military and nonmilitary activity is the total mobi-

---

[42] Stig Förster, ed., *An der Schwelle zum totalen Krieg. Die militärische Debatte über den Krieg der Zukunft, 1919–1939* (Paderborn: Ferdinand Schöningh, 2002); Jeremy Black, *The Age of Total War, 1860–1945* (Lanham, MD: Rowan & Littlefield Publishers, 2006); David A. Bell, *The First Total War* (Boston, MA: Houghton Mifflin Company, 2007); Alya Aglan and Robert Frank, eds., *1937–1947: La guerre-monde*, 2 vols. (Paris: Gallimard, 2015).

[43] Enzo Traverso, "Prologue. 1914–1945: Le monde au prisme de la guerre," *1937–1947: La guerre-monde*, ed. Alya Aglan and Robert Frank, vol. 1/2 (Paris: Gallimard, 2015), 27.

[44] A recent contribution to total war studies is the important monograph by Paul K. Saint-Amour on interwar culture and literature, *Tense Future: Modernism, Total War, Encyclopedic Form* (New York: Oxford University Press, 2015).

lization of the social. A total war is not necessarily an absolute war. The First World War, for instance, was a total war in Germany, Great Britain, and France, but it rarely reached the levels of absolute war. Moreover, except for its depiction by propaganda departments, the enemy was not considered in absolute terms, and in this sense it is instructive to read the literature on that war, which on not a few occasions depicts the enemy as a brother and victim of obscure transnational economic interests: Adam Scharrer's novel *Vaterlandslose Gesellen* (Fellows without Fatherland) (1930) is a case in point. The Second World War was, in contrast, both a total war and an absolute war. Total war is a modern phenomenon. In turn, absolute war has probably always been practiced, although it is also true that it has reached its deadliest degree only in modern times due to its undeniable synergy with total war.

Colonial wars fought in the nineteenth century and early twentieth century clearly demonstrate that absolute wars can be waged without overlapping with a total war. The protracted war fought between the US Army and the Native American Nations (1840–90); the French invasion, devastation, and occupation of Algeria (1830–47); the wars of extermination waged by the Germans against the Hehe in East Africa (1890–98) and the Herero in Southwest Africa (1904–7); and the cruel, merciless military conflict between the US Army and pro-independence forces in the Philippines (1899–1913) were all wars fought with the utmost ferocity. Combatants did not discriminate between enemy fighters and civilians, while the "other" was invariably considered as an absolute enemy that had to be exterminated.[45] The murder of women and children, the erection of concentration camps for the local population, the devastation of fields and crops, the killing of livestock, the razing to the ground of local towns: anything went in the colonial wars waged since the French invasion of Algeria in 1830. None of those colonial absolute wars were total, for the state did not mobilize the entire society in support of the war effort. On the other hand, colonial wars prepared the ground for the absolute wars fought in the twentieth century. A look at the number of casualties is in this sense rather instructive. They are invariably staggering. In the

---

[45] On colonial warfare in the nineteenth century and early twentieth century, see Thoralf Klein and Frank Schumacher, eds., *Kolonialkriege. Militärische Gewalt im Zeichen des Imperialismus* (Hamburg: Hamburger Edition, 2006); and Bruce Vandervort, *Wars of Imperial Conquest in Africa, 1830–1914* (Bloomington, IN: Indiana University Press, 1998). Isabel V. Hull's *Absolute Destruction: Military Culture and the Practices of War in Imperial Germany* (Ithaca, NY: Cornell University Press, 2005) is very helpful for understanding the connections between colonial warfare and the world wars to come.

231 major combats fought in German East Africa between May 1889 and June 1910, the German expeditionary forces killed approximately 150,000 local men and women.[46] In turn, the crushing of the Maji rebellion (1905–7) left a death toll that ranges from 250,000 to 300,000 indigenous people.[47] In that conflict, Germans resorted to all sorts of violent measures (e.g., setting towns ablaze, the destruction of all food supplies, the devastation of the fields, the displacement of the livestock) to force "peace" on the indigenous population.[48] Germans usually conducted colonial warfare in absolute terms. In Southwest Africa, they deliberately and openly carried out a war of extermination against the Herero. Known as the Herero War (1904–7), this colonial military conflict prefigured the sheer ruthlessness of the Second World War and the Vietnam War (1955–75). Historians do not agree on the number of Herero and Nama killed by the German expeditionary troops. Comparing the approximate data of the population before and after the war, Susanne Kuß concludes that the Germans exterminated at least one third of the Herero and Nama population.[49] The colonial war fought by the US Army in the Philippines in 1899–1913 needs to be considered, too, as a war of annihilation. Around 125,000 American soldiers fought in that war; 4,200 were killed, and 3,500 were wounded. On the side of the Filipinos, 20,000 pro-independence fighters died in combat. The striking figures are, however, those of the civilian Filipinos who died as a result of confinement in concentration camps, starvation, or murder; they range from 250,000 to one third of the population dead, namely 750,000 people.[50]

All those colonial military conflicts constitute absolute wars conducted without an overlapping simultaneous total war. In the twentieth century, the Russian Civil War (1918–20); to an extent, the Spanish Civil War (1936–39); the war waged on the eastern front by Germany and the Soviet Union (1941–45); the Pacific War (1941–45); the Vietnam War (1955–75); and the conflict between Hutus and Tutsis in Rwanda

[46] Thomas Morlang, "'Die Wahehe haben ihre Vernichtung gewollt.' Der Krieg der 'kaiserlichen Schutztruppe' gegen die Hehe in deutsch-Ostafrika (1890–1898)," *Kolonialkriege. Militärische Gewalt im Zeichen des Imperialismus*, ed. Thoralf Klein and Frank Schumacher (Hamburg: Hamburger Edition, 2006), 80.
[47] Ibid., 80.   [48] Ibid., 93–94.
[49] Susanne Kuß, "Kriegführung ohne hemmende Kulturschranke. Die deutschen Kolonialkriege in Südwestafrika (1904–1907) und Ostafrika (1905–1908)," *Kolonialkriege. Militärische Gewalt im Zeichen des Imperialismus*, ed. Thoralf Klein and Frank Schumacher (Hamburg: Hamburger Edition, 2006), 212.
[50] Frank Schumacher, "'Niederbrennen, plündern und töten sollt ihr.' Der Kolonialkrieg der USA auf den Philippinen (1899–1913)," *Kolonialkriege. Militärische Gewalt im Zeichen des Imperialismus*, ed. Thoralf Klein and Frank Schumacher (Hamburg: Hamburger Edition, 2006), 114.

(April–July 1994), which caused 800,000 deaths in only 100 days, are also cases of wars close to their absolute degree, in which the enemy was seen with absolute animus – and fought accordingly. In some cases, as in the war between Germany and the Soviet Union, and also that waged between the United States and Japan, war was at once absolute and total within the wider context of a global war. Despite the undeniable fact that before 1789 there are instances of wars fought on behalf of absolute, transcendental categories (e.g., "true religion"), the extraordinary number of human and material resources, the fact that the wars would be fought, as in the French Revolution, on behalf of the nation, and not merely the crown, the political and emotional commitment of the citizen-soldier, the prominent role played by ideology, as well as the universalism of the Enlightened ideals underpinning that revolution, conferred a new dimension to warfare and exponentially increased the brutality with which the "absolute enemy" was treated. Clausewitz was wrong in believing that the Napoleonic Wars were the first instance of absolute war. As John Keegan has written in his history of warfare, wars of extermination are perhaps as old as war itself.[51] However, Clausewitz was prescient in one thing: the magnitude of violence increases exponentially with the modern industrial nation-state and the almost unlimited human and material resources that it can muster. Because of the specific constituents of modern warfare, it would be plausible to argue for the existence of "modern absolute warfare."[52]

War Writing

As is well known, writing about war is intrinsically difficult. Yet with the increasing complexity of warfare in modern times, the means for fully comprehending and portraying military conflicts have become still harder to grasp and articulate.[53] Ever since its emergence in the Napoleonic

---

[51] John Keegan, *A History of Warfare* (New York: Vintage Books, 1994), 3–60.
[52] For an introduction to modern warfare, see Roger Chickering, Dennis Showalter, and Hans van de Ven, eds., *The Cambridge History of War*, vol. 4: *War and the Modern World* (Cambridge University Press, 2012). For a brief but cogent description of modern war, see Richard English, *Modern War: A Very Short Introduction* (Oxford University Press, 2013), 5–16.
[53] For the cognitive challenge of warfare to human understanding and modes of representation, see Fredric Jameson, *The Antinomies of Realism* (London: Verso, 2013), 232–58; Kate McLoughlin, *Authoring War: The Literary Representation of War from the Iliad to Iraq* (Cambridge University Press, 2011), 232–58, and her "War and Words," *The Cambridge Companion to War Writing*, ed. Kate McLoughlin (Cambridge University Press, 2009), 15–24; and Peter Paret, *The Cognitive Challenge of War: Prussia 1806* (Princeton University Press, 2009).

campaigns, modern warfare has posed formidable challenges to epistemology, ethics, and language. As Anders Engberg-Pedersen has demonstrated in *Empire of Chance*, the Napoleonic Wars brought about an epistemic change in the history of knowledge; with them, a discourse on war developed – one that considered war as both a "problem of knowledge" and a very complex contingent activity mostly led by chance. This multi-faceted complexity of modern warfare since the Napoleonic Wars has proven elusive to mimetic representation. Take, for instance, Tolstoy and Stendhal, two writers who were keenly aware of the fact that modern war did not seamlessly fit within their realist project. In Tolstoy's *War and Peace* (1865–69) the Battle of Borodino is narrated through the gaze of Peter Bezukhov, a character who not only lacks the technical knowledge necessary for fully understanding what he observes; in addition, he cannot properly see the battle because his eyeglasses slip off as he rides his mare, leaving the nearsighted Peter Bezukhov in a precarious situation. By depicting the Battle of Borodino in this fashion, Tolstoy satisfies realism's rule of verisimilitude, but he does so by placing war on the margins of representation: in spite of the many pages devoted to its narration, the battle becomes utterly unknowable. Thirty years before Tolstoy finished *War and Peace* Stendhal had already offered a similar answer to the problem of representing modern warfare. In *La Chartreuse de Parme* (The Charterhouse of Parma) (1839) the French writer famously narrated the Battle of Waterloo through a focalizer – Fabrice del Dongo – intoxicated by the excessive ingestion of alcohol. The chaos of battle is thus refracted through the blurred perception of someone who understands nothing of what he sees. The battle is something beyond Fabrice del Dongo's grasp and therefore beyond accurate representation.[54] As would later happen in Tolstoy, Stendhal applies a formula for representing war that paradoxically undermines realist fiction: narrative unreliability does not constitute a solid scaffold for building a house of fiction as conceived by the great masters of classic realism, from Honoré de Balzac to Henry James.[55] Basically, both Stendhal and Tolstoy novelized a notion that would be pervasive in future war writing,

---

[54] On viewing war, see Jan Mieszkowski, *Watching War* (Stanford University Press, 2012); Susan Sontag, *Regarding the Pain of Others* (New York: Picador, 2003); and Anders Engberg-Pedersen and Kathrin Maurer, eds., *Visualizing War: Emotions, Technologies, Communities* (London: Routledge, 2018).

[55] For the impact of the Napoleonic Wars on realist literature, see Engberg-Pedersen, *Empire of Chance*, 184–245. Cf. Mary A. Favret's book on the Romantic representation of warfare: *War at a Distance: Romanticism and the Making of Modern Wartime* (Princeton University Press, 2010).

most particularly in writing on absolute war, namely the impossibility of cognitively mastering modern warfare.[56]

But it was the military conflict of 1914–18, not the wars fought in the nineteenth century, that truly demonstrated the poverty of language for conveying the experience of modern warfare. As it has been repeatedly pointed out, the First World War affected in fundamental ways the human capacity for understanding and representing war. The First World War's sheer vastness, its global dimension, its huge number of casualties, the alienation experienced by many soldiers in confronting a mechanized and industrialized war, as well as its ruthless command and control, long duration, and total nature, undermined the power of reason to understand the world and the ability of language to represent it, thereby shattering the very foundations of fiction as it had been practiced hitherto.[57] A "crisis of meaning" arose as an aftershock of the First World War.[58] Profoundly baffled and traumatized by the magnitude of the tragedy, European and American artists and writers had to figure out – as it has been repeatedly noted – how to represent an experience lived and perceived by many as unspeakable, unaccountable, incommunicable.[59] Among the different poetics that shaped the artistic and literary expressions of the First World War the most radical of them all stands out, the one that came closest to capturing the nature of total war: modernism.[60] This literary and artistic correlate of the dismantling of the myths of nineteenth-century Western

---

[56] For general approaches to war writing, see, among other works, David Bevan, ed., *Literature and War* (Amsterdam: Rodopi, 1990); Jim Hicks, *Lessons from Sarajevo: A War Stories Primer* (Amherst, MA: University of Massachusetts Press, 2013); Samuel Hynes, *The Soldiers' Tale: Bearing Witness to Modern War* (London: Penguin, 1997); McLoughlin, *Authoring War*; and her edited volume *The Cambridge Companion to War Writing* (Cambridge University Press, 2009); Margot Norris, *Writing War in the Twentieth Century* (Charlottesville, VA: University Press of Virginia, 2000); and James Anderson Winn, *The Poetry of War* (Cambridge University Press, 2008).

[57] See, among other studies, Paul Fussell's classic book *The Great War and Modern Memory* (Oxford University Press, 1975).

[58] James Dawes, *The Language of War: Literature and Culture in the U.S. from the Civil War through World War II* (Cambridge, MA: Harvard University Press, 2002), 131.

[59] For an analysis of this issue in British writing, see Randall Stevenson, *Literature and the Great War, 1914–1918* (Oxford University Press, 2013), 1–120.

[60] In this book, modernism is conceived of as a *longue-durée* literary practice, and not as a movement circumscribed to a specific historical period. Furthermore, in contrast to scholars who have argued for the existence of postmodernism, I consider modernism and postmodernism to be one and the same, for they share the same family resemblances. On modernism, see Peter Childs, *Modernism* (London: Routledge, 2000); Astradur Eysteinsson, *The Concept of Modernism* (Ithaca, NY: Cornell University Press, 1990); Michael Levenson, ed., *The Cambridge Companion to Modernism* (Cambridge University Press, 1999); Nil Santiáñez, *Investigaciones literarias: Modernidad, historia de la literatura y modernismos* (Barcelona: Crítica, 2002); and Vincent Sherry, ed., *The Cambridge History of Modernism* (Cambridge University Press, 2017).

society produced apropos of the First World War works as diverse as
Dadaist poetry, the war poems of Georg Trakl and Guillaume Apollinaire,
T. S. Eliot's "The Waste Land" (1922), avant-garde paintings, etchings,
and lithographs by Umberto Boccioni, Natalia Goncharova, Paul Nash,
Max Beckmann, Otto Dix, and George Grosz, as well as plays and novels
entirely or partially related to the war such as Karl Kraus's *Die letzten Tage
der Menschheit* (The Last Days of Mankind) (1922), Virginia Woolf's
Jacob's Room (1922), *Mrs. Dalloway* (1925), and *To the Lighthouse*
(1927), Ford Madox Ford's tetralogy *Parade's End* (1924–28), Edlef
Köppen's *Heeresbericht* (Army Communiqué) (1930), and Louis-
Ferdinand Céline's *Voyage au bout de la nuit* (Journey to the End of the
Night) (1932).[61] While the vast majority of literature written on the First
World War falls within the parameters of realism, or follows traditional
patterns and models, the poetics and practice of modernism provided
writers with an innovative language for expressing a new phenomenon
(i.e., total war within the context of a global war), thereby opening new
grounds for the representation of modern warfare.

An investigation on the writing of absolute war reveals that the general
labels usually employed to describe modern fiction – "realism" and "modernism" – are somewhat insufficient for capturing the specificity of the
works devoted to its representation. To be sure, this phenomenon is
already present in the literature on the First World War I have just referred
to, but it was exacerbated in the works written on the world war of
1939–45. Michael Rothberg is one of the scholars who has tackled this
problem in his analysis of a war-related event: the Nazi destruction of the
European Jews.[62] The "demands of Holocaust representation" are such
that traditional realism as practiced since the nineteenth century proved to
be unable to capture the experience of the *Lager*. To solve the challenges
posed by the *Endlösung* or Final Solution to representation, survivors and
writers came up with a form of realism that differs in significant ways from
traditional realism. Rothberg calls this new kind of realism "traumatic
realism." According to him, traumatic realism is "a form of documentation

---

[61] On the Anglo-American modernism produced apropos of the First World War, see Saint-Amour,
Tense Future, 90–132, 179–302; and Vincent Sherry, *The Great War and the Language of
Modernism* (New York: Oxford University Press, 2006). For an overview of the avant-garde in
the context of that military conflict, see Modris Eksteins, *Rites of Spring: The Great War and the
Birth of the Modern Age* (Boston, MA: Mariner Books, 2000); and Ernst Piper, *Nacht über Europa.
Kulturgeschichte des Ersten Weltkriegs* (Berlin: List Taschenbuch, 2014), 98–150, 291–314.
[62] Michael Rothberg, *Traumatic Realism: The Demands of Holocaust Representation* (Minneapolis,
MN: University of Minnesota Press, 2000).

and historical cognition attuned to the demands of extremity."[63] It seeks to bring forth traces of trauma and to preserve and expose "the abyss between everyday reality and real extremity."[64] It is precisely that abyss that "frustrates the mechanisms that make up realism's conditions of possibility."[65] "The problematics of representing and coming to terms with an extreme historical event," Rothberg writes, "push[ed] the realist project ... to its limits." Traumatic realism exceeds, accordingly, the framework of classic realism. "Traumatic realist texts," he argues, "search for a form of documentation beyond direct reference and coherent narrative but do not fully abandon the possibility for some kind of reference and some kind of narrative."[66] Hence the alternation of realist techniques with modernist devices in traumatic realist works. Put differently: there is a socially shared universe of meaning under conditions of traumatic realism – which is one of the preconditions for practicing realist literature – , "but it is defamiliarized by its inextricability from another world," that is to say, the concentrationary universe.[67] This sort of dual nature explains the points of overlap with modernism and also the differences between the two forms of writing: traumatic realism shares with modernism a distrust of representation; at the same time, "it nevertheless cannot free itself from the claims of mimesis, and it remains committed to a project of historical cognition through the mediation of culture."[68] The traditional theory of reflection does not apply to traumatic realism because this form of writing does not attempt to reflect the traumatic event mimetically, "but to *produce* it as an object of knowledge and to *transform* its readers so that they are forced to acknowledge their relationship to post-traumatic culture."[69] On account of its providing access to something previously unknowable, and also because of its drive to teach readers how to approach that object, "the stakes of traumatic realism are at once epistemological and pedagogical, or, in other words, political."[70] Although Rothberg uses this category solely in the context of the literature produced on the *Endlösung*, traumatic realism is a term that can be perfectly applied to works on modern warfare, most particularly to mimetic works on war in its absolute degree.

We encounter similar problems when we use the term "modernism" to describe certain experimental literary works on absolute war. Often, the label "modernism" does not properly convey the specific characteristics, function, and purpose of modernist artifacts on a catastrophe such as war

---

[63] Ibid., 14. [64] Ibid., 139. [65] Ibid., 139. [66] Ibid., 99, 100–1. [67] Ibid., 140.
[68] Ibid., 140. [69] Ibid., 140. [70] Ibid., 140.

in its absolute degree. Whether their cause is human agency (e.g., wars, genocide) or a lack thereof (e.g., natural phenomena like earthquakes or hurricanes), catastrophes challenge the human capacity for processing, understanding, remembering, and representing experience. As we all know, catastrophic events may even temporarily knock down the mental tools used by human beings for their cognition and storage of reality, thereby triggering in survivors of catastrophes a post-traumatic stress disorder. In his book on the "writing of disaster," Maurice Blanchot has argued that disasters constitute a break with any form of totality. They mean the "ruin of the word" and entail the fragmentation of the unity of the subject who has lived it. A disaster is a reminder that "would cross out through invisibility and illegibility all that shows itself and all that is said."[71] Hence a disaster, according to Blanchot, "unwrites"; it limits and erodes the individual's ability to understand and express it through language. Catastrophes may be considered, therefore, as the "end of meaning."[72] Given such an effect of catastrophic events on cognition and verbal expression, given, also, the *excess* inherent in catastrophes, a crucial question immediately arises: Which are the most cogent literary practices, rhetorical strategies, and linguistic tools for narrating catastrophes and their impact on language, space, cultural memory, and social relations, as well as on the human body and mind?

Modernist literary works refract the "unwriting" caused by disasters with more precision than realist literature does. Through experiments with style, language, and literary conventions, they formally display the disruptive, massive, and shattering nature of disasters. Because of this interconnection between catastrophes and the language of modernism, modernist works written on catastrophic events belong to what I suggest calling *catastrophic modernism*. By *catastrophic modernism* I refer to the specific type of modernism produced in response to catastrophes such as absolute war, total war, the Nazi extermination program, natural disasters, and global terrorism. Its family resemblances (to use Wittgenstein's notion) are similar to those of interwar modernism.[73] However, in addition to the usual family resemblances of modernism, catastrophic modernist works

---

[71] Maurice Blanchot, *L'écriture du désastre* (Paris: Gallimard, 1980), 68–69.

[72] Matthew Gumpert, *The End of Meaning: Studies in Catastrophe* (Newcastle upon Tyne: Cambridge Scholars Publishing, 2012).

[73] The notion of "family resemblances" (*Familienähnlichkeiten*) was developed by Ludwig Wittgenstein in *Philosophical Investigations*, trans. G. E. M. Anscombe, 2nd ed. (Oxford: Blackwell Publishers, 1997), sections 65–71, 92, 108, 114. For a detailed analysis of the family resemblances of modernism, see Santiáñez, *Investigaciones literarias*, 121–35, 247–380.

share several core features that set them apart from other modernist literary artifacts. First, catastrophic modernist texts are determined, to a certain extent, by disaster. Catastrophes such as absolute war somehow seem to partly mold the creativity of authors who intend to represent them, their substance leading writers towards choosing those literary devices most cogent for portraying the many dimensions, as well as the variegated consequences, of disasters. In their attempt to bear witness to disaster, these kinds of work are decisively shaped by the very structure of catastrophic events. The modernism of catastrophic modernist texts is, therefore, a *function* of the horror that they depict. Second, catastrophic modernist artifacts subvert by formal means the traditional ways used to communicate and reflect on catastrophe (e.g., historical accounts, journalistic chronicles, essays). In so doing, they defamiliarize the usual representation of disasters, thereby offering potentially enriching new insights on them. Third, catastrophic modernism usually contains an ethical dimension. When that is the case, it demands from readers a reflection at once political and ethical on disastrous events caused by human agency. This is most true of many instances of modern war writing. Fourth, catastrophic modernism seeks to transfer the destructive effects of catastrophes to the readers' understanding and affectivity. The literary artifacts comprised within catastrophic modernism may be characterized as "passionate utterances," a notion put forth and developed by Stanley Cavell to designate perlocutionary speech acts produced to have consequential effects on the reader's feelings, affects, thoughts, and actions.[74] As passionate utterances, catastrophic modernist works are intended to lead the reader, through literary experiments, to somehow feel the emotional distress, existential precariousness, and cognitive disorientation experienced by individuals who have endured a disaster. Fifth, catastrophic modernism is permeated, in different degrees, by what we could term *the writing of cruelty*. The graphic description and narration of barbaric forms of human violence can make the reading of catastrophic modernist texts an unpleasant experience. Catastrophic modernist works that openly indulge in the explicit and vivid narration, for instance, of absolute war's excesses, cruelly perform on the reader a symbolic violence that refracts the physical violence perpetrated by troops in the battlefield.

The use of modernist devices to represent catastrophes needs to be understood in connection with all those five essential characteristics.

---

[74] Stanley Cavell, *Philosophy the Day after Tomorrow* (Cambridge, MA: The Belknap Press of Harvard University Press, 2005), 186.

Certainly, modernist literary techniques have a complex history, and they have been employed in countless texts that have nothing to do with catastrophe. However, whenever I single out for analysis one modernist device it is important to bear in mind that such particular technique, insofar as it is specifically used to represent absolute war, automatically relates to a set of basic features that partly shape catastrophic modernism, thereby acquiring a new specific function and meaning. The boundaries of catastrophic modernism comprise all the possible combinations of the aforementioned core features with the family resemblances of modernism in general.

Catastrophic modernist writing on absolute war as it was fought in the Second World War stems, to a degree, from the catastrophic modernist tradition started by literary works on the First World War. However, it is also true that the absolute war fought in the Second World War has its own specificity – a specificity that projects itself onto the themes and forms of the literature that represents it. Fighting to death; bringing combat to the extremes Clausewitz spoke of; the drive to annihilate the enemy; the systematic assassination of enemy civilians (e.g., the Germans' murder of political commissars, members of the Communist Party, and Jews after their invasion of the Soviet Union); the perpetration of sexual violence (Soviet troops raped over 2 million German women of all ages); the extermination of entire segments of the population (e.g., the Nazi industrial mass murder of Jews, homosexuals, the Roma people, and the mentally ill or handicapped); the breaking up of all boundaries, including the lifting of all moral reservations with respect to the aerial bombardment of civilian targets; the use of atomic weapons against urban centers – these are phenomena that differentiate the Second World War from the world war of 1914–18. The differences between absolute war in 1939–45 and total war in 1914–18 created the basis for new ways of practicing the poetics of catastrophic modernism. A number of modernist literary texts on the Second World War reproduced the push towards the extremes performed by absolute war, their authors radicalizing the modernist discourse on catastrophe. The extreme reality of absolute war seemed to demand an extreme kind of literature at both the thematic and formal levels. As we will see, the catastrophic modernist works analyzed in *The Literature of Absolute War* bring us closer to the catastrophe of absolute war by means of all sorts of experiments with vocabulary, syntax, imagery, and generic conventions.[75] These literary

---

[75] Cf. Marina MacKay, *Modernism, War, and Violence* (London: Bloomsbury, 2017).

works employ a rich, complex language for narrating the experience of catastrophe. They acknowledge the difficulty, if not the outright impossibility, of cognitively mastering the catastrophic event. Their awareness of the utter incommensurability of disaster allows us to conclude that catastrophic modernism is a modern sublime.

Finally, I would like to underscore that in this book the terms "realism" and "modernism" do not describe two discrete groups that comprise works of fiction. Instead, they are conceived of as constituting the ideal poles of what I have elsewhere called *the spectrum of possibilities*.[76] Most of the modern fiction written since *Don Quixote* (1st part 1605, 2nd part 1615) has been produced within the spectrum of possibilities. This spectrum functions like a magnetic field of sorts. Literary works gravitate towards one or the other pole, never reaching either of them because in the spectrum of possibilities realism and modernism constitute ideal notions; there is no work that fulfills *all* the criteria for belonging to modernism or to realism. The spectrum of possibilities is a structure of the modern age.[77] As an epochal structure, the spectrum of possibilities is, therefore, the condition of possibility for the production of any work of fiction written in modernity, from the seventeenth century to the present. I will tacitly use the spectrum of possibilities as an analytic tool for exploring works of fiction produced to represent absolute war, always bearing in mind that the pole of modernism contains a class of modernist works that I call "catastrophic modernism," and also that half-way between the pole of modernism and the pole of realism there is the poetics of traumatic realism.

---

[76] Santiáñez, *Investigaciones literarias*, 76–77.

[77] I use the notion of "structure" in the sense given by Fernand Braudel. According to the French historian, *longue durées* or long-time spans are articulated by structures. Braudel writes: "a structure is no doubt an assemblage, a reconstruction, and an architecture, but even more than that it is a reality that time uses poorly and transmits throughout a long period of time. Certain structures, extremely long-lived, turn into stable elements for an infinity of generations ... Other structures are more prone to disappear. But all of them are at once foundations and obstacles" (*Écrits sur l'histoire* [Paris: Flammarion, 1969], 50).

CHAPTER ONE

The Horror

Extermination

Expressed in the context of late nineteenth-century European colonialism, Kurtz's suggestion to "Exterminate all the brutes!"[1] would be followed to the letter in many battlefields and several key fronts of the Second World War. Combats in Eastern Europe, Southeast Asia, and the Pacific were fought with the racism, savagery, and absolute animosity that had defined earlier instances of absolute war, namely the colonial conflicts waged in the "age of empire" – to use a periodological label developed by Eric J. Hobsbawm – mentioned above. Whether in the forbidding frozen steppes of Ukraine and Russia, or in the thick, treacherous jungles of the South Pacific islands, each warring force perceived the enemy as "brutes" that deserved nothing short of extermination.

We can get a glimpse of what Kurtz's desideratum entailed for the troops on the ground by reading the closing chapter of Norman Mailer's 1948 novel *The Naked and the Dead* – a chapter that fictionalizes a not uncommon practice of the US armed forces in the war against Japan. In these final pages, the narrator elliptically describes the mopping up operation undertaken by the American troops that have just seized Anopopei, a fictional island located somewhere in the South Pacific. As if to reassure the postwar American reader from the outset, the narrator states that the operation "was eminently successful."[2] Dispersed in small units, the remnants of the Japanese garrison were an easy prey for American patrols combing the island. By the end of the mopping up "the casualty figures were unbelievable," the narrator acknowledges without the slightest sign of irony or disapproval. He even adds specific information on the number of cold-blooded kills: on the fifth day, 278 Japanese were killed while only

[1] Joseph Conrad, *Heart of Darkness. The Congo Diary* (London: Penguin, 2007), 62.
[2] Norman Mailer, *The Naked and the Dead* (New York: Picador, 1998), 715. Further references in text.

two Americans died in the operation; on the eighth day, "the most productive of the campaign," American squads killed 821 Japanese and captured nine at the cost of three American lives (715). General Cummings, the commander-in-chief of the American forces that invaded Anopopei, "had handled the mopping up with brilliance" (716). In order to alleviate the nervousness caused by his awareness of the secondary role that he had played in the decisive action that defeated the Japanese defending the island, he "carried out the mopping up with a ceaseless concentration on details" (718). Accordingly, General Cummings verifies that on the sixth day of the mopping up operation 347 Japanese were killed, while on the ninth up to 502 Japanese had been shot dead by American troops (718). Adding up those figures to the ones provided earlier by the narrator, we learn that 1,948 Japanese were massacred in just four days of the nine-day mopping up operation at the cost of only six American lives. The enormous disproportion between the casualties on each side clearly shows that Japanese soldiers were hunted down and liquidated without mercy. If we are to believe the narrator, the troops enjoyed this murderous activity. Considering the dangers that the American soldiers had faced while fighting their way through the island, "the mopping up was comparatively pleasant, almost exciting" (718). Not only this: in fact, "The killing lost all dimension, bothered the men far less than discovering some ants in their bedding" (718). Remarkably, Americans also killed defenseless wounded Japanese lying in bed in improvised field hospitals (718–19). According to the narrator, prisoners were taken only occasionally and under very specific circumstances (719–20).[3] Indeed, the Japanese soldiers hunted down by patrols of GIs were visited by "the horror!" Kurtz cries out twice before he dies.[4]

In the Pacific War Americans displayed racism and a genocidal disposition. The racist mentality of the Americans vis-à-vis the Japanese underpinned a barbarous behavior during the war that led to horrific scenes, the ultimate of them being, of course, those produced by the atomic bombs dropped on Hiroshima and Nagasaki. American novels, war dispatches, and memoirs on the Pacific theater of war provide a close and detailed view of the ruthless actions performed by the US armed forces against the Japanese Imperial army. From a psychological and ideological standpoint,

---

[3] Cf. James Jones's *The Thin Red Line* (1962; New York: Dial Press Trade Paperbacks, 2012), a classic novel on the Battle of Guadalcanal that vividly portrays the Americans' brutal treatment of the Japanese during the Second World War.

[4] Conrad, *Heart of Darkness*, 86.

the US armed forces conducted the war in the Pacific driven by two powerful destructive forces. One of them was the profound resentment caused by the Japanese attack on Pearl Harbor on December 7, 1941. Pearl Harbor did not demoralize Americans, as the Japanese had expected with misplaced optimism. On the contrary: the "sneak attack," as the Japanese onslaught would be contemptuously known in the United States, served as "a rallying cry that motivated Americans to greater efforts and hardened their hearts."[5] It was precisely this "hardness of the heart," among other factors, that made the war in the Pacific "one of the most merciless, brutal and intense conflicts in history."[6] In a seminal book on the racism that led both the Americans and the Japanese to fight each other in 1941–45 with such ferocity and absolute animus, John W. Dower underscores that the attack on Pearl Harbor "provoked a rage bordering on the genocidal among Americans. Thus, Admiral William Halsey ... vowed after Pearl Harbor that by the end of the war Japanese would be spoken only in hell, and rallied his men thereafter under such slogans as 'Kill Japs, kill Japs, kill more Japs.' Or as the US Marines put it in a well-known variation on Halsey's motto: 'Remember Pearl Harbor – keep 'em dying.'"[7] The dropping of two atomic weapons on Japan was partly motivated by this anger, at least if we are to believe President Truman's speech of August 6, 1945, announcing to the world the atomic bombing of Hiroshima. Early in the speech, Truman inadvertently reveals the resentment that under-pinned the fateful decision to drop the bomb: "The Japanese began the war from the air at Pearl Harbor. They have been repaid manifold."[8]

The second force that powered American brutality in the Pacific was racism, which antedates the outbreak of the war in the Pacific.[9] After December 7, 1941, this racism acquired in not a few quarters a genocidal character. While Americans usually, if not always, differentiated between "bad" and "good" Germans, they considered all Japanese as being essentially "treacherous" and "barbaric." Likened to all sorts of animals, as well as children, primitive people, and madmen, the Japanese had by no means a good press in the United States.[10] It is no coincidence, in this sense, that the

---

[5] John T. Kuehn, "The War in the Pacific, 1941–1945," *The Cambridge History of the Second World War*, ed. John Ferris and Evan Mawdsley, vol. 1/3 (Cambridge University Press, 2015), 425.
[6] Ibid., 425.
[7] John W. Dower, *War without Mercy: Race and Power in the Pacific War* (New York: Pantheon Books, 1986), 36.
[8] Harry S. Truman, "Statement by the President Announcing the Use of the A-Bomb at Hiroshima," The American Presidency Project, 1999–2017, www.presidency.ucsb.edu/ws/?pid=1216, accessed August 6, 2017.
[9] Dower, *War without Mercy*, 8.   [10] Ibid., 77–200.

American armed forces had drafted plans, before December 1941, to incinerate Japanese cities.[11] Atrocities, hatred, and absolute violence in the Pacific and Southeast Asia can only be understood in the context of racism and a genocidal drive. A poll taken by the US armed forces in 1943 revealed that half of the American soldiers believed that killing all Japanese was necessary in order to achieve peace.[12] "By the final year of the war," Dower reminds us, "one out of four US combatants stated that his primary goal was not to help bring about Japan's surrender, but simply to kill as many Japanese as possible."[13] Even more remarkable are, however, the polls taken among American civilians; they indicate that between 10 and 13 percent of Americans "consistently supported the 'annihilation' or 'extermination' of the Japanese as a people, while a comparable percentage were in favor of severe retribution after Japan had been defeated."[14] A vast majority of Americans demanded nothing short of Japan's absolute, complete defeat.[15] Such attitudes and expectations reflected the GIs' mentality and behavior on the ground. American troops in the field mutilated, or saw being mutilated, Japanese corpses in order to take "souvenirs" (ears, noses, teeth, even skulls), sunk hospital ships, shot at sailors who had abandoned ship and pilots who had bailed out of their planes, killed defenseless wounded soldiers, tortured enemy troops, and were notoriously reluctant to take prisoners, often executing on the spot Japanese soldiers who had just surrendered.[16]

In turn, Japanese troops had committed all sorts of atrocities ever since their invasion of China in September 1931. The war in Southeast Asia took on from the very beginning a colonial and racial dimension. Accordingly, officers and the rank-and-file acted with deliberate cruelty and the utmost violence on countless occasions during the Second Sino-Japanese War (1937–45), in their conquest of territory in Southeast Asia, and later in their war against the United States. The perpetration of mass massacres of noncombatants; the mistreatment, torture, and sometimes even murder of prisoners of war; the use of prisoners as forced labor and women from conquered areas as prostitutes in brothels for the troops; the conducting of medical experiments on enemy combatants and noncombatants alike – these were the most common dishonorable practices of the Japanese armed forces. The so-called Rape of Nanjing stands as the most notorious war crime ever perpetrated by the Japanese against the enemy. Nanjing was seized by the Japanese on December 13, 1937, after they had indiscriminately strafed, shelled, and bombed the city. But the real mass

[11] Ibid., 41–42.   [12] Ibid., 53.   [13] Ibid., 53.   [14] Ibid., 53.   [15] Ibid., 55.
[16] Ibid., 61–72.

massacre began in fact when the Japanese took over the city. Over a period of six weeks, the Japanese troops sacked Nanjing with zest, looting its shops, raping thousands of women, and killing at will combatants and noncombatants alike. Although there are no precise, definitive figures concerning the number of casualties, it is commonly agreed that up to 200,000 people were slaughtered in Nanjing by the Japanese Imperial army. It was not the first time that Japanese troops murdered Chinese citizens. In the early 1930s Japan had already persecuted and liquidated Chinese "bandits." However, the mass massacre of Nanjing set a new standard for future Japanese actions in South Asia and in the Pacific, this time against the Americans.

The racism and absolute enmity displayed by both the Japanese and the American troops were often expressed in the ferocity of combats. The history of the Pacific War has been told many times, which renders it unnecessary to rehearse here events and figures.[17] Suffice it to say that the fierce battles for Guadalcanal, Iwo Jima, and Okinawa constitute three emblems of the merciless absolute war waged by Japan and the United States. In Iwo Jima, the 21,000 troops commanded by General Kuribayashi Tadamichi fought almost literally to the last man, inflicting in five weeks around 28,000 casualties (6,800 of them fatal) on the American troops that had landed on the beaches of Iwo on February 19, 1945. These figures would be dwarfed by those of the Battle of Okinawa. In eighty-two days, the defending Japanese troops killed over 21,000 sailors and soldiers and wounded around 55,000 Americans. The Japanese losses were far more staggering: the 100,000-man-strong garrison would be completely annihilated, while the civilian losses totaled at least 80,000. Other instances of mass massacres would be the American firebombing of Tokyo on the night of March 9–10, 1945 (with a death toll of 85,000 civilians), and the atomic bombing of Hiroshima and Nagasaki, which resulted – as already mentioned in the Preface – in 200,000 deaths by November 1945. The final death toll of the war in Southeast Asia and the Pacific will probably never be known with precision. Recent estimates of the casualties of war in that region of the world since the beginning of the Second Sino-Japanese War in 1937 until the surrender of Japan announced by Emperor Hirohito on August 15, 1945, have established that over 25 million people died, out of

---

[17] For a comprehensive one-volume introduction to the Pacific War, see John Costello, *The Pacific War, 1941–1945* (New York: Harper Perennial, 2009). A much more detailed account can be found in Jerome Hagen's multi-volume history of that conflict: *War in the Pacific*, 5 vols. (Honolulu, HI: Hawaii Pacific University, 1998–2010).

which more than two thirds were civilians.[18] In the Japanese Imperial army 2,121,955 men lost their lives, while the deaths and men missing in action in the American armed forces totaled, in the Pacific War, 111,606.[19]

As vicious as the Pacific War was, the classic instance of absolute war in the Second World War is the one fought between Nazi Germany and the Soviet Union in 1941–45.[20] This military conflict was, from beginning to end, a colonial war of extermination. The German designs with respect to the Soviet Union had an obvious colonial basis. The National Socialists never concealed their view that the Soviet Union was the enemy to beat, and they usually talked or wrote about it in colonial terms: the ultimate purpose of a war against the USSR was to colonize and exploit all land from the western borders to the Urals. Therefore, when Germany invaded the Soviet Union it did it with two main objectives in mind: the extermination of an absolute enemy and the conquest and occupation of as much land as possible for the expansion of Germany's "living space." Deeply conditioned by the National Socialists' theory of *Lebensraum*, as well as their ideological animus against the Slavs, the Jews, Bolshevism, and the Soviet Union, the war in the East was, from its early stages, a vicious war of annihilation.[21] Shortly before the invasion, a series of directives were issued to commanders in the field stipulating the murder on the spot of captured Soviet commissars (i.e., the *Kommissarbefehl* or "commissar order" issued by the German High Command), *Ostjuden*, and partisans, as well as the approval of reprisals against entire villages (i.e., the "Barbarossa decree," described by Christopher R. Browning as a "'shooting license' against Russian civilians").[22] Combats were usually to the finish, and detachments

---

[18] Kuehn, "The War in the Pacific, 1941–1945," 454.

[19] "Casualties," in Kent G. Budge, "The Pacific War Online Encyclopedia," 2007–13, www.pwencycl .kgbudge.com, accessed September 12, 2017.

[20] See Chris Bellamy, *Absolute War: Soviet Russia in the Second World War* (New York: Alfred A. Knopf, 2007), 16–38. He rightly claims that two kinds of war overlapped in the military conflict between Nazi Germany and the Soviet Union: absolute war and total war.

[21] The bibliography on the war between Nazi Germany and the USSR is quite extensive. See, for instance, Bellamy, *Absolute War*; Stephen G. Fritz, *Ostkrieg: Hitler's War of Extermination in the East* (Lexington, KY: University Press of Kentucky, 2011); Richard Overy, *Russia's War: A History of the Soviet War Effort, 1941–1945* (New York: Penguin Books, 1998); and Timothy Snyder, *Bloodlands: Europe between Hitler and Stalin* (New York: Basic Books, 2010). For compact histories of military operations on the eastern front, see David R. Stone, "Operations on the Eastern Front, 1941–1945," *The Cambridge History of the Second World War*, ed. John Ferris and Evan Mawdsley, vol. 1/3 (Cambridge University Press, 2015), 331–57; and Masha Cerovic, "Le front Germano-Soviétique (1941–1945): Une apocalypse européenne," *1937–1947: La guerre-monde*, ed. Alya Aglan and Robert Frank, vol. 1/2 (Paris: Gallimard, 2015), 913–62.

[22] Christopher R. Browning, *Ordinary Men: Reserve Police Battalion 101 and the Final Solution in Poland*, revised ed. (New York: Harper Perennial, 2017), 11.

of *Einsatzgruppen* or task forces (aided on not a few occasions by the Wehrmacht)[23] rounded up in the rearguard Jews, political commissars, and people suspected of being dangerous, and summarily executed them. It has been estimated that the *Einsatzgruppen* murdered, in open-air shootings in 1941–43, over 1.3 million people.[24] Political indoctrination had prepared German soldiers to fight an absolute war, and the war in the East reached from its outset extreme levels of savagery.[25] Operation Barbarossa had been thought out as yet another *Blitzkrieg*, but the Soviets, after the initial setbacks of their army, dug in and defended themselves with determination and ferocity; by December 1941 they had already killed 300,000 Germans. The Nazis conceived of the war as an extermi-nating "crusade" against "Judeobolshevism." In the terse words of Field Marshal Wilhelm Keitel, the war against the Soviet Union was "an ideological war of extermination."[26] The German officers as well as the rank-and-file who fought against the Soviet Union were "not only military combatants but political warriors as well" whose purpose was the complete annihilation of the Soviet Union.[27] What led the war in the East to its exceptionally murderous power was the priority given to racial (anti-Semitic) and ideological (anti-communist or anti-fascist) principles. After the initial debacle, which rendered Stalin literally speechless for days, the Soviet troops reorganized themselves, imposed a strict discipline (e.g., Stalin's Order 227, which stipulated for his soldiers "not one step back!"), and were encouraged to kill as many Germans as possible, a murderousness that exponentially increased as soon as they recovered lost territory and saw the levels of destruction caused by the Germans. This would ultimately lead to a heightened violence that found a tragic emblem in the rape of approximately 2 million German women by Red Army troops. From June 1941 to early May 1945, the war of annihilation fought between Nazi Germany and the Soviet Union was, in effect, an instance of absolute war. That war was "absolute" on account of its sheer brutality, the savagery of

[23] On the willing participation of the Wehrmacht in the perpetration of war crimes in Eastern Europe, see Hannes Heer and Klaus Naumann, eds., *Vernichtungskrieg. Verbrechen der Wehrmacht, 1941–1944* (Hamburg: Hamburger Edition, 1995).
[24] Raul Hilberg, *The Destruction of the European Jews* (New York: Holmes & Meier, 1985), 338. For a historical account of the *Einsatzgruppen*, see Richard Rhodes's book *Masters of Death: The SS-Einsatzgruppen and the Invention of the Holocaust* (New York: Vintage Books, 2003).
[25] Omer Bartov's book *Hitler's Army: Soldiers, Nazis, and War in the Third Reich* (New York: Oxford University Press, 1991) provides an accurate account of the German armed forces' political indoctrination.
[26] Quoted in Bellamy, *Absolute War*, 27.
[27] Arno J. Mayer, *Why Did the Heavens Not Darken? The "Final Solution" in History* (New York: Pantheon Books, 1988), 210.

the fighting, the atrocities committed against partisans, civilians, wounded enemies, and prisoners of war, and the huge number of casualties. Approximately 3 million German soldiers died or went missing in action fighting the Red Army, a figure that exceeds the total number of German deaths from all the other fronts combined (2 million). Half of them died between January and May 1945 as a result of the increased brutalization of the war in its final stages. In turn, the Red Army lost 9 million men and women, combining those killed in action, the ones who were missing in combat, and those who died in German concentration camps, while Soviet civilian losses exceeded 20 million people dead.[28]

In the remaining pages of this chapter I will concentrate all my attention on one single instance of absolute war, the most radical and brutal of them all: the war fought by Nazi Germany and its allies against the Soviet Union. I will revisit the absolute war in the Pacific theater when I discuss, in the next chapter, the literature on the atomic bomb. The goal of this chapter is the exploration of the interplay between the practice of absolute war and its written representation on the one hand, and the determination of several key family resemblances of the literature of absolute war on the other. I will develop six basic propositions: (i) the unbracketing of war leads to the fragmentation of both the individual's psyche and narrative; (ii) there is a correlation between the dissolution of the limit in absolute war and abjection; (iii) the brutality of combat in absolute war is textually replicated by the writing of cruelty; (iv) absolute enmity may be connected, in absolute war, to genocide and radical evil; (v) the destruction of limits in absolute war leads to useless suffering and to the erosion of meaning, turning warfare into something altogether absurd; and (vi) several literary devices, such as multiple or variable internal focalization, the prominence of dialogue, the presence of multiple narrators, and the practice of collage and montage may be considered as discursive antidotes to the absolute animosity that characterizes absolute war.

Kaput, the Abject, and the Writing of Cruelty

Moving away from the ordinary use and connotations that the word has in the English language, I employ *kaput* as an analytical term because of its ability to condense important meanings connected to war in its absolute degree. *Kaput,* or the condition of being utterly finished, worn out, defeated, destroyed, or dead, is a pervasive trait shared by numerous texts

[28] Stone, "Operations on the Eastern Front, 1941–1945," 356–57.

on absolute war. To be sure, this family resemblance of much writing on absolute war is already apparent in works published before the world war of 1939–45: take, for instance, several texts written on the First World War, such as Henri Barbusse's *Le Feu* (Under Fire) (1916) and Edlef Köppen's *Heeresbericht* (Army Communiqué) (1930). The state of being or going kaput plays nonetheless a more prominent role in narratives focused on complete military annihilation. More than in the representation of any other kind of war, in narratives on absolute war everything and everybody seems to go or to be kaput. Such is the intensity of this family resemblance of the literature on absolute war that the very discourse used to narrate it may internalize the representation of kaput within its own texture; when that is the case, the language, plot, discourse, rhetorical devices, and narrative strategies used to portray unlimited violence and destruction on a vast scale are, as it were, broken up. Kaput finds its climactic expression in works on the Second World War, particularly in those that concentrate on the eastern front, on the strategic bombing of Germany, and on the war waged in Southeast Asia and the Pacific. All the narratives analyzed in this chapter contain kaput in varying degrees. The main issues that I would like to address here concern, above all, the literary strategies used to express kaput in two of the first narratives ever written on the eastern front, the different levels of intensity in which kaput penetrates and determines those narratives, the representation of the victims of absolute war, the connection between the depiction of kaput and the writing of cruelty, and finally the close links between kaput and the abject.

Kaputt is precisely the title of one of the first works of fiction that took up the extreme challenge posed to language and rhetoric by absolute war as it was fought on the eastern front. Authored by the disenchanted fascist Curzio Malaparte (pen name of Kurt Erich Suckert), this novel published in 1944 constitutes an extraordinary literary achievement, not only because it is one of the most remarkable catastrophic modernist masterpieces produced on the world war of 1939–45, but also because, contrary to a common belief among scholars (i.e., that *Kaputt* is not exactly a war novel, its main preoccupation being, so this interpretation goes, the decadence of Europe), Malaparte's novel both captures and internalizes essential aspects of absolute war.[29] This rather singular instance of modernist autofiction

---

[29] For other approaches to Malaparte's *Kaputt*, see Peter-André Alt, "Der Schelm und die Nazis. Ordnungsstörung als pikareskes Prinzip im Erzählen über das Dritte Reich: Malaparte, Grass und Littell," *Wilde Lektüren. Literatur und Leidenschaft*, ed. Wiebke Amthor, Almut Hille, and Susanne Scharnowski (Bielefeld: Aisthesis, 2012), 383–407; Colman Andrews, "Eating Malaparte,"

(the narrator and main character of *Kaputt* is a morally ambiguous and well-connected Italian war correspondent who bears the same surname as the author's) partly follows the experience of Malaparte himself as the war correspondent for the Italian daily *Corriere della sera*.[30] Thanks to his literary reputation, fascist credentials, and Italian nationality (Italy would send expeditionary troops to fight alongside the Wehrmacht against the Red Army), Malaparte enjoyed a relatively privileged position at the front while working for the aforementioned newspaper which allowed him to have access to individuals and places beyond the reach of most people. A seasoned reporter (he had already worked for *Corriere della sera* in East Africa in 1939) and war writer (in 1941 he published a novel on the Franco-Italian front titled *Il sole è cieco* [The Sun is Blind]), he would collect his war dispatches in a volume titled *Il Volga nasce in Europa* (The Volga Starts in Europe) (1943).

One of the first things that catches the reader's attention is *Kaputt*'s modernist plotlessness as well as the remarkable centrality in the novel of the act of telling war stories. In a way, *Kaputt* may be described as a novel about the act of telling stories on absolute war. Unlike novels on the horrors of the eastern front such as Viktor Nekrasov's popular award-winning *Front-Line Stalingrad* (1946), Theodor Plievier's *Stalingrad* (1945), or Gert Ledig's *Die Stalinorgel* (Stalin's Organ) (1955), *Kaputt* does not depict battles or hand-to-hand combat. Its approach to absolute war is elliptic. *Kaputt* consists of eighteen chapters grouped into six thematic parts. The six parts that make up the novel are not organized within a lineal logic. Neither the events, nor the different narrative frameworks of the novel, are chronologically arranged. This classic instance of war writing follows the conventions of a spatial form, a notion developed by Joseph Frank to

Malaparte: A House Like Me, ed. Michael McDonough and Tom Wolfe (New York: Clarkson Potter, 1999), 150–55; Charles Burdett, "Changing Identities through Memory: Malaparte's Self-Figurations in *Kaputt*," *European Memories of the Second World War*, ed. Helmut Peitsch, Charles Burdett, and Claire Gorrara (New York: Berghahn Books, 1999), 110–19; Gianni Grana, *Curzio Malaparte* (Milan: Marzorati editore, 1961), 60–88; William Hope, *Curzio Malaparte* (Market Harborough: Troubador, 2000), 81–94, and his "The Narrative Contract Strained: The Problems of Narratorial Neutrality in Malaparte's *Kaputt*," *Italianist: Journal of the Department of Italian Studies, University of Reading* 19 (1999), 178–92; Gary Indiana, "A Million Little Theses: Curzio Malaparte Became the Proust of the Abattoir of Europe's Upheaval. Does It Matter That He Made It Up?," *BookForum: The Review for Art, Fiction, & Culture* 13.2 (2006), 8–10; Ursula Link-Heer, "Versuch über das Makabre. Zu Curzio Malapartes *Kaputt*," *LiLi. Zeitschrift für Literaturwissenschaft und Linguistik* 19.75 (1989), 96–116; and Giampaolo Martelli, *Curzio Malaparte* (Turin: Borla, 1968), 121–37.
[30] On Malaparte's multiple self-figuration in *Kaputt*, see Alt, "Der Schelm und die Nazis," 383–407; Burdett, "Changing Identities through Memory," 110–19; and Hope, "The Narrative Contract Strained," 178–92.

characterize the kind of narratives in which space, and not time, is the main
constructing device.[31] By means of this modernist technique Malaparte tells
many stories stamped by the destruction of limits, the excess, depravity,
abjection, brutality, primal violence, and sheer horror that are so distinctive
of absolute war. Rooted in the tradition of European high modernism
(particularly as practiced by Marcel Proust), Malaparte's novel is a spatial
experiment with style and narrative construction.[32] By breaking up the
chronological sequence and concatenating a remarkable number of overlapping war-related stories, Malaparte produces a cubist canvas of absolute
war. As happens with other authors of war narratives, the implied author of
Kaputt seems to think that the best procedure for representing absolute war
resides in putting together disjoined sketches of warfare – or scenes related
to it. Consequently, the condition of going or being kaput depicted in the
stories told by Malaparte projects itself onto the entire narrative. The title of
the novel refers, therefore, not only to the contents of the stories embedded
therein, but to the whole narrative as well. *Kaputt* is in this sense a self-
referential title.

A striking feature of *Kaputt* lies in the narrator's conspicuous enjoyment
in narrating stories utterly abject, macabre, and horrifying.[33] This enjoyment shows itself in Malaparte's readiness to tell stories and in the fact that
he narrates many throughout the novel. Contravening an unwritten rule of
etiquette for formal gatherings, the narrator and main character Malaparte
stands up in the middle of a dinner party (which is the situation of most of
the embedded narrative frameworks of this novel) and starts telling stories
whose atrocious nature cannot but be disagreeable to his refined audience.
In certain situations, he may even be perceived as an "unwelcome guest."[34]
Telling horrifying war stories becomes itself a cruel act akin to the brutal
acts mentioned by Malaparte, as well as the cruelty that he attributes to the
Germans throughout the novel. This is most evident when Princess Louise
von Preussen begs him to not tell her the story of the glass eye ("I cannot
bear to listen to these harrowing stories," she complains),[35] a request that

---

[31] Joseph Frank, *The Idea of Spatial Form* (New Brunswick, NJ: Rutgers University Press, 1991),
     31–132.
[32] See Grana, *Curzio Malaparte*, 64.
[33] On Malaparte's enjoyment in telling stories in *Kaputt*, see, for instance, Grana, *Curzio Malaparte*,
     63. In "Versuch über das Makabre," 96–116, Link-Heer has written on Malaparte's penchant for
     the macabre.
[34] Hope, *Curzio Malaparte*, 81–94.
[35] Curzio Malaparte, *Kaputt*, trans. Dan Hofstadter (New York Review Books, 2005), 255. Further
     references in text.

ultimately goes unheeded because Malaparte manages to tell that story anyway (262–66).

It could be argued that the repeated act of telling stories on absolute war constitutes an instance of the jouissance that Roland Barthes attributes to certain kinds of (modernist) texts. In his book-length essay on pleasure and literature, Barthes differentiates between texts of pleasure and texts of jouissance ("bliss" in the American translation). A text of pleasure is that which fulfills the reader and provides euphoria; it finds its roots within the history of culture without breaking up with it, while it is closely linked to comfortable practices of reading.[36] In contrast to this, a text of jouissance "imposes a state of loss," "discomforts," "unsettles the reader's historical, cultural, psychological assumptions, the consistency of his tastes, values, memories, brings to a crisis his relation with language." Barthes underscores that jouissance is a brutal pleasure, one that lacks mediation, pointing out its asocial nature, which is defined as "the abrupt loss of sociality." Texts of jouissance, he claims elsewhere in the book, can be characterized as "pleasure in pieces; language in pieces, culture in pieces," they are perverse "in that they are outside any imaginable finality … nothing is reconstituted, nothing recuperated." Barthes famously concludes that the text of jouissance is "absolutely intransitive."[37] The stories told in *Kaputt* by the narrative voice, as well as the entire novel, clearly belong to the category of jouissance. The horrifying stories on Siegfried (the name stands here for "SS trainees") and the cat (259–61), the glass eye (262–66), the reindeer and the salmon (333–55), and the one on the forty pounds of human eyes sent by squads of ustashis to the Croatian fascist leader Ante Pavelić (269–78) need to be seen as instances of Malaparte's cruel jouissance as storyteller. *Kaputt* makes the reader uncomfortable, shaking up his horizon of expectations and his moral sense. Malaparte has a talent for the grotesque, for the abject, for refined cruelty – and he *enjoys* it. Atrocity, perversity, absolute enmity, and the abject are the main motifs of most of the stories told in *Kaputt*. This is a motivation designed to unsettle the reader. Moreover, Malaparte breaks up the plot into pieces as much as he dissolves the literary tradition by eroding the boundaries between genres and sub-genres. Following Barthes's theoretical remarks on textual perversity, Malaparte's text is perverse in two senses: it lacks finality and it deals with the abject. The narration of stories in *Kaputt* is inserted

[36] Roland Barthes, *The Pleasure of the Text*, trans. Richard Miller (New York: Farrar, Strauss and Giroux, 1975), 14.
[37] Ibid., 14, 39, 51–52, 52.

into social situations, but their nature and contents place them outside of the sphere of sociality – yet another characteristic of jouissance as described by Roland Barthes. For all these reasons, *Kaputt* is a clear instance of the writing of cruelty.

All that is in keeping with Julia Kristeva's assessment of the abject, which she describes as "a terror that dissembles."[38] In fact, Kristeva's view of abjection relates, to a certain extent, with Barthes's notion of jouissance and Malaparte's writing of cruelty. According to her, abjection is a perversion and a danger that at once causes fascination and even jouissance:

> It is simply a frontier, a repulsive gift that the Other, having become alter ego, drops so that "I" does not disappear in it but finds, in that sublime alienation, a forfeited existence. Hence a jouissance in which the subject is swallowed up but in which the Other, in return, keeps the subject from foundering by making it repugnant. One thus understands why so many victims of the abject are its fascinated victims.[39]

As she writes in another passage of her essay on abjection, "The abject is perverse because it neither gives up nor assumes a prohibition, a rule, or a law; but turns them aside, misleads, corrupts; uses them, takes advantage of them, the better to deny them."[40] Hence a text of abjection may perfectly be a text of jouissance. The intertwining of jouissance and the abject within Malaparte's writing of cruelty strengthens the narrator's constitutive moral ambiguity (as an Italian, he is on the side of the perpetrators; his stories, however, are indictments of the perpetrators' immoral and criminal actions).[41] The ideological and ethical distance kept by the narrator are such that readers may have the morally distressing impression that the narrative voice tells stories on war and abjection for no particular reason, apart from the obvious pleasure that he experiences by telling them. In this sense, his storytelling somehow approaches the intransitivity that Roland Barthes attributes to texts of jouissance.

The presence of cannibalism within the narrative is a clear instance of the novel's admixture of kaput, abjection, and jouissance.[42] Malaparte's interest in cannibalism is part and parcel of his writing of cruelty. Early in the novel, the narrator talks about the cannibalism practiced by Soviet prisoners of war in a concentration camp in Smolensk (15). However,

---

[38] Julia Kristeva, *Powers of Horror: An Essay on Abjection*, trans. Leon S. Roudiez (New York: Columbia University Press, 1982), 4.
[39] Ibid., 9.   [40] Ibid, 15.
[41] On this score, see Alt, "Der Schelm und die Nazis," 383–407; Grana, *Curzio Malaparte*, 74–75; and Hope, "The Narrative Contract Strained," 178–92.
[42] Cf. Andrews, "Eating Malaparte," 150–55.

Malaparte views cannibalism not only as an abject act of desperation and survival. For him, cannibalism is something consubstantial with absolute warfare and (in the case of the Second World War) its German perpetrators. In a banquet organized by the Governor-General of Poland, Malaparte describes the main course – a goose – within a context of cannibalism. Looking at the goose with the eye of a connoisseur, the narrator has the impression that it has been executed by an SS firing squad (74). Malaparte relates that he "felt on the side of the goose. Oh, yes! I sided with the goose, not with those who were aiming their rifles, nor with those who were shouting 'Fire!' nor with all those who were saying 'Gans kaputt!' – The goose is dead!" (75). The dinner party may be considered, therefore, as a gathering of cannibals. The association of German hosts and guests with cannibals is no coincidence given the Germans' criminal brutality in Poland and on the eastern front. In yet another dinner party assembling again the perpetrators of the world war of 1939–45, Malaparte describes the ceremony of "honor of the knife," or the slicing up of the main course, which on this occasion is a deer. The honor falls on Frau Frank, who sinks the knife into the deer's back. Once again, Malaparte turns a social event that has gathered some members of the new aristocracy of Nazi Germany into a reunion of cannibals – of cannibals who feed on Jews: "The knife remained stuck in the deer's back, next to the little red flag with the black swastika, and I confess that the sight of that knife and that flag implanted in the back of the noble animal gave me an uncomfortable feeling with which was mixed a subtle sense of horror as the conversation of the guests, little by little drifted back to ghettos and Jews" (102). In *Kaputt* such acts of symbolic cannibalism mimic the logic of absolute war – both the cannibal and war eat up bodies. Malaparte is explicit on this score. For him, the Germans are the true cannibals of the Second World War. German soldiers, he claims, have been lucky because the war has not devoured them – not as yet, that is. "The war does not eat corpses – it only eats living soldiers," he writes, "It gnaws the legs, the arms, the eyes of living soldiers, mostly while they sleep, just as rats do. But men are no more civilized; they never eat living men . . . . I saw Russian prisoners at Smolensk eating the corpses of their comrades who had died of hunger and cold"; and Malaparte decisively concludes: "The Germans are a sentimental people, the most sentimental and the most civilized people in the world. The German people will not eat corpses; they eat living men" (254).

The consideration of absolute warfare as a form of cannibalism on the one hand, and of the Germans as cannibals on the other, is far from arbitrary. As Maggie Kilgour has written in her book on communion and cannibalism, "eating is a means of asserting and controlling individual and also cultural identity."[43] Following Kilgour's characterization of cannibalism, as well as her own terminology, I argue that by "eating" their enemies, in *Kaputt* the Germans aim at finding a lost "unity," turning what is "external" to them into a part of themselves, namely the German social body. Led by the myths of "total unity" and "oneness," the Germans' conduct of absolute war-as-cannibalism eliminates a threatening "alien outsideness," incorporating it into the subject's "inside." The German "body" tolerates nothing outside of itself.[44] In fact, this is the ultimate meaning of the German cruelty discussed by Malaparte in several passages from the novel. In *Kaputt* Malaparte underscores that Nazis "kill and destroy out of fear ... they are afraid of all that is living, of all that is living outside of themselves and of all that is different from them" (12); they fear the defenseless, the weak, the sick, the oppressed, women, Jews (91); what drives the Germans to cruelty in Poland, Malaparte writes, "to deeds most coldly, methodically and scientifically cruel, is fear" (91). From this standpoint, it could be claimed that the Nazi destruction of European Jewry represents the ultimate expression of the Germans' cannibalization of the "other." Kilgour considers eating as "the most material need yet [it] is invested with a great deal of significance, an act that involves both desire and aggression, as it creates a total identity between eater and eaten while insisting on the total control ... of the latter by the former."[45] This intrinsic aggressiveness, as well as the cannibal's drive to assimilate the "other" through bodily absorption, makes cannibalism a suitable image for condensing an essential feature of absolute war. The image of cannibalism, to quote Kilgour again, "is frequently connected with the failure of words as a medium, suggesting that people who cannot *talk* to each other *bite* each other."[46] In contrast to limited conventional warfare, absolute war excludes "talking" to the enemy (to follow Kilgour's image), and it aims, like cannibalism, at "biting" him, that is to say at his complete annihilation and assimilation. Malaparte concentrates on those points of overlap between cannibalism and absolute war by setting many narrative frameworks on absolute war at dinner parties. Aside from the obvious

---

[43] Maggie Kilgour, *From Communion to Cannibalism: An Anatomy of Metaphors of Incorporation* (Princeton University Press, 1990), 6.

[44] For information on cannibalism and cultural identity, see Kristen Guest, ed., *Eating Their Words: Cannibalism and the Boundaries of Cultural Identity* (Albany, NY: State University of New York Press, 2001).

[45] Kilgour, *From Communion to Cannibalism*, 7.   [46] Ibid., 16.

connection between food and talk,[47] through the recurrence of banquets in *Kaputt* Curzio Malaparte conveys something crucial about absolute war: it is a cannibalistic activity. In a way, the guests at those dinner parties perform an activity (eating food) akin to the one conducted by the German army (the cannibalization of the enemy). When they gather German perpetrators, dinner parties in *Kaputt* can be said to refract absolute war's constitutive cannibalism. This means that there is a subtle, internal connection between the elegant dining rooms described by Malaparte and the horrific landscape of absolute war cruelly narrated during dinner. Contrary to what it may seem on first inspection, at dinner parties Malaparte is not far removed from absolute war, but is rather in close proximity to its essential cannibalism.

Putrefaction and social decadence are two major manifestations of kaput in Malaparte's novel on absolute war. In fact, the first stories that the narrator tells his audience are precisely related to those two topics. These stories set the tone for the rest of the book. In chapter 2 Malaparte narrates the story of a dead horse rotting outside a house where he lodged near the front (32–48), pointing out that "everywhere hung that smell of things rotting, of decomposing matter" (36), while in chapter 3 he relates the episode of the horses trapped in the ice of Lake Ladoga by the sudden freeze of the water – corpses that as soon as the ice melts in the spring spread an unbearable stench (48–60). "That huge decomposing body," underscores the narrator somewhat morbidly, "tainted the air with its lean smell of rotten wood, and the first spring breeze was already bringing its tired scents, its tepid odors, its intimate and bestial dog's breath" (52). Those two episodes lead Malaparte to list for the benefit of his audience a series of things whose rotting smell he remembers (39), a remembrance on putrefaction that correlates to "the new odor of the new war" (37) mentioned by the narrative voice earlier in the text. In *Kaputt*, putrefaction – yet another manifestation of the abject in absolute war – functions also as a symptom of the death of Europe as well as everything that is noble. Malaparte has an elegiac view of the old continent, which he sees in the process of self-destruction, as the closing paragraphs of the first part of the novel make apparent.

In *Kaputt* Malaparte is particularly interested in massacres and the description of corpses – two additional instances of kaput and abjection. In chapter 6 he narrates the pitiless, savage pogrom of Jassy (105–45), and in chapter 7 he relates an incident that involves the dead bodies of Jews

---

[47] See ibid., 8–9.

who had been herded onto a train (168–77). Malaparte went with the Italian consul to Poduloea, a Romanian town around 30 kilometers beyond Jassy, searching for the Jewish owner of the villa where the consul lodges. They found him among the dead taken out by soldiers from the train where Jews had been placed (174). What is remarkable, however, is what comes next: suddenly, one of the doors of the wagon yields, and dozens of corpses fall upon the Italian consul, literally burying him (174). The dead become alive again; the abject acquires a spectral quality. Malaparte writes: "The dead are wrathful, stubborn, ferocious . . . *The dead are crazy.* Woe to the living if a dead man hates him . . . The dead are jealous and vengeful. They fear no one, they fear nothing . . . They even have no fear of death. They fight tooth and nail, silently, without yielding a step" (174). The victims come back to life to take revenge on their murderers (Sartori, as an Italian, is an ally of the Germans and the Romanians, who are the ones that carried out the pogrom in Jassy and shipped out on a train the Jews who were still alive). The "struggle" between the corpses and the Italian consul is fierce:

> Some, attempting to crush him, hurled themselves with all their weight upon Sartori, others dropped on him coldly, rigidly, sluggishly; others butted their heads into his chest, or hit with him their knees and their elbows. Sartori grasped their hair, clutched at their clothing, caught hold of their arms, tried to push them back by gripping their throats or hitting their faces with clenched fists. (174–75)

In the end, Sartori frees himself from the corpses with the help of Romanian soldiers. This lively quality of the corpses imagined by Malaparte, along with their capacity to seriously threaten the living, is significant. In Julia Kristeva's view, the corpse condenses the dissolution of the border between subject and object; it upsets whoever confronts it. "Refuse and corpses," Kristeva argues, "show me what I permanently thrust aside in order to live."[48] Body fluids, defilement, corpses, and excrement "are what life withstands" and every time we contemplate such things we are at the border of our condition as living beings. "The corpse," according to Kristeva, "is the utmost of abjection. It is death infecting life. Abject. It is something rejected from which one does not part, from which one does not protect oneself as from an object. An imaginary uncanniness and real threat, it beckons to us and engulfs us."[49] In that episode from *Kaputt*, that threat is very real, for the corpses literally "engulf" the Italian consul, almost suffocating him to death.

[48] Kristeva, *Powers of Horror*, 3.   [49] Ibid., 3, 4.

By means of its constitutive writing of cruelty, *Kaputt* makes us stare at the abject. Malaparte has a clear preference for telling stories on abjection – stories on cannibalism, on the stench of the rotting corpses of animals or humans, on the "new odor" of war, on haggard Jews barely surviving in the ghetto of Warsaw, on the gouged-out eyes of cats or human beings, on sordid prostitution. Given the extensive attention granted to the abject, the novel itself becomes an instance of abjection. *Kaputt* establishes, on the one hand, a connection between absolute war and abjection, and on the other, between the abject and Malaparte's own writing. Ultimately, the condition of being kaput is in Malaparte synonymous to that of being abject. This is precisely the meaning and function of the abject in *Kaputt*: it is a threat, it is death infecting life – and infecting fiction, for Malaparte's relation with the abject is ambivalent; it is marked at once by repulsion and by attraction. This never-resolved ambivalence lies at the core of the novel's writing of cruelty.

Like Curzio Malaparte's *Kaputt*, Theodor Plievier's 1945 novel *Stalingrad* constitutes yet another early response to the extreme challenges posed by absolute war to representation.[50] This was not Plievier's first attempt at writing on war. Based on his service in the German Navy during the First World War, Plievier had published several books on the world war of 1914–18 and its immediate aftermath. However, the novel *Stalingrad* would be his greatest literary accomplishment. Plievier wrote it in the Soviet Union, the country where he had been living since 1934. In 1943, he had been commissioned by the Soviet authorities to read the correspondence and personal diaries confiscated from the Germans after their defeat in the Battle of Stalingrad. Reading those documents awakened in

---

[50] For more information on Plievier's *Stalingrad*, see, among other works, Joan F. Adkins, "Sacrifice and Dehumanization in Plievier's *Stalingrad*," *War, Literature, and the Arts* 2.1 (1990), 1–22; Samson B. Knoll, "*Moskau–Stalingrad–Berlin*: Theodor Plievier's War Trilogy Revisited," *Literatur und Geschichte*, ed. Karl Menges, Michael Winkler, and Jörg Thunecke (Amsterdam: Rodopi, 1998), 171–203; Hans Harald Müller, "Nachwort. *Stalingrad*. Zur Geschichte und Aktualität von Theodor Plieviers Roman," *Stalingrad*, by Theodor Plievier, 2nd ed. (Cologne: Kiepenheuer & Witsch, 2011), 443–63; Gunther Nickel, "Faction: Theodor Plievier: *Stalingrad* (1945)," *Von Böll bis Buchheim. Deutsche Kriegsprosa nach 1945*, ed. Hans Wagener (Amsterdam: Rodopi, 1997), 49–62; Helmut Peitsch, "Theodor Pliviers *Stalingrad*," *Faschismuskritik und Deutschlandbild*, ed. Christian Fritsch and Lutz Winckler (Berlin: Argument, 1981), 83–102; Michael Rohrwasser, "Theodor Plieviers Kriegsbilder," *Schuld und Sühne? Kriegserlebnis und Kriegsdeutung in deutschen Medien der Nachkriegszeit (1945–1961)*, ed. Ursula Heukenkamp (Amsterdam: Rodopi, 2001), 139–53; and Dieter H. Sevin, *Individuum und Staat. Das Bild des Soldaten in der Romantrilogie Theodor Plieviers* (Bonn: Bouvier, 1972). See Alan F. Bance, "The Brutalization of Warfare on the Eastern Front: History and Fiction," *The Second World War in Literature: Eight Essays*, ed. Ian Higgins (Edinburgh: Scottish Academic Press, 1986), 97–114, for a balanced exploration of the German literature written on the eastern campaign.

Plievier a profound interest in the battle, particularly for its tragic dimension and human drama. Thanks to the mediation of Johannes R. Becher,
he was allowed to interview German survivors of Stalingrad who were held
captive near Moscow. His extensive interviews with battered, demoralized,
undernourished soldiers and officers, together with the documents he had
previously consulted, offered him a view at once intimate and kaleidoscopic of the Battle of Stalingrad – a double perspective that would shape
the very structure of *Stalingrad*.[51] The manuscript would be published first
in several installments in *Internationale Literatur* in 1943–44, and as a
book in late 1945. Today basically read only by experts in German Studies,
Theodor Plievier's *Stalingrad* was in fact the first best-seller in postwar
Germany; moreover, together with Thomas Mann's 1947 *Doktor Faustus*,
it was the novel that merited more reviews in Germany in the first decade
after the end of the war.[52] After moving out of the Soviet Zone in 1947, no
longer feeling under political scrutiny, Plievier would write two more
novels on the Second World War, this time centering his attention not
only on the German side, but also on the Soviets', in *Moskau* (Moscow)
(1952) and *Berlin* (1954).

Although both *Kaputt* and *Stalingrad* concentrate on destruction and
abjection, Plievier's narrative on the Battle of Stalingrad is, formally
speaking, a very different undertaking from Malaparte's account of absolute war. In contrast to Malaparte, who opted for concatenating, as we saw
earlier, vignettes of the war, Plievier aims at totality. In effect, Plievier's
Stalingrad offers the most comprehensive literary portrait of absolute
destruction and abjection in the conditions of absolute war met at Stalingrad. In this sense, *Kaputt* and *Stalingrad* could hardly be more dissimilar.
Plievier's novel offers a vast, complex canvas of the predicament of General
Paulus's 6th Army in Stalingrad, from November 19, 1942, until the
German surrender on February 2, 1943. With the exception, perhaps, of
demoted non-commissioned officer August Gnotke and Colonel (later
promoted to general) Manfred Vilshofen, *Stalingrad* lacks psychologically
well-delineated characters. The writer prefers to concentrate on a great
multiplicity of characters of all ranks and walks of life, some of whom
serve, too, as focalizers of the action narrated by the extradiegetic narrator.
Stalingrad comprises eight unnumbered chapters. Although properly
speaking its story covers the span of time that goes from the eve of

---

[51] On the genesis of *Stalingrad*, see Müller, "Nachwort," 446–53; and Sevin, *Individuum und Staat*,
     13–14.
[52] On the reception of this novel, see Peitsch, "*Stalingrad*," 93–98.

Operation Uranus (November 19–23, 1942) to the first week after General Paulus surrendered to the Red Army, the focus falls, however, on the last three weeks of the battle, starting with the Soviet offer, tendered on January 9, 1943, for a German surrender. The narrator briefly relates the Soviet encirclement, summarizes in no more than eleven pages events that took place in November, December, and early January, and then moves on to the phase of the battle he is keen to represent: its last three weeks, in which the absolute debacle of the German army in Stalingrad was consummated.[53] Remarkably, the narrator does not represent the atrocities committed by the Germans before the encirclement of their army (although he does mention some of them, as we will see further on). The Battle of Stalingrad had started on August 23, 1942. The Luftwaffe had bombed the city and destroyed many of its buildings, killing thousands of people and creating the lunar landscape of rubble that would dramatically determine the kind of urban warfare waged there. All these aggressive actions of war are never mentioned. Instead, the narrator seems more interested in providing a tale of German victimhood, while occasionally digging into several factors that led to the tragedy – for tragedy, in the literary sense of the word, it is, as Helmut Peitsch has shrewdly noticed.[54] Plievier centers all his attention on the plight of the German army, the suffering of the common soldier, the dilemmas of the officers from the general staff – caught as they were between Hitler's explicit order to fight to the last bullet and their realization that it was senseless, almost criminal, to send more men to their death. The story is entirely told from the point of view of the Germans. The narrative voice never relates the story from the point of view of the Soviet civilians trapped in the city, or the troops doing the fighting. Although the narrator occasionally does mention, almost in passing, the war crimes committed by the German armed forces prior to their defeat in Stalingrad, the reader may nonetheless have the unpleasant impression that in this novel the Germans are the unwitting victims of the battle, instead of its perpetrators.

While it is unquestionable that Plievier endeavors to represent the battle in all of its complexity, *Stalingrad* is not, as it has always been considered, a realist novel. The German writer somehow sensed that a phenomenon as unfathomable as absolute war may exceed the capabilities of the realist mode, requiring in its stead the deployment of a modernist poetics.

---

[53] Theodor Plievier, *Stalingrad*, 2nd ed. (Cologne: Kiepenheuer & Witsch, 2011), 20–27, 28–39, 39–440. Further references in text.
[54] Peitsch, "*Stalingrad*," 90.

Stalingrad's otherwise evident representational drive, backed by the author's pre-textual work at documenting himself through interviews with German prisoners of war, is undermined once and again by a series of modernist literary techniques that draw the readers' attention away from the nonlinguistic reality represented in the novel, bringing them closer towards *Stalingrad*'s own literary, fictional nature. Clearly indebted to the Austro-German literary expressionism of the 1910s and 1920s,[55] Plievier deploys several modernist devices. One of them consists of the specific technique of focalization followed in the novel. *Stalingrad* is told through several focalizers, the most important of them being Gnotke and Vilshofen, whose views are interspersed with authorial summaries or comments (e.g., 21, 53, 60–61, 153). The multiple and variable internal focalization of *Stalingrad* follows in the steps of a strand of modernist war writing initiated apropos of the First World War. John Dos Passos's *Three Soldiers* (1921) and R. H. Mottram's *The Spanish Farm Trilogy* (1924–26) are two predecessors, within the sub-genre of war writing, of the kind of focalization used by Plievier. The German writer employs other techniques that bring *Stalingrad* closer to modernism than to realism within the spectrum of possibilities mentioned in the Introduction: the literal reproduction of passages from letters written by combatants (18–19, 37–39) or addressed to them by relatives and friends (186–89), which breaks down the boundaries between fiction and non-fiction; the embedding of multiple simultaneous conversations (50); the overlapping of simultaneous scenes, connected either through the poetic repetition of phrases such as "Here sat," "Here stood," or "Here was" (257–62), or by anaphorically starting each scene with the phrase *"At the same time"* (137–40); the underscoring of the novel's driving force and chief perlocutionary speech act – stated for the first time by an officer of the general staff to an audience of fellow officers in captivity (10) – through the anaphoric repetition of the phrase "also that must not be forgotten" (341, 346), a motif that underscores Plievier's basic reason for writing the novel: the German ordeal in Stalingrad must never be forgotten; the insertion of anaphoras reminiscent of prose poetry (142–43); and above all, the use of a prose focused on the truculent, the macabre, and the abject, which makes the novel's expressionism a function of an underlying writing of cruelty. To be sure, *Stalingrad* does not attain the levels of literary experimentation of Alexander Kluge's *Schlachtbeschreibung* (Description of a Battle) (1964), a

---

[55] Knoll (*"Moskau–Stalingrad–Berlin,"* 181) and Rohrwasser ("Theodor Plieviers Kriegsbilder," 139–53) have also remarked the presence of expressionism in Plievier's *Stalingrad*.

montage of fictional and non-fictional texts on Stalingrad whose story roughly covers the same weeks as Plievier's novel (i.e., from the third week of November 1942 to the first week of February 1943). And yet, in a literary context in which realism was the dominant mode of writing, Plievier's use of modernist literary devices makes of *Stalingrad* a remarkable, unique literary undertaking, an instance of catastrophic modernism that prefigured more technically daring narratives on the Second World War.

All the expressionist passages from *Stalingrad* are directly connected to warfare, as if actions of absolute war needed expressionism for its proper conveyance to the reader. In that sense, *Stalingrad* is reminiscent of classic expressionist novels on the First World War, such as Leonhard Frank's *Der Mensch ist gut* (Men Are Good) (1917), Fritz von Unruh's *Opfergang* (Path to Sacrifice) (1918), and Ernst Johannsen's *Vier von der Infanterie. Ihre letzten Tage an der Westfront 1918* (Four from Infantry: Their Last Days on the Western Front, 1918) (1929). One of the first instances of Plievier's use of an expressionist prose is to be found in chapter 2. Gnotke's sensing of the Soviet pincer movement that ended with the encirclement of the German 6th Army and its allies is narrated in terms that recall the diction so characteristic of Austro-German expressionism. The staccato rhythm that distinguishes expressionist prosody mimics here Gnotke's shocked and confused perception of an unexpected enemy attack whose nature and consequences required time to understand: "The earth trembles. A subterranean tremor. It shivers up. The hands, from where does it come ... The earth, the sky! The sky is ablaze, in the north as well as over the Don ... Artillery. Mortars. Roaring canons, thousands of pounds of powder blow up. The calendar shows November 19" (21). The fierceness of the Soviet onslaught is described with similar expressionist means and in a staccato style that rhetorically imitates the nature of the attack: "Vortex. Funnel. Lightning of fire. Balls of smoke. Beams falling back, pieces from the ceiling of the bunker" (24). Elsewhere in *Stalingrad*, the narrator chooses an expressionist prose for describing the violence and chaos set off by a Soviet offensive: "Minutes later. From the lower sky Russian bombers free themselves. The echelon seemed to bounce out as if in a ball ... Howling of motors. Impact of bombs. Fountains spraying up – earth, pieces, car sections ... from the railway yard black bags of smoke" (170). The effects of this attack are equally told in an expressionist style; now, however, the staccato syntax used earlier gives way to a chaotic enumeration that reproduces the sense of chaos and disorientation experienced by the Germans: "Blown up garages, ammunition dumps, artillery emplacements, amongst them human beings, or pieces, trunks, heads of men, the rubble flew forty meters up, fell down, was taken up again with the whirl to be finally ground up and pulverized" (170–71). The same expressionist style had been used earlier to describe a situation of pande-monium and complete destruction: "The earth white, the sky above gray. On the snow dead, dying men, the living. On the snow stalled cars and cursing drivers. Men, who with helmets, with hands, shovel out the wheels, excavate parts of a driveway. Sweat on foreheads ... frozen motors ... On the sides, tossed sleighs, upended cars, shattered wheels, lone horses with muted steps, disappearing into the night" (131). Cer-tainly, in *Stalingrad* the reader will not find the experiments with language that pervade avant-garde novels about multitudes of people, such as John Dos Passos's *Manhattan Transfer* (1925) and Alfred Döblin's *Berlin Alexanderplatz* (1929). *Stalingrad* lacks the formal audacity of those openly modernist works. However, it does contain literary experiments of an expressionist nature that reveal its driving catastrophic modernism. All the above-mentioned literary strategies are characteristic of a modernist work, while at the same time the novel reveals through its form and themes the homology between its constitutive catastrophic modernism on the one hand, and the nature of absolute war on the other.

After a short initial chapter in which a captive German officer from the general staff delivers a speech on the battle to fellow officers and prisoners of war (7–10), the story proper on Stalingrad begins, rather significantly, with kaput and abjection. The first scene shows a demoted non-commissioned officer, August Gnotke, doing abject work, namely burying corpses and body parts in mass graves as a member of a penal battalion (11–12). He and his comrades are "undertakers" (15) and move like "specters" (14). Placed near the front line, these "men of the dead" (16), these "hauling specters" (16) are the only ones capable of moving freely in the area. They all look alike and remain silent all the time; having lost the habit, they never speak to each other, thereby mimicking the absolute silence of the corpses that they carry and bury (17). The scene depicts Gnotke and his comrades assembling body parts (17–18) or piling up corpses (26). The narrator portrays him as a man without hope (19). His past has been taken away from him with the demotion, his present is empty (19). According to the narrative voice, "Gnotke had become someone without ideas ... his consciousness had not been able to hold. Such a kernel of being, with demands, will, feelings, commiseration, love ... existed no more in him" (22). In contrast, he had kept a sharp eye and hearing; his sensory organs functioned very well (22). A man who works on the abject (corpses are, let us remember, the epitome of the abject according to Julia Kristeva), Gnotke has been reduced to a being who merely perceives reality through his senses, and in the process has become abject himself.

This first scene from *Stalingrad* condenses a favorite theme of Plievier's in this novel: the horror. From the very beginning, the narrator displays a strong inclination for graphically narrating all kinds of horrible scenes of German suffering, thereby deploying a writing of cruelty. The destruction of material, places, and human bodies constitutes the basis of the horror cruelly depicted by Plievier in *Stalingrad*. Some scenes are difficult to bear. Take, for instance, the description of Captain Steiger's terrible wounds on his knee and leg (86). When First Lieutenant Rohwedder tries to help out his captain and takes off Steiger's boot, he involuntarily amputates his foot: "Rohwedder pulled out the boot, and along with the boot – leather, cloth, skin, flesh were all a single mass – he pulled out the short-frozen foot, and on his lap he had the clean cut-off skeleton of Steiger's foot" (87). The narrator intersperses on occasion his own opinion on the terrible scenes he describes, thereby underscoring the human drama and the ethical discourse of the novel (e.g., 89). Stalingrad has become a huge hospital and a vast cemetery. We read about trains full of "frozen human flesh" (196). We read that in "Krawzow and Petschanka, in Voroponovo, Jeschowa, Gumrak, Stalingradski, on all the cursed streets to Stalingrad" there are buildings in ruins "crowded with abandoned wounded men" (197). We read that house cellars equally contain countless "wounded men who have never received medical care" (199). We read that in the center of the city "even the former *Ortskommandantur* had been transformed into a military hospital" overcrowded by "over one thousand hungry severely wounded men" whom no doctor can take care of properly due to the lack of medicines; the only occupation of medical personnel consists of "dragging the corpses out" (200). Soldiers healthy enough to fight on are described as "ghosts" (239) or as shadows of themselves (112). Major General Cönner considers that "We are only objects!" (103, 109). The ongoing butchery is absolutely senseless. As Captain Steiger exclaims, "We die for nothing" (90). The vast canvas of the German predicament ultimately portrays, in the narrator's own words, "the agony of an army" (200).

The climactic scene of kaput and abjection in *Stalingrad* is one that takes place in the building where the *Ortskommandatur Mitte* used to be located (378–95). An order from the general staff directs all wounded military personnel to go there. The narrator tells about the arrival of a group of wounded men led by Chief Staff Surgeon Simmering. What they find upon arrival is arresting and leaves them literally motionless: endless piles of corpses lying by the walls of the building. The scene is reminiscent of works on German *Lager* that also describe the piling up of the corpses of executed or gassed inmates. The narrator writes: "This pile, thrown on top of each other, six feet high, extended from the passage route to the corner of the courtyard and from the corner to the door of the wings of the building, and behind the door the pile continued. The entire building, as long as it was, was surrounded by a wall of corpses" (379). A non-commissioned officer explains the situation to Simmering: "due to the enemy shelling and the frozen ground, it is impossible to think of a proper burial. We have deposited the corpses there in a warehouse. The warehouse is full, from floor to ceiling … The only job left for the sanitary personnel is to take out the dead" (379–80). The novel provides an instance of such a kind of death: badly wounded Lieutenant Loose is taken by the medical personnel outside the building, and he is abandoned there, to die alone; there is simply nothing else to be done for him (381–82).

The narrator sets the abject and kaput in the context of the absolute war waged between Nazi Germany and the Soviet Union. He depicts Stalingrad as an instance of absolute war, but also as retribution *and* atonement for the war crimes committed by the Germans in the Soviet Union. Stalingrad, according to the narrator, meant "the expiation of all sins" (34). He immediately goes on to enumerate all these "sins." "The crowds of Russian refugees, elderly men and women, and mothers with breast-fed babies … under the sharp east wind laying out on the tracts with a temperature of −20°, −30° Celsius, attentively listening to trains, trains that wouldn't ride ever again … and prisoners of war, to whom only plucks of intestines of dead horses were thrown" (34–35). The narrator goes on, and mentions the trains crowded with kidnaped slave workers en route to Germany, the half-deserted local towns, the despotism of the Gestapo (35). Stalingrad "stood at the end of all paths, and the vanquished Stalingrad should expiate each atrocity, erase each crime" (35). The narrator insists that it should never be forgotten: "the place of a lost battle, of a lost war, the zenith of the German striving for power, of the hardest defeat in German military history, the most profound moral and political downfall of the German people" (336). A dying man, Captain Steiger acknowledges his own responsibility for his tragic end, for he has fought in an army that has committed war crimes; only for that reason he must die (126). A soldier named Vidomec (437) and Captain Thomas (157–59) think in similar terms. Likewise, a group of generals acknowledge their guilt in the war crimes perpetrated by the German army (314–16,

332–33). The narrator himself elaborates on the war crimes committed by the Germans (427–28). Captain Steiner (90) and Colonel Vilshofen (424) believe that "They have aimed at the impossible" (90), and now Germans must pay for their hubris. All these expressions of guilt indirectly manifest absolute war's unrestricted violence as well as its rupture of all limits.

Useless Suffering and the Absurd

Extreme suffering like that experienced by the characters that populate Theodor Plievier's *Stalingrad* resists linguistic expression. This is particularly true of their physical pain. According to Elaine Scarry, physical pain is not merely language-resistant; it actively destroys language, "bringing about an immediate reversion to a state anterior to language, to the sounds and cries a human being makes before language is learned."[56] Bodily pain lacks referential content, "it is not of or for anything," Scarry argues, "It is precisely because it takes no object that it, more than any other phenomenon, resists objectification in language."[57] In the chapter on torture from his book *Jenseits von Schuld und Sühne* (Beyond Guilt and Atonement), Jean Améry has likewise stressed that physical pain defies communication.[58] In turn, Emmanuel Levinas makes a similar point in his phenomenology of what he terms "useless suffering." According to Levinas, suffering is both "unassumable" and "unassumability." The unassumability of suffering does not derive from the excessive intensity of a sensation. Rather, the philosopher argues, "It results from an 'excess,' a 'too much' which is inscribed in a sensorial content, penetrating as suffering the dimensions of meaning which seem to be opened and grafted to it."[59] This penetration of suffering in the "dimension of meaning" is one of its crucial characteristics, and, as we will see, it plays an important role in the writing on absolute war. In Levinas's view, suffering cannot be "synthesized" (in the Kantian sense of the word), which means that it cannot be comprehended by reason. Consequently, suffering lies beyond comprehension; in a way, it is unsayable. In connection to that resistance to rationalization and understanding, all suffering disturbs and is itself this disturbance. In Levinas's own words, "it is as if

---

[56] Elaine Scarry, *The Body in Pain: The Making and Unmaking of the World* (Oxford University Press, 1985), 4.
[57] Ibid., 5.
[58] Jean Améry, *At the Mind's Limits: Contemplations by a Survivor on Auschwitz and Its Realities*, trans. Sidney Rosenfeld and Stella P. Rosenfeld (Bloomington, IN: Indiana University Press, 1980), 33.
[59] Emmanuel Levinas, "Useless Suffering," *The Provocation of Levinas: Rethinking the Other*, ed. Robert Bernasconi and David Wood, trans. Richard Cohen (London: Routledge, 1988), 156.

suffering were not only a given refractory to synthesis, but the way in which the refusal opposed to the assembling of givens into a meaningful whole is opposed to it."[60] Suffering, in sum, *resists* meaning. It is passivity, a "submission," but not as the reverse of "activity." The passivity of suffering is more profoundly passive, according to Levinas, than the receptivity of our senses. In suffering sensitivity is a vulnerability, it is an evil. For this reason, the understanding of suffering can be attained through the understanding of evil. The negativity of evil is the source of all apophatic negations. Evil's "no" is negative "right up to 'non-sense'."[61] Therefore, evil ultimately refers to suffering; it is the true impasse of life and being, its absurdity. For Levinas, the evil of pain is an explosion and the most profound articulation of pain itself.[62] Hence the uselessness of pain: in its phenomenality, suffering is senselessness, it is useless, it is "for nothing."[63]

Literary works devoted to absolute war abound in depictions of useless suffering and its utter meaninglessness. To be sure, any war may be seen as an absurd activity. In Kate McLoughlin's view, the absurdity of war resides in the discrepancy between the hyperlogic of the war machine, which consists of a system of rules and regulations, and the war machine's incapability of attending to the complexities of the individual. The war machine is therefore "seemingly independent of human creation, antithetical to human needs, literal-minded, endlessly repetitive and insane."[64] While McLoughlin's assessment is correct, in warfare the absurd may be related to other factors as well. Even if the war machine attended or cared for the individual, facing death on a daily basis or fighting in very difficult circumstances may lead combatants to perceive war and their own predicament as lacking in meaning and purpose. Such a feeling of being in an absurd situation is exacerbated when troops fight in an absolute war. In a context as hard for troops and civilians as war in its absolute degree is, human beings seem to exist in an irrational, meaningless world; life is usually seen as devoid of purpose, cohesiveness, and signification. The only logic in place is the logic of absolute war.

Absolute violence and the senseless suffering that it triggers permeate a significant number of narratives on the eastern front of the Second World War. Such works center on both the absurdity of war and the equally absurd suffering of its victims. Poignant descriptions of useless suffering can be found, for instance, in the articles and sketches that Vasily

---

[60] Ibid., 156.   [61] Ibid., 157.   [62] Ibid., 157.   [63] Ibid., 157–58.
[64] Kate McLoughlin, *Authoring War: The Literary Representation of War from the Iliad to Iraq* (Cambridge University Press, 2011), 182.

Grossman wrote on the massive Soviet retreat in the second half of 1941; most of those pieces were published in the Red Army periodical *Krasnaya Zvezda*. With rare sensitivity and empathy Grossman relates the retreat of civilians from approaching German troops,[65] the "Terrible Retreat" of August–September 1941,[66] scenes of human tragedy amongst the people from Gomelin or Ukraine,[67] people fleeing Orel or gloomily leaving Moscow in October 1941.[68] All of those vignettes describe instances of useless, meaningless, "for-nothing" suffering. Grossman has captured the suffering of the Soviet people caused by the German invasion and the Germans' pitiless, often outright criminal treatment of the civilian population. The military retreat and the suffering that it causes depicted by Grossman would be captured, too, by Viktor Nekrasov in *Front-Line Stalingrad* (1946). In Part 1 of that novel, Nekrasov narrates the chaotic withdrawal and dispersal of many Red Army units in the weeks that followed the German invasion of the Soviet Union. Additional instances of useless suffering experienced in the absolute war waged by Nazi Germany and the Soviet Union can be drawn from a great variety of narratives. Some center on the challenging war experience of a single soldier, such as Carlos María Ydígoras's 1957 autobiographical novel *Algunos no hemos muerto* (Some of Us Have Not Died), on the soldier's anxious fatalistic anticipation of his own death, as is the case with the main character of Heinrich Böll's *Der Zug war pünktlich* (The Train Was on Time) (1949), or on his defection to the enemy as a result of his sense of the utter absurdity of war and its useless suffering, a situation narrated by Siegfried Lenz in his novel *Der Überläufer* (The Defector), written in 1950 and posthumously published in 2016. A few texts address the mass rape of German women by the invading Soviet troops, as for instance in the anonymous diary *Eine Frau in Berlin* (A Woman in Berlin) (English translation 1954, German original 1959). Others relate the absurd suffering of soldiers and civilians in different theaters of the war on the eastern front, like Heinrich Böll's 1951 traumatic realist novel *Wo warst du, Adam?* (Where Were You, Adam?), or the ordeal undergone by an entire city: A. Anatoli Kuznetsov's novel *Babi Yar: A Document in the Form of a Novel* (1970, censored first edition 1966), which describes the German occupation of Kiev through the eyes of a teenager – a refraction of the author himself – is a case in point.

---

[65] Vasily Grossman, *A Writer at War: A Soviet Journalist with the Red Army, 1941–1945*, trans. and ed. Antony Beevor and Luba Vinogradova (New York: Vintage Books, 2005), 12–14.
[66] Ibid., 18–26.   [67] Ibid., 23, 39–40.   [68] Ibid., 48–49, 52–65.

Several novels establish a direct correlation between useless suffering and the absurdity of absolute war, projecting both to the very narrative texture. I am referring, above all, to Gert Ledig's *opera prima*, *Die Stalinorgel* (Stalin's Organ), a novel published in 1955.[69] Based on the author's combat experience on the eastern front and well-received by critics and lay readers alike, *Die Stalinorgel* constitutes one of the most interesting responses to absolute war produced at the time, and needs to be considered as a catastrophic modernist experiment with language, style, and literary convention. Like Malaparte in *Kaputt*, Ledig shapes his novel as a spatial form, frequently shifting scenes, warring sides, and focalizers in the same chapter. The narrator often uses an expressionist staccato style (in *Die Stalinorgel* there is a striking abundance of nominal sentences) that refracts the potentially broken, discontinuous nature of a military offensive, embeds in the novel passages typeset in italics that usually provide additional information on the biography and past war activities of specific characters, and shows the action through a number of focalizers, alternating multiple internal focalization (the same action as seen through different focalizers) with variable internal focalization (different actions are perceived by different focalizers). This multi-sided presentation of the story produces a modernist multi-perspective effect. Ledig narrates through a writing of cruelty (the descriptions of deaths and bodily mutilation are very graphic) the absurd, militarily pointless two-day Soviet offensive against a small area occupied by the Germans on the Leningrad front.

As regards the useless suffering experienced by combatants in absolute war, the first scene from the prologue sets the tone of the novel. It narrates the absurd and grotesque death of a German lance-corporal in a modernist key marked by a dark humor that somehow anticipates Joseph Heller's in his 1961 classic *Catch-22*. The modernism and the humor used to describe something utterly horrendous – a dissonance at the time of the publication of *Die Stalinorgel* – captures with a carnivalesque laughter the *décalage* between the logic of military planning and the logic of individual action, as well as the absurd effects of the former on the latter and the transformations of the body as a result of deadly

---

[69] Little has been written on *Die Stalinorgel*: Jörn Ahrens, "Macht der Gewalt. Hannah Arendt, Theodor W. Adorno und die Prosa Gert Ledigs," *Literatur für Leser* 24.3 (2001), 165–78; Sigfrid Hoefert, "Zur Darstellung von Kampfhandlungen mit technischen Mitteln – Anhand von Werken von Gert Ledig und Stefan Heym," *Wahrheitsmaschinen. Der Einfluss technischer Innovationen auf die Darstellung und das Bild des Krieges in den Medien und Künsten*, ed. Claudia Glunz and Thomas F. Schneider (Göttingen: Vandenhoeck & Ruprecht, 2010), 253–62; and Florian Radvan, "Nachwort," *Die Stalinorgel*, by Gert Ledig (Frankfurt am Main: Suhrkamp, 2003), 203–29.

violence.[70] The passage is long, but on account of the novelty of the tone, worth quoting at length:

> The lance-corporal couldn't turn in his grave because he didn't have one. Some three versts from Podrova, forty versts south of Leningrad, he had been caught in a salvo of rockets, been thrown up in the air, and . . . been impaled on the skeletal branches of what once had been a tree . . . Half an hour later, when the crippled tree trunk was taken off an inch or two above the ground by a burst of machine-gun fire, his wrecked body came down. Meanwhile, he had also lost a foot . . . By the time he hit the ground, he was just half a man . . . Once the tank-tracks had rolled over the lance-corporal, a combat plane fired into the mass of shredded uniform, flesh, and blood. After all that, the lance-corporal was left in peace.[71]

Graphically narrated by means of the writing of cruelty so as to effectively communicate to the reader the extreme nature of absolute war, this brutal death finds an echo in a scene from chapter 7 in which the corporal commanding the position on Hill 308 blows himself up in order to destroy a Soviet tank, killing all its occupants as well as the remaining German defenders of the hill (106–8). Ledig does not spare his readers the horror of war. On the contrary: he tends to center his attention on the representation of sheer violence. His writing of cruelty contains a carnivalesque dimension that effectively conveys the absurdity of war.

The novel describes several cases of useless suffering. One such instance is Major Schnitzer's. He feels a profound and sustained pain due to the recent death of his wife and their only daughter in an air raid. The narrative voice, through free indirect speech, explains the logic of suffering breeding resentment: the telegram that notified him about the deaths of his wife and daughter was "a blow. Either you fall back on your knees and pray and try to atone. Or else you strike back. He thought: I will strike back. He wanted everyone to suffer for the child: the Runner, the company in the barrier position, the whole world" (32). Out of resentment, Schnitzer orders Runner Braun to take thirty unseasoned replacements to reinforce an unimportant and untenable position. The Runner tries to resist this absurd order but ends up accepting it. Unsurprisingly, this character reflects on the absurdity of everything (47). In general, the missions of Runner Braun are considered by the narrative voice as "pointless" (11–12). The narrator describes the suffering of Runner Braun, the

[70] On the function and meaning of laughter in war literature, see McLoughlin, *Authoring War*, 164–88.
[71] Gert Ledig, *Die Stalinorgel* (Frankfurt am Main: Suhrkamp, 2000), 7–8. Further references in text.

defenders of Hill 308, Captain Sostschenko, the non-commissioned officer accused of deserting in the face of an enemy attack, and the officer in charge of executing a deserter. All those characters feel trapped by the war, which they invariably consider to be meaningless. The absurdity of war is felt by the Germans as well as the Russians. Captain Sostschenko, for instance, is perfectly aware that the order he has been given makes little sense. In his conversation with the general – he remembers – Sostchenko realized that the order to attack the hill was simply a diversionary, hopeless operation whose sole function was to dupe the enemy (60–61). He experiences the entire situation as unreal: "In front of him fog, next to him the tank . . . Sostschenko failed to realize that they were all waiting for him, for him to set an example. He wasn't in the real world" (65). This sense of living in an unreal reality accompanies him throughout (e.g., 74–75). The sham trial, condemnation to death, and execution of a German sergeant accused of deserting narrated at the end of the novel is yet another absurd event, especially given the fact that under the Russian attack many German soldiers abandoned their units, thereby becoming deserters de facto (137). Ironically, shortly afterwards the Judge Advocate is absurdly shot by a stray bullet that disfigures his face and kills him (148).

Die Stalinorgel ends with a dialogue between a non-commissioned officer and the major after the burial of several soldiers and the prayers of a military priest. This dialogue hints at the possible absurdity of the entire action and therefore of the extreme suffering and deaths caused by the attack. "'Don't think I am glad to get away. I actually find it rather pleasant. Makes a change. Anyway . . . I secretly hope there is some truth in it.' 'Yes', said the Major. 'I would hate to think that was just another trick'" (201). The major may be referring to what the chaplain said during the burial, or to something we don't know about. However, it is fair to assume that the implied author refers through these two characters to the meaning, or lack thereof, of the events narrated in *Die Stalinorgel*. In short: he may be alluding to useless suffering and the absurdity of absolute warfare. In a way, it could be argued that the novel itself formally embraces war's absurdity, and not only through the formal chaos achieved through a radical use of spatial form. In addition, this instance of catastrophic modernism may be considered, to an extent, as being itself absurd. In *Die Stalinorgel* there is a striking lack of logical correlation between the detailed attention given to military events and their utter meaninglessness. By focusing on the absurd, Ledig's novel becomes itself somewhat absurd, devoid of a clear meaning, cohesiveness, or narrative purpose, aside of course from its depiction of absolute war's absurdity.

The highest literary achievement in the representation of useless suffering in conditions of absolute war is Vasily Grossman's monumental novel *Life and Fate*.[72] Together with Viktor Nekrasov's *Front-Line Stalingrad* (1946), this novel is the greatest Russian fictional account of the Second World War.[73] Finished in 1960 but published posthumously in Switzerland in 1980, Grossman's masterpiece attempts, in contrast to Malaparte's *Kaputt*, Plievier's *Stalingrad*, and Ledig's *Die Stalinorgel*, a total, comprehensive portrayal of absolute warfare vis-à-vis its socio-political context, covering a period that runs from the fall of 1942 to the weeks that followed the German surrender at the Battle of Stalingrad in early February 1943. Although Stalingrad is at the center of the novelist's attention, the action takes place in many other places as well, thereby laying before the reader a huge canvas depicting a country at war. Written after the poetics of socialist realism and with obvious intertextual traces of Tolstoy's *War and Peace* (1865–69), this portrayal of absolute war, which is also a fierce attack on fascism and Stalinism, intertwines many storylines through a number of specific recurring characters, such as the physicist Viktor Pavlovich Shtrum, his sister-in-law Yevgenia (Zhenya) Nikolaevna Shaposhnikova, the political commissar Nikolay Grigorevich Krymov, and Colonel Pyotr Pavlovich Novikov. *Life and Fate* contains combat scenes (particularly interesting are the passages devoted to hand-to-hand fighting around House 6/1 in Stalingrad in chapters 57–60 of Part 1, and chapters 16–22 from Part 2), and it also narrates the Soviet pincer maneuver that led to the encirclement of the German 6th Army and its allies (on this score see especially Part 3, chapters 1–2, 7–9, 11–19). However, and to a higher degree than Theodor Plievier in *Stalingrad*, Grossman gives precedence to the senseless suffering behind the personal tragedies triggered by absolute war over the representation of combat.

---

[72] Vasily Grossman, *Life and Fate*, trans. Robert Chandler (New York Review Books, 2006). All references in text. For more information on Vasily Grossman and *Life and Fate*, see John Garrard and Carrol Garrard, *The Life and Fate of Vasily Grossman*, 2nd ed. (Barnsley: Pen & Sword, 2012); Katharine Hodgson, "The Soviet War," *The Cambridge Companion to the Literature of World War II*, ed. Marina MacKay (Cambridge University Press, 2009), 120–22; S. Shankman, "God, Ethics, and the Novel: Dostoevsky and Vasily Grossman," *Neohelicon* 42.2 (2015), 371–87; Kenneth Sherman, "Vasily Grossman's Treblinka," *Brick* 82 (2009), 138–46; and Vladimir Voinovich, "The Life and Fate of Vasily Grossman and His Novel," *Survey: A Journal of East & West Studies* 29.1 (1985), 186–89.

[73] Three useful surveys of the Russian literature on the Second World War are Hodgson, "The Soviet War," 111–22; Arnold McMillin, "The Second World War in Official and Unofficial Russian Prose," *The Second World War in Literature: Eight Essays*, ed. Ian Higgins (Edinburgh: Scottish Academic Press, 1986), 19–31; and Don Piper, "Soviet Union," *The Second World War in Fiction*, ed. Holger Klein, John Flower, and Eric Homberger (London: Macmillan Press, 1984), 131–72.

Within the Soviet literary field devoted to the Second World War Vasily Grossman's *Life and Fate* stands on the antipodes to Viktor Nekrasov's *Front-Line Stalingrad*, a war novel that narrates warfare exclusively from the point of view of the front-line combatant. Nekrasov never provides, as Grossman does, general views of the ongoing war, or reflections on the psychology of warfare, nor does he relate the war to social conditions and political determinants. His is a gripping action novel in which characters are little more than functions of the chief preoccupation of the narrator, namely the relation of the great dispersal and withdrawal of the Red Army in the first months of the German invasion of the Soviet Union (Part 1) and the Battle of Stalingrad (Part 2). Concerning the battle itself, from *Front-Line Stalingrad* the reader simply learns about it through the eyes of those who directly fought off the attacking German forces. Grossman's *modus operandi* is quite different from Nekrasov's. He supplies, for instance, much background information on the planning, troop training, and military operations carried out to set up Operation Uranus (code name of the Soviet pincer movement executed between November 19 and 23, 1942, to encircle the German forces and their allies). Consistent with this panoramic view of the Battle of Stalingrad, the author of *Life and Fate* shows the complex reality of absolute war through both sides – a multi-perspective procedure that we already saw in Ledig's *Die Stalinorgel* – , even if there is an otherwise understandable asymmetry between the narrative attention given to the Germans and that granted to the Soviet side. After all, Grossman's novel is not on the predicament of the German army, but rather on the heroic resistance and great victory of the Soviet people over the Germans.

In his literary rendering of the war, Grossman – who had indeed seen war at close range as a reporter for the Red Army periodical *Krasnaya Zvezda* (he covered the battles of Moscow, Stalingrad, Kursk, and Berlin) – shows a clear awareness of its absolute character. At the end of *Life and Fate* war is defined by the omniscient extradiegetic narrator as a "war of all against all" (870). This is a statement that must be understood literally, for the war waged on the eastern front in 1941–45 was no ordinary military conflict opposing two armies. It was that, of course: the German armed forces fought the Red Army. But it was also a war waged by the Germans against the Jews, political commissars, and in fact all sorts of Soviet civilians, and it was, too, a war fought by Stalin's secret police against defeatism and political dissidence. Grossman portrays the interconnection among all those simultaneous conflicts and displays through his characters an awareness of the absolute nature of the Great Patriotic War (as the war is known in Russia and other former republics of the Soviet Union) and the suffering that it brings. As early as in chapter 4 from Part 1, a Russian inmate in a German concentration camp called Ikonnikov claims to have witnessed a terrible war crime: "On the fifteenth of September last year [1941] I watched twenty thousand Jews being executed – women, children and old men" (27–28). Shortly afterwards the narrator adds: "Then the war had begun and Byelorussia had been invaded. Ikonnikov had witnessed the torments undergone by the prisoners-of-war and the executions of Jews in the towns and shetls" (29). This is clearly a description of several situations related to absolute war. Apropos of Stalingrad, the narrator writes about the "remorseless advance" of the German forces and "the iron teeth of the German offensive" (37). The narrative voice also correlates absolute war, the planned destruction of the European Jews, and German fascism in several passages (e.g., 195).

Unlike *Die Stalinorgel*, *Life and Fate* does not present war as a necessarily meaningless activity. Indeed, it is senseless for the many victims of the German or Stalinist oppression depicted in the novel, but at the same time under specific circumstances war may confer a purpose to people's lives. This is exactly what political commissar Krymov finds in Stalingrad. United in their struggle against a common enemy, the people of Stalingrad have carried out, in Krymov's view, the ideals of the November Revolution of 1917. Commissar Krymov notices the deployment in Stalingrad of the revolutionary ideals. For the German soldiers depicted in Plievier's *Stalingrad*, fighting on is pointless. By contrast, in Grossman's *Life and Fate* war provides meaning and purpose to the people defending Stalingrad. As the narrator writes further on, "Stalingrad was the only beacon of freedom in the kingdom of darkness. / A people's war reached its greatest pathos at the time of the defense of Stalingrad" (665). Since his arrival at Stalingrad, Krymov had the feeling that in the city the Party had no power (236–37). "Stalingrad had changed everything," he adds in another passage (259). Krymov thinks, "This war, and the patriotic spirit it aroused, was indeed a war for the Revolution ... Stalingrad, Sebastopol, the fate of Radischev, the power of Marx's manifesto, Lenin's appeals from the armored car near the Finland station – all these were part of one and the same thing" (516). For the Soviet defenders, Stalingrad at war is a space of meaning in which there is true democracy and a sense of individual freedom momentarily beyond the grasp of the Soviet state. For this very reason, after the German surrender the people of Stalingrad will feel a loss of purpose and meaning, finding instead a sense of emptiness (796–98).

In *Life and Fate* the narrator places absolute enmity in the nature of both fascism and Stalinism. Krymov is quite explicit on this score: the enemy of the people is an absolute enemy; accordingly, he "had never doubted the sacred right of the Revolution to destroy its enemies" (512), which is an idea that he expresses in several passages of the novel. Interestingly, Krymov differentiates between his – in his view – legitimate absolute enmity and the absolute enmity expressed by the Red Army snipers, which he finds somewhat distasteful. In a meeting with the famed sharp-shooters of Stalingrad, Krymov has mixed feelings towards their way of fighting the Germans: "he had never felt the least pity for enemies of the Revolution, but it was wrong to rejoice at the killing of German workers. There was something horrible about the way these soldiers talked" (235–36). But on further reflection, Krymov concludes that the Party itself has mobilized the fury of the masses to destroy the Germans, and after all "War's war!," concluding that the Germans "deserve what they get" (237). In turn, National Socialists followed the same notion of absolute enmity to extirpate from the so-called *Volksgemeinschaft* all the "alien" and "noxious" elements. As a character named Chalb says of the Nazis, "We never hesitated not only to cut out infected tissue from the body of the people, but also to cut out apparently healthy tissue that might become infected at a critical moment" (733). The points of overlap between National Socialism and Stalinism as regards their respective ways of dealing with the "inner enemy" are underscored at length by camp commandant Liss in an important conversation with prisoner Mostovskoy (393–403).

For its proper realization, absolute animosity needs to stimulate the people's animus towards a collective of declared enemies, and "in this case it is not enough to rely merely on the instinct for self-preservation; it is necessary to stir up feelings of hatred and revulsion" (213). A minority of people is in charge of creating such an atmosphere of absolute animosity (213–14), and while there is always resistance, in the end "the obedience of the vast mass of people is undeniable" (214). In addition to the life instinct and ideological influence, terror and limitless violence at the service of the state cooperate in making of mass murder an accepted everyday activity (215). The paradigmatic instance of absolute enmity is the one expressed against the Jewish people (484–87). Absolute animosity is instilled in people who in principle should not feel any. This is the case, for instance, of Private Roze, whose job "was to watch through the inspection-window [of the gas chamber]; when the process was completed, he gave the order for the gas chamber to be emptied. He was also expected to check that the dentists worked efficiently and honestly" (532). According to the narrator, "Gentleness and friendliness had seemed the fundamental traits of his character," and for this simple reason even Roze himself "was surprised how much hatred lay inside him and how long he had kept it hidden" (533). Another case of absolute animosity instilled in someone who should not feel any can be found in Lieutenant Bach. In the German field hospital at Stalingrad, Bach has changed his mind regarding the extermination of the Jews. "Previously it had sent shivers down his spine. Even now, if he were in power himself, he would immediately put a stop to this genocide" (376). Nevertheless, he also believed that there is "such a thing as a German soul and a German character – which meant that there must also be a Jewish soul and a Jewish character" (376). Lieutenant Bach thinks that "The most extraordinary thing of all is that whereas for years I felt I was being suppressed by the state, I now understand that it alone can give expression to my soul" (378).

There are many scenes in which absolute enmity and, consequently, useless suffering, are played out: a *Brenner* counting bodies in a *Lager* (200–2), life in a ghetto (203, 205), Jews in a cattle-wagon (203–4), Nazi bureaucrats solving the technical problems involved in the extermination of people (471–78), and of course the many chapters whose action takes place in a German *Lager* (Part 1, chapters 1–2, 4–6, 44, 67–71; Part 2, chapters 14, 39, 41–49), a Soviet concentration camp (Part 1, chapters 40–41), and the Lubyanka prison (Part 3, chapters 2–6, 42–43, 56–57). All these scenes establish a link between absolute war, useless suffering, and the absolute animosity that has led to the extermination of many people. The concentration camp is an outcome of the war, and its goal is extermination (478). The description of the German *Lager* contains one of the key messages of the novel – a message against fascism, Stalinism, and the war that has facilitated their exterminating drive: "This is a world of straight lines: a grid of rectangles and parallelograms imposed on the autumn sky, on the mist and on the earth itself . . . Their very uniformity was an expression of the inhuman character of this vast camp" (19). In contrast to that repressive geometry, "Among a million Russian huts you will never find even two that are exactly the same" (19), a fact that the narrator connects to life itself: "Everything that lives," he claims, "is unique. It is unimaginable that two people, or two briar-roses should be identical . . . If you attempt to erase the peculiarities and individuality of life by violence, then life itself must suffocate" (19).

Before absolute war, fascism, and Stalinism, Grossman defends throughout the novel democracy and individual freedom. In *Life and*

Fate, both manifest themselves through the predominance of dialogue. The narrator claims that "What constitutes the freedom, the soul of an individual, is its uniqueness" (555). A character that functions as an authorial voice, Chepyzhin, categorically affirms that "Freedom is the fundamental principle of life" (690). The individual's uniqueness and freedom counterbalance in the novel the useless suffering and absolute enmity that are at the heart of absolute war and totalitarianism. These claims are consistent with the ethical message suggested in the novel. *Life and Fate* does not put forth an ethical message based on the fundamental dual structure made up by good and evil. Its portrayal of the war and totalitarianism cannot be understood by invoking that binary structure. *Life and Fate* opposes any absolute, be it absolute evil or absolute good, for both are predicated on the violent imposition of abstract values onto something that exceeds the abstract, namely the individual. The moral philosophy underpinning the novel is condensed in an embedded text written by Ikonnikov, who argues against people who believe in absolute good, which they tend to impose onto other people whether they like it or not: "They say: my good coincides with the universal good; my good is essential not only to me but to everyone ... / And so the good of a sect, class, nation or state assumes a specious universality in order to justify its struggle against an apparent evil" (405). He also expresses criticism of all the suffering caused by Christianity (405–6) and questions the idea of good underlying the November Revolution on account of all the suffering that it has brought (406–7). In his view, the only way to true goodness is not through a universal abstract notion of good, but rather by means of human kindness: "The kindness of an old woman carrying a piece of bread to a prisoner, the kindness of a soldier allowing a wounded enemy to drink from his water-flask, the kindness of youth towards age, the kindness of a peasant hiding an old Jew in his loft ... A kindness outside any system of social or religious good" (407–8). This kindness, he claims, is "what is most truly human in a human being," "what sets man apart," it is, in sum, "the highest achievement of his soul" (409). In the *Lager* Ikonnikov has despaired of the good, even of human kindness, and yet he has also discovered there that not even fascism, not even gas chambers can conquer human kindness (410). The text concludes with what may be taken as an authorial ethical message: "Human history is not the battle of good struggling to overcome evil. It is a battle fought by a great evil struggling to crush a small kernel of human kindness" (410). To his literary depiction of senseless, useless suffering, Grossman adds, therefore, meta-ethical passages that comment on that suffering while putting forth an ethics that overcomes the supposedly noxious binary structure made up of good and evil.

Life and Fate contains an important self-referential metatext that connects the twin notions of individual freedom and democratic polity, incorporating them into the very texture of the novel. A character named Madyarov defends Chekhov as the bearer of true freedom. Chekhov, Madyarov argues, "took Russian democracy on his shoulders, the still unrealized Russian's freedom" (282). According to Madyarov, "Chekhov brought Russia into our consciousness in all its vastness – with people of every estate, every class, every age ... He said something no one in Russia had ever said. He said that first of all we are human beings – and only secondly are we bishops, Russians, shopkeepers, Tartars, workers ... he said that people are equal because they are human beings" (283). Chekhov is considered as the banner of a "true, humane, Russian democracy, of Russian freedom, of the dignity of the Russian man" (283); in contrast to this kind of humanism, "Our Russian humanism has always been cruel, intolerant, sectarian ... It has always mercilessly sacrificed the individual to some abstract idea of humanity" (283). The narrative prominence of dialogue, as well as the wide spectrum of characters from all walks of life novelized by Grossman, constitutes the literary embodiment of Grossman's defense of the uniqueness of the individual, the democratic polity, and the kind of humanism put forth by Chekhov, as well as the novelist's way of countering the absolute animosity described in his work. Upon such devices Grossman builds up a polyphonic world that somehow counterbalances the injustices and the senseless suffering endured by many of his characters in the context of the absolute war fought by Nazi Germany and the Soviet Union.

Radical Evil

Vasily Grossman's reflections on the evil underpinning both National Socialism and Stalinism can also be found in other coeval works, including scholarly monographs. A few years before Grossman finished *Life and Fate*, a book by the German philosopher and political scientist Hannah Arendt which addressed, from a historical and philosophical perspective, the very issues that preoccupied Grossman at the time, saw the light of day. I am referring, of course, to *The Origins of Totalitarianism* (1951). As part of her reflections on the Nazi *Lager* system and the Soviet Gulag elaborated in that monograph, Arendt writes on the same pivotal problem that Grossman would novelize in his *magnum opus* – the

problem of evil. Specifically, she revisits and redefines the notion of
"radical evil," a term originally coined by Kant in *Die Religion innerhalb
der Grenzen der bloßen Vernunft* (1793).[74] Her concept of radical evil is,
however, significantly different from Kant's. Kant does not use this term
in reference to a type of evil, or to an inconceivable one, but rather to
the propensity (i.e., the subjective principle of the possibility of an
inclination, such as concupiscence) of the person to deviate from the
moral law. Radical evil is thus the subordination of the moral law to
selfish human interests. For Kant, the statement "someone is evil" means
that the individual is aware of the moral law, in spite of which he has
incorporated into his maxims a deviation from such law. "Radical" does
not mean, therefore, a "higher stage," or a "greater intensity," of evil.
Evil is "radical" because it is "rooted" in human nature as a propensity
and also because it is the "ground" that corrupts all maxims. Finally,
Kant argues that the subordination of selfish interests to evil would not
be human, but diabolic. In other words, for Kant there can be no
diabolical evil, that is, people who practice evil qua evil. Profoundly
disturbed by the immense destructiveness brought about by the war and
by the extermination of almost 6 million European Jews, Arendt tacitly
concluded that Kant had not gone far enough in his discussion of radical
evil. In *The Origins of Totalitarianism* Hannah Arendt pushed the
Kantian notion of radical evil beyond Kant by assuming the real possibility of a diabolical evil. Thus, in the last phase of totalitarianism, which
Arendt locates in the Nazi death camps and the Gulag, there appears an
"absolute evil," a concept that alternates in her work with "radical
evil."[75] For Arendt, this evil is "absolute" because it cannot be deduced
from humanly comprehensible motives, such as self-interest, cowardice,
the will to power, or resentment, unless one would ground it in the
undeniable idealism of many Nazis willing to sacrifice everything,
including themselves and their own families, for the sake of their ideas.[76]
In Arendt's own words, "The disturbing factor in the success of
totalitarianism is rather the true selflessness of its adherents."[77] This
disposition to self-sacrifice makes absolute evil a most troubling phenomenon, because the willingness to die for one's ideals identifies good

---

[74] Immanuel Kant, *Religion within the Boundaries of Mere Reason and Other Writings*, trans. and ed. Allen Wood and George di Giovanni (Cambridge University Press, 1998), 45–73.
[75] Hannah Arendt, *The Origins of Totalitarianism*, new ed. (New York: Harcourt Brace and Company, 1979), viii–ix, 437–59.
[76] Ibid., 307–8, 322.   [77] Ibid., 307.

and evil: evil behavior underpinned by maxims that prescribe self-sacrifice has the structure of an ethically good act.[78]

While Hannah Arendt does not relate radical evil to war, it could be argued that under specific circumstances absolute war may be a realm propitious for the deployment of radical evil. The Second World War as it was fought on the eastern front allows for making that connection. The Nazi project to purge the *"Volksgemeinschaft,"* or people's community, of *"Untermenschen"* (sub-humans), whose existence, it was thought, endangered the purity and health of the Aryan race, displayed all its murderousness only after the war broke out on September 1, 1939. *Aktion* T4, the euthanasia program devised by the Nazis to kill patients deemed incurable, started to function right after the German invasion of Poland. More than 70,000 persons would be gassed from September 1939 until T4 was suspended on August 24, 1941. Partly caused by mounting social opposition to the euthanasia program within the Reich itself, this suspension coincided in time with a new phase in the Nazis' drive to murder the "enemies" of the Aryan *"Volksgemeinschaft."* Immediately after the German invasion of the USSR on June 22, 1941, *Einsatzgruppen* or mobile killing units followed in the steps of the Wehrmacht with the mission of rounding up Jews, political commissars, and other "subversive" Soviet civilians, and executed them on the spot. This new stage in the Nazi destruction of the European Jews was, therefore, part and parcel of the absolute war unleashed by Germany against the Soviet Union. As was the case with the operations undertaken by the *Einsatzgruppen*, the systematic mass murder of Jews in death camps set in full motion after the Wannsee Conference on January 20, 1942, cannot be dissociated from the war either. As specialized scholarship has amply demonstrated, the final form of the *Endlösung der Judenfrage* (or Final Solution of the Jewish Question, the projected physical extermination of European Jewry) was not inevitable. Regardless of its constitutive murderousness, the anti-Semitism intrinsic to National Socialism might have taken a different path had the Germans invaded Great Britain, or had the Wehrmacht taken Moscow and pushed the Soviets beyond the Urals. But none of that happened, and the different plans sketched for "cleansing" Europe of its Jewish population (e.g., through mass deportation of the European Jews to Madagascar or to

---

[78] For more information on radical evil, see Richard J. Bernstein, *Radical Evil: A Philosophical Interrogation* (Cambridge: Polity, 2002); Joan Copjec, ed., *Radical Evil* (London: Verso, 1996); and Slavoj Žižek, *Tarrying with the Negative: Kant, Hegel, and the Critique of Ideology* (Durham, NC: Duke University Press, 1993), 95–101.

the coldest regions in northern Russia) had to be abandoned for good. The defeat of the Germans at the Battle of Moscow turned out to be strategically decisive. The fight for *Lebensraum* had been lost, and with it the possibility of solving once and for all the "Jewish problem" through mass deportation. More radical measures were adopted, almost improvised, by Nazi administrators in Poland and bureaucrats in Berlin as a result of the course taken by the eastern campaign.[79] The Wannsee Conference and the construction of death camps cannot be understood without a proper comprehension of the avatars of the war in the East, particularly the German military failures. Although based on ideological considerations laid out prior to the outbreak of hostilities, and despite the fact that the harassment, discrimination, and persecution of Jews began in Germany almost as soon as the Nazis seized power in late January 1933, the extermination program as it finally developed was in a literal sense at once an *intension* and *extension* of the absolute war fought on the eastern front. As António Horta Fernandes has written, "without the chaos inherent to war itself and the fact that war creates its own objectives, this multiplication of violence would hardly have taken place as it did."[80] To argue, as Arendt does, that the extermination of the Jews took important manpower and resources away from the war effort is to miss the point that killing Jews was, for the Nazis, part of the war. The National Socialists believed themselves to be at war with "international Jewry."[81] The evil that powered the activities of the *Einsatzgruppen* in the East and the death camps in Poland and elsewhere constituted, consequently, a *function* of absolute war.[82] Given the fact that the German death camps analyzed by Arendt in connection with totalitarianism are closely linked to warfare, the notion of radical evil may be related to the very war whose course determined the

[79] See, for instance, Saul Friedländer, *Nazi Germany and the Jews, 1939–1945: The Years of Extermination* (New York: Harper Perennial, 2008); Hilberg, *The Destruction of the European Jews*; and Ian Kershaw, *Hitler, the Germans, and the Final Solution* (New Haven, CT: Yale University Press, 2008).

[80] António Horta Fernandes, *Livro dos contrastes: Guerra & política* (Porto: Fronteira do Caos Editores, 2017), 298.

[81] On the Nazis' "war against the Jews," see Lucy S. Dawidowicz's *The War against the Jews, 1933–1945* (New York: Holt, Rinehart and Winston, 1975), which establishes two phases in that war: the "internal war" (the anti-Jewish legislation passed in Germany between 1933 and 1935) and the "world war" (deportation and extermination of the European Jews during the world war of 1939–45).

[82] For the connections between war and genocide, see Doris L. Bergen, *War & Genocide: A Concise History of the Holocaust*, 2nd ed. (Lanham, MD: Rowman & Littlefield Publishers, 2009); and Eric Markusen and David Kopf, *The Holocaust and Strategic Bombing: Genocide and Total War in the Twentieth Century* (Boulder, CO: Westview Press, 1995).

Final Solution for the European Jews and the extermination of homosexuals, the Roma people, the mentally ill or handicapped, as well as other kinds of so-called *Untermenschen*. For all those reasons, radical evil may be considered as a family resemblance of absolute war.

One of the finest literary works to triangulate absolute war, radical evil, and genocide saw the light of day in 2006: I am referring to Jonathan Littell's 1,400-page-long bestselling novel *Les Bienveillantes* (The Kindly Ones).[83] Awarded the Prix Goncourt in 2006 as well as the Grand prix du roman granted by the Académie Française, this *succès de scandale* takes a path that differs in substantial ways from the usual one followed by the literature on the extermination of the European Jews and the Second World War: the novel is entirely narrated by a former high-ranking SS officer attached to the SD or *Sicherheitsdienst* (intelligence agency of the SS) named Maximilien Aue, who offers a comprehensive view of the *Endlösung* and absolute war in a "war memoir" which includes the activities of the *Einsatzgruppen* in Ukraine and the Caucasus, the Battle of Stalingrad, the Allied aerial bombing of Berlin, the death camps in Poland, and the final days of the Battle of Berlin. *Sensu stricto*, choosing a perpetrator instead of (as had hitherto been the norm) a victim for exploring the Nazi destruction of the European Jews in the context of the war was not something entirely new. There are precedents of novels whose main character and/or narrator is a Nazi: remember, for instance, Robert Merle's *La mort est mon métier* (Death is My Trade) (1952), Michel Tournier's *Le roi des Aulnes* (The Ogre) (1970), Michel Rachline's *Le bonheur nazi ou la mort des autres* (The Nazi Happiness, or, The Death of the Others) (1972), and Bernhard Schlink's *Der Vorleser* (The Reader) (1995). And yet, never before had a writer dared to narrate with such comprehensiveness and thoroughness the problem of radical evil and the entire extermination program, from beginning to end, through the gaze and voice of a former high-ranking SS officer. In that sense Littell violated a literary taboo – a taboo that tacitly forbade the narration of the destruction of the European Jews from the henchmen's point of view. His violation of the taboo is part and parcel of the novel's writing of cruelty.

---

[83] To date, in addition to a growing number of scholarly articles, four books on *Les Bienveillantes* have seen the light of day: Aurélie Barjonet and Liran Razinsky, eds., *Writing the Holocaust Today: Critical Perspectives on Jonathan Littell's The Kindly Ones* (Amsterdam: Rodopi, 2012); Murielle Lucie Clément, ed., *Les Bienveillantes de Jonathan Littell* (Cambridge: Open Book, 2010); Élise Lamy-Rested, *Parole vraie, parole vide: Des Bienveillantes aux exécuteurs* (Paris: Garnier, 2014); and Édouard Husson and Michel Terestchenko, *Les complaisantes: Jonathan Littell et l'écriture du Mal* (Paris: François-Xavier de Guibert, 2007).

Les Bienveillantes takes on the structure of the standard testimonial book produced by a survivor from a *Lager* and replaces that point of view with that of a perpetrator. The American writer does so by placing the *Endlösung* within the context of the war, specifically the absolute war waged by Nazi Germany and the Soviet Union. Littell's triangulation of absolute war, radical evil, and the extermination of European Jewry through a Nazi narrator is a true innovation in the otherwise vast field constituted by the fictional works on the Second World War and the destruction of the European Jews. An interesting after-effect of this triangulation through the voice of a perpetrator is that precisely by choosing such a kind of narrator Littell produces a narrative that challenges the reader's capacity to understand the very world portrayed in such detail by Maximilien Aue. The narrator's evil morality and deeds (as we will see, in addition to participating in the mass killing of Jews and commissars as a member of an *Einsatzgruppe*, Aue is also a cold-blooded assassin) undermine his own trustworthiness and reliability. The unreliability consubstantial with this narrator, to which I will come back later, reveals important aspects of radical evil, the extermination program, absolute war, and also the kind of literature that the admixture of all those themes seems to demand.

The narrator of *Les Bienveillantes* embeds in his memoir substantial meditations on absolute war (which he terms, unsurprisingly, "total war") in order to explain the world war of 1939–45. Aue sets off in counterpoint his general considerations on absolute war and his task force's mass murder of Jews, political commissars, and other Soviet civilians. It is certainly not coincidental that these reflections on absolute war overlap with the narration of Aue's exploits in Ukraine as a member of an *Einsatzgruppe* unit. In Hitler's Germany, killing Jews, like shooting political commissars, was after all an ideologically motivated act of war. Aue's interlacing of excursuses on absolute war and the narration of the indiscriminate murder of civilians who are perceived as absolute enemies that must be exterminated indicates, by itself, the close connection established in the novel between the nature of absolute war, absolute enmity towards the Jews and the Slavs, and radical evil. The narrator and main character points this out very early in his memoirs. In the first part of the novel he categorically affirms that the arbitrary distinction established after the war between, on the one hand, "military operations," and on the other, "the atrocities" perpetrated by an alleged minority of sadists and head cases (*détraqués*), is nothing else but "a comforting phantom of the victors of the war."[84] Shortly after this

---

[84] Jonathan Littell, *Les Bienveillantes* (Paris: Gallimard, 2006), 33. Further references in text.

statement, Maximilien Aue adds a comment on his own participation in the war. Although it is a defensive, self-exculpatory passage, at the same time it reflects something substantial about absolute war. Aue writes: "What I have done, I have done knowingly, thinking that it was my duty and that it was necessary to do it, regardless of how disagreeable or unfortunate it was. Total war is also this: civilians don't exist any longer, and between the gassed or shot Jewish child and the German child killed by incendiary bombs the only difference concerns the means employed" (34). For the autodiegetic narrator of *Les Bienveillantes*, in absolute war there is really no difference between fighting a regular army and mass murdering civilians. The novel shows in detail those two mutually complementary dimensions of absolute war. On the one hand, the second part centers on the mass killings of civilians conducted by the *Einsatzgruppe* unit to which Aue belongs. Maximilien Aue actively participates in the murder of defenseless people (e.g., 118–19, 123–25, 132–33), including the *große Aktion* at Babi Yar, a ravine on the outskirts of Kiev where on September 29–30, 1941, about 35,000 Jews were assassinated by German and local killing squads (181–95).[85] On the other hand, the third part of the novel focuses on a military conflict between two armies – the Battle of Stalingrad. Therefore, Aue formally places in tandem the extermination of civilians during the war (part two) and the struggle to death against enemy regular troops (part three). The claim that it is impossible to differentiate between military operations proper and atrocities committed against civilians is one of the leitmotivs of Littell's novel.

Maximilien Aue is well aware of the essential difference between the Second World War and all previous wars. Precisely by undertaking the mass murder of Jews and all sorts of civilians on the eastern front, Germans have brought something new and disturbing to the practice of warfare. Aue reminds us that war has always been perceived "as the greatest evil" (193). However, the narrator writes, "we invented something next to which war looked like something proper and pure" (193). Even the butcheries committed during the First World War, Aue goes on, "looked almost proper and just compared to what we had brought to the world" (194). He is surely referring to the activities of the *Einsatzgruppen* and the extermination program. Aue senses that such atrocities introduced something new into the practice of war, and that in this novelty there is the key for

[85] Cf. A. Anatoli Kuznetsov's treatment of the massacre, narrated through the point of view of a survivor, in his 1970 (censored first edition 1966) novel *Babi Yar: A Document in the Form of a Novel*, trans. David Floyd (New York: Farrar, Straus and Giroux, 1970), 99–120.

understanding everything (194). Sometimes Aue gets close to the truth, as
for instance when he realizes that his own psychology and inclinations have
much in common with the rupture of limits that is so characteristic,
according to Clausewitz, of absolute war. The narrator establishes a
correlation between his own frame of mind, his murderous activities
against Soviet civilians, and the nature of the war fought on the eastern
front: ever since his childhood, he writes, "I was haunted by the passion for
things absolute as well as by the overtaking of limits; at the time, that
passion had led me to the edge of the mass graves in Ukraine" (144). The
extermination of Jews is precisely the epitome of such subversion of all
sorts of limits, and therefore it is the highest point of absolute war. This is
so because killing them serves no practical purpose; it is a breakup with the
world of the economy and politics, it is a "waste" (*gaspillage*), "the pure
loss" (209). The annihilation of the enemy has meaning only in itself: the
only gain will be the genocide of the Jewish people. It does have one
additional sense, however: "that of a definitive sacrifice which entangles us
forever, which hinders us once and for all from turning back ... With
that ... there is no reverse any longer. Final victory or death" (209–10).
The extermination of the Jews hinders the Germans from retrieving
themselves back into regular warfare, or from seeking honorable peace
with their enemies; because of the genocide of the Jewish people, that will
not be a viable option. A red line, a point of no return has been crossed. At
the end of the war, there will only be destruction, that of the Allies, or of
the Germans themselves. These two possible scenarios describe one of the
two goals of the armies involved in absolute war: the complete annihilation
of the enemy (the other possible goal, as will be remembered, consists of
expecting from the enemy an unconditional surrender).

Aue performs evil deeds not on selfish grounds, but rather out of his
unwavering faith in National Socialism. He wants his deeds to fulfill
ethical criteria – National Socialist ethical criteria, that is. After witnessing
the first executions of civilians, he develops symptoms of post-traumatic
stress (i.e., vomiting, diarrhea, nausea, among others), which indicates
that, at least at the subconscious level, he is aware of the evil nature of
his actions, in spite of which he keeps performing them.[86] Aue the narrator
still suffers from the post-traumatic stress disorder developed during the
war (17–18). On account of these reasons and symptoms, Aue's evil

---

[86] On this score, see Scott M. Powers, "Jonathan Littell's *The Kindly Ones*: Evil and the Ethical Limits
of the Post-Modern Narrative," *Evil in Contemporary French and Francophone Literature*, ed. Scott
M. Powers (Newcastle upon Tyne: Cambridge Scholars Publishing, 2011), 189–92.

activities can be said to have the structure of ethical acts: he insists that he did not want to become a murderer, but when he was asked to be one, Aue did not refuse;[87] he *sacrificed* his sense of goodness for the sake of the evil ethics of National Socialism. Throughout *Les Bienveillantes* the narrator intersperses reflections on ethics, as well as on the crucial need to fully understand and thus embrace the intrinsic rationality underlying the orders that one is given. Early in the novel he expresses this imperative need – a need at once personal and ethical: "If we committed an injustice, one had to reflect on it and decide if it was necessary and inevitable, or if it was only the outcome of laziness, of a lack of mental consideration … I knew that such decisions were taken at a higher level. Yet we were not automata, it was imperative not only to obey the orders, but also to adhere oneself to them" (69).

This Kantian demand of awareness of the moral law and the individual's duty to fulfill it for its own sake are further emphasized when Aue underscores how vital it is to understand *in itself* the necessity of Hitler's orders. This is so, Aue explains, because "if one bent oneself simply because of a Prussian sense of obedience … without understanding them [the orders] and without accepting them, that is to say without *submitting* to them, then one was nothing but a calf, a slave, and not a man" (153–54). National Socialism must be "a living Law" (154). Killing is a horrible thing, he says, "But it was possible that that terrible thing was also a necessary thing; in which case one had to submit to such necessity" (153–54). To be sure, Aue acknowledges the existence of selfish passions in his involvement in the murder of Jews (160–61). At the same time, he recognizes the objective necessity of killing all Jews, and by so doing he surmises an underlying ethics in mass murder. The moral law, Kant claimed in his *Kritik der praktischen Vernunft* (Critique of Practical

---

[87] Georges Bataille's *La littérature et le mal* (Paris: Gallimard, 1957) provides a good literary context for Littell's treatment of evil. For more information on evil in Littell's novel, see Karl Heinz Bohrer, "Der Skandal einer Imagination des Bösen. Im Rückblick auf *Die Wohlgesinnten* von Jonathan Littell," *Merkur. Deutsche Zeitschrift für europäisches Denken* 65.2 (2011), 129–46; Youssef Ferdjani, "*Les Bienveillantes*: Le National-Socialisme comme mal métaphysique," *Les Bienveillantes de Jonathan Littell*, ed. Murielle Lucie Clément (Cambridge: Open Book, 2010), 263–76; Margaret-Anne Hutton, "Jonathan Littell's *Les Bienveillantes*: Ethics, Aesthetics and the Subject of Judgment," *Modern & Contemporary France* 18.1 (2010), 1–15; Julia Kristeva, "A propos des *Bienveillantes* (De l'abjection à la banalité du mal)," *Infini* 99 (2007), 22–35; Nadia Louar, "Is Kindly Just Kinky? Irony and Evil in Jonathan Littell's *The Kindly Ones*," *Evil in Contemporary French and Francophone Literature*, ed. Scott M. Powers (Newcastle upon Tyne: Cambridge Scholars Publishing, 2011), 136–58; Powers, "Jonathan Littell's *The Kindly Ones*," 159–202; and Liran Razinsky, "We Are All the Same: Max Aue, Interpreter of Evil," *Yale French Studies* 121 (2012), 140–54.

Reason) (1788), is the sole ground of the pure will. Individuals freely choose their maxims, that is to say the propositions or general determinations of the will that underlie any action. Since moral behavior consists of fulfilling the moral law for its own sake, and not out of self-interest or because it brings pleasure or happiness, it follows that attaining the highest good by sheer accident does not describe ethical behavior. On the contrary: Kant thinks that this coincidence derives from an evil maxim. He writes: "whenever incentives other than the law itself ... are necessary to determine the power of choice to lawful actions, it is purely accidental that these actions agree with the law, for the incentives might equally well incite its violation. The maxim ... is therefore still contrary to law, and the human being, despite all his good actions, is nevertheless evil."[88] The moral law must be fulfilled by a deliberate choice of a free will, which by reason finds itself bound to the law. This is exactly what Aue complains about in regard to his comrades: they followed orders *without thinking*. Theirs was not an inner free choice; therefore, their actions were not properly ethical, but, to put it in Kantian language, "juridical": Aue's comrades fulfill not the moral law, but the law of the state. If we take as a point of reference Kant's book on the metaphysics of morals, one could say that their maxims fall into the doctrine of right, while Aue strives to follow maxims that belong to the doctrine of virtue. If in Nazi Germany fulfilling the moral law lies in the murdering of Jews, of the "enemies" of the "*Volksgemeinschaft*," individuals must understand that law first and freely choose it as the determining ground of their actions. That is precisely Aue's impossible, unattainable goal: to internalize and incorporate into his maxims what cannot be rationally internalized and incorporated, that is to say the extermination of an entire race. Racial extermination cannot be a practical law because individuals who incorporate into their maxims the need to annihilate an entire race fall into a contradiction, in the sense that they are legislating their own potential extermination by other people. In other words: practical reason would establish a priori its own elimination – and that is a logical impossibility.

Closely following two of his sources,[89] Littell makes his narrator insist on the banality of those who perpetrated evil (38–39).[90] In other passages

---

[88] Kant, *Religion within the Boundaries of Mere Reason*, 54.

[89] Hannah Arendt, *Eichmann in Jerusalem: A Report on the Banality of Evil*, revised and expanded ed. (New York: Penguin, 1994); and Browning, *Ordinary Men*.

[90] For more information on the banality of evil in *Les Bienveillantes*, see, for instance, Ferdjani, "*Les Bienveillantes*," 269–70; Hutton, "Jonathan Littell's *Les Bienveillantes*," 9–13; and Kristeva, "A propos des *Bienveillantes*," 22–35.

of his memoirs he describes the ordinariness of the men who participated in the mass killing of Jews in the Soviet Union, or who worked in the death camps (e.g., 53, 94, 143–44). Despite those statements, the truth is that Maximilien Aue was far from banal during the war. His evil is radical indeed, but rarely banal in the sense given to that notion by Hannah Arendt in her book *Eichmann in Jerusalem*.[91] Aue is no Eichmann. According to Arendt, "The trouble with Eichmann was precisely that so many were like him, and that the many were neither perverted nor sadistic, that they were, and still are, terribly and terrifyingly normal."[92] Such normality implied the existence of a new type of criminal, that is to say the criminal who commits his crime "under circumstances that make it well-nigh impossible for him to know or to feel that he is doing wrong."[93] Eichmann, Arendt claims, was not a monster. "Except for an extraordinary diligence in looking out for his personal advancement," she writes, "he had no motives at all. And this diligence in itself was in no way criminal . . . He *merely*, to put the matter colloquially, *never realized what he was doing*."[94] The problem was not stupidity – Eichmann was a competent administrator; it was *thoughtlessness* that predisposed Eichmann "to become one of the greatest criminals of that period."[95] None of this applies to Maximilien Aue. First, he is a thoughtful, reflective character; Aue says that in Ukraine he sought to find the ethical grounds for his evil actions. And second, in his private life he has committed incest with his sister, he is a homosexual dominated by transgenderism, and on occasion he behaves like a sociopath, suddenly assassinating six people. He strangles his mother and kills with an ax his stepfather in Antibes (757–59); he unexpectedly and without saying a word shoots to death an old *Junker* after he has skillfully played a Bach piece in an old church (1328–29); also without saying a word, he beats to death an old lover of his in a restroom in the Hotel Adlon (1353–54); he breaks the skull of a policeman and escapes (1374) after being arrested for tweaking with his fingers Hitler's nose in the Führer's bunker (1368–71); and without a warning, for no apparent reason, he kills his good friend Thomas with an iron bar (1389). All these murders are described in detail, but the narrator never accompanies his narration with an explanation or a justification, nor feels any remorse.

These matters bring us to Aue's narratorial credibility. Precisely because he performed evil acts, precisely because he is an unrepentant Nazi assassin, Aue needs to be considered as an unreliable narrator. According

---

[91] See, especially, Arendt, *Eichmann in Jerusalem*, 252, 280–98.   [92] Ibid., 276.   [93] Ibid., 276.
[94] Ibid., 287.   [95] Ibid., 288.

to Wayne C. Booth's famous formulation, a narrator is "reliable when he speaks for or acts in accordance with the norms of the work (which is to say the implied author's norms), unreliable when he does not."[96] In Seymour Chatman's reader–response definition,

> In "unreliable narration" the narrator's account is at odds with the implied reader's surmises about the story's real intentions. The story undermines the discourse. We conclude, by reading out, between the lines, that the events and existents could not have been "like that," and so we hold the narrator suspect ... The implied reader senses a discrepancy between a reasonable reconstruction of the story and the account given by the narrator.[97]

Unreliable narrators, however, are hardly always unreliable. For this reason, the reader must discern the truthfulness, or lack thereof, behind the three main functions performed by any narrator according to James Phelan, namely reporting, interpreting, and evaluating.[98] Instead of thinking of a binary system composed of reliable and unreliable narrators, it is more productive "to recognize that narrators exist along a wide spectrum from reliability to unreliability."[99] Narrators may have personalities or traits that serve as signposts to warn the reader of their possible unreliability. The factors that identify a narrator as unreliable usually stem from codes shared and accepted by the implied author and his readers, such as for instance the narrator's idiocy, his alcoholism, his naivety, his acknowledged lack of information, his excessive youth, his psychological problems, and dubious, questionable, or problematic moral values. This last dimension of unreliability is crucial in novels like *Les Bienveillantes*. William Riggan has written, with respect to the moral dimension of narrative unreliability, that "the narrator's unreliability is most often revealed by a facetiousness of tone ... by an insufficiency or a fallaciousness of foundation for his moral philosophy, or simply by the unacceptability of that philosophy in terms of normal moral standards or of basic common sense and human decency,"[100] a definition that serves to characterize Aue's

---

[96] Wayne C. Booth, *The Rhetoric of Fiction*, 2nd ed. (University of Chicago Press, 1983), 158–59. For theoretical approaches to unreliable narrators, see, in addition to Booth's seminal pages from *The Rhetoric of Fiction* (6–7, 158–59, 174–75, 239–40, 295–96, 300–8, 311–36), Seymour Chatman, *Story and Discourse: Narrative Structure in Fiction and Film* (Ithaca, NY: Cornell University Press, 1978), 233–37; James Phelan, *Living to Tell about It: A Rhetoric and Ethics of Character Narration* (Ithaca, NY: Cornell University Press, 2005), 49–53; and William Riggan, *Picaros, Madmen, Naïfs, and Clowns: The Unreliable First-Person Narrator* (Norman, OK: University of Oklahoma Press, 1981), 17–37, 171–83.
[97] Chatman, *Story and Discourse*, 233.   [98] Phelan, *Living to Tell about It*, 50.   [99] Ibid., 53.
[100] Riggan, *Picaros, Madmen, Naïfs, and Clowns*, 36.

unreliability on account of his political ideology, his evil deeds, and his National Socialist interpretation of Kantian ethics.

True: Aue is a trustworthy historical witness.[101] Similarly, Aue's statements on absolute war and on the relation of identity between military operations and atrocities against defenseless civilians in conditions of absolute war coincide with this monograph's assessment of war in the absolute degree. However, Aue's private life and the way he treats it in the narrative, together with his fascist ideology and his explicit unwillingness to apologize for his crimes (he claims that anyone in his situation would have done the same), make of him an unreliable narrator. Because of his past deeds, Maximilien Aue is by definition not trustworthy; his truthfulness must be put into brackets, and his words need to be examined carefully.[102] In addition to his problematic ethics, political ideology, murderous actions during the war, and his series of assassinations, there are several elements that emphasize Aue's unreliability. One of them is his feeling of emptiness after the war ("I came out of the war as an empty man," he says [25]). His present post-traumatic stress disorder (17–18), which started during the war when he saw the first mass killings of civilians (e.g., 170), is yet another factor that clearly indicates the determining negative effect that absolute war had on him. In certain phases of his war experience, he suffered from high fever or head injuries that seriously hampered his perception of reality and his remembrance of it. He spent the last weeks in Stalingrad under a very strong and lasting fever (591). To narrate the events of those days, "I quote books, not my remembrance, because the calendar had become for me an abstract notion" (591). At that time, he worked "like a sleepwalker" (592). Another important element that makes Aue unreliable is the head wound caused by a bullet in

[101] Susan Rubin Suleiman, "When the Perpetrator Becomes a Reliable Witness of the Holocaust: On Jonathan Littell's *Les Bienveillantes*," *New German Critique: An Interdisciplinary Journal of German Studies* 106 (2009), 5–11.

[102] On the reliability or unreliability of the narrator of Littell's novel, see Antoine Compagnon, "Nazism, History, and Fantasy: Revisiting *Les Bienveillantes*," *Yale French Studies* 121 (2012), 118; Jakob Lothe, "Authority, Reliability, and the Challenge of Reading: The Narrative Ethics of Jonathan Littell's *The Kindly Ones*," *Narrative Ethics*, ed. Jakob Lothe, Jeremy Hawthorn, and Leonidas Donskis (Amsterdam: Rodopi, 2013), 177–84, 187–88; Luc Rasson, "How Nazis Undermine Their Own Point of View," *Writing the Holocaust Today: Critical Perspectives on Jonathan Littell's The Kindly Ones*, ed. Aurélie Barjonet and Liran Razinsky (Amsterdam: Rodopi, 2012), 106–8, and his "Le narrateur SS a-t-il lu Sade?," *Paroles de salauds: Max Aue et cie*, ed. Luc Rasson (Amsterdam: Rodopi, 2013), 111–12; and Susan Rubin Suleiman, "Performing a Perpetrator as Witness: Jonathan Littell's *Les Bienveillantes*," *After Testimony: The Ethics and Aesthetics of Holocaust Narrative for the Future*, ed. Jakob Lothe, Susan Rubin Suleiman, and James Phelan (Columbus, OH: Ohio State University Press, 2012), 112–13, and her "When the Perpetrator Becomes a Reliable Witness of the Holocaust," 5–11, 17–18.

Stalingrad. In the hospital, the doctor tells him that "a bullet had traversed my head" (623). Aue writes: "a hole traversed my head, a narrow circular corridor, a fabulous well, closed, inaccessible to thinking, and if this was true, then nothing was like before ... My thinking of the world had to reorganize itself around that hole" (624). While still in recovery, he had problems understanding written or spoken language (625, 627). In Berlin, his *trou* or hole in the skull seems to seriously affect his perception of things, making him see things that others could not perceive (634). In relation to his head wound, on occasion he believes he is hallucinating and is afraid of losing his mind (668). As he says elsewhere with a series of questions, "What did that bullet do to my head? Did it forever blur the world, or had it really opened a third eye – the one that sees through the opacity of things?" (671). His memory of the facts is uneven. For instance, in a locker room with Thomas he does not remember the cause of his friend's scar on the stomach, despite the fact that they were together when Thomas was shot in Stalingrad. "Suddenly," Aue notes, "I had the impression that I could not be sure of anything" (990–91). Finally, Aue never acknowledges having killed his mother and stepfather, despite the damning circumstantial evidence gathered by the police. The reader easily infers that Aue killed them, but the narrator does not confirm this suspicion. The story undermines Aue's reliability. His personal recollection of events is suspect on account of all these factors. In sum: Littell deploys in his novel four of the six types of unreliability established by James Phelan, namely misreporting, misreading, misregarding, and underreporting.[103]

Maximilien Aue's unreliability has the same function as the silences, gaps, ellipses, and insinuations that are omnipresent in the letters sent home from the eastern front as well as in the war journal kept by Uwe Timm's brother, who fought in a Waffen-SS unit in Ukraine until he died in the fall of 1943. In his book *Am Beispiel meines Bruders* (In My Brother's Shadow) (2003), the noted German writer Uwe Timm endeavored to ascertain whether his older brother Karl-Heinz had participated, or at least witnessed, the atrocities committed by the Germans in the Soviet Union. The burning, insidious question is this: "Was his unit, the 3rd Battalion of the SS-Totenkopf Division, used for the so-called mopping up [*Säuberung*]? Against partisans, civilians, against Jews?"[104] Karl-Heinz's diary only records daily occurrences and actions of war, but

---

[103] Phelan, *Living to Tell about It*, 51–52.
[104] Uwe Timm, *Am Beispiel meines Bruders*, 4th ed. (Munich: Deutscher Taschenbuch Verlag, 2007), 34. Further references in text.

never the horror. There is no mention of taking prisoners, the murder of civilians, or any atrocity likely to have been witnessed, if not committed, by the Waffen-SS unit in which Timm's brother served. Neither feelings nor opinions have been recorded. A "partial blindness" speaks through the journal: it only registers what could be considered as normal actions and events in the context of a military conflict (148). According to Uwe Timm, "The diary deals exclusively with the war" (28). As an intradiegetic narrator, Karl-Heinz misregards and underreports: first, readers may legitimately suspect that on account of his Nazi ideology and ethical values (he joined the Waffen-SS, according to his mother, out of "idealism") Timm's brother is unreliable at the level of ethical evaluation (misregarding); second, the reader must supplement the information not provided in Karl-Heinz's journal (underreporting). Throughout *Am Beispiel meines Bruders*, Uwe Timm keeps asking himself why his brother did not find worth mentioning the abuse or murder of civilians, the round up and assassination of Jews and political commissars, the taking of prisoners, the execution of hostages, in short, the perpetration of atrocities that in all likelihood Karl-Heinz had seen, perhaps even performed. An undated entry of the brother's war diary, placed between the last dated entry and the note in which Karl-Heinz mentions that he has been seriously wounded, seems to suggest the reason for not recording the horror in his journal: "*I hereby end my diary, for I find it senseless to keep a record of things as horrible as those that I have sometimes seen*" (120). Initially, the narrator attributes this silence to a reluctance to face guilt (120). Further on in the text, however, Uwe Timm puts forth another tentative interpretation of that intriguing, obscure passage in the form of a question: "Does this insight that one cannot write a book on horrible things include also the enemies and victims, the Russian soldiers and civilians?" (147). Timm ends his book by reproducing again the last entry of Karl-Heinz's journal (155), thereby underscoring the key importance of that undated entry, its irreducible ambiguity on the horror, and the centrality of Timm's hesitant hermeneutics of the passage, according to which the text's silences may express the refusal to face one's own guilt as a perpetrator of violence as well as the constitutive incommunicability of the horror of absolute war. Unreliability, therefore, serves to underscore essential elements of radical evil and absolute war as it was fought on the eastern front.

A modernist literary device, the unreliability of Littell's narrator shows likewise that both radical evil and absolute war challenge communication; as in Uwe Timm's book, they resist language and representation.

Narrating evil from within entails hermeneutic and ethical complications, for one cannot take at face value the words uttered by a narrator who has been radically evil. *Les Bienveillantes* belongs to the catastrophic modernist tradition on absolute war. Like other catastrophic modernist texts, Littell's novel is a passionate utterance addressed at having a consequential effect on the reader. It also deploys a writing of cruelty, projecting to the reader the unbracketed violence of absolute war. The very fact that Littell adopts for his novel the genre of the testimonials by survivors of concentration and death camps while replacing the voice of the victim with that of the perpetrator is, in itself, a form of perverse cruelty with respect to his readership. At the same time, thanks to his use of an unreliable narrator, Littell opens new paths for narrating absolute war in connection with evil and the destruction of European Jewry. Malaparte, Plievier, and Ledig had already understood the extreme epistemological challenges and the representational difficulties implied in writing about absolute war, making their literary choices accordingly. Jonathan Littell provides an innovative literary work to add to that tradition of writing on war in its absolute degree. The literary device of narrative unreliability can be interpreted as a trope that stands for the utter unsayability of the extreme horror of both absolute war and the genocide of the Jewish people. If this reading is correct, we could even go one step further and suggest a radical thesis, namely that *Les Bienveillantes* tacitly claims, by way of a *reductio ad absurdum* (the unreliable narrator is, after all, an unrepentant Nazi assassin), that *any* account of absolute war and the destruction of European Jewry is, *inevitably*, unreliable.

Total Representation and the Ethics of Otherness

Some of the texts studied above suggest, so to speak, antidotes to the absolute war that they describe. Theodor Plievier and Gert Ledig built up their narratives on multiple or variable internal focalization. By privileging multiple perspectives, those novelists somehow counter the absolute animosity described at the level of the story – an animosity that excludes, by definition, multiplicity. For his part, Vasily Grossman, who also uses multiple and variable internal focalization, favors dialogue as the main narrative technique. *Life and Fate* is organized around an immense, never-ending conversation among its characters; it could be argued that Grossman tacitly propounds dialogue as a means for overcoming the absolute animosity that pervades the story of his great novel. Therefore, one may argue that the production of discourse and the technique of focalization oppose the proliferation of absolute animosity narrated in the stories of *Stalingrad, Die Stalinorgel,* and *Life and Fate.*

The most radical ethical overcoming of absolute enmity in the Second World War is to be found, however, in Walter Kempowski's ten-volume *Das Echolot. Ein kollektives Tagebuch* (The Sonar: A Collective Diary) (1993–2005).[105] This work constitutes one of the most interesting literary representations of warfare (absolute or otherwise) ever produced. A monumental montage of thousands of texts, *Das Echolot* offers an original and penetrating answer to the thorny question that has confronted many writers since Stendhal and Tolstoy, namely, how to represent through language and literary convention a phenomenon as complex and multi-layered as modern warfare. Posing as someone who, by means of a figurative sonar, charts the depths of history and detects long-forgotten voices amidst its folds and crevices, Kempowski seeks to depict the Second World War by combining excerpts from already published sources with passages and photographs taken from the unpublished material he had collected for his *Archiv für unpublizierte Autobiographien und Alltagsfotografen* (Archive of unpublished autobiographies and photographs of everyday life) – a unique repository created in 1980 containing about 300,000 photographs and 7,000 documents that span German history from the nineteenth century to the present.[106] The resulting collage, organized in the form of a "collective diary," is a vast, multi-perspective panorama of war. Kempowski skillfully orchestrates the voices of famous individuals and completely unknown people, bringing their experiences, activities, feelings, and thoughts to the fore. *Das Echolot,* a 7,700-page-long work that lacks an extradiegetic narrator and does not contain a single text by Kempowski himself (although it does include a photograph of him with other members of his family; in *Januar,* vol. 4, 445), tacitly asks its readers not to forget the war and the genocide of the European Jews, expecting

[105] Walter Kempowski's *Das Echolot* comprises four books: *Das Echolot. Ein kollektives Tagebuch. Januar und Februar 1943,* 2nd ed., 4 vols. (Munich: btb, 1997); *Das Echolot. Fuga furiosa. Ein kollektives Tagebuch, Winter 1945,* 2nd ed., 4 vols. (Munich: btb, 2004); *Das Echolot. Barbarossa'41. Ein kollektives Tagebuch,* 5th ed. (Munich: btb, 2004); and *Das Echolot. Abgesang'45. Ein kollektives Tagebuch,* 4th ed. (Munich: btb, 2007). Further references will be given in the text preceded by the corresponding abbreviated title (i.e., *Januar, Fuga, Barbarossa, Abgesang*).

[106] For more information on Kempowski's archive, see, for instance, Dirk Hempel, *Walter Kempowski. Eine bürgerliche Biographie* (Munich: btb, 2004), 173–76; and Maren Horn and Christina Möller, "'Sie erzählen, und ich werfe die Geschichten mit dem Bildwerfer an die Wand'. Der Schriftsteller Walter Kempowski als Archivar – Der Archivar Walter Kempowski als Schriftsteller," *Akten-Kundig? Literatur, Zeitgeschichte und Archiv,* ed. Marcel Atze et al. (Vienna: Praesens, 2007), 316–37.

them to draw from it, all by themselves, after reading the compiled testimonies, an ethical lesson.[107]

One striking aspect of *Das Echolot*'s treatment of war is its predominant focus on the eastern front of the Second World War. If the ten volumes are arranged not by their date of publication, but rather by their internal chronology, one readily notices that Kempowski essentially chronicles key episodes of the entire eastern campaign, from the eve of Germany's onslaught on the Soviet Union on June 22, 1941, to the day after Germany's unconditional surrender on May 8, 1945: thus *Barbarossa'41* (Barbarossa'41) (2002) deals with the first six months of the German invasion of the Soviet Union; *Januar und Februar 1943* (January and February 1943) (1993) pays special attention to the last month of the Battle of Stalingrad and the reverberations in Germany of the destruction and surrender of the 6th Army; *Fuga furiosa* (1999) represents the first two months of 1945 mostly, if not only, as they were lived in the eastern territories of the Reich, starting on January 12, with the beginning of the Red Army's final offensive, and ending on February 13–14, with the Allied aerial bombing of Dresden; finally, *Abgesang'45* (Swansong 1945) (2005) zooms in on a few days of the last two weeks of the war, from Adolf Hitler's birthday on April 20, 1945, to the day after the war ended in Europe. Kempowski himself has highlighted his focus on the eastern front

---

[107] Critics have referred only in passing to the war depicted in *Das Echolot*: Raul Calzoni, "Vielstimmigkeit der Zeitgeschichte in Walter Kempowskis *Das Echolot*," *Keiner kommt davon. Zeitgeschichte in der Literatur nach 1945*, ed. Erhard Schütz and Wolfgang Hardtwig (Göttingen: Vandenhoeck & Ruprecht, 2008), 137, 141, 150; Stefanie Carp, "Schlachtbeschreibungen. Ein Blick auf Walter Kempowski und Alexander Kluge," *Vernichtungskrieg. Verbrechen der Wehrmacht, 1941–1944*, ed. Hannes Heer and Klaus Naumann (Hamburg: Hamburger Edition, 1995), 664–79; Jörg Drews, "Die Toten sind nicht wirklich tot. Zu Walter Kempowskis literarischem Memorial *Das Echolot*," *Vergangene Gegenwart – gegenwärtige Vergangenheit. Studien, Polemiken und Laudationes zur deutschsprachigen Literatur, 1960–1994*, ed. Jörg Drews (Bielefeld: Aisthesis, 1994), 232, 234; Ulrich Herbert, "Zwischen Beschaulichkeit und Massenmord. Die Kriegswende 1943 aus der Perspektive des Alltags," *Neue politische Literatur* 40.2 (1995), 185–89; Peter Höyng, "From Darkness to Visibility: Walter Kempowski's *Das Echolot* [Sonar] and Günter Grass' *Im Krebsgang* [Crab Walk] as Two Overdue Narratives Facing World War II in Germany," *Reconstructing Societies in the Aftermath of War: Memory, Identity, and Reconciliation*, ed. Flavia Brizio-Skov and Susanna Delfino (Boca Raton, FL: Bordighera, 2004), 175, 185; Ulrich Krellner, "'Aber im Keller die Leichen sind immer noch da'. Die Opfer-Debatte in der deutschen Literatur nach 1989," *Moderna Språk* 99.2 (2005), 162; Helmut Lethen, "Das Echolot des Geschichtszeichens Stalingrad," *Walter Kempowski. Bürgerliche Repräsentanz, Erinnerungskultur, Gegenwartsbewältigung*, ed. Lutz Hagestedt (Berlin: De Gruyter, 2010), 323; Martin Rehfeldt, "Archiv und Inszenierung. Zur Bedeutung der Autorinszenierung für Walter Kempowskis *Das Echolot* und Benjamin von Stuckrad-Barres *Soloalbum*," *Walter Kempowski. Bürgerliche Repräsentanz, Erinnerungskultur, Gegenwartsbewältigung*, ed. Lutz Hagestedt (Berlin: De Gruyter, 2010), 379; and Gisela Zimmermann-Thiel, "'Echolot': A Warning," *Kultur-Chronik* 12.4 (1994), 4.

in the preface to *Barbarossa'41*: *Das Echolot* consists, he writes there, of several parts, whose "exemplary stations" are "Leningrad, Stalingrad, Auschwitz, Dresden, and Berlin" (5). On account of the evidence, it is therefore a misrepresentation to argue without qualification, as is usually done, that *Das Echolot* is a book on the Second World War.

Kempowski's decision to concentrate on the eastern front was significant, as it presumably led him to reflect on how to represent a rather peculiar front – one that saw the intertwining of two different types of war: absolute war and total war. *Das Echolot* is a twofold reflection on the dual nature of war on the eastern front. If one considers the conception of the book, its structure, its vast montage of materials of all sorts, the national, professional, ideological, and social diversity of all the authors included, and the book's drive for totality, then one may conclude that *Das Echolot* refracts total war. But if we take into account what Hayden White calls the "content of the form,"[108] if we focus our attention on the ethics of otherness interwoven with the montage of other people's texts, if our critical gaze falls upon Kempowski's almost fetishistic respect for everybody's right to speak and to be remembered, then we must come to the conclusion that *Das Echolot* overturns the logic of absolute war, especially in regards to its treatment of the "other." Taken as a whole, then, *Das Echolot* is both a formal refraction of total war and an ethical reversal of war in its absolute degree. Kempowski has captured the composite nature of the war fought on the eastern front, building an original way of representing warfare on the simultaneous formal absorption and ethical negation of the substance of that military conflict. And it is from within this twofold relationship with the war on the eastern front that Kempowski seeks to answer the questions of how to represent warfare, and with what purpose. The answer to the first question is a duplicate, in a sense, of the structure of the war depicted in the book, while the answer to the second is a negation of absolute war's annihilation of the "other." The reason behind this seemingly paradoxical attitude towards absolute and total war can be found, I believe, in two ethical imperatives underlying *Das Echolot*: the I's infinite responsibility towards the "other" and the I's unnegotiable need to preserve the "other's" voice. In the final analysis, *Das Echolot* formally internalizes the structure of total war in order to denounce, subvert, and ultimately cancel out the negative, deadly notion of the "other" implied in absolute war – a notion that characterizes the enemy as an "absolute

---

[108] Hayden White, *The Content of the Form: Narrative Discourse and Historical Representation* (Baltimore, MD: Johns Hopkins University Press, 1987).

enemy," as a completely unreasonable and evil opponent who must be destroyed at all costs.

Through his montage of other people's texts, Kempowski aims at portraying war in all of its complexity. Even in a superficial reading of *Das Echolot* the will to achieve totality is readily detectable. Kempowski reproduces a great number of texts written from the front, from Germany, and from many other countries around the world, by all sorts of people related in one way or another to the war. Medical military personnel, officers and enlisted men, members of the SS, conscripts of the Red Army, American GIs, war refugees, civilians trapped in front-line positions or bombed out of their homes, Jews about to be deported to concentration camps, famous writers and painters living in exile who analyze the war in their journals or private correspondence, world leaders who meet to discuss the war – this is just a brief sample of the enormous variety of people who portray, from many angles, places, stations in life, and ideological positions, the multi-dimensionality of modern war. Kempowski deploys in *Das Echolot* what may be termed a "poetics of total representation." Partly born as a response to the representational challenges posed by total and absolute warfare, the main objective of this poetics is to depict war in a manner at once comprehensive and fragmentary, and it can be found at work in the various narrative levels that constitute *Das Echolot*.[109]

At the level of the story the enormous quantity of texts that Kempowski puts together yields a multi-layered and highly nuanced image of absolute war. Entries relating combat experiences and the daily lives of soldiers deployed in forward positions coexist with others that describe, for instance, marches into enemy territory (the German invasion of the Soviet Union, in *Barbarossa*, 9–303; the Red Army's penetration into the Reich, in *Fuga*, vols. 1–4), the increasing hardship upon advancing farther behind enemy lines (e.g., *Barbarossa*, 76, 183, 249), the retreat of troops before an enemy attack (*Barbarossa*, 318–703; *Fuga*, vols. 1–4), the medical care administered to the wounded (e.g., *Januar*, vol. 1, 429–30; vol. 3, 618; vol. 4, 192; *Fuga*, vol. 1, 235–36), the discussions among and decisions taken by general staffs and the supreme high command of the German armed forces (e.g., *Barbarossa*, 73–74, 535–38, 675–76), or the thoughts, meetings, and agreements of various world leaders, whose decisions influenced the course of war as well as its aftermath (the Casablanca

---

[109] Carla A. Damiano has studied the formal devices used by Kempowski in the first four volumes of *Das Echolot* in her book *Walter Kempowski's Das Echolot: Sifting and Exposing the Evidence via Montage* (Heidelberg: Universitätsverlag Carl Winter, 2005).

Conference, in *Januar*, vols. 1–2; the Yalta Conference, in *Fuga*, vols. 3–4). Kempowski's poetics of total representation also seeks to capture the worries, fears, hopes, and activities of many Germans at home, as well as the hardships endured by the civilian population caught at the front. This is the case, for instance, in the pages devoted to the flight of Germans living in the eastern provinces of the Reich (*Fuga*, vols. 1–4), to the Germans who were subjected to all sorts of humiliations, including rape and murder, by the invading Soviet troops (*Fuga*, vols. 1–4; *Abgesang*, 115), to the Allied aerial bombings of German cities (*Januar*, vols. 1–4; *Fuga*, vols. 1, 3–4; *Abgesang*, 43–45), and to the extremely harsh conditions under which the inhabitants of Leningrad had to live during the siege of their city (e.g., *Barbarossa*, 354–62, 488–95, 698–702).

As part of his total representation of war, Kempowski also embeds passages into *Das Echolot* that discuss the war in general terms. These overarching comments provide both a historical context and an ideological framework for the entries that narrate specific war events. In *Januar und Februar 1943*, such comments are often voiced by Wilhelm Muehlon, who offers a useful context for understanding the war as it is described in many other texts. However, Kempowski's usual practice in this regard consists of distributing global views of the war among several authors. Some passages, for instance, point out and analyze the decisive strategic implications of the entry of the United States into the war (e.g., *Barbarossa*, 337, 382–83, 439). Other entries, most of them by Joseph Goebbels and other Nazi leaders, refer to the radicalization of Germany's way of conducting war as a result of its defeat at Stalingrad (*Januar*, vols. 1–4; *Fuga*, vol. 2, 787). Apropos of the first months of the war between Germany and the Soviet Union, several authors had already underscored the absolute and total nature of the military conflict. This can be inferred, for example, from the words of Heinrich Heim – an assistant at Hitler's headquarters in East Prussia – in a passage that illustrates the close connection between the practice of modern war and industrial output (*Barbarossa*, 664–65). A few passages emphasize the differences between absolute war on the eastern front and the various earlier *Blitzkriege* in Poland and Western Europe (*Barbarossa*, 113, 139, 278–79). For some people, the war against the Soviet Union was essentially an ideological war (*Barbarossa*, 42, 158–59, 249–50). Others express ideas on the war that align *grosso modo* with the Nazi official version of it (e.g., *Barbarossa*, 135, 366).

In contrast to the above viewpoints, there are entries that point out absolute war's absurdity. In a text from the closing pages of *Barbarossa '41* that sounds like an authorial comment on war, we read the following words scribbled by the Russian pediatrician Anna Lichatscheva: "I think of the millions of children in the entire world, whose childhood was stolen by the war. Russian children, German children. What is the sense of this war?" (699). Likewise, Bruno Kaliga observes that "Sometimes I pray, and sometimes I curse my fate. On that score all is senseless and aimless. When and how will the deliverance be? Will death come through a bomb or a grenade? Is it illness and infirmity? All these questions preoccupied us constantly" (*Januar*, vol. 1, 35). In wartime, life loses its old meaning and certainties, as can be deduced from a passage by Konrad Wilhelm Henckell: "I know, everything was only the beginning. But the sense – life cannot be taken for granted any longer, it is a gift" (*Januar*, vol. 1, 181). In *Fuga furiosa* Werner Hütter muses that "everything is unreal – the exertions, the victims, let alone the defeat," asking himself: "What will be achieved? Above all, what should be achieved? The flush of victory at the beginning, where has it gone? ... War should end right now ... Why is war so insatiable, so senselessly long?" (vol. 3, 435). Together, these entries on the war's senselessness function as an echo of the general authorial view of war that the reader can piece together while reading *Das Echolot*.

Similar observations could be made about a few entries devoted to the connections between war, language, and representation. Several authors argue, with varying degrees of directness, that it is impossible for one individual to capture the war's vastness. Pjotr Samarin addresses this issue in what may be read as a metacommentary on the notions of absolute and total war implied in *Das Echolot*: events on the battlefield, he writes, are "so dramatic, they occur in such fullness, that one cannot keep track of everything" (*Barbarossa*, 636). According to Paul Hübner, it is difficult to express war (*Barbarossa*, 278), and for the writer Wolfgang Borchert war is a phenomenon that resists communication. In a letter to his parents that may be read as yet another authorial metatext on the writing of war, Borchert states that "The things related to the war, as well as what one experiences in warfare, are not suitable for letters addressed to you – and everything else seems so unessential to me" (*Januar*, vol. 4, 158). A text by André Gide claiming that the war will produce new kinds of writing that differ from traditional realist accounts is endowed with a similar self-referential metatextual function: "One of the consequences of this war will undoubtedly be that art will be snatched away from realism. The reportage ... will liberate literature, in the same way that photography could liberate painting through a catharsis of sorts" (*Januar*, vol. 2, 582). It is difficult not to interpret Gide's words as a metatextual comment on the experimental poetics underpinning *Das Echolot*.

Kempowski's poetics of total representation articulates the level of discourse as well. *Das Echolot* comprises texts written in a wide range of linguistic registers. The variety of genres is equally considerable. Passages stemming from letters, personal diaries, and autobiographies abound, but the reader will also find secret reports, newspaper articles, military communiqués, telegrams, death certificates, submarine logs, restaurant menus, radio programs, train schedules, public speeches, poems, and cemetery records, among others. The polyphony of voices and the variety of linguistic registers is thus mirrored by the considerable diversity of genres included in the work. In addition to texts, Kempowski intersperses a significant number of photographs of people or scenes that relate in some way to the entries in each volume.

In keeping with Kempowski's poetics of total representation, the texts comprising *Das Echolot* are also connected on the level of the plot. In *Culpa*, Kempowski outlines the main techniques that he utilized in order to give artistic form to his collage.[110] Two of them need to be mentioned here: the principle of horizontality and the principle of verticality. The principle of horizontality refers to the reappearance of certain authors throughout *Das Echolot*. As Drews and Zimmermann-Thiel have already observed, the multiple appearances of the same author create a novelistic effect, for the reader ends up identifying them as characters.[111] The principle of verticality refers to the relationships between entries by different authors. Though diverse in their origins and viewpoints, the texts comprised in *Das Echolot* are connected in a variety of ways. The most common connection is based in dialogue – a dialogue that, itself, is constructed by means of various technical devices. Often, consecutive entries are interconnected because they were written in, or are about, the same place (e.g., Leningrad, *Barbarossa*, 37–45; Stalingrad, *Januar*, vol. 1, 555–61; Dresden, *Fuga*, vol. 4, 707–825) or the same situation (e.g., the fleeing of Germans from the approaching Soviet troops, *Fuga*, vol. 1, 685–90; the deportation of Germans to the Soviet Union, *Fuga*, vol. 3, 7–15), or because they address the same theme (e.g., the German invasion of the Soviet Union, *Barbarossa*, 21–25; Victory Day in Paris, *Abgesang*, 315–18). Consecutive entries may also relate to each other on account of being written in the same genre (letters by different authors, *Barbarossa*, 674) or by the same kind of people (e.g., series of entries written by world leaders, *Abgesang*, 311; by Nazi leaders and bureaucrats, *Januar*, vol. 2,

---

[110] Walter Kempowski, *Culpa. Notizen zum "Echolot"* (Munich: btb, 2007), 336.
[111] Drews, "Die Toten sind nicht wirklich tot," 228; Zimmermann-Thiel, "'Echolot'," 8.

158–63; or by people from the same hometown, *Fuga*, vol. 1, 101–6).
However, the relationships between different passages are just as frequently
marked by contrast. Entries by high-ranking German officers and administrators ominously referring to the imminent invasion of the Soviet Union
(*Barbarossa*, 10–12), for example, are contrapuntally offset by entries from
Soviet leaders and military personnel who did not believe that Germany
would invade their country (*Barbarossa*, 12–14, 15–17).

The polyphony of voices resulting from the montage of thousands of
texts is the literary expression of the preeminence of the "other" in *Das
Echolot*. Kempowski's total representation of absolute war is inextricably
linked to an ethics of otherness, which projects moral meaning onto the
texts, the ways they interrelate, and their final assemblage. Kempowski has
sketched out this ethics on several occasions, most notably in *Culpa*. There
he explains that the composition of *Das Echolot* was driven by ethical
considerations, noting that a strong stimulus for working on the book lay
"in the denunciatory dimension of the undertaking."[112] While many
would have eventually given up on such a monumental endeavor, Kempowski's perseverance can perhaps be explained by his vision for the work
as a way of redressing what he considered to be an unjust situation: "It is a
feeling for justice. I have the impression that the generation born in those
times has not been treated justly."[113] In other words, *Das Echolot* is
conceived of as a reparation to the generation that lived through the war.
But this "*Kurskorrektur*" or course correction, which is supposed to bring
us nearer the truth,[114] will only be effective if the author and his readers let
everyone talk. There can be no moral restrictions governing the detection
and reproduction of the voices of the "other": "I have listened to the good
ones, who also are always a bit bad, and the bad ones, who also had a
mother, and I have placed [*formiert*] the texts into a dialogue" (*Januar*,
vol. 1, 7). As Kempowski puts it, the most important thing in *Das Echolot*
"is precisely the flow of events on good and evil."[115] Kempowski's ethics of
otherness comprises, therefore, the whole ethical spectrum of maxims.
However, as Calzoni has rightly argued, this inclusiveness does not place
victims and perpetrators on the same level, nor does it preclude the passing
of moral judgment.[116] As Zimmermann-Thiel and other critics have
already noted, the lack of an extradiegetic narrator leaves the determination
of the entries' moral value (not to mention the moral value of *Das Echolot*

---

[112] Kempowski, *Culpa*, 189.   [113] Ibid., 235.   [114] Ibid., 235.   [115] Ibid., 281.
[116] Calzoni, "Vielstimmigkeit der Zeitgeschichte in Walter Kempowskis *Das Echolot*," 134.

as a whole) to the reader.[117] That being said, sometimes the location of the entries is intended to suggest moral meaning. This is the case, for instance, with the passages relating to the extermination of the European Jews, which in *Januar und Februar 1943*, *Fuga furiosa*, and *Barbarossa'41* are typically situated at the end of the calendar days – a strategic position that highlights their significance. Guided by the entries' relative position, the reader may (or may not) pass moral judgment by comparing ethical attitudes. The author deliberately avoids stating an explicit ethical message. To use a formulation suggested by Ludwig Wittgenstein in his *Tractatus Logico-Philosophicus*, the ethical message woven into *Das Echolot* is not said, but shown, and it is the reader's job to *see* it.[118]

A crucial element in Kempowski's treatment of otherness is the absolute enmity derived from the absolute war fought on the eastern front. *Das Echolot* provides many instances of absolute enmity. To begin with, the Germans perceive the Soviets as "cruel combatants" (*Barbarossa*, 120), as pitiless, inhuman people, barbarians who torture and mutilate their prisoners (e.g., *Barbarossa*, 122, 260). The general sentiment of hatred underlying this view is clearly accompanied by the desire to exact vengeance, and so it is no surprise that after finding the mutilated corpses of several comrades, an unnamed German soldier recalls that "The revenge came immediately. Yesterday we were gracious to the SS, for the Jews that we took were immediately shot" (*Barbarossa*, 260). Initially, at least, this kind of fighting was foreign to the soldiers. Although absolute war is nothing other than the unconditioned actualization of war's essence, the nature of combat in the East was felt by some troops to be something new and deeply menacing (e.g., *Barbarossa*, 25). The soldiers adjusted quickly, though, and the Wehrmacht participated shoulder to shoulder with the *Einsatzgruppen* in the killing of thousands of innocent civilians. In *Barbarossa'41* a significant number of entries are devoted to the massacres of civilians in the occupied territories of the eastern front. Most of these massacres are perpetrated against Jews, an issue to which Kempowski devotes a great deal of attention. In fact, this particular instance of absolute enmity is of such importance to Kempowski that he occasionally narrates individual episodes of its occurrence more than once. This is the case with the massacre of Jews in Kovno

---

[117] Zimmermann-Thiel, "'Echolot'," 6.
[118] On "saying" and "showing," see Ludwig Wittgenstein, *Tractatus Logico-Philosophicus*, trans. D. F. Pears and B. F. McGuinness (London: Routledge, 2001), propositions 3.262, 4.115, 4.121–4.122, 4.126, 4.461, 5.61–5.63, 6.12, 6.36, 6.51, 6.53.

(present-day Kaunas), reported first by Corporal Röder (*Barbarossa*, 65–66) and later on by a photographer (101–2). In other places this literary technique is reversed, meaning that the same person can be found narrating different scenes of mass murder; this is what happens, for example, with Felix Landau, a member of the SS who describes with gruesome detail several mass murders of Poles and Jews (*Barbarossa*, 215–16, 243–45). The mass execution of Jews in Gargzdai (Garsden in German) (*Barbarossa*, 86–89) is narrated in a similarly brutal manner. Massacres of Jews as retaliatory measures (*Barbarossa*, 227–28) or simply as the result of policy (*Barbarossa*, 245) are also included.

Soviet troops also viewed their enemies with absolute enmity – and behaved accordingly. In *Fuga furiosa* Kempowski includes texts that show the extent to which the murderous behavior of many Soviet soldiers toward German civilians living in East Prussia and other eastern territories of the Reich was officially condoned, even encouraged. From a Red Army broadsheet soldiers could read things like this: "Kill! Kill! Germans are guilty of everything, the living ones and those who are not born yet! Follow the directive of comrade Stalin and reduce to a pulp the fascist beast in its cave. Crush with violence the racial pride of the German women! Take them as rightful booty!" (*Fuga*, vol. 1, 8). Another broadsheet of the Red Army reproduced by Kempowski portrays the Germans in a similar manner and prescribes correspondingly ruthless behavior on the part of the Soviet soldiers (*Fuga*, vol. 1, 8–9). These two texts, embedded right after passages that announce the beginning of the final Soviet offensive in February 1945, set the tone for the remaining pages of *Fuga furiosa*. So as to remind the reader of the Soviet policy of encouraging absolute animosity, Kempowski inserts further on in the same volume the comments of Red Army soldier Janek Tyrczynski, who recounts the measures taken by Soviet officials to spur their soldiers to violence against German civilians: "Moreover, we had been educated into hating the Germans. In broadsheets that we received on the front, there always appeared 'Kill the German men and defile the German women. Crush their racial pride.' Not only wasn't it forbidden to us, actually we were encouraged to do it" (*Fuga*, vol. 1, 717). Fueling such hatred was easy on account of the resentment most Soviets already felt toward the Germans for their criminal behavior in the Russian territories they had occupied. As Marshal Ivan Tschernjakovski put it, there was no mercy for the Germans because none was granted to the Soviet people when the Germans invaded their country (*Fuga*, vol. 1, 12). In *Fuga furiosa* the reader will find a number of texts written by Soviet soldiers in which Germans are described as *Untiere* or "beasts" that must be eradicated (e.g., *Fuga*, vol. 1, 11–12; vol. 2, 837–38; vol. 4, 475–76).

The embedded texts written by German exiles and Jews form another crucial component of *Das Echolot*'s ethics of otherness. During the Third Reich the exiles and the Jews both figuratively and literally lived outside or on the margins of German society. In *Barbarossa'41* Kempowski represents this extraterritoriality formally by placing the texts by German exiles on one "margin," namely at the beginning of each calendar day, and those dealing with the persecution and extermination of the European Jews at the end, that is to say on the closing "margin" of the calendar day. Certainly, texts by exiles are scattered throughout *Das Echolot*, and passages describing the persecution and extermination of the Jewish people (written by Jews and non-Jews alike) can be found in many different parts of the work. But it is in *Januar und Februar 1943*, and most particularly in *Barbarossa'41*, that these texts acquire prominence by their position at the beginning or the end of calendar days. Their placement on the edges not only formally emphasizes the social marginality of the groups they describe, and their exclusion from German society, but it also projects an ethical message upon the inner entries. Exile and extermination were the outcomes of the same National Socialist politics and policies that triggered a world war. The privations and anxieties of exiles as well as the suffering and utter destruction of the Jews frame and put into perspective the otherwise very real privations, anxieties, and suffering of German troops at the front and German civilians at home. Kempowski wants the readers never to forget that the condition that made the suffering of an untold number of Germans during the war possible was in fact their connivance with a totalitarian regime that forced so many into exile and persecuted whole segments of German society, such as the Jewish population. Kempowski does not deny the reality of the suffering endured by many Germans; on the contrary, he even organizes *Das Echolot*'s passages in such a way that the reader will likely feel compassion. What he aims to do is to qualify that suffering.

To a certain degree, it could be argued that the ethics of otherness woven into *Das Echolot* is an ethics without ontology. In a way that is reminiscent of Emmanuel Levinas's ethics, in *Das Echolot* the "other" is irreducible to the same, to a totality; it is altogether other. The immense polyphony of Kempowski's multi-volume book is predicated on both the uniqueness and precedence of the voice of the "other." As it happens in the philosophy of Levinas, Kempowski advances an ethics of otherness in which the "other" precedes the I, and the I is infinitely indebted to him.

It is by recovering the "other's" voice from the depths of memory and history and letting him speak that Kempowski chooses to pay off this debt, and, equally importantly, it is his way of overturning absolute war's notion and treatment of the "other." By bringing together all sorts of individuals, *Das Echolot* may be viewed as a homage to the "other's" irreducible singularity, as well as a confirmation of the absolute respect that the I owes to the "other." Kempowski conveys this idea in an ekphrasis in the prefaces to *Barbarossa'41* and *Abgesang'45*, namely his reference to Velázquez's *The Surrender of Breda* in which the victor shows mercy to the defeated enemy. Kempowski's description of the painting focuses on this very aspect in a tone that insinuates his agreement with Velázquez's message: "In this painting a victorious man and a vanquished person stand face to face. The victorious general has not put his foot on the neck of the defeated commander [*Unterlegenen*], who gives him, in humiliation, the keys to the city. Instead of doing that, he graciously leans towards him, yes, he raises the bowing defeated commander!" (*Barbarossa*, 5; *Abgesang*, 5). And indeed, the core message of *Das Echolot* seems to be the importance of showing compassion for the "other." The encircled Wehrmacht soldiers in Stalingrad, the Germans bombed out of their houses, the American prisoners of war, and the Auschwitz inmates all deserve compassion, even if some of their actions are questionable or deplorable, and even if we acknowledge that in very fundamental senses they are not equally inno-cent. Not to feel compassion for a German soldier going through the ordeal of Stalingrad means not to follow the maxim implied in *The Surrender of Breda*, a maxim that, according to Kempowski, has never been "honored" (*Barbarossa*, 5). Kempowski puts before the reader the whole range of suffering brought about by war, thereby eliciting in the readers a feeling of empathy and *Mitleid* or compassion. War is a destruc-tive activity in which most people lose. The acknowledgement of this loss and the absolute compassion and respect for the "other" underpinning *Das Echolot* revert and ultimately cancel out the absolute animus intrinsic to the absolute war waged on the eastern front.

Das Echolot may be read as an immense canvas of absolute war, as well as a compendium of all the topics and literary devices characteristic of the writing on absolute war that I have explored in this chapter, for it contains numerous instances of kaput, the abject, the writing of cruelty, useless suffering, the absurd, multi-perspectivism, and narrative unreliability. Furthermore, it represents absolute war in a novel format. To be sure, *Das Echolot* partly stems from a specific tradition of war writing, a tradition that bears the stamp of catastrophic modernism. Karl Kraus's *Die letzten*

Tage der Menschheit (The Last Days of Mankind) (1922), Edlef Köppen's *Heeresbericht* (1930), John Dos Passos's novel *1919* (1932), Alexander Kluge's *Schlachtbeschreibung* (1964), Claude Lanzmann's *Shoah* (1985), and Hans Magnus Enzensberger's *Europa in Ruinen* (Europe in Ruins) (1990) are books on war and its aftermath built upon the montage of other people's texts. But *Das Echolot* goes beyond these works, putting forth a much more radical and comprehensive collage of war. Unlike Kraus, Köppen, Dos Passos, and Kluge, Kempowski does not include fictional texts in his work; and in contrast to Lanzmann, who centers exclusively on the destruction of the European Jews, and to Enzensberger, whose book basically aims to describe the physical and moral ruin of European cities between 1944 and 1948, he does not limit himself to one single objective only. Instead, he chronicles almost the entire war in all its dimensions, with a particular emphasis on the eastern front, shaping his collage – yet another novelty – as a collective journal. Focusing on the eastern front was a momentous decision, as it led Kempowski to develop a poetics of total representation, which refracts the structure of total war, in order to formally capture the essential elements of absolute war. The merging of that poetics with an ethics of otherness has produced a unique literary work – a practical lesson on how to represent an event as multi-layered as absolute war, and a critique of an ethical problem closely linked to absolute war that sadly persists: the perception and treatment of those who do not agree with us as absolute enemies who must be annihilated.

CHAPTER TWO

Terror

Obliteration

In 1921, the Italian Ministry of War published a groundbreaking book on aerial warfare: *Il dominio dell'aria: Saggio sull'arte della guerra aerea* (The Command of the Air: An Essay on the Art of Aerial Warfare).[1] Its author, General Giulio Douhet, elaborated therein the thesis that when the air force is the main attacking weapon war should develop in two phases. First, the air force must reach command of the air by destroying the enemy's aerial forces. Second, after attaining the command of the air it must relentlessly bomb the enemy's urban centers "with the intention of crushing the material and moral resistance of the enemy."[2] The emergence of military aviation has radically changed the art of war. By virtue of the air force, Douhet claims, "the repercussions of war . . . can be directly felt for hundreds and hundreds of miles over all the lands and seas of nations at war"; the battlefield is no longer limited to "the boundaries of the nations at war," which means that "all of their citizens will become combatants since all of them will be exposed to the aerial offensives of the enemy"; Douhet ominously adds: "There will be no distinction any longer between soldiers and civilians" (10).[3]

Il dominio dell'aria vigorously defends strategic bombing as the most efficient means for winning a war. It effectively reverses the usual relation between civilians and military personnel: in Douhet's view, one of the main goals of strategic bombing consists of saving the lives of one's own

---

[1] On Douhet's strategic thinking, see Thomas Hippler, *Bombing the People: Giulio Douhet and the Foundations of Air-Power Strategy, 1884–1939* (Cambridge University Press, 2013).

[2] Giulio Douhet, *The Command of the Air*, trans. Dino Ferrari (Washington, DC: Office of Air Force History, 1983), 128. Further references in text.

[3] For an introduction to the targeting of civilians in modern warfare, see Alexander B. Downes, *Targeting Civilians in War* (Ithaca, NY: Cornell University Press, 2008); and Yuki Tanaka and Marilyn B. Young, eds., *Bombing Civilians: A Twentieth-Century History* (New York: New Press, 2009).

troops by killing enemy civilians in such a proportion that their government will be forced to surrender. In this kind of war, the decision will be quick because the "decisive blows will be directed at civilians," which is "the element of the countries at war least able to sustain them" (61). He admits that massive aerial bombing of targets such as cities may be inaccurate, but this should be no cause for concern for the general staff; this is so for one reason: "*the objective must be destroyed completely in one attack, making further attack on the same target unnecessary*" (20). Douhet underscores that the bombing raid (or raids, if several are needed) has to be directed against large urban centers (22). The attacking squadrons should bomb "peacetime industrial and commercial establishments; important buildings, private and public; transportation arteries and centers; and certain designated areas of civilian population as well" (20). In order to destroy such targets, the air force should use the three kinds of bombs at its disposal at the time: explosive bombs (which would demolish the targets), incendiary bombs (which would set them ablaze), and chemical weapons (whose task would be to hinder the firefighters from extinguishing the fires). "The complete destruction of the objective," Douhet believed, "has moral and material effects, the repercussions of which may be tremendous. To give us some idea of the extent of these repercussions, we need only envision what would go on among the civilian population of congested cities once the enemy announced that he would bomb such centers relentlessly, making no distinction between military and nonmilitary objectives" (20).

Interestingly, Douhet does not conceal the fact that bombing civilians on such a scale and with such annihilating force amounts to committing an act of terror.[4] The use of indiscriminate terror as a means of coercion is in truth the whole point of strategic bombing, according to Giulio Douhet. The mission of the air force would consist of terrifying and killing as many civilians as possible so as to quickly defeat their country. As soon as it has total command of the air, the air force "will be able to unleash without risk all their offensive power to cut off the enemy's army and navy from their bases of operation, *spread terror and havoc* in the interior of his country, and break down the moral and physical resistance of the people" (35; emphasis added). Terrorizing the civilian population is, therefore, at the

---

[4] See Antulio J. Echevarria II, *Military Strategy: A Very Short Introduction* (New York: Oxford University Press, 2017), 66–77, for a consideration of the bombing of civilian populations as "strategic terror bombing"; and Peter Sloterdijk, *Terror from the Air*, trans. Amy Patton and Steve Corcoran (Los Angeles: Semiotext(e), 2009), 52–70, on aerial bombing in the context of his discussion about "terror from the air."

core of Douhet's notion of strategic bombing. General Douhet describes with chilling detachment the spreading of terror caused by the massive bombing of civilians:

> What could happen to a single city in a single day could also happen to ten, twenty, fifty cities. And, since news travels fast ... what, I ask you, would be the effect upon civilians of other cities, not yet stricken, but equally subject to bombing attacks? What civil or military authority could keep order, public services functioning, and production going under such a threat? ... In short, normal life would be impossible in this constant nightmare of imminent death and destruction. (58)

Strictly speaking, in the theory developed by Douhet strategic bombing is not described in terms of absolute war. Douhet's main objective in propounding his ideas on strategic bombing was not exactly the breakup of all limits hindering war from approaching or reaching its absolute degree, but rather the *shortening* of the war. Certainly, the massive terror bombing of a city in order to compel the enemy into surrender implies the practice of an all-encompassing, non-discriminating violence. However, this is not a sufficient reason for viewing Douhet's notion of strategic bombing as a specific expression of war in its absolute degree. The crucial, decisive factor that has turned strategic bombing into a manifestation of absolute war rests, paradoxically, in the failure of Douhet's theory to materialize as he expected. Douhet underestimated people's resilience when they are under heavy aerial attack, as well as their willingness to remain loyal to their government despite its inability to defend them from carpet bombing. He also failed to understand that the air force cannot win a war by itself. The history of warfare in the twentieth- and twenty-first centuries has demonstrated that bombers need ground troops to finish the job. The systematic, relentless, and ruthless pursuance of the strategic bombing of urban centers in spite of its obviously dubious results – *this* is what makes strategic bombing an instance of absolute war.

Although it merited a mixed reception, Giulio Douhet's *Il dominio dell'aria* came to have a strong influence on military doctrine in Great Britain and the United States. Two early advocates of strategic bombing, Marshall Hugh Trenchard (commonly portrayed as the "Father of the Royal Air Force") and General William "Billy" Mitchell (regarded by many as the father of the US Air Force), developed their military doctrine on the strategic use of the air force partly as a result of their attentive reading of Douhet's seminal treatise. Embraced, therefore, by key figures of the armed forces in Britain and the United States, Douhet's adamant defense of the need to conduct massive strategic bombing in order to terrorize the enemy civilian population would be mercilessly applied in the Second World War, most particularly by the Allies, less so by the Germans, fundamentally because German military doctrine viewed the air force as a tactical weapon, that is, as operating in preparation for, or in conjunction with ground troops to destroy military objectives.

The aerial bombing of civilian targets in Europe and Asia during the Second World War claimed the lives of over a million people.[5] Under the bombs dropped by British and American squadrons, in Germany alone around 410,000 civilians perished.[6] In Britain 60,000 people were killed as a result of the Luftwaffe's campaign, while the Anglo-American air raids on Italy and France left 60,000 and 70,000 dead respectively.[7] The figures concerning the Japanese casualties occasioned by the bombing missions of the US Army Air Forces are equally, if not more, staggering.[8] The torching of Tokyo on the night of March 9–10, 1945, carried out by 334 American aircraft flying at low altitude, to give but one example, killed more than 85,000 men, women, and children, leaving 1 million people homeless, a "feat" that surpassed the horrifying massacres of Hamburg (45,000 deaths during Operation Gomorrah, conducted by the RAF between July 24 and August 3, 1943) and Dresden (25,000 people killed in three waves of attack by British and American squadrons on February 13–14, 1945). It has been estimated that the number of Japanese civilians killed by

---

[5] See Sven Lindqvist, *A History of Bombing*, trans. Linda Haverty Rugg (New York: New Press, 2001). For a survey of aerial warfare, see Frank Ledwidge, *Aerial Warfare: The Battle for the Skies* (New York: Oxford University Press, 2018). For comprehensive studies of the aerial bombing in Europe in 1940–45, see Richard Overy, *The Bombing War: Europe, 1939–1945* (London: Allen Lane, 2013); and Claudia Baldoli, Andrew Knapp, and Richard Overy, eds., *Bombing, States and Peoples in Western Europe, 1940–1945* (London: Continuum, 2011).

[6] On the air war against Germany: Jörg Friedrich, *Der Brand. Deutschland im Bombenkrieg, 1940–1945* (Munich: Propyläen, 2002); and Overy, *The Bombing War*, 237–485.

[7] On the bombing of Great Britain: Angus Calder, *The Myth of the Blitz* (London: Pimlico, 1991); Juliet Gardiner, *The Blitz: The British under Attack* (London: Harper Press, 2010); Tom Harrisson, *Living through the Blitz* (New York: Schocken Books, 1976); and Overy, *The Bombing War*, 59–234. On the air raids on France: Claudia Baldoli and Andrew Knapp, *Forgotten Blitzes: France and Italy under Allied Air Attack, 1940–1945* (London: Continuum, 2012); Eddy Florentin (with the collaboration of Claude Archambault), *Quand les Alliés bombardaient la France, 1940–1945* (N.p.: Perrin, 1997); Jean-Claude Valla, *La France sous les bombes américaines, 1942–1945* (Paris: Éditions de la Librairie Nationale, 2001); and Overy, *The Bombing War*, 556–82. On the aerial bombardment of Italy: Baldoli and Knapp, *Forgotten Blitzes*; and Overy, *The Bombing War*, 486–546.

[8] For the American bombing of Japan, see Downes, *Targeting Civilians in War*, 115–55; Mark Selden, "A Forgotten Holocaust: U.S. Bombing Strategy, the Destruction of Japanese Cities, and the American Way of War from the Pacific War to Iraq," *Bombing Civilians: A Twentieth-Century History*, ed. Yuki Tanaka and Marilyn B. Young (New York: New Press, 2009), 77–96; and Barrett Tillman, *Whirlwind: The Air War against Japan, 1942–1945* (New York: Simon & Schuster, 2010).

conventional or atomic bombs dropped by the Americans is close to 400,000.[9] All moral reservations against bombing civilians – reservations that had found legal expression in international treaties forbidding the targeting of undefended cities, buildings, and noncombatants since the Hague Convention of 1899 – were lifted in the world war of 1939–45.[10] More often than not, in those years the enemy was seen as an absolute enemy, as a criminal opponent who had to be annihilated or forced to an unconditional surrender. Absolute animosity or indifference to the suffering of the enemy prevailed over moral considerations in the massive, sustained, and systematic aerial bombing of civilians. With characteristic perceptiveness, the American critic Edmund Wilson remarked in April 1945 that at the time human life no longer had any value, and very few people paid attention to or were upset by the murder of innocent civilians. Wilson adds that in the United States, after the initial shock felt upon hearing about the nature and devastating consequences of the massive bombing of Germany, Americans would follow "the contest" between the RAF and the Luftwaffe as if it were a "football game."[11]

Indiscriminate aerial bombing brought about the deaths of many people, but it meant the destruction of human habitation as well.[12] In the summer of 1945, the urban landscape in Europe and Japan was one of utter desolation. More than 130 German cities and almost all Japanese urban centers had been heavily bombed. The destruction was immense: 61 percent of Cologne, 60 percent of Dresden, 64 percent of Düsseldorf, 75 percent of Hamburg, and 69 percent of Kassel – to give but a few examples – had been obliterated. The damage done to Japanese cities was no less appalling: 58 percent of Yokohama, 51 percent of Tokyo, 81 percent of Fukuyama, and 99 percent of Toyama – for instance – were

---

[9] John W. Dower, *War without Mercy: Race and Power in the Pacific War* (New York: Pantheon Books, 1986), 41.

[10] See Tami Davis Biddle's "Air Power," *The Laws of War: Constraints on Warfare in the Western World*, ed. Michael Howard, George J. Andreopoulos, and Mark R. Shulman (New Haven, CT: Yale University Press, 1994), 140–59, for an overview of the international laws concerning aerial warfare.

[11] Quoted in Hans Magnus Enzensberger, *Europa in Ruinen. Augenzeugenberichte aus den Jahren 1944–1948* (Munich: Deutscher Taschenbuch Verlag, 1995), 112–13. On the ethics, or lack thereof, of strategic bombing, see C. A. J. Coady, "Bombing and the Morality of War," *Bombing Civilians: A Twentieth-Century History*, ed. Yuki Tanaka and Marilyn B. Young (New York: New Press, 2009), 191–214; and A. C. Grayling, *Among the Dead Cities: The History and Moral Legacy of the World War II Bombing of Civilians in Germany and Japan* (New York: Bloomsbury, 2006).

[12] For a general discussion on the meaning and consequences of the destruction of architecture in times of war, see Robert Bevan, *The Destruction of Memory: Architecture at War*, 2nd expanded ed. (London: Reaktion Books, 2016).

destroyed by American bombers. To get a glimpse of the devastating effect of the bombing war of 1940–45 on the urban landscape of the belligerent countries, one only needs to consult Hans Magnus Enzensberger's sobering *Europa in Ruinen* (Europe in Ruins) (1990) – a montage of excerpts from chronicles and personal diaries on the moral and physical ruin of many European cities – or watch the so-called cinema of the rubble (*Trümmerfilme*).

In their obliteration of urban centers, the bombers eroded two essential constitutive dimensions of social life and human experience. The first one is cultural memory. In relation to the strategic bombing of Germany, Jörg Friedrich has highlighted this consequence of the Allied aerial campaign, providing extensive descriptions of the German monuments, churches, libraries, archives, and museums that were destroyed or seriously damaged by the Allies' bombing campaign.[13] In their annihilation of cities and towns, the bombers turned into rubble a good deal of the community's cultural memory, thereby wiping out crucial foundations of communal and national identity. Suddenly lacking some of the familiar memory sites by which individuals negotiated a shared past, lacking, also, a place of their own, bombed-out people found themselves forcefully expelled from their personal and collective past. Everybody's being-in-the-world acquired an entirely unexpected aspect. Those who remained in bombed cities had to adjust to a *new* place. The people's sense of place had been altered. Since many streets and neighborhoods had been destroyed beyond recognition, orienting oneself through the rubble was not an easy or safe undertaking, particularly at night. The urban grammar of destroyed German cities and the new and precarious being-in-the-world of their inhabitants have been represented, in much detail, in numerous literary works. The obliteration of cultural memory placed many people in a discontinuous space in which many traces of a shared communal and national past had disappeared *à jamais*. As a result, in part, of the destruction of landscape and urban space (which may be viewed as bridges to the past), social ties were eroded or severed. Thus, in cities like Hamburg people lived, according to Otto Erich Kiesel, "on the margins of civilization."[14]

The time continuum is the second constituent of social life and human experience that was affected by the bombs. Gert Ledig was no doubt thinking of this when he wrote, in the closing pages of his novel *Vergeltung*

[13] Friedrich, *Der Brand*.
[14] Otto Erich Kiesel, *Die unverzagte Stadt* (Hamburg: Volksbücherei-Verlag Goslar, 1949), 409.

(Payback) (1956), that bombing "annihilated the past and the future."[15] Humankind, an authorial character from Hermann Kasack's *Die Stadt hinter dem Strom* (The City beyond the River) (1947) argues, has fulfilled its dream of flying only to use airplanes "in order to reciprocally blow up the past of all human accomplishments."[16] "Time has been shattered," Hans Erich Nossack wrote in a novella published in 1947 against the backdrop of the bombing of Germany.[17] In his account of the annihilation of Hamburg in July–August 1943, written in November 1943 but not published until 1948 under the title *Der Untergang* (The End), Nossack would put it tersely: "We no longer have a past."[18] Realizing that, like so many inhabitants of Hamburg, he and his wife had lost everything in the bombing, including the cultural memory of the city, Nossack observes that they had "no time, none at all"; they had been taken "out of time"; because of this temporal discontinuity, everything they did immediately became "senseless."[19] Forcefully expelled from time, they had become sheer present devoid of meaning.[20] What goes missing in *Der Untergang* is not, therefore, a constellation of sites of memory, but *their very condition of possibility* – time. It is not surprising that Nossack experienced the bombing of Hamburg as a true *Untergang* or downfall.[21] The city had been destroyed to such an extent, that one felt a radical sense of estrangement in relation to it: "What surrounded us," Nossack writes, "by no means reminded us of what had been lost. It had nothing to do with it. It was something different, it was something strange, it almost was, in fact, the Not-Possible";[22] living there cannot be merely considered as hard; it is simply inconceivable.[23] Being literally exiled from his private space, from the urban grammar, and from time, Nossack had become a *new* man. This was literally a *Stunde Null* or zero hour, in the sense that upon witnessing the vast destruction of Hamburg, after looking into nothingness and learning that he had lost everything, living in a space that he did not recognize any longer, Nossack felt excluded from the time continuum. Time and existence had been spatialized. By razing to the ground 75 percent of Hamburg's urban space, the Royal Air Force had taken the inhabitants of that city out of their spatio-temporal habitat, erasing, as Hubert Fichte put it, their concept of *"Dauer"* or "continuity."[24] With

[15] Gert Ledig, *Vergeltung* (Frankfurt am Main: Suhrkamp, 2001), 198.
[16] Hermann Kasack, *Die Stadt hinter dem Strom* (Frankfurt am Main: Suhrkamp, 1996), 142.
[17] Hans Erich Nossack, *Nekyia. Bericht eines Überlebenden* (Frankfurt am Main: Suhrkamp, 1961), 35.
[18] Hans Erich Nossack, *Der Untergang* (Frankfurt am Main: Suhrkamp, 1976), 30.   [19] Ibid., 36.
[20] Ibid., 71.   [21] Ibid., 40.   [22] Ibid., 45.   [23] Ibid., 62.
[24] Hubert Fichte, *Detlevs Imitationen "Grünspan"* (Frankfurt am Main: Fischer, 2005), 34.

many of them lacking a house of their own (in Operation Gomorrah the British bombers destroyed 250,000 homes), having lost most of their possessions, the people of Hamburg – like the inhabitants of so many bombed-out cities – found themselves living in a present without a past; they had become both *homeless* and *pastless*.

Air war was nothing new in 1939–45. The first aerial bombing in history took place in present-day Libya during the Italo–Ottoman War (1911–12);[25] Germany and Great Britain had bombed each other from the air in the world war of 1914–18, the Japanese had raided Shanghai in 1936, and German and Italian squadrons regularly bombed Spanish towns and cities during the civil war fought in Spain in 1936–39. Having said this, the amount and scale of the air raids in 1939–45, the erasure of all moral considerations, the absolute animosity that led to the merciless bombing of enemy civilians, the intensity of the bombardments, the horrible effect of the bombs on the human body (e.g., disintegration, incineration, dismemberment), and the huge devastation that they inflicted on the receiving end make aerial bombing in the Second World War an instance of absolute war, as well as a new, and in many cases a traumatic experience, one of a sort that challenges ethics, epistemology, and representation in the extreme. Again, the extremes of absolute war examined in the Introduction correlate with the extremity of its effects. One may wonder whether language can depict, for example, the firestorms of Hamburg and Dresden or the atomic bombings of Hiroshima and Nagasaki, or whether literature can represent them without falsifying or trivializing human experience, or whether there are suitable narrative modes and linguistic means for making air raids believable to readers who have never been bombed. Charged with ethical implications, these questions could hardly be dismissed by writers interested in representing aerial bombing. Nossack was one of the first writers to point out the enormous difficulty of narrating the bombing of Hamburg, the firestorm that it triggered, and its effects on the city and the population. He faced an epistemological, ethical, and literary challenge – a triple challenge perceptible even when he just listened to the testimony of survivors: "what they tell when they speak about it," Nossack underscores early in *Der Untergang*, "is so ghastly inconceivable, that it is not possible to understand how they could survive."[26] It is true that the difficulty lies partly in obvious

---

[25] See Michael Paris, "The First Air Wars – North Africa and the Balkans, 1911–13," *Journal of Contemporary History* 26.1 (1991), 97–109.
[26] Nossack, *Der Untergang*, 7.

epistemological limitations, in the fact, that is, that everybody's point of view is necessarily limited.[27] But the real trouble resides in the fact that the firestorm produced ungraspable individual experiences. Interestingly, Nossack noticed that people hosting refugees from Hamburg seemed to feel envy towards them, not only on account of the goods that the latter received, but also because had they been there, they might have gazed into the abyss of nothingness.[28] The essential question here is, therefore, how to narrate the "jump into nothingness" performed by the surviving inhabitants of Hamburg. It is there, in that unrepresentable nothingness or *Nichts*, where the clue for understanding the catastrophic event is to be found. At once a metaphysical void, an existential emptiness, a traumatic hole, and a textual negativity, in *Der Untergang* the abyss is narrated by omitting it, by suggesting it, by placing it within a narrative void.

In the remaining sections of this chapter I will explore the literary response to the aerial bombings' radical challenge to understanding, ethics, and representation. The transnational comparison of texts on air raids sheds new light on the literary strategies chosen by their authors as well as the ethical implications of such strategies. Transnationalism reveals, for instance, that there is usually, if not always, a correlation between the intensity of the destruction and the level of experimentation with form, language, and genre in the works that represent it. The heavier the represented bombing was, the more radical the means for its representation are likely to be. In other words: the destruction of literary form and language in experimental texts is often commensurate with the destruction of cultural memory, the epistemological challenges, the ontological changes, and the psychological and psycho-social traumata which arose as a result of the bombing. This proposition, I would like to underscore, does not describe a rule, but rather a tendency. I claim that within the spectrum of possibilities novels tend towards the pole of realism or the pole of modernism depending in part on the kind of bombing that they represent. In the next sections I will examine four clusters of literary responses to the multiple and extreme challenge posed by aerial bombing to epistemology, ontology, ethics, and language: (i) a catastrophic modernist response built upon the representation of disaster through experiments with form and language; (ii) a representational response organized around mimesis and storytelling; (iii) modernist responses centered on a narrative voiding of the bombing that mirrors the psychic void characteristic of severe trauma; and (iv) a response intimately connected to the

[27] Ibid., 70.   [28] Ibid., 60.

writer's existential, literary, and moral imperative to tell and retell the experience of being bombed by an atomic weapon. If in the previous chapter the horror of the battlefield was the thread that unified its different sections, here the common background is the terror perpetrated by military personnel on the civilian population.

Strategic Bombing and Catastrophic Modernism

A significant number of the literary works on the bombing of Germany undertook the task of experimenting with language, form, and literary conventions in order to capture the multiple dimensions of aerial bombing, its destruction of human lives, space, and cultural memory, as well as its traumatic effects on survivors.[29] A catalogue of catastrophic modernist representations of the aerial bombardment of Germany would include Arno Schmidt's *Aus dem Leben eines Fauns* (Scenes from the Life of a Faun) (1952), Gert Ledig's *Vergeltung* (1956), Louis-Ferdinand Céline's *Rigodon* (Rigadoon) (1969), Kurt Vonnegut's *Slaughterhouse-Five* (1969), Hubert Fichte's *Detlevs Imitationen "Grünspan"* (Detlev's Imitations) (1971), Alexander Kluge's *Der Luftangriff auf Halberstadt am 8. April 1945* (The Air Raid against Halberstadt on April 8, 1945) (1977), and Walter Kempowski's *Der rote Hahn* (The Red Rooster) (2001). To this list we could add experimental works devoted to the aerial bombing of

---

[29] On the literature and culture concerned with the aerial bombing of Germany, see Jörg Arnold, *The Allied Air War and Urban Memory: The Legacy of Strategic Bombing in Germany* (Cambridge University Press, 2011); Raul Calzoni, "Chasms of Silence: The *Luftkrieg* in German Literature from a Reunification Perspective," *Memories and Representations of War: The Case of World War I and World War II*, ed. Elena Lamberti and Vita Fortunati (Amsterdam: Rodopi, 2009), 255–72; Volker Hage, *Zeugen der Zerstörung. Die Literaten und der Luftkrieg* (Frankfurt am Main: Fischer, 2003), and his edited volume *Hamburg 1943. Literarische Zeugnisse zum Feuersturm* (Frankfurt am Main: Fischer, 2003); Julia Hell, "Ruins Travel: Orphic Journeys through 1940s Germany," *Writing Travel: The Poetics and Politics of the Modern Journey*, ed. John Zilcosky (University of Toronto Press, 2008), 123–62; Colette Lawson, "The Natural History of Destruction: W. G. Sebald, Gert Ledig, and the Allied Bombings," *Germans as Victims in the Literary Fiction of the Berlin Republic*, ed. Stuart Taberner and Karina Berger (Rochester, NY: Camden House, 2009), 29–41; Heinz-Peter Preußer, "Regarding and Imagining: Contrived Immediacy of the Allied Bombing Campaign in Photography, Novel and Historiography," *A Nation of Victims? Representations of German Wartime Suffering from 1945 to the Present*, ed. Helmut Schmitz (Amsterdam: Rodopi, 2007), 141–59; Fritz Joachim Sauer, "Der Luftkrieg der Literatur," *Sprache – Literatur – Kultur. Text im Kontext*, ed. Bo Andersson, Gernot Müller, and Dessislava Stoeva-Holm (Uppsala University, 2010), 263–77; W. G. Sebald, *Luftkrieg und Literatur. Mit einem Essay zu Alfred Andersch*, 5th ed. (Frankfurt am Main: Fischer, 2005); Susanne Vees-Gulani, *Trauma and Guilt: Literature of Wartime Bombing in Germany* (Berlin: Walter de Gruyter, 2003); and several contributions to a book edited by Wilfried Wilms and William Rasch: *Bombs Away! Representing the Air War over Europe and Japan* (Amsterdam: Rodopi, 2006), 149–229, 281–94, 329–42.

countries other than Germany: I am thinking of Céline's *Féerie pour une autre fois* (Fable for Another Time) (1952–54) – whose second part narrates at length an Allied air raid on Paris – , and Curzio Malaparte's *Kaputt* (1944) – in the last chapter of which the narrator describes an air raid on Naples – , and of course the experimental narratives on the aerial bombing of Britain: Thomas Pynchon's *Gravity's Rainbow* (1973), Michael Moorcock's *Mother London* (1988) and, to a certain extent, Henry Green's *Caught* (1943), Elizabeth Bowen's *The Heat of the Day* (1948), and James Hanley's *No Directions* (1943). In varying degrees, all these works put forth new, experimental ways of representing catastrophic events derived from absolute war that somehow elude cognition, integration, and representation. They may also be considered as passionate utterances aimed at having consequential effects on the reader. Furthermore, some of them practice the writing of cruelty, for they bring to the reader a symbolic violence that mimics the violence of the bombing. All these works are instances, therefore, of catastrophic modernism.

In order to show the complexity of the catastrophic modernism devoted to aerial bombing and its effects, I will examine closely three of its different strands or modalities. First, I study a catastrophic modernism centered on collage, montage, and spatial form that disrupts the readers' demand for narrative unity and cognitive cohesiveness. Due to the similarity of these family resemblances with those of cinema, I will call this first strand of catastrophic modernism "cinematic." Second, I analyze an expressionist kind of catastrophic modernism. This time I am using the term "expressionism" not as it is commonly employed in literary studies (i.e., to characterize a literary movement that was hegemonic in Germany and Austria in the 1910s and 1920s). Instead, here it is conceived of as an artistic style that renders nonlinguistic reality through the subjective responses and emotions that it awakens in the author. These responses and emotions are conveyed through distortion and exaggeration, as well as extreme and vivid experiments with language and style. In addition to its search for an adequate language and imagery to represent the violence of, and the chaos unleashed by, aerial bombing, this expressionist strand of catastrophic modernism communicates the emotional intensity and affective charge involved in the human experience of that specific manifestation of absolute war. Third, I concentrate on a catastrophic modernism that gravitates around an impressionistic approach to air raids; in this third strand authors attempt to render the ephemeral effects of light, color, and sound. This modality captures the sensory richness of bombing, as well as the perceptual and cognitive disorientation felt by its victims. The boundaries between these three modalities are not fixed, but fluid. Some authors may practice only one of them, while others may combine in one single work, in different degrees, two or more strands of catastrophic modernism. Finally, it could be said that the modernist works studied below reveal the existence of a homology between catastrophic modernism and strategic bombing.

Gert Ledig's novel *Vergeltung* belongs to the cinematic strand of catastrophic modernism.[30] Published in 1956, and criticized at the time, in the German *Feuilletons*, for its experimental depiction of aerial bombing and its effects on space and people,[31] *Vergeltung* is divided into fifteen unnumbered chapters; each chapter comprises a varying number of scenes, and interspersed between each chapter there is an autobiographical or biographical short narrative typeset in italics that summarizes the life of a specific character from the novel. By means of interweaving several storylines, in *Vergeltung* Ledig exclusively represents a sixty-nine-minute aerial bombing of an unnamed German city conducted by American bombers. The extradiegetic narrator moves quickly from one story to the next. His narrative is a fragmented succession of juxtaposed scenes that covers several spaces and places of the city. Some characters remain trapped in the same place, while others move across the city during the air raid. Sergeant Strenehan, the American airman who bails out of his airplane after being hit by flak fire and who, once in the city, wanders around before being captured and eventually murdered, mirrors the double movement followed by the narrator of the novel: a vertical one, which covers the different heights of the spaces and places depicted in the novel (the sky, a flak tower's roof, house interiors and staircases of buildings, the streets of the city, and the cellar of an apartment building), and a horizontal one, a movement that mirrors the narrator's shifting from one storyline to the

[30] I use the following edition: Gert Ledig, *Vergeltung* (Frankfurt am Main: Suhrkamp, 2001).
[31] On the reception of *Vergeltung*, see Dominic Berlemann, "Das soziale Gedächtnis und der Nebencode des Literatursystems am Beispiel von Gert Ledigs Luftkriegsroman *Vergeltung*," *Kanon, Wertung und Vermittlung. Literatur in der Wissensgesellschaft*, ed. Matthias Beilein, Claudia Stockinger, and Simone Winko (Berlin: De Gruyter, 2012), 88–92; Gabriele Hundrieser, "Die Leerstelle der Leerstelle? Das Phänomen Gert Ledig, die Ästhetik der Gewalt und die Literaturgeschichtsschreibung," *Weimarer Beiträge. Zeitschrift für Literaturwissenschaft, Ästhetik und Kulturwissenschaften* 49.3 (2003), 361–79; and Gregor Streim, "Der Bombenkrieg als Sensation und als Dokumentation. Gert Ledigs Roman *Vergeltung* und die Debatte um W. G. Sebalds *Luftkrieg und Literatur*," *Krieg in den Medien*, ed. Heinz-Peter Preußer (Amsterdam: Rodopi, 2005), 303–12. For additional studies on that novel by Ledig, see Jörn Ahrens, "Macht der Gewalt. Hannah Arendt, Theodor W. Adorno und die Prosa Gert Ledigs," *Literatur für Leser* 24.3 (2001), 165–78; Fritz Gesing, "Sterben im Bombenhagel. Hans Erich Nossacks *Der Untergang* und Gert Ledigs *Vergeltung*," *Deutschunterricht. Beiträge zu seiner Praxis und wissenschaftlichen Grundlegung* 54.1 (2002), 48–58; and Lawson, "The Natural History of Destruction," 29–41.

next. Moreover, in its all-encompassing gaze *Vergeltung* provides a vertical view of the action in the two possible directions, from above (the American bomber before being hit) and from below (gunners shooting the attacking squadrons and people in the city looking up and seeking refuge), as well as a horizontal one, thanks to several characters, among them the teacher assigned to serve in an anti-aircraft battery who leaves his combat station in order to search for his missing son, the rescue party mustered to save the people buried alive in a cellar, and a group of Russian prisoners of war wandering through the graveyard and the city while bombs are falling all over the place. To use the two terms developed by Michel de Certeau, spatially speaking in Ledig's novel the "tour" (i.e., the set of discursive operations needed to proceed from one place to the other) alternates with the "map" (i.e., the description of a place in terms of the distribution of all its elements as well as their static relation with other places).[32] The narrator's motion from scene to scene is as quick as the movement of the firestorm caused by the bombs, and it creates in the reader the impression that the catastrophic event is lived simultaneously by a multitude of individuals. In addition, the rapid succession of scenes and the resulting plotlessness make *Vergeltung* a difficult novel to read. Spatial form and the complex cinematic montage of discontinuous scenes and chapters seek to disrupt the readers' cognition of reality in order to place them in a situation similar to the one experienced by the disoriented and panic-ridden characters of *Vergeltung*. Ledig's novel on absolute war is, therefore, a passionate utterance criss-crossed by the writing of cruelty.

Like the story and the plot, the discourse of *Vergeltung* is discontinuous. Sentences are unusually short, and they are articulated by a staccato style that refracts at once the plot's fragmentary structure as well as the bombing and the explosion of the bombs told at the level of the story. Form underscores the fact that violence is *Vergeltung*'s protagonist. As Colette Lawson has rightly claimed,[33] Ledig's novel fits within the parameters of what W. G. Sebald has called, apropos of the representation of the aerial bombing of Germany, "a natural history of destruction."[34] There is no teleology or justification of violence in *Vergeltung*; there is no explanation of the bombing according to preconceived cultural paradigms; there is no promise of redemption; there is no possible empathy with the characters, who are portrayed as lacking agency: the Germans described by Ledig are

---

[32] Michel de Certeau, *The Practice of Everyday Life*, trans. Steven Rendall (Berkeley, CA: University of California Press, 1984), 119–22.
[33] Lawson, "The Natural History of Destruction," 33–40.   [34] Sebald, *Luftkrieg und Literatur*, 40.

not subjects, but rather objects of raw destructive historical forces. *Vergeltung* is a phenomenology of war and violence in which both war and violence are the real subjects of the narrative.[35] The true hero of the novel is "destruction itself."[36] Few novels on aerial bombing have described with such rawness and pitilessness the aerial bombing of civilian targets. In what is perhaps the most experimental and original novel ever written on the strategic bombing of Germany, *Vergeltung* sets the tone with the crude narration, in the first chapter, of the bombing of a graveyard that kills women and children who had sought shelter there.[37] With detachment and an ostensibly laconic tone, the narrative voice relates with much detail the atrocious deaths of people, the destruction of buildings and streets, the firestorm triggered by the bombs. The terse tone and the matter-of-fact language used for describing destruction are ultimately addressed at stirring and unsettling the affects and emotions of readers. Violence is present, therefore, at the level of the story told by the narrative voice, at the level of discourse in the syntax and words chosen by the narrator and some characters, and at the level of the plot due to the broken-up, choppy, spatial articulation of Ledig's narrative. The violence performed on space, places, bodies, and language is also deployed, in other words, by the authorial shattering of the very form that represents it.

In 1977 the writer and filmmaker Alexander Kluge published, as part of his *Neue Geschichten. Hefte 1–18* (New Stories: Notebooks 1–18), a novella entirely devoted to the aerial bombing of his hometown at the end of the war: *Der Luftangriff auf Halberstadt am 8. April 1945*.[38] Like *Vergeltung*, Kluge's novella is a narrative centered on a single air raid that belongs to

---

[35] Ahrens, "Macht der Gewalt," 165; Lawson, "The Natural History of Destruction," 35.
[36] Vees-Gulani, *Trauma and Guilt*, 90.   [37] Ledig, *Vergeltung*, 9–10.
[38] I have used a modern edition: Alexander Kluge, *Der Luftangriff auf Halberstadt am 8. April 1945* (Frankfurt am Main: Suhrkamp, 2008). All references are given in the text. For other approaches to Kluge's novella, see Stefanie Carp, "Schlachtbeschreibungen. Ein Blick auf Walter Kempowski und Alexander Kluge," *Vernichtungskrieg. Verbrechen der Wehrmacht, 1941–1944*, ed. Hannes Heer and Klaus Naumann (Hamburg: Hamburger Edition, 1995), 664–79; Klaus Meyer-Minnermann, "Die (Un)Sagbarkeit des Schreckens: Alexander Kluge, Hans Erich Nossack und Ralph Giordano über Bombentod und Zerstörung," *Etudes Germaniques* 67.2 (2012), 351–76; Richard Murphy, "History, Fiction, and the Avant-Garde: Narrativisation and the Event," *Phrasis: Studies in Language and Literature* 48.1 (2007), 87–93; Walter Pape, "'Mich für mein ganzes Leben verletzendes Geschehen als Erlebnis'. Die Luftangriffe auf Salzburg (1944) in Thomas Bernhards *Die Ursache* und Alexander Kluges *Der Luftangriff auf Halberstadt am 8. April 1945*," *Bombs Away! Representing the Air War over Europe and Japan*, ed. Wilfried Wilms and William Rasch (Amsterdam: Rodopi, 2006), 181–97; W. G. Sebald, "Zwischen Geschichte und Naturgeschichte. Versuch über die literarische Beschreibung totaler Zerstörung mit Anmerkungen zu Kasack, Nossack und Kluge," *Orbis Litterarum: International Review of Literary Studies* 37.4 (1982), 345–66; and Cyrus Shahan, "Less than Bodies: Cellular Knowledge and Alexander Kluge's 'The Air Raid on Halberstadt on 8 April 1945'," *Germanic Review* 85.4 (2010), 340–58.

the cinematic strand of catastrophic modernism. As he had already done in
his 1964 novel on the Battle of Stalingrad, *Schlachtbeschreibung* (Description of a Battle), Kluge here puts together fictional texts and documentary
material (i.e., journalistic interviews, archival documents, photographs,
drawings, and diagrams). Divided into two parts and thirty short chapters,
the resulting collage zooms in on a number of simultaneous scenes of the
bombing of Halberstadt as well as situations that took place later on. In a
way somewhat reminiscent of Ledig's procedure in *Vergeltung*, Kluge offers
both the view from above, that is from the perpetrators of the bombing,
and the view from below, namely the one natural to those being bombed.
In the first part of the novella the narrator focuses on situations lived by a
handful of characters: the woman in charge of administering a movie-
theater (7–10), a company of soldiers (10–11), a photographer who takes
pictures of the bombing (12–16), the gardener of the local cemetery
(16–18), two female volunteers of the *Öffentliche Luftwarnung* or Civil
Aerial Alert (18–22), the guests of a wedding (22–25), sixty people who
seek shelter in a cellar (25–27), the narrator's family in the cellar of their
house (27–29), the editorship staff of a periodical in their office (29–30),
and the citizens who live on 9 Domgang Straße (30–31), ending with a
scene that describes the burning of a local *Kneipe* or pub (31). The second
half of *Der Luftangriff auf Halberstadt am 8. April 1945* is a bit more
complex. It begins with two chapters that offer what Kluge calls "Strategie
von unten" (strategy from below) (31–38) and "Strategie von oben"
(strategy from above) (39–53). In the first of these two chapters, the
narrator relates in much detail the superficially rational strategy followed
by Gerda Baethe to save herself and her children during the bombing. She
counts the seconds between explosions, calculates accordingly the time
needed to move from one point to another, evaluates, in sum, the different
aspects of the bombing in order to make rational choices. The chapter on
"Strategie von oben" provides the reader with an account, accompanied by
graphics and drawings, of the tactics and strategy of the Allied air-force
high command, as well as the reason that led the squadron's leader to order
the bombing of the exceedingly insignificant town of Halberstadt. The
remaining chapters complement this chapter or give the reader additional
information on the bombing. Thus Kluge includes, amongst other materials, an interview with Brigadier Anderson (53–61), an interview published in a Swiss newspaper with a high-ranking officer from the general
staff (61–65), passages on the fate of several places in Halberstadt (73–75),
and a chapter on the firefighters' actions during the bombing as told by an
officer of a firefighting squad from Cologne (81–84), closing his novella

with an account of a survey conducted by the Americans in order to measure the effect on people of the aerial bombing of Germany (86–90).

In *Der Luftangriff auf Halberstadt am 8. April 1945* bombing is represented through the collage of texts, voices, focalizers, and several types of discourse (i.e., visual language and written speech). The violence narrated in the story projects itself onto a shattered plot, even onto the discourse, for while the narrator's tone and voice are detached and rational, both detachment and reason somehow mimic the detachment and rationality that Kluge detects as the main elements behind the industrial production and delivery of the bombs. It is true that the author projects himself onto one of his characters: in his novella Kluge proceeds not unlike a photographer who means to bear witness to the event by taking photographs of the catastrophe (12). Kluge's style is indeed documentary; it has the detached quality of a photographer's assignment. At the same time, however, Kluge's cold and analytical approach to the topic, which appeals not only to the readers' emotions, but to their intelligence as well, is not unrelated to the equally detached rationality underlying the planning of the bombing itself. In short: whereas the fragmentation of the plot and discourse perfectly mimics – as in Ledig's *Vergeltung* – the catastrophic destruction described in the novel, the narrative tone as well as the approach adopted by Alexander Kluge uneasily reproduce the logic followed by the perpetrators. This unexpected complicity of Kluge's novella with the dehumanizing rationality that underpins the production and dropping of bombs places readers in an uncomfortable situation, one that somehow duplicates the role of victims in an air raid. Because of that complicity, the experimental form that articulates *Der Luftangriff auf Halberstadt* is much more than an innovative response to the challenges posed by bombing to representation; in addition, it may be read as imposing on the reader the same disturbing logic that led to the bombing of Halberstadt.

The expressionist strand of the catastrophic modernism devoted to the representation of strategic bombing is epitomized by the oeuvre of Louis-Ferdinand Céline published after the Second World War. Céline's first postwar novel constitutes a fascinating instance of expressionistic catastrophic modernism: I am referring to *Féerie pour une autre fois*, published in two installments in 1952 and 1954.[39] The first of a series of four novels

---

[39] On the experimental devices of *Féerie pour une autre fois*, see Marie-Christine Bellosta, "*Féerie pour une autre fois* I et II: Un spectacle et un prologue," *La Revue des Lettres Modernes* 543–546 (1978), 31–62; Annie Gillian, "*Féerie pour une autre fois* et le cinéma," *La Revue des Lettres Modernes*

based on Céline's life from June 1944 to the end of the war and its immediate aftermath, *Féerie pour une autre fois* represented, as other scholars have already pointed out, a sharp departure from Céline's previous fiction. In addition to introducing an authorial character and narrator named after himself, Céline blurred in this novel the boundaries between history and fiction, and took to new extremes his conversational *style émotif*. In *Féerie pour une autre fois* he also radicalized his tendency to produce plotless, digressive narratives, offering the reader a unique, to a certain extent difficult and unpleasant-to-read novel that was received with relative indifference when it saw the light of day. Compared to *Voyage au bout de la nuit* (Journey to the End of the Night) (1932) or his so-called German trilogy (i.e., *D'un château l'autre* [From Castle to Castle] [1957], *Nord* [North] [1960], and *Rigodon* [1969]), *Féerie pour une autre fois* cuts the figure of the poor relation. This is, of course, no place to delve into the reasons for this relative silence on this novel.[40] Instead, I would like to advance several hypotheses to explain the formal radicalism of *Féerie pour une autre fois*. The air raid narrated in the second part of the novel is much more than a simple "*décor* for the absurd events that constitute the novel's minimal plot."[41] In marked contrast to this and similar views that minimize the air raid described at length in *Féerie pour une autre fois*, I claim, first, that the second part of the novel is in fact a reflection on aerial bombing in general, as well as on the epistemological and ontological problems and the psychological and psycho-social traumata that it may cause. Second, it constitutes a practical lesson on how to represent an air raid. And third, *Féerie pour une autre fois* is, to a degree, a literary artifact written against the readers. Céline's overt hostility towards the readers is a pragmatic refraction of the aerial bombing described in the novel; by relentlessly "bombing" them with aggressive remarks, as well as an expressionist language and imagery that seek to stir their feelings, Céline wants

543–546 (1978), 83–106; Patrick McCarthy, "La multiplicité des narrateurs dans *Féerie pour une autre fois*," *Céline: Actes du Colloque International de Paris (27–30 Juillet 1976)* (Paris: Société d'Etudes Céliniennes, 1978), 231–46; Colin W. Nettelbeck, "Temps et espaces dans *Féerie pour une autre fois*," *La Revue des Lettres Modernes* 543–546 (1978), 63–81; Rosemarie Scullion, "Writing and Resistance in Louis-Ferdinand Céline's *Féerie pour une autre fois* I," *Esprit créateur* 38.3 (1998), 28–39; Alice Stašková, "Transfigurations d'un procès: Les narrataires céliniens dans *Féerie pour une autre fois* I," *Classicisme de Céline*, ed. André Derval (Paris: Société d'Etudes Céliniennes, 1999), 339–54; Allen Thiher, *Céline: The Novel as Delirium* (New Brunswick, NJ: Rutgers University Press, 1972), 138–68, and his "*Féerie pour une autre fois*: Mythe et modernisme," *La Revue des Lettres Modernes* 560–564 (1979), 107–21.

[40] On this score, see J. H. Matthews, *The Inner Dream: Céline as a Novelist* (Syracuse, NY: Syracuse University Press, 1978), 129–31.

[41] Thiher, *Céline*, 156.

his readers to experience the fear, the existential precariousness, and the cognitive disorientation triggered by an air raid. Céline's *style émotif* is meant, therefore, not only to render the emotion of spoken French; it also purports to have consequential effects on the readers' affects vis-à-vis aerial bombing. Consequently, *Féerie pour une autre fois* is, like the novels previously analyzed, a passionate utterance – one that can hardly leave anyone indifferent. The three foci that I have just mentioned are important factors powering Céline's radical experimentation with language, imagery, and form.

The Allied air raid on Paris is told in the second part of *Féerie pour une autre fois*.[42] It covers a temporal spectrum of a few hours only, from the outset of the attack early in the evening up to the small hours of the following day. Significantly, Céline frames his narration of the bombing with a reference to memory and the trauma triggered by bombing. "To tell about it afterwards . . . it is easier said than done," writes Céline, "One still has the echo within . . . *brroum!* . . . time is nothing, but the memory! . . . and the explosions of the world! . . . people whom one has lost . . . the sorrows . . . and the echo that still shakes you up . . . I will be thrown to the tomb with them! . . ."[43] Céline talks about the "echo" of the bombing in his mind, connecting that traumatic experience to his equally traumatic war experience in the world war of 1914–18 (245). While he complains that "the memories of the event rock me," the narrator assures his readers that "I will catch them all! . . ." (246). Given the little impact that the Allied bombardments of France have had on French literature and historiography, given also the fact that this lack of interest does not correspond to the magnitude of the bombing campaign (about 70,000 Frenchmen died as a result of aerial bombings, which means that more people died in France because of the air war than civilians perished in Britain under the German bombs), it is tempting to define *Féerie pour une autre fois*, in its attempt at re-inscribing a traumatic event in public discourse, as an instance of "cryptowriting." In psychoanalytic terms, Céline practices a cryptowriting that uncovers a phenomenon (the aerial war) that has been

---

[42] See Bellosta, "*Féerie pour une autre fois* I et II," 41–58; Nettelbeck, "Temps et espaces dans *Féerie pour une autre fois*," 73–74; and Philip Watts, "An Introduction to Céline," *Fiction* 12.1 (1994), 37, for an analysis of the aerial bombing narrated by Céline. Cf. Llewellyn Brown, "L'esthétique du cataclysme: *Féerie pour une autre fois* II de L.-F. Céline," *Littératures* 42 (2000), 115–25, and Anna Élaine Cliche's study "Féerie pour un temps sans mesure: Louis-Ferdinand Céline chroniqueur du désastre," *Des fins et des temps: Les limites de l'imaginaire*, ed. Jean-François Chassay, Anne Élaine Cliché, and Bertrand Gervais (Les Presses de l'Université de Montréal, 2005), 59–113.

[43] Louis-Ferdinand Céline, *Féerie pour une autre fois* (Paris: Gallimard, 1995), 245. Further references in text.

"buried" by fellow Frenchmen into what Nicolas Abraham and Mária Török have called a "crypt."[44] The crypt is the psychic locus where we hide those phantoms to whom we cannot, or are unwilling to, give their due. They are unacknowledged, locked into a crypt that is transmitted from one generation to the next. In this case, Frenchmen have repressed a memory that is doubly painful: in addition to being extremely violent, the events were performed by *friends* because the French government had surrendered and signed an armistice with Nazi Germany.[45] The French refusal to remember and recreate the bombing of their country is understandable, if not politically and morally justified. With a few exceptions (I am thinking, for example, of Julien Guillemard's harrowing account of the Allied destruction of Le Havre),[46] in France there is almost no cultural memory of the aerial bombing of the country by the Allies. At the same time, with or without trauma, it is also true that Céline felt at home with disasters such as the bombing of Paris. He says it himself: "Nothing intoxicates me as much as great disasters do, I easily get drunk with calamities" (34). Céline's interest in the bombing of Paris was, therefore, grounded on an attitude at once socio-historical and personal.

Céline compares the Allied bombing to natural disasters (e.g., 373), the biblical Deluge (e.g., 294, 385–86, 463), the eruption of Mount Vesuvius (e.g., 288, 473, 475), and the Apocalypse (e.g., 387, 388–89). The bombing of Paris is seen as an event that belongs (to quote Sebald again) to the "natural history of destruction."[47] Céline does not explain or justify violence, nor does he relate it to a promise of redemption; with the exception perhaps of Jules, characters lack agency vis-à-vis the air raid, and the narrator does not let the reader feel any empathy for them. Instead, he focuses on destruction itself, namely on the grammar and pragmatics of aerial bombing. To begin with, the destruction wrought by the Allied bombers is correlated to a peculiar kind of writing. This is how Céline describes the formation of the squadrons flying towards their targets: "the giant S's! . . . the O's! . . . the Z's! . . . phenomenal speeds! . . . They made

---

[44] See Nicolas Abraham and Mária Török, *The Shell and the Kernel: Renewals of Psychoanalysis*, trans. and ed. Nicholas T. Rand (University of Chicago Press, 1994).

[45] Gabriele Schwab has analyzed the "burial" of the memory of war into a "crypt" in her study of the legacies and transgenerational trauma in Germany, *Haunting Legacies: Violent Histories and Transgenerational Trauma* (New York: Columbia University Press, 2010). It would be interesting to explore from that perspective the repression in France of the memory of the Allied air war against that country.

[46] Julien Guillemard, *L'enfer du Havre, 1940–1944: Témoignage* (Paris: Les Éditions Médicis, 1945).

[47] Sebald, *Luftkrieg und Literatur*, 40.

Z's! ... O's! U's! ... but that meant this! and that! ... messages! They knew them all! They knew! ... it was necessary to decipher! ... scrutinize! ... The O! the Z! ... it was writing on the clouds!" (204). Even the bombs, when dropped, have a writerly order (258). Flying and bombing are types of writing that need deciphering. In the sky there are "signs," and the writer's duty resides in "knowing how to decipher them" (264). This is precisely what *Féerie pour une autre fois* does for the reader: it deciphers the complex writerly nature of aerial bombing by means of experiments with expressionist language and imagery, as well as the complete fragmentation of both the story and the plot.

Bombing is described as a stunningly beautiful spectacle of colors and sounds not unlike painting and music (e.g., 252–53, 255–56, 263–64). Céline is also fascinated by the orderly movement of the airplanes (e.g., 253, 256–57, 306–7). This writing, this pictorial and musical spectacle of colors, sounds, and movement, this deadly ballet on the sky mimicked by Céline in his own writing, radically transforms the usual spatial order. The bombers on the sky rewrite spatial relations on the ground in unexpected ways. Céline mirrors in his experimental novel this multiple rewriting. Thus, the bombing of some areas of Paris and its banlieue is depicted as inverting the spatial order: "I see the houses ... they are pulled off, they climb up, they get tangled up with each other ... everything up there, very high up! I recognize the boulevard de Lorraine! ... they swirl around even farther away! ... there is an entire city in the air! ... upside down! ... it's an optical effect, everything! ... everything is projected above the clouds!" (295). Trees are taken off the ground and start flying (298); the Luxembourg Gardens are also in the air (320). The usual spatial relation between sky and earth has been inverted (346). There has been, in short, a "revolution of the space" (346) that has altered not only the geometry of places, but also the usual hierarchy of moral values (386). As the narrator says with more detail in another passage, the city has been turned upside down by the bombing (351–52). Once the bombing is over, the city goes back to its usual spatial order (e.g., 502–3, 509, 515–16).

The inversion of the spatial geometry is reproduced in the novel's plotlessness, in its digressions, in the endless delirious monologue of the narrator, in its spatial form, in short: in its radical *inversion* of the traditional realist novel. It is not by chance that Céline chose the *féerie* or fable for shaping his novel.[48] The plot structure, as well as the

[48] See Bellosta, "*Féerie pour une autre fois* I et II," 31–62, for a critical consideration of that novel as *féerie*.

experiments with time, space, imagery, syntax, and morphology are closely related to that sub-genre: "confusion of places, of times! . . . This is the fable, you understand, fable is this . . . the future! The past! False! True!" (36). In the context of this novel, *féerie* means at once "theatrical play, spectacle where supernatural characters appear," "splendid, marvelous spectacle," and "irrational and poetical universe."[49] The generic rules of a *féerie* reflect, in *Féerie pour une autre fois*, the confusion of time and space characteristic of any aerial bombing, the murderous beauty and spectacular dimension of such kinds of attack, and the sense of absurdity caused by the bombs among the people. *Féerie pour une autre fois*, with its multiple digressions and analepses, is one of the most extraordinary expressionist catastrophic modernist artifacts ever devoted to aerial bombing. There is a connection between the bombers' destruction of space, cultural memory, and people's sense of time on the one hand, and the novel's expressionist experimentalism and spatial form on the other. As Céline himself acknowledges, he simply reports what he saw. Throughout the novel the narrator insists once and again on the historicity of everything he tells in it. Despite appearances to the contrary, he underscores that his is the procedure of a historian who has witnessed the events (e.g., 259, 261, 390). Hence his comparison of himself with Pliny the Elder (e.g., 272, 463, 475). But most important, the nature of the bombing *determined* both the author's language and the narrative form. He says as much: "You will tell me: not very organized your chronicle! . . . Is there an order in deluges? . . . and a lousy liar, be sure about that, that who tells you calmly that he has seen melting, in certain order! . . . the proof: my last start! . . . Try to narrate that calmly! . . ." (424). Therefore, the carnivalesque expressionist language, the plotlessness, the verbal excesses, the mystifications, the broken-up syntax, and the spatial form of *Féerie pour une autre fois* have to be considered as Céline's deliberate and self-aware response to the challenge posed to representation by an instance of absolute war such as the aerial bombing of civilian targets.

   The last mode of catastrophic modernism on air raids that I have chosen to scrutinize in this section – the impressionist strand – is represented by James Hanley's *No Directions* (1943).[50] Fragmented and plotless, this

---

[49] "Féerie," *Le Grand Robert de la langue française*, ed. Alain Rey (Paris: Dictionnaires Le Robert, 2001), definitions 1–3.
[50] There is a dearth of critical studies on Hanley's *No Directions*. Exceptions to the norm are Rod Mengham, "Broken Glass," *The Fiction of the 1940s: Stories of Survival*, ed. Rod Mengham and N. H. Reeve (Basingstoke: Palgrave, 2001), 124–33; and Jean-Christophe Murat, "City of Wars: The Representation of Wartime London in Two Novels of the 1940s: James Hanley's *No Directions*

claustrophobic novel focuses on what goes on in a building of flats in Chelsea shortly before a German air raid (part 1) and during the attack until it is over (part 2). With the exception of chapters 3 (which narrates Lena Stevens's walk through an impressionistically depicted blacked-out London) and 7 (devoted to relating the artist Clement Stevens's wandering on the neighboring streets during the last phase of the bombing), the rest of the chapters narrate events that take place inside the building. In *No Directions*, space is far more important than time. Temporal indications are sparse and vague. Thus, the narrator writes that "A nearby clock was striking" without indicating the hour,[51] and the same happens on other occasions (e.g., 58, 68). In none of these cases does the reader learn the exact time marked by the clock. The same indetermination can be found in the presentation of the characters. Except for Clement and Lena Stevens, whose biographies are briefly summarized (63–68), all the characters lack a past. Little is known about them, aside from their professions. The only thing that counts is the present – the present of destruction. In contrast to this scarcity of temporal markers and biographical details, space is treated with much more specificity.

In *No Directions* spatial form refracts the nature of the bombing and its destruction of continuities. The main storylines may be arranged into three groups. The first group covers stories that are closely connected with the new ways of experiencing private and public space caused by the bombing and by the regulations issued by the British authorities on air-raid defense. Mrs. Emily Frazer, for instance, does not want to leave her flat (whose door has been off its hinges since the previous air raid), and she refuses to move away from the door (14–16). She defends a sense of privacy that has been shattered by the war. Her awareness that the usual meaning of "private" and "public" space has been altered because of the war worries her to the point of obsession. Mr. Frazer tries hard to persuade his wife to seek shelter in the cellar when the air raid starts (100–2), and after much resistance they go down to the cellar, but not for long, since Mrs. Frazer goes back to her flat before the All Clear (122, 124–25). Part of the problem lies in the fact that life in the cellar is alienating and lacks meaning, at least for some characters. According to Gwen, in the cellar "nothing seemed to have meaning" (18). The tempo of life and even the language are new "down there"; mixing his voice with

and Patrick Hamilton's *The Slaves of Solitude*," *Anglophonia: French Journal of English Studies* 25 (2009), 329–40.
[51] James Hanley, *No Directions* (London: André Deutsch, 1990), 10. Further references in text.

the thoughts and emotions of Mr. Frazer, the narrator writes: "Sitting in a cellar where people talked, but you didn't understand very much, the tempo of everything was new, even the language they used was new, you didn't seem to have the right key to it" (101). In the second group of storylines we can see the treatment of existential issues. Thus, chapter 2 narrates the casual sexual encounter between a former model of Clem's, Celia Downs, and the unknown sailor taken by the warden into the building at the beginning of the novel. Both characters break into an unoccupied flat, and after drinking and flirting they end up having sexual intercourse. This story shows the loosening during the war of sexual strictures usually imposed on people by social conventions, as well as the vindication of life in the face of the deadly danger posed by the air raids. The other storyline within this second group centers on Clem and Lena's efforts to take to the cellar an unfinished painting by Clem (72–75, 109, 112, 126, 129–31). If we are to believe his wife, Clem "always takes it down below whenever there's a raid" (126). While in the sexual affair between Celia and the sailor there is a vindication of the body and life, in Clem's attempt to save his art from destruction there is a defense of the spiritual world and cultural memory.

The third group comprises the two vanishing points of the novel: Lena's walk shortly before the bombing starts, and Clem's wandering through the streets as the bombing is ebbing away. The visual contrast between the two scenes is quite striking. In the former, the entire city is immersed in darkness, while in the latter the explosions produce colors and sounds and alter shapes: Clem is clearly contemplating a sort of impressionist painting as it is being made by the bombers. In Lena's walk, Hanley presents a ghostly and threatened city, repeatedly compared to a "dark sea" whose black-out engulfed and protected everything, establishing a new spatial grammar. The last chapter, which is obviously in dialogue with chapter 3 (each of them closes one part of this two-part novel), depicts an entirely different urban landscape. Clem cannot resist the temptation to leave the sheltering cellar and go out to see the bombing ("I must see this. I must see this" [134], he keeps saying, fascinated by the visual spectacle that he imagines is going on in London). This is the only chapter that truly describes the bombing. In the previous chapters it had been narrated through what the tenants of the building hear from their cellar. Initially, mentions of the on-going raid as well as of the Germans are understated (91–92, 93, 103, 109). But at some point, the bombing increases in intensity, and the bombers drop their loads near or over Chelsea (e.g., 134). Characters sense the bombing, but they do not see it. In contrast, chapter 7 describes the air raid directly. Like Henry Green (pen name of Henry Yorke) in his 1943 novel *Caught*, which does not describe an aerial bombing until the last twenty pages of the novel,[52] Hanley's *No Directions* defers the visual depiction of bombing until the closing chapter. Also like Green, Hanley depicts the bombing as a painter would, that is by focusing on and describing in impressionistic terms its visual elements, thereby introducing into the novel the principle of ekphrasis, a metatextual device characteristic of modernist literature that underscores the very texture of the novel by emphasizing the sculptural or pictorial dimension of a scene or character. This is achieved by focalizing the description of bombed-out London through the painter Clement Stevens (see, for instance, 135–36). The narrator occasionally points out this "artist's gaze": "He didn't hear, didn't feel, he only saw" (136). From the roof of a high building, Clem sees the following impressionist view of the city: "Wood and stone and steel alive with wrecking power. Roads opened, streets collapsed, hollow sounds where once old giants had stood, great gaps, fissures, rivers in tumult, showering glass, old giants flat. He looked down from the heights. An orgy of movement, in one direction, moving under the light. An ocean of floating trash" (136). This is precisely what Clem admires: the pictorial dimension of the bombing. Clem's attitude is rather similar to the one displayed by Guy Crouchback, the main character of Evelyn Waugh's trilogy *Sword of Honor* (1966). Back in England after a tour of duty, Crouchback exclaims after contemplating an air raid on London – something that he finds "most exhilarating" – "Pure Turner."[53] Chapter 7 of *No Directions*, therefore, contains a pictorial description of bombing. A disturbing and ambiguous projection of Clement Stevens himself, the German squadrons "paint" an impressionist canvas of London.

Strategic Bombing and Storytelling

Mimetic literature can narrate situations of absolute war as well. This is most true of the literary texts produced to depict the German strategic bombing of Great Britain.[54] Although realism is dominant in fictional

[52] Henry Green, *Caught* (New York Review Books, 2016), 168–91.
[53] Evelyn Waugh, *Sword of Honor* (New York: Back Bay Books, 2012), 250, 249.
[54] On the literature produced on the air war against Great Britain, see Calder, *The Myth of the Blitz*, 153–79; Lara Feigel, *The Love-Charm of Bombs: Restless Lives in the Second World War* (New York: Bloomsbury, 2013); Susan R. Grayzel, *At Home and under Fire: Air Raids and Culture in Britain from the Great War to the Blitz* (Cambridge University Press, 2012), 295–314; Leo Mellor, *Reading the Ruins: Modernism, Bombsites and British Culture* (Cambridge University Press, 2011); Kristine

texts on aerial bombing written within different national literary fields, this poetics has been predominantly practiced by writers who have centered on the aerial bombing of Britain. In general terms, the authors who wrote about the Battle of Britain (summer–fall 1940), the Blitz (fall 1940–spring 1941), or German bombing missions undertaken against Great Britain later in the war did it within the framework of the poetics of realism. Most of the novels that today constitute the literary canon on the aerial bombing of Britain are realist narratives: this is the case, for instance, with Graham Greene's two novels *The Ministry of Fear* (1943) and *The End of the Affair* (1951), as well as a novel that portrays in detail London's bombed-out urban landscape in 1946: Rose Macaulay's *The World My Wilderness* (1950). Even Henry Green's *Caught* (1943) and Elizabeth Bowen's *The Heat of the Day* (1948), two novels that use modernist literary techniques (most notably an elaborate syntax, a convoluted style, the exploration of fragmented consciousness, semantic ambiguity, and the disruption of temporal chronology),[55] may be perfectly read as representational works driven by one of the "twin sources" of realism according to Fredric Jameson: storytelling, that is the "narrative impulse."[56] Lesser-known novels such as Phyllis Bottome's *London Pride* (1941), Elinor Mordaunt's *Blitz Kids* (1941), Doris Leslie's *House in the Dust* (1942), R. F. Delderfield's *The Avenue Goes to War* (1958), and Robin Jenkins's *Fergus Lamont* (1979) can be equally characterized as books written after the poetics of realism. On first inspection, the Blitz and other German aerial incursions against Britain did not seem to seriously challenge the writers' ability to represent aerial bombing and related events, nor did they hinder storytelling, nor did they question or undermine the laws underlying the existing repertoire of genres. In fact, some important novels follow the conventions of time-tested popular subgenres: *The Ministry of Fear* is a spy thriller, both *The Heat of the Day* (also a spy novel) and *The End of the Affair* can be considered as love stories, and one may characterize Doris Leslie's *House in the Dust*, Rosamond Lehmann's *The Echoing Grove* (1953), and Patrick Hamilton's *The Slaves of Solitude* (1947) as novels of manners.

A. Miller, *British Literature of the Blitz: Fighting the People's War* (New York: Palgrave Macmillan, 2009); and Sara Wasson, *Urban Gothic of the Second World War: Dark London* (New York: Palgrave Macmillan, 2010).

[55] For an exploration of British modernist works produced apropos of the Second World War, see Marina MacKay, *Modernism and World War II* (Cambridge University Press, 2007).

[56] Fredric Jameson, *The Antinomies of Realism* (London: Verso, 2013), 15–26.

It is remarkable indeed that, except for the last chapter of Henry Green's *Caught* and of James Hanley's *No Directions*,[57] the most important novels on the bombing of Britain *eschew* the direct description of aerial bombardments. While significant in symbolic and structural terms, in those novels the air raids usually remain in the background, echoing the main characters' psychology, moral dilemmas, and existential predicament (e.g., *The Ministry of Fear*), enhancing the dramatic atmosphere of key conversations (e.g., *The Ministry of Fear*, *The Echoing Grove*, and *The Heat of the Day*), or providing the perfect ambiance for endless flirting and amorous liaisons (e.g., *Caught*) and pleasurable sexual intercourse (e.g., *The End of the Affair*). Sometimes, the aerial raids are simply mentioned, almost *en passant*, as the determinants of the main characters' specific circumstances or mental pathologies, such as the temporary lodging of Miss Roach, to draw an example from Hamilton's *The Slaves of Solitude*, in a boarding-house away from embattled London, or Mrs. Grant's amnesia, caused by aerial bombing according to her doctor, in Henry Green's *Back* (1946).[58] In contrast, low-brow novels such as Phyllis Bottome's *London Pride* and Elinor Mordaunt's *Blitz Kids* provide a more extensive panorama of the aerial bombings, of what people did while London was under attack, of the consequences of the air raids on their lives and the urban landscape. In most cases, the Blitz does not undermine the novelists' attempt at story-telling, nor does it lead writers to come up with new, original literary expressions for narrating the bombing and its consequences. They tend to follow existing British literary models. Unlike the experimental narratives on the air raids on Germany studied or cited in the previous section, literature on the bombing of Britain does not usually project to form and language the destruction that it represents or mentions. Compared to the works studied earlier, in narratives devoted to the Blitz there is no true shattering of form, with the exception of the impressionist techniques in James Hanley's *No Directions*, the twisting of syntax and the discontinuous temporality in Elizabeth Bowen's *The Heat of the Day* and Henry Green's *Caught*, or the rupture with linear time in Graham Greene's *The Ministry of Fear*. These modernist devices refract the important alterations caused by aerial bombing on urban space, consciousness, and the human perception and experience of space and time.[59] At the thematic level, there is a

[57] Green, *Caught*, 168–91; Hanley, *No Directions*, 135–42.
[58] Henry Green, *Back* (Champaign, IL: Dalkey Archive Press, 2009), 154.
[59] See Beryl Pong's study of the temporal and spatial dislocation in *The Heat of the Day* and *The Ministry of Fear* ("Space and Time in the Bombed City: Graham Greene's *The Ministry of Fear* and Elizabeth Bowen's *The Heat of the Day*," *Literary London: Interdisciplinary Studies in the*

partial disintegration of traditional social mores, a blurring of the boundaries between the public sphere and domestic spaces, and a redefinition of the social roles traditionally assigned to men and women. In general, modernist techniques are embedded in narratives with a strong representational, mimetic dominant. Realism predominates over catastrophic modernism in novels such as Greene's *The Ministry of Fear*. Only in openly experimental narratives such as Thomas Pynchon's *Gravity's Rainbow* (1973) and Michael Moorcock's *Mother London* (1988) is this pattern reversed. While the representational narratives on the Blitz differ in important ways, they do share family resemblances in their depiction of the aerial bombing of British cities that warrant further explanation.

The most remarkable family resemblance of the canonical representational novels on the bombing campaign against Britain is the predominance of love stories. Significantly, this family resemblance is absent from the literary accounts of the strategic bombing of Germany. Scenes such as one from Rosamond Lehmann's *The Echoing Grove* in which two characters talk at length about acquaintances, relationships, and personal feelings without paying much notice to the sirens' warning of the end of a German aerial attack cannot be found in narratives on the bombing of Germany: "Wait for the All Clear," says Georgie to Rickie, "It hasn't sounded, has it? Surely we can't have been cut off even from that?"[60] Such absent-mindedness and nonchalance, as well as the topics themselves discussed by these two characters, are almost unthinkable in literature on the aerial bombing of Germany. Bearing in mind the data on the aerial bombings of Britain and Germany, one might conclude that the greater severity of the Allied bombardment on Germany somehow precluded the possibility of imagining and narrating love relationships as the bombs fell on the population. To be sure, German fictional works written in connection with the air war relate love stories, but amorous liaisons only flourish, as can be seen, for example, in Heinrich Böll's *Der Engel schwieg* (The Silent Angel) and Otto Erich Kiesel's *Die unverzagte Stadt* (The Undaunted City), once the war is over.

Some British authors established a connection between bombing, a relaxation of social mores as a result of war conditions, and love affairs. As Patrick Hamilton put it in *The Slaves of Solitude*, "Love, like drink,

---

Representation of London 7.1 [2009], www.literarylondon.org, accessed June 4, 2016). Pong interprets the "Blitz writing" of these two novels by Bowen and Greene as a literary refraction of aerial bombing.
[60] Rosamond Lehmann, *The Echoing Grove* (London: Virago, 2000), 265.

under the influence of the war, was exerting a new sort of pressure everywhere, affecting people it would not have affected before, and in an entirely fresh way."[61] Take, for instance, Graham Greene's *The End of the Affair*, a novel centered on the adulterous relationship between the novelist Maurice Bendrix (main character and narrator of the novel) and Sarah Miles, a woman married to a suave civil servant.[62] Within the novel's narrative economy, in *The End of the Affair* air raids are a function of the two main characters' love affair, and not the other way around. War, the narrator acknowledges, helped their relationship "in a good many ways," so much so that it is even considered by Bendrix as an "accomplice in my affair."[63] Sexual intercourse is never interrupted by an air raid or a flying-bomb attack. Following a pattern of behavior well known by psychologists, life at its most basic reasserts itself in its close encounter with death. Actually, danger seems to enhance pleasure. Bendrix is rather explicit in this regard:

> We had only just lain down on the bed when the raid started. It made no difference. Death never mattered at those times ... No, the V1s didn't affect us until the act of love was over. I had spent everything I had, and was lying back with my head on her stomach and her taste – as thin and elusive as water – in my mouth, when one of the robots crashed down on to the Common and we could hear the glass breaking further down the south side.[64]

Sarah Miles corroborates in her journal Bendrix's words: "We paid no attention to the sirens. They didn't matter. We weren't afraid of dying that way."[65] While war is an accomplice of that clandestine love relationship, it also functions as the catalyst for its interruption. The breakup of the relationship derives from a V-1 attack on London on June 16, 1944.[66] Believing him to be dead under the debris produced by a near-hit, Sarah Miles prays to God for a miracle, promising that should

[61] Patrick Hamilton, *The Slaves of Solitude* (New York Review Books, 2007), 238.
[62] For more information on *The End of the Affair*, see Feigel, *The Love-Charm of Bombs*, 245–46, 407–13; Jean-Michel Ganteau, "'A Conflict between an Image and a Man': The Visual Diction of Romance in Graham Greene's *The End of the Affair*," *Etudes Britanniques Contemporaines: Revue de la Société d'Etudes Anglaises Contemporaines* 31 (2006), 69–81; Lucy S. Pake, "Courtly Love in Our Own Time: Graham Greene's *The End of the Affair*," *Lamar Journal of the Humanities* 8.2 (1982), 36–43; Ray Snape, "Plaster Saints, Flesh and Blood Sinners: Graham Greene's *The End of the Affair*," *Durham University Journal* 74.2 (1982), 241–50; and John A. Stotesbury, "A Postcolonial Reading of Metropolitan Space in Graham Greene's *The End of the Affair*," *London in Literature: Visionary Mappings of the Metropolis*, ed. Susana Onega and John A. Stotesbury (Heidelberg: Universitätsverlag Carl Winter, 2002), 107–21.
[63] Graham Greene, *The End of the Affair* (New York: Penguin, 2004), 44.   [64] Ibid., 55.
[65] Ibid., 75.   [66] Ibid., 54–58, 73–76.

Bendrix live she will believe in him and give up the relationship. Bendrix does survive (he was simply unconscious under the weight of a door that had fallen onto him), and Sarah Miles keeps her promise, altogether giving up her affair with Bendrix. In sum: while air raids have a secondary presence in Greene's novel, they play a crucial role as regards the motivation of the story. Aerial bombing is for the most part a back-ground, a dramatic echo of love-making, an efficient cause that alters the individuals' mores and facilitates (or breaks up) adulterous liaisons. Most importantly, bombing does not deter writers from storytelling; on the contrary: it *produces* stories.

The connection between war and love, which of course has a long tradition that goes back to Greek literature, is omnipresent in *Caught*, Henry Green's classic novel on the travails of the volunteers who served in London's Auxiliary Fire Service (AFS) during the conflict.[67] War brought to British society a relaxation of social mores, opening up the field for tolerated clandestine love relations.[68] In the categoric words of a secondary female character from *Caught*, "War ... is sex."[69] Indeed, the narrator of Green's novel devotes a great deal of attention to the flirting and occasional love affairs between AFS volunteers and young women. According to Hilly, war has brought "a tremendous release for most"; Hilly does not believe that "there is anyone who hasn't enjoyed the change."[70] Thanks to the war, anything is possible. The narrator elaborates this view of love in times of war, stating that "This was a time when girls, taken out to night clubs by men in uniform, if he was a pilot she died in his arms that would soon, so she thought, be dead. In the hard idiom of the drum these women seemed already given up to the male in uniform so soon to go away, these girls, as they felt, soon to be killed themselves, so little time left, moth deadly gay, in a daze of giving."[71] Sometimes, when Richard Roe, the protagonist of the novel, is on the street, "Girls looked him straight, long in the eyes as never before, complicity in theirs blue, and blue, and blue. They seemed to drag as they passed."[72] Roe notices a similar atmosphere in the pubs and night clubs where he and the other AFS volunteers spend a good deal of their free time.[73] Determined "to join in the delights he

---

[67] See Feigel, *The Love-Charm of Bombs*, 45–46, 97–100; Rex Ferguson, "Blind Noise and Deaf Visions: Henry Green's *Caught*, Synaesthesia and the Blitz," *Journal of Modern Literature* 33.1 (2009), 102–16; MacKay, *Modernism and World War II*, 98–103; Miller, *British Literature of the Blitz*, 83–115; and Lyndsey Stonebridge, "Bombs and Roses: The Writing of Anxiety in Henry Green's *Caught*," *Diacritics: A Review of Contemporary Criticism* 28.4 (1998), 25–43.
[68] On this score, see Feigel, *The Love-Charm of Bombs*.   [69] Green, *Caught*, 114.   [70] Ibid., 95.
[71] Ibid., 46.   [72] Ibid., 47.   [73] Ibid., 61.

imagined men and girls were sharing out to each other in the desperation of the times,"[74] he starts an extramarital love affair.

Although the novel's main action takes place from September 1942 to September 1944, that is to say, one and a half years after the end of the Blitz (the major German aerial attacks went on from September 7, 1940, to May 21, 1941), Elizabeth Bowen's *The Heat of the Day* depicts events, social interactions, urban landscape, moral ambiguities, and love relationships as determined, one way or another, by absolute war.[75] In *The Heat of the Day* important conversations are held during air raids. The last interview between counterintelligence officer Robert Harrison and Stella Rodney, for instance, occurs while London is being bombed.[76] War also affects the self. The bombing of London decisively changed Stella's personality. Between the fall of France in June 1940 and the autumn of that year, "She had the sensation of being on furlough from her own life" (102). The Blitz altered that: throughout the raids of September 1941, Stella "had been awed, exhilarated, cast at the very most into a sort of abstract of compassion . . . To be at work built her up, and when not at work she was being gay in company whose mood was at the pitch of her own . . . The existence, surrounded by one another, of these people she nightly saw was fluid, easy, holding inside itself a sort of ideality of pleasure" (102). Moreover, the Blitz, the narrator writes, intensified the senses and gave London a new, unexpected "organic power" (98). The new self as well as

---

[74] Ibid., 63.

[75] The reader will find additional information on Bowen's *The Heat of the Day* in, for instance, Robert L. Caserio, "*The Heat of the Day*: Modernism and Narrative in Paul de Man and Elizabeth Bowen," *Modern Language Quarterly: A Journal of Literary History* 54.2 (1993), 263–84; Thomas Dukes, "Desire Satisfied: War and Love in *The Heat of the Day* and *Moon Tiger*," *War, Literature, and the Arts* 3.1 (1991), 75–97; Feigel, *The Love-Charm of Bombs*, 29–30, 249–51, 307–13, 429–30; S. Kapoor, "Chaos and Order in Elizabeth Bowen's *The Heat of the Day*," *Panjab University Research Bulletin (Arts)* 22.2 (1991), 119–23; Phyllis Lassner, "Reimagining the Arts of War: Language & History in Elizabeth Bowen's *The Heat of the Day* & Rose Macaulay's *The World My Wilderness*," *Perspectives on Contemporary Literature* 14 (1988), 30–38; Céline Magot, "Elizabeth Bowen's London in *The Heat of the Day*: An Impression of the City in the Territory of War," *Literary London: Interdisciplinary Studies in the Representation of London* 3.1 (2005), www.literarylondon.org/, accessed August 9, 2016; Miller, *British Literature of the Blitz*, 26–58, and her "'Even a Shelter's Not Safe': The Blitz on Homes in Elizabeth Bowen's Wartime Writing," *Twentieth Century Literature* 45.2 (1999), 138–58; Pong, "Space and Time in the Bombed City," n.p.; Petra Rau, "The Common Frontier: Fictions of Alterity in Elizabeth Bowen's *The Heat of the Day* and Graham Greene's *The Ministry of Fear*," *Literature and History* 14.1 (2005), 31–55; Anna Teekell, "Elizabeth Bowen and Language at War," *New Hibernia Review/Iris Éireannach Nua: A Quarterly Record of Irish Studies* 15.3 (2011), 61–79; and Barbara Bellow Watson, "Variations on an Enigma: Elizabeth Bowen's War Novel," *Southern Humanities Review* 15.2 (1981), 131–51.

[76] Elizabeth Bowen, *The Heat of the Day* (New York: Anchor Books, 2002), 355–63. Further references in text.

that new London correlate to the emergence of what the narrator denominates a "new society," one (basically upper and upper-middle class) that
enjoys the sense of danger (102–3). The two main characters of *The Heat
of the Day*, Stella Rodney and Robert Kelway, belong to that "loose little
society" (103). Their relationship was born out of the war, and it was made
possible partly because of the relaxation of social mores. According to the
narrator, "Wartime, with its makeshifts, shelvings, deferrings, could not
have been kinder to romantic love" (109). London, the "embattled city,"
was indifferent to private lives (109). It is no coincidence that the two
lovers met the day the Blitz started in early September 1940 (97–98). To a
great extent, love is a product of war. "For Stella," the narrator points out,
"her early knowing of Robert was associated with the icelike tinkle of
broken glass being swept up among the crisping leaves, and with the
charred freshness of every morning" (100–1). The bombing is both the
background, the efficient cause, and the enhancing power of their love. In
the first weeks of their relationship, which are also the first weeks of the
Blitz, "they did not know how much might be the time, how much
themselves. The extraordinary battle in the sky transfixed them; they
might have stayed for ever on the eve of being in love" (105). Stella is
perfectly aware of the secret links between their love and combat; as she
tells Robert, "we *are* friends of circumstance – war, this isolation, this
atmosphere in which everything goes on and nothing's said. Or we began
as that: that was what we were at the start – but *now*, look how all this
ruin's made for our perfectness! You and I are an accident, if you like"
(209–10). The narrator elaborates this point further on: "They were the
creatures of history, whose coming together was of a nature possible in no
other day" (217), adding later that "War at present worked as a thinning of
the membrane between the this and the that, it was a becoming apparent –
but then, what else is love?" (218).

Next to love, some novels on the aerial bombing of Britain focus on
espionage and mystery. The most prominent work of this genre is of
course Graham Greene's *The Ministry of Fear*.[77] In this taut spy thriller

---

[77] See, among other studies on *The Ministry of Fear*, Damon Marcel DeCoste, "Modernism's Shell-
Shocked History: Amnesia, Repetition, and the War in Graham Greene's *The Ministry of Fear*,"
Twentieth Century Literature 45.4 (1999), 428–52; Mary Ann Melfi, "The Landscape of Grief:
Graham Greene's *The Ministry of Fear*," *South Atlantic Review* 69.2 (2004), 54–73; Miller, *British
Literature of the Blitz*, 134–51, and her "'The World Has Been Remade': Gender, Genre, and the
Blitz in Graham Greene's *The Ministry of Fear*," *Genre: Forms of Discourse and Culture* 36.1–2
(2003), 131–50; Pong, "Space and Time in the Bombed City," n.p.; Rau, "The Common
Frontier," 31–55; and Victoria Stewart, "The Auditory Uncanny in Wartime London: Graham
Greene's *The Ministry of Fear*," *Textual Practice* 18.1 (2004), 65–81.

aerial bombing has a determining effect on morality, subjectivity, inter-
personal relations, and urban space. The aerial bombing of London has a
much stronger presence in this novel than in the ones we have seen thus
far. At the level of the plot, bombing is a dynamic motif. Thus, two main
scenes, Arthur Rowe's tense conversation in his flat with a stranger who
turns out to be a German secret agent,[78] as well as his confrontation, at the
closing of the novel, with Willi Hilfe – yet another German spy –
(193–200), take place during air raids that have an impact on the outcome
of those encounters. Rowe's amnesia, which is another turning point in the
novel, is the result of a bomb explosion, while his tortured past, fragmented personality, and precarious professional status somehow mirror the
scarred urban space. The narrator associates the destruction of London
with Rowe's personality and existence. As he puts it, "Now in the strange
torn landscape where London shops were reduced to a stone ground-plan
like those of Pompeii he moved with familiarity; he was part of this
destruction and he was no longer part of the past" (31). At times, Rowe
feels "a kind of evil pride like that a leopard might feel moving in harmony
with all the other spots on the world's surface, only with greater power"
(31). Like London, Rowe is in an emotionally ruinous state: "'What
frightens me," he confesses, "is knowing how I came to terms with it
before my memory went. When I came in to London today I hadn't
realized there would be so many ruins. Nothing will seem as strange as
that. God knows what kind of ruin I am myself'" (146). Finally, the spatial
discontinuities in London correspond to the amnesia suffered by Rowe,
which obviously disconnects him from his own past. All this is told in a
section of the novel titled, rather significantly, "Bits and Pieces."

The Ministry of Fear describes in some detail the effects of the aerial
bombing on London's buildings and urban landscape. The narrator sets
the scene of a bombed London almost from the very beginning. Thus, the
reader learns at the beginning of *The Ministry of Fear* that "Arthur Rowe
lived in Guilford Street. A bomb early in the blitz had fallen in the middle
of the street and blasted both sides, but Rowe stayed on. Houses went
overnight, but he stayed. There were boards instead of glass in every room,
and the doors no longer quite fitted and had to be propped at night" (12).
Further on the narrator tells about the destruction brought on to Clapham
(57), St. James's Church, Chelsea, and Battersea (68). Climbing up the
stairs of a building, Rowe has a good view of the partial destruction of
London; from up there, "the war came back into sight. Most of the church

---

[78] Graham Greene, *The Ministry of Fear* (New York: Penguin, 2005), 105. Further references in text.

spires seemed to have been snapped off two-thirds up like sugar-sticks, and there was an appearance of slum clearance where there hadn't really been any slums" (68). In this realist novel, the first thing Rowe notices upon returning to London after his internment in a fake sanatorium is precisely London's altered landscape as the result of bombing (170).

The realist mode is also the dominant one in several novels written on aerial bombings of countries other than Britain. In Japan, Morio Kita's *The House of Nire* (1963) constitutes one of the most illustrious realist novels devoted to the war and prewar period; its last eighty pages vividly describe, through a network of internal focalizers, the firebombing of Tokyo on March 9–10, 1945, and life in the city thereafter. In the Soviet Union, Viktor Nekrasov describes in his 1946 novel, *Front-Line Stalingrad*, the German bombing of that city.[79] There is also a corpus of realist novels devoted to the strategic bombing of Germany. The first to appear was a long novel by Otto Erich Kiesel published in 1949, *Die unverzagte Stadt*, in whose second part the author gives a 250-page-long account of the British bombing of Hamburg in late July and early August 1943. The bombing of Dresden has merited the attention of realist narratives as well: I am thinking of Henri Coulonges's *L'adieu à la femme sauvage* (Farewell to the Wild Woman) (1979), and three novels authored by writers from East Germany: *Phosphor und Flieder* (Phosphor and Lilacs) (1954) by Max Zimmering, and the novels *Die Feuer sinken* (The Fires Recede) (1961) and *Leben für Leben* (Life for Life) (1987) by Eberhard Panitz.[80] To that list we could perhaps add two novels exclusively devoted to the aftereffects of bombing, that is to the devastation of space and the precariousness of human life amidst the ruins: Heinrich Böll's *Der Engel schwieg* (The Silent Angel) (finished in 1950 but not published until 1992) and Peter de Mendelssohn's *Die Kathedrale* (The Cathedral) (also published many years after it was written in the immediate aftermath of the war: 1983).

The differences between all these works and the British realist narratives on aerial bombing are quite striking. First, the aforementioned realist novels on the bombing of Germany devote much more attention to aerial

---

[79] Viktor Nekrasov, *Front-Line Stalingrad*, trans. David Floyd (Barnsley: Pen & Sword Military, 2012), 78–82.

[80] The novels by Zimmering and Panitz are manifestations of the vivid interest shown in the German Democratic Republic for revisiting and commemorating the bombing of German cities, particularly Dresden. On this score, see Anne Fuchs, *After the Dresden Bombing: Pathways of Memory, 1945 to the Present* (New York: Palgrave Macmillan, 2012). For more information on the literary treatment of the bombing of Dresden in the cultural artifacts produced in East Germany, see Thomas C. Fox, "East Germany and the Bombing War," *Bombs Away! Representing the Air War over Europe and Japan*, ed. Wilfried Wilms and William Rasch (Amsterdam: Rodopi, 2006), 113–30.

bombing and destruction than their British counterparts, giving far more detailed information on air raids and their effects on urban space and people. Second, some of them address openly and directly the issue of the trauma caused by bombing, most particularly Coulonges's *L'adieu à la femme sauvage*. Third, realist works on the strategic bombing of Germany partly take up the challenge posed by aerial bombing to representation, something that, for the most part, is absent from the British realist fiction on the bombardment of Britain. Finally, some authors seem to have understood that a simple, straightforward representational narrative is not enough for capturing catastrophic events like the bombings of Hamburg, Dresden, and Tokyo. Consequently, Kiesel, Zimmering, Panitz, and Kita represent aerial bombing by interweaving simultaneous scenes focalized through different characters.[81] The fragmentary, chaotic, multi-plot structure of their novels, as well as the use of multiple or variable internal focalization, places the reader in a discursive maze that duplicates the destruction, chaos, and confusion produced by the bombing. In the sense that they represent the intersection of daily life and extreme historical events and experiences, these novels are traumatic realist works.

Otto Erich Kiesel's *Die unverzagte Stadt* is the most significant instance of traumatic realism on aerial bombing. With the exception of the first chapter and a passage in the last chapter of the second part, the action of the novel takes place exclusively in Hamburg. In fact, *Die unverzagte Stadt* can be read as a history of Hamburg during the war and its aftermath. Divided into three parts and a short epilogue, the novel mentions and dates the main historical events in the world and in Hamburg. Its historical perspective is therefore wider than the British realist accounts on aerial bombing, and so too is the ideological density of the novel. But what makes Kiesel's work interesting lies in its formal inconsistencies, probably caused by the novelist's intuition of the fact that the bombing of Hamburg in July and August 1943 constituted something extraordinary, beyond reason, measure, and justice that surpassed the usual means of realist representation. In other words, the obliteration of Hamburg was such an extraordinary event that it shattered the realist poetics underpinning *Die unverzagte Stadt*, turning this novel into a traumatic realist narrative. This is something that does not usually happen in the British representational

---

[81] Kiesel, *Die unverzagte Stadt*, 273–524; Max Zimmering, *Phosphor und Flieder. Vom Untergang und Wiederaufstieg der Stadt Dresden* (Berlin: Dietz, 1954), 5–59; Eberhard Panitz, *Die Feuer sinken. Roman der Dresdner Februartage 1945* (Schkeuditz: Schkeudizer Buchverlag, 2000), 5–48, and his *Leben für Leben. Roman einer Familie* (Halle: Mitteldeutscher Verlag, 1987), 150–81; Morio Kita, *The House of Nire*, trans. Dennis Keene (Tokyo: Kodansha International, 1990), 649–723.

narratives on aerial bombing. As mentioned earlier, generally speaking the Blitz did not truly undermine the human capacity for representing it. In contrast, in *Die unverzagte Stadt* the bombing of Hamburg is perceived as an event that defies cognition, understanding, and representation. The implied author argues that the bombing itself *lacks* meaning, that is to say it is absolutely out of proportion; in turn, this very excess of the bombing *destroys* meaning. For those who survived it, the narrator writes, the firestorm triggered by the bombs was something "unimaginable, indescribable."[82] The firestorm "unsettles meaning" (310), it is a "symphony of madness" (389). As the narrative voice points out, "the unsettling of meaning caused by the bluster of the fires" paralyzed thinking (392). People were living in a sort of gray zone of uncertainty: what had been "valid" so far had no meaning any longer, and what was new lacked a "verifiable relation to the present situation" (307–8). This lack of sense of the British bombing of the city, as well as its destruction of meaning, brings Alfred Berger, the main character of the novel, to the brink of madness (405) and constitutes one of the pillars of the traumatic realism that underpins Kiesel's novel. The bombing of Hamburg is clearly perceived as a potentially traumatic event because it damages the usual mental mechanisms used for the cognition of reality. In the theory produced to understand it, trauma is generally considered as the structure of the experience of an overwhelming and disruptive event that has not been fully experienced at the time of its occurrence; such event resists comprehension, integration into consciousness, and expression because the ordinary mechanisms of memory and consciousness have been temporarily destroyed.[83] That apparent realization of the traumatic nature of the bombing is supplemented, in *Die unverzagte Stadt*, by the sorrow felt by a character after witnessing the destruction of cultural memory (305).

All these aspects of the aerial attack on Hamburg may be correlated to Kiesel's employment of modernist techniques for describing the bombing. The main modernist techniques consist of the occasional practice of spatial form and the attempts at expressionist diction and rhetoric in passages

[82] Kiesel, *Die unverzagte Stadt*, 306. Further references in text.

[83] On trauma and cultural representations, see, among many other works, Gert Buelens, Sam Durrant, and Robert Eaglestone, eds., *The Future of Trauma Theory: Contemporary Literary and Cultural Criticism* (London: Routledge, 2014); Cathy Caruth, *Unclaimed Experience: Trauma, Narrative, and History* (Baltimore, MD: Johns Hopkins University Press, 1996), and her edited volume *Trauma: Explorations in Memory* (Baltimore, MD: Johns Hopkins University Press, 1995); and Dominick LaCapra, *Writing History, Writing Trauma,* 2nd ed. (Baltimore, MD: Johns Hopkins University Press, 2014).

written in a way remindful of poetry (nominal sentences, parataxis, paralle-listic structures, anaphoras, visual organization of sentences as if they were the lines from a poem, prose poetry). Although the first time the narrator writes in such a style is when he narrates the bombing of Hamburg on June 3, 1940 (137–38), which among other casualties caused the death of a group of children (139), this kind of language is used mostly to describe specific scenes of the British bombing of July–August 1943. For instance:

> Unending boom in the air.
> Is it a tornado, chasing faraway, the city?
> A range of flames in the East.
> Fir trees: red, glaring white.
> Over the houses, the murderous droning of bombers flying at low altitude.
> To the cellar! To the cellar!
> Let it burn! Let it burn!
> Fire sings – it sings the song of the victorious flame.
>
> (298)

As if to emphasize the importance of these changes in style, the end of the second part of the novel is written in an expressionist mode as well:

> Alfred let his eyes look around. There they still were, the youngsters, hardened through sorrow, undaunted, willing … to survive. When the storm is over, they will build a new world …
> And that world will not be one in which the powerful sit above the powerless below,
>
> – in which few have much, and many possess little,
> – in which thousands sow and one harvests,
> – in which dying is easy, because living is so hard,
> – in which people speak about peace while they mean war,
> – in which people praise loyalty but practice treason,
> – in which brothers abandon brothers in hard times, and say: "I don't know you!" …
> – in which hatred inhabits, where nothing but love should dwell!
>
> (523–24)

The representation of trauma should not be confined to the boundaries of catastrophic modernism. While it has been considered that fragmented, non-linear experimental texts come closer to accurately representing trau-matic experience – itself characterized by the dissociation of the mind and alterations in the experience of time – than realist works,[84] the truth is that realism is capable of capturing trauma as well. As Stef Craps has noted,

---

[84] For instance: LaCapra, *Writing History, Writing Trauma*, 23.

"the crisis of representation caused by trauma generates narrative *possibility* as much as narrative *impossibility*."[85] From a similar theoretical standpoint, Roger Luckhurst states that "a wide diversity of high, middle and low cultural forms have provided a repertoire of compelling ways to articulate that apparently paradoxical thing, the trauma narrative."[86] What I claim is not that realism cannot depict trauma, but rather that traumatic events related to absolute war like the devastating aerial bombing of Hamburg in the summer of 1943 seem to exceed a purely mimetic account. A realist text such as Kiesel's turns into a traumatic realist novel as soon as the author tries to accommodate within his mimetic narrative the experience of war in its absolute degree. Some authors, however, went even further than Kiesel did: believing absolute war to be beyond traditional representation, they gave up the representation of the air raids and chose instead to void them altogether in their narratives.

The Void

In the last section of his 1977 novella, *Der Luftangriff auf Halberstadt am 8. April 1945*, Alexander Kluge writes about a survey conducted by the American armed forces in Halberstadt after the Second World War. Soon the person in charge of interviewing the inhabitants of Halberstadt realized that, while people were more than willing to share with him their "experiences," whenever they narrated the bombing of their town they invariably resorted to clichés and empty statements, similar, if not identical, to the ones that he had already heard from the surveyed citizens of Nuremburg, Würzburg, Frankfurt, and other bombed-out German cities.[87] Apparently, the true experiences, feelings, and memories of the catastrophic event had been erased from the minds of those Germans interviewed by the American officer. The narrator recapitulates the thoughts of the officer on this score with the following words: "it seemed to him as if all those people ... had lost their ability to remember within the destroyed plains of the city."[88] From the episode narrated by Kluge, one may draw the conclusion that the bombing of Halberstadt was in fact a traumatic event that had severely impeded the survivors' capacity to witness, process, feel, remember, and express the aerial bombing that they

[85] Stef Craps, "Beyond Eurocentrism: Trauma Theory in the Global Age," *The Future of Trauma Theory: Contemporary Literary and Cultural Criticism*, ed. Gert Buelens, Sam Durrant, and Robert Eaglestone (London: Routledge, 2014), 51.
[86] Roger Luckhurst, *The Trauma Question* (London: Routledge, 2008), 83.
[87] Kluge, *Der Luftangriff auf Halberstadt am 8. April 1945*, 87.   [88] Ibid., 89.

had undergone. On account of their use of clichés and empty phrases, as well as their lack of emotion, it is plausible to presume that the inhabitants of Halberstadt had either repressed the event or been numbed by it.[89] In short: a *void* had been formed in the minds of those Germans interviewed by the American officer – a void that was *embedded* also in their narratives on the bombing.[90]

This void must have been experienced by victims of aerial bombing throughout Germany. Although there are no systematic and comprehensive epidemiological studies of the psychological effects of the strategic bombing of Germany during the Second World War,[91] it is generally acknowledged that the massive bombardment of German cities in 1940–45 had a traumatic effect on many Germans. This must be particularly true of the men and women who survived the bombings and ensuing firestorms of Hamburg and Dresden. Even W. G. Sebald, ever so critical of the Germans' alleged silence in regard to the systematic bombing of their country, acknowledges that "The death by fire within a few hours of an entire city ... must inevitably have led to overload, to paralysis of the capacity to think and feel in those who succeeded in surviving."[92] The data that we have on the catastrophic damage inflicted by the Allied air raids on Germany seem to confirm these inferences: in addition to the enormous destruction of human lives and urban space summarized at the beginning of this chapter, 900,000 men and women were injured and 7.5 million Germans became homeless. It has been estimated that a total of 20 million Germans experienced aerial bombing. After examining these data and opinion polls conducted in the wake of the war, Alice Förster and Birgit Beck suggest that probably a high number of

[89] I am using a distinction suggested by Robert Jay Lifton in *Death in Life: Survivors of Hiroshima* (New York: Random House, 1967) between the responses of psychic "numbing" (or blocking of the traumatized individual's feelings) and "repression" (by means of which the traumatized person excludes or forgets an idea or event) to trauma.

[90] The inscription of a void in the psyche of the traumatized individual constitutes a phenomenon widely known by medical practitioners and theorists of trauma alike. See Cathy Caruth, "Introduction," *Trauma: Explorations in Memory*, ed. Cathy Caruth (Baltimore, MD: Johns Hopkins University Press, 1995), 7, and her *Unclaimed Experience*, 17; Henry Krystal, "Integration and Self-Healing in Post-Traumatic States: A Ten-Year Retrospective," *American Imago* 48 (1991), 114; and Dori Laub, "Bearing Witness, or the Vicissitudes of Listening," *Testimony: Crises of Witnessing in Literature, Psychoanalysis, and History*, by Shoshana Felman and Dori Laub (London: Routledge, 1992), 57.

[91] Alice Förster and Birgit Beck's study is an exception to the norm: "Post-Traumatic Stress Disorder and World War II: Can a Psychiatric Concept Help Us Understand Postwar Society?," *Life after Death: Approaches to a Cultural and Social History of Europe during the 1940s and 1950s*, ed. Richard Bessel and Dirk Schumann (Cambridge University Press, 2003), 15–35.

[92] Sebald, *Luftkrieg und Literatur*, 32–33.

Germans suffered from post-traumatic stress.[93] Certainly, the otherwise
obvious proposition that many Germans suffered because of the Allied air
raids over their country does not minimize in the least the culpability of
Germans for supporting or acquiescing to a murderous regime, nor does it
equate at all the victims of the air war to the victims of the Nazi
extermination program.[94] But it does indeed add an element of complexity
to the assessment of postwar German culture and society.

There is a remarkable family resemblance between a significant number
of novels devoted, one way or another, to narrating the air war against
Germany that has largely gone unnoticed by the increasing number of
scholars who study the cultural representations of the Allied aerial raids on
Nazi Germany. I am referring to the striking fact that several novels *void*
the representation of the bombing, either in the mind of certain characters,
or else within the narrative discourse.[95] When they choose the former
device, the narrator may represent the bombing; what happens is that
some of the characters cannot recall it due to their being traumatized by
the event. When the latter is the case, the novel eschews altogether the
direct depiction of the bombing. Either way, the void is closely related to
psychological, epistemic, and literary problems. This void articulates
novels such as Max Zimmering's *Phosphor und Flieder* (1954), Eberhard
Panitz's *Die Feuer sinken* (1961), Kurt Vonnegut's *Slaughterhouse-Five*
(1969), Hubert Fichte's *Detlevs Imitationen "Grünspan"* (1971), Henri
Coulonges's *L'adieu à la femme sauvage* (1979), and Dieter Forte's second
volume of his trilogy *Das Haus auf meinen Schultern* (The House on My
Shoulders) (1999).

Unlike the novels that do openly narrate the aerial bombing of German
towns studied in previous sections, in the aforementioned novels there is a

---

[93] Förster and Beck, "Post-Traumatic Stress Disorder and World War II," 27–29.

[94] In recent years, there has been in Germany a reassessment of German suffering and victimhood in
the last world war. See Aleida Assmann, *Der lange Schatten der Vergangenheit. Erinnerungskultur und
Geschichtspolitik* (Munich: C. H. Beck, 2006), 183–204; Bill Niven, ed., *Germans as Victims:
Remembering the Past in Contemporary Germany* (New York: Palgrave Macmillan, 2006); Helmut
Schmitz, ed., *A Nation of Victims? Representations of German Wartime Suffering from 1945 to the
Present* (Amsterdam: Rodopi, 2007); and Helmut Schmitz and Annette Seidel-Arpaci, ed.,
*Narratives of Trauma: Discourses of German Wartime Suffering in National and International
Perspective* (Amsterdam: Rodopi, 2011).

[95] By contrast, the void embedded in texts produced by survivors of the Nazi destruction of the
European Jews has been studied by several scholars. See Sara R. Horowitz's book *Voicing the Void:
Muteness and Memory in Holocaust Fiction* (Albany, NY: State University of New York Press, 1997),
as well as Giorgio Agamben's influential comments on the "unwitnessing" of the traumatic event
and the "lacunae" contained in testimonies written by survivors of German death camps, in his
Remnants of Auschwitz: The Witness and the Archive, trans. Daniel Heller-Roazen (New York: Zone
Books, 1999).

deliberate voiding of the main event that correlates to psychological trauma as described earlier. I would like to underscore, however, that in these novels the discursive voiding of the traumatic event – a manifestation of the language of silence – does not have a relation of identity with the void of trauma. They constitute two different realities: one is a narrative, formal void, while the other belongs to the realm of mental pathologies. Having said this, the narrative void and the void of trauma need to be considered as homologous entities: the narrative voiding of the catastrophic event in fictions on air raids on the one hand, and the traumatic void caused by aerial bombing in the psyche of those who underwent them on the other, mirror each other, the former being a literary image of the latter. Thus, when read in relation to the traumatic event the narrative void reveals, as we shall see, crucial aspects of the experience and representation of trauma. By voiding the direct representation of the cause of the post-traumatic stress (i.e., the aerial bombing of civilians), the novels formally refract at once the aforementioned workings of acute trauma and the extreme difficulty of bearing witness to absolute war. The writers seem to have sensed the defining presence of a "hole" in the minds of people traumatized by aerial bombing; accordingly, in order to explore, understand, and represent such a psychic voiding they have placed a gap within their novels. Furthermore, through their voiding technique the novels studied in this section suggest the manifold consequences and implications of the traumatic event, as well as the moral meaning of the bombing and the means for overcoming a post-traumatic stress disorder. In this sense, they invite us to reflect on the psychological, social, and transgenerational traumata triggered by the air raids, deploy a hermeneutics of silence, consider narratives as coping mechanisms vis-à-vis trauma, and ponder on the ethics (or lack thereof) of strategic bombing.

In addition to keeping a relation of homology with the psychic void, the narrative voiding of the traumatic event also brings out the resistance of aerial bombing to representation. Put differently: not only does the discursive void in the novels mirror and dialogue with the void of psychological trauma; it is also an answer given to the great challenge posed by absolute warfare to cognition and linguistic representation. Like much war writing, representations of air raids are tinged with excess and ineffability. The voiding of the main event is a literary strategy that places the selected novels within what Kate McLoughlin has termed as "not-writing," namely a mode of writing common to war texts that "functions analogously to military diversion tactics: attention is diverted away from the main action, but with the inevitable result that the true target eventually becomes clear ... such tactics are means of *deliberately* circumventing the direct depiction of the conflict."[96] Omissions, ellipses, indexical signs, parapolemics, circumlocutions, euphemisms, and lacunae are some of the rhetorical devices deployed in not-writing. Although one can find them in all sorts of literature, such devices "are particularly apposite responses to the representation-resistant phenomenon that is armed conflict."[97] Therefore, an exploration of the narrative void inevitably addresses two different intersecting problems: first, there is the problem of expressing in a literary text the effects of the catastrophic event on the human psyche and on the language used to talk about it; and second, we have the problems intrinsic to representing the catastrophic event itself. The two novelists examined here found in the void a solution to those intertwining problematic issues. One may ultimately claim that the void is a figure for the elusiveness of both trauma and absolute warfare as manifested through strategic bombing. The embedding of negativity in fiction had a significant effect on novelistic language and form, as well as on the reading experience.

The discursive voiding of the air raid plays an important role in catastrophic modernist novels. Take, for instance, Hubert Fichte's *Detlevs Imitationen "Grünspan,"* an experimental novel in which the void refers at once to the void of trauma and to the difficulty of finding adequate strategies for narrating an extreme and complex event such as the British bombing of Hamburg in the summer of 1943.[98] On first inspection, it is counterintuitive to argue for the existence of such a void. After all, the novel narrates several scenes from the bombing. But a more careful reading reveals that those narratives of the bombardment are not only partial and very fragmentary; in addition, they center more on its effects on the human body than on the event itself. The first time the novel relates the air raid against Hamburg is in chapter 14.[99] Here the bombing is described through the eyes of Detlev – the main character of the novel – as a child; he spends one of the several air raids undertaken by the RAF

[96] Kate McLoughlin, *Authoring War: The Literary Representation of War from the Iliad to Iraq* (Cambridge University Press, 2011), 139.
[97] Ibid., 151.
[98] For more information on Fichte's novel, see Hartmut Böhme, *Hubert Fichte. Riten des Autors und Leben der Literatur* (Stuttgart: J. B. Metzlersche Verlagsbuchhandlung, 1992), 163–82; Calzoni, "Chasms of Silence," 265–66; and Claudio Kasperl, "'Nun ist alles anders'. Zur narrativen Gestaltung einer Grenzsituation in Hubert Fichtes Roman *Detlevs Imitationen 'Grünspan',*" *Grenzsituationen. Wahrnehmung, Bedeutung und Gestaltung in der neueren Literatur*, ed. Dorothea Lauterbach, Uwe Spörl, and Uli Wunderlich (Göttingen: Vandenhoeck & Ruprecht, 2002), 303–30.
[99] Fichte, *Detlevs Imitationen "Grünspan,"* 20–25. Further references in text.

against Hamburg during Operation Gomorrah in a cellar together with his mother, grandparents, and neighbors. The unreliability and epistemological limitations implied in narrating the bombing from this point of view are evident: from the cellar, no one could see anything, and the main focalizer, the eight-year-old Detlev, is too little to fully understand the events that took place; in this sense, Detlev constitutes an unreliable focalizer. To be sure, Detlev and his family could hear the bombing, the flak fire, and they also felt the hopping of the cellar caused by the pounding of the bombs. But this is all we learn about the bombardment in this chapter. The narrator uses a paratactic syntax, with a remarkable presence of nominal sentences, inserting in a syncopated way the interventions of the characters who had sought shelter in the cellar – literary devices that reproduce the staccato rhythm of the bombing and its shattering effects on urban space and human bodies. In *Detlevs Imitationen "Grünspan"* Fichte does not really portray the bombing. Instead, he narrates it through ellipsis and the unreliability of a child. The author captures the horror by suggesting the facts as perceived by a little boy. After the bombing, the family decides to leave the city. When they cross Hamburg towards the train station, the narrator portrays through Detlev's point of view the effects of the bombing on the urban landscape. The destruction of the city is told in short sentences in a staccato style in counterpoint to other events. The fragmentary nature of these passages is related to Detlev's partial and somewhat unreliable understanding of the situation, and it also reflects the very destruction brought on the city. For example:

- The home for cripples was here.
- A mine fell on it.
- Cripples and then to be killed by a blockbuster as well.

(32)

The difficulty inherent in representing the bombing itself and the firestorm it triggered is further emphasized with a scene that describes Detlev's family fleeing Hamburg by train. His mother tries to explain to a diplomat aboard the train what has just happened in Hamburg. The diplomat's reaction of incredulity clearly suggests the impossibility of effectively communicating certain experiences: "You are exaggerating!" (33), he replies to Detlev's mother. Detlev notes: "Finally mother realizes . . . that things here have not yet got so far . . . that here the war is still being won . . . and that her distress appears improper in the superior atmosphere of the first-class compartment" (33).

In *Detlevs Imitationen "Grünspan"* Fichte establishes a counterpoint between the chapters on the bombing and its immediate aftermath as experienced by little Detlev (chapters 14 and 16) and a chapter that describes Detlev's alter ego, Jäcki, conducting research in 1968 on the bombardment of Hamburg. In chapter 17 Jäcki goes to the State Library, the Medical School in Eppendorf, the Hamburg History Museum, and the central fire station in Hamburg in order to gather documents produced on the bombing of his hometown. In each place, he consults or checks out material devoted to the aerial raids, inserting or summarizing in the novel passages that either describe the effects of the bombing or narrate very brief scenes of the bombardment itself. Most of Jäcki's attention falls on the findings of pathological anatomical examinations relating to the attacks on Hamburg from 1943 to 1945, produced by Dr. Siegfried Graeff (34–36, 48–49, 50–54). As a result, Jäcki centers on the disturbing effects of the bombing on the human body, describing at length the horrible aspect of a number of corpses, thereby practicing a writing of cruelty. Less attention is given to the bombing itself, parts of which are narrated through the insertion or summary of very short passages from *Hamburg und seine Bauten* (Hamburg and its Buildings) – a document produced by the Municipal Statistical Office – , Martin Caidin's *The Night Hamburg Died*, a short film held in the central fire station, Karl Detlev Moeller's *Das letzte Kapitel* (The Last Chapter), and Curzio Malaparte's *La pelle* (The Skin); the narrator also embeds fragments written by Carl Heinrich Hagenbeck.

Intertextuality is a decisive structural device in Hubert Fichte's experimental novel. The main character, who as previously said was in Hamburg during the bombing as a child, cannot properly represent the air raid. What he remembers is clearly insufficient, and the only thing he can do, aside from remembering his experience of the air raid in a cellar, is to reproduce or summarize excerpts on different aspects of the bombardment. Perhaps the most extraordinary of these different texts put together by Jäcki is the summary of a film held at the central fire station. There Jäcki sees a short silent film that shows different scenes lived during the bombing: a family that runs into the flames, the burning of neo-Gothic towers, bloated bodies, and so on (42–43). But what makes this passage interesting is the fact that the narrator, after watching the film, rewinds it, seeing everything in reverse order. Someone from the fire station tells Jäcki that in an aerial bombing people lose their sense of time and the capacity to orient themselves in space: "Anyone who hasn't experienced such events finds it hard to understand that any sense of time gets lost in such situations. In the middle of an environment that changes completely within seconds or minutes, there is perhaps no 'in time' [*rechtzeitig*] anymore" (43). The rewinding of the film, and by extension the multitemporal non-chronological organization of the plot, reproduces precisely this abnormal reality produced by the bombing.

Crucially, at the end of chapter 17 the narrator intersperses passages from different sources with a sentence uttered by a "Spokesman" that is repeated, with variations (51, 52), several times, thereby establishing a leitmotif: "Speech fails before the huge dimensions of horror" (50). An English Spokesman conveys the same idea in English: "Speech is impotent to portray the measure of the horror" (50). These two statements constitute metatextual comments on the passages in the novel devoted to the bombing: indeed, language cannot capture the real dimensions of the horror brought about by the air raid of Hamburg. Hence the fragmentary nature of Fichte's depiction of the bombing of the city: it is impossible to find a unified voice on such a multidimensional event. The protagonist's experience and perspective are clearly insufficient. This justifies the fact that the representation of the air raid and its effects is done through other people's texts, and not through recreating direct experience. The inscription of the void on the novel's discourse is directly associated with the irrepresentability of the bombing itself and with a possible trauma developed by the main character. The narrator himself stresses the challenge posed to representation by the bombing of Hamburg in the summer of 1943 in a metafictional passage that helps us understand the narrative voiding of the main event:

> Is there an expression for that? / Let letters burn? Lead type melt? ... / Should writers set themselves alight? / Or invent pictograms ... ? ... / Do pictograms convey the fire itself and the ashes? /... Color two pages of this book black. / – This is the destruction! / Or print a black, shining, fat mark on two pages of the book – in the middle leave empty a minuscule, five-pointed American star – and let syllables peep out from the edge of the blot ... What would be very bold for literature, would probably be pretty weak as an illustration. (47–48)

Significantly, this is precisely what Fichte does throughout *Detlevs Imitationen "Grünspan,"* namely experiments with form and language. That metatextual passage refers, therefore, both to the difficulty of representing bombing in fiction and to the catastrophic experimentalism in Fichte's novel. The untold destruction of Hamburg relates to the dissolution of the subject's unity (Detlev/Jäcki), the superposition of temporalities (the novel contains two temporal levels: the war and immediate postwar on the one hand, and 1968 on the other), the spatial form of the novel, and the play with style and syntax, as for instance chapter 51, which imitates the structure of Wittgenstein's *Tractatus Logico-Philosophicus*.

The pinnacle of the catastrophic modernist voiding of the air bombardment is to be found in Kurt Vonnegut's 1969 novel, *Slaughterhouse-Five*. To begin with, Billy Pilgrim, its memorable protagonist, represents an instance of psychological void. His post-traumatic stress disorder has already been commented on, so there is no need here to rehearse the arguments made by other scholars.[100] However, I do want to underscore the link, in Vonnegut's novel, between the void in the psyche of the protagonist and a void stamped on the narrative, namely the diegetic omission of the traumatic event. Such association, which has been largely neglected by scholars, emerges in chapter 8. In a scene from that chapter devoted to narrating a wedding-anniversary party organized by him and his wife, Billy Pilgrim listens to a song played by a barbershop quartet. At some point, Pilgrim has a psychosomatic response to the "changing chords" of the musicians.[101] He looks so bad that his worried wife asks what is wrong with him. He replies reassuring her that he is all right. The narrator provides an important clarification: "And he was, too, except that he could find no explanation for why the song had affected him so grotesquely. He had supposed for years that he had no secrets from himself. Here was proof that he had a great big secret somewhere inside, and he could not imagine what it was" (173). After thinking "hard about the effect the quartet had on him," Billy Pilgrim "found an association with an experience he had long ago" (177). And it is then, and only then, that the novel tackles at last what it has promised from the first page: the bombing of Dresden (177–78). The "great big secret" Pilgrim did not suspect himself of having is none other, therefore, than the unacknowledged – and unwitnessed – traumatic event. The link connecting the barbershop quartet and the bombing is the resemblance between the musicians and the guards who kept watch on Pilgrim and the other American prisoners of war in Dresden (178). By means of a chain of free associations (musicians/guards/bombing), Pilgrim unveils something crucial about himself.

[100] See, for instance, Kevin Brown, "The Psychiatrists Were Right: Anomic Alienation in Kurt Vonnegut's *Slaughterhouse-Five*," *South Central Review: The Journal of the South Central Modern Language Association* 28.2 (2011), 101–9; Susanne Vees-Gulani, "Diagnosing Billy Pilgrim: A Psychiatric Approach to Kurt Vonnegut's *Slaughterhouse-Five*," *Critique: Studies in Contemporary Fiction* 44.2 (2003), 175–84, and her *Trauma and Guilt*, 161–71.
[101] Kurt Vonnegut, *Slaughterhouse-Five, or, The Children's Crusade: A Duty-Dance with Death* (New York: Dell Publishing, 1991), 173. Further references in text.

The void of psychological trauma inscribed on Billy Pilgrim's psyche correlates with a structural void in the novel. In the same way that the bombing has created a hole in Pilgrim's existence, the bombardment of Dresden is inscribed in the novel as an *absence*. Vonnegut refracts the void of trauma into the very discourse produced to represent it. *Slaughterhouse-Five* constitutes a prominent instance of the textual voiding of the traumatic event. The void plays a crucial role in Vonnegut's narrative. In this 215-page-long novel, Vonnegut defers for almost 180 pages the narration of the bombing of Dresden. Even though the authorial extradiegetic narrator insists, in chapter 1, on the extreme importance of the bombing of Dresden in his life, even though that bombing seems to be at the root of Billy Pilgrim's post-traumatic stress disorder, the narration of the traumatic event is constantly deferred, and it is only related *elliptically* at the end of the novel.[102] The ellipsis of the bombing is achieved by narrating it through the eyes of someone who did not see the bombardment: Billy Pilgrim spent the entire aerial raid in the meat locker of the slaughterhouse where the Germans had placed him and other American prisoners of war (177–78). The narrator sums it up thus: "He was down in the meat locker on the night that Dresden was destroyed" (177). To underscore the implied irony in that statement, the narrative voice adds that it was a "very safe shelter," and "All that happened down there was an occasional shower of calcimine" (177), thereby summarizing the quality of great safety that was already implied in an earlier description of the shelter (165). The American POWs and their guards do not get out of the meat locker until noon of the following day, finding out that "Dresden was like the moon now, nothing but minerals ... Everybody else in the neighborhood was dead" (179). To be sure, Billy Pilgrim could hear from the meat locker the burst of the high-explosive bombs (177), but that is the only thing Pilgrim experienced of the air raid. He did not see the bombs fall, nor did he witness the horrifying situations produced by the ensuing firestorm. Strictly speaking, in *Slaughterhouse-Five* there is no narration of the bombing of Dresden. Pilgrim learns bits of what goes on above the meat locker

---

[102] Peter Freese argues likewise that the thematic center of Vonnegut's novel – Dresden – "is endlessly circumnavigated but never fully encountered" ("Kurt Vonnegut's *Slaughterhouse-Five*: Or, How to Storify an Atrocity," *Historiographic Metafiction in Modern American and Canadian Literature*, ed. Bernd Engler and Kurt Müller [Paderborn: Ferdinand Schöningh, 1994], 221). Similar observations in Alberto Cacicedo, "'You Must Remember This': Trauma and Memory in *Catch-22* and *Slaughterhouse-Five*," *Critique: Studies in Contemporary Fiction* 46.4 (2005), 363–64; Ann Rigney, "All This Happened, More or Less: What a Novelist Made of the Bombing of Dresden," *History and Theory* 48.2 (2009), 18; and Vees-Gulani, *Trauma and Guilt*, 169.

by eavesdropping on what the guards say to each other, which is not much: "A guard would go to the head of the stairs every so often to see what it was like outside, then he would come down and whisper to the other guards. There was a firestorm out there. Dresden was one big flame. The one flame ate everything organic, everything that would burn" (178). That is all the narrator of *Slaughterhouse-Five* has to say about the air raid on Dresden. The most important event in the novel, the event that decisively determined the lives of the authorial extradiegetic narrator and his character Billy Pilgrim, is conspicuously absent. The bombing of Dresden may be viewed as a sort of black hole in *Slaughterhouse-Five*: in spite of its psychological and textual importance, it takes place *outside* the narrator's visual field. In this sense, one may argue that the very title of the novel emphasizes the void. It refers not to the bombing of Dresden, not to death, but rather to the place where Billy had found protection from it and from where he could not see anything. The slaughterhouse number five is the place of the un-witnessing. Paradoxically, it stands for survival, for life. The narrative voiding of the event may be seen here as a trope that stands for Billy's psychic repression of the traumatic event. The title of Vonnegut's novel is, therefore, the ultimate emblem of both the psychic void and the discursive void.

Within the logic of the novel, two main reasons explain this voiding of the main event. First of all, Billy Pilgrim and his fellow veterans do not remember much of what they went through during the bombing. In psychological terms, Dresden is so painful an event that it has been repressed. Pilgrim's comrade-in-arms Bernard V. O'Hare says that "he couldn't remember much" about Dresden (4). In his summary of a conversation with O'Hare, Pilgrim acknowledges that "neither one of us could remember anything good. O'Hare remembered one guy who got into a lot of wine in Dresden, before it was bombed, and we had to take him home in a wheel-barrow. It wasn't much to write a book about. I remembered two Russian soldiers who had looted a clock factory" (13–14), concluding: "*That* was about *it* for memories" (13–14). Indeed, it isn't much. At the end of the novel, when asked by another patient at the hospital "what it had been like" in Dresden, Pilgrim merely tells him "about the horses and the couple picnicking on the moon" (197–98). Again, there is no story of the bombing of Dresden. If the first reason that explains the voiding of the traumatic event has to do with the repression of memories, the second one is connected to the insufficiency of language for capturing trauma as well as extreme, catastrophic events such as a specific instance of absolute war. The novel itself suggests as much a couple of times. Once the bombing is over, Billy Pilgrim and the rest of the American POWs are forced to help the Germans with rescue missions. Pilgrim writes the following about their walking through Dresden's lunar landscape: "Nobody talked very much as the expedition crossed the moon. There was nothing appropriate to say" (180). According to the narrative voice, the aerial bombardment of Dresden had been planned with the objective of killing everybody: "One thing was clear: Absolutely everybody in the city was supposed to be dead ... and anybody that moved in it represented a flaw in the design" (180). Naturally, an event designed for killing everybody precludes, if successful, all possible witnessing. The extradiegetic narrator had already touched on this issue earlier in his explanation to his editor as to why his book on Dresden is somewhat short and disorganized: "It is so short and jumbled and jangled, Sam, because there is nothing intelligent to say about a massacre. Everybody is supposed to be dead, to never say anything or want anything ever again. Everything is supposed to be very quiet after a massacre, and it always is, except for the birds" (19).

These narratorial interventions may be read as meta-ethical commentaries as well as self-referential metatextual passages, for they provide a key to understanding why the bombing is not represented in *Slaughterhouse-Five*: there is nothing appropriate or intelligent to say about the bombing of Dresden. As both a catastrophic event and the source of trauma, the bombardment of that city resists witnessing, cognition, integration, and linguistic expression. We lack the adequate words for expressing that air raid. Writing about it is not an easy task. As the extradiegetic narrator of *Slaughterhouse-Five* puts it at the very beginning of the novel,

> I would hate to tell you what this lousy little book cost me in money in anxiety and in time. When I got home from the Second World War twenty-three years ago, I thought it would be easy for me to write about the destruction of Dresden, since all I would have to do would be to report what I had seen ... / But not many words about Dresden came from my mind, anyway. And not many words come now, either. (2)

In part, the difficulty lies in finding the right strategies to narrate a void that encapsulates the death brought on people and space, as well as the trauma caused to those who survived but *did not really see it*. The solution to this predicament is the language of silence, specifically the representation of the void of trauma through the void in the psyche and the void of form. The inexpressibility of the bombing relates to the unsayability of trauma. *Slaughterhouse-Five* formally duplicates the structure of trauma, for it builds upon a void by means of excluding from memory and narrative

discourse the representation of the core event of the traumatic experience –
aerial bombing.

In *Leben für Leben* (1987) a character named Michael Simrock asks
himself, apropos of the bombing of Dresden, a question that many people
have kept asking ever since: "Why?"[103] This collapse of meaning derives
from the overwhelming character of the bombing as well as the lack of a
sound justification for targeting Dresden, and it indirectly refers to a
fundamental element in the experience of trauma. The Allied air raids
on Hamburg and Dresden in the novels analyzed above are clearly perceived as potentially traumatic events because they may damage the mental
mechanisms used for the cognition, storage, and linguistic representation
of reality. As we have seen, the answer given by some novelists to the
double challenge of representing the act of bombing as well as its psychological effect on people consists precisely of voiding the traumatic catastrophic event in the mind of specific characters and in the narrative
discourse. In these narratives there is a crucial dialogue between silence
and remembrance that reproduces the structure of trauma. At the same
time, the novels explored in this section are also manifestations of the not-
writing that characterizes, according to Kate McLoughlin, much war
literature, particularly those works that try to capture the resistance of
warfare to representation.[104] In these novels, not-writing emerges as the
recognition that the condition of possibility for writing – absolute war – is
in itself narrative-resistant. The void is a way of tackling this difficulty.

The narrative embedding of the void and the difficulty of truly bearing
witness to the catastrophic event needs to be understood, too, vis-à-vis
language and the generic conventions of the novel. For the void is not only
a narrative correlate of trauma, or a literary device characteristic of not-
writing. It is also a shaping force, a pivotal element that disrupts at once
language and narrative form by emptying them out of all positivity. As
Robert Martin Adams has noted in his book on nothingness in nineteenth-
century literature, the void is much more than a mere theme or literary
device: "by its positioning in the scale of experiential values, it has sooner
or later an influence on all the other elements in the literary register."[105] In
truth, it is a symptom of a failure, in the sense that negativity is predicated
on language's inability to give an account of the destruction caused by the
bombs. Considering the novels explored here, not even catastrophic

---

[103] Panitz, *Leben für Leben*, 159.   [104] McLoughlin, *Authoring War*, 135–63.
[105] Robert Martin Adams, *Nil: Episodes in the Literary Conquest of Void during the Nineteenth Century*
(Oxford University Press, 1966), 242.

modernist works seem capable of fully capturing the horrific violence unleashed by absolute war without acknowledging the failure of the word by inserting, within their texture, language's double – silence. In order to let the unsayable speak, the novelists introduced in their fictions a radical device – the principle of negativity – that greatly contributed to their formal implosion. "What allows the unsayable to speak," Sanford Budick and Wolfgang Iser have written, "is the undoing of the spoken through negativity. Since the spoken is doubled by what remains silent, undoing the spoken gives voice to the inherent silence"; the unsayable, they add, "can only speak for itself."[106] In key passages from the two novels explored earlier, the language of silence replaces the written word, thereby introducing in the text a vanishing point. A no man's land that exceeds the boundaries of any literary practice, the narrative void may be viewed as an extraterritoriality, as a "beyond" of sorts that decisively determines the grammar and meaning of the entire work.

In the fiction on the strategic bombing of Germany, negativity relates *formally* to the terror triggered by the bombers. Bombing civilians is an instance of "horrorism," a notion that describes a mode of inordinate violence grounded on the massacre of helpless victims and the disfiguration and dismemberment of the human body.[107] Despite their voiding of the destruction of urban space and human bodies, the novels commented on previously could not escape from being themselves casualties of horrorism: formally speaking, they have been broken up, emptied out, destructured, "dismembered," traumatized as it were, by the very catastrophe circumvented by the narrator. The experimentation with form, style, imagery, and language in the novels by Fichte and Vonnegut textually refracts the effects on space and people of the horrific violence that those authors chose to void. The horror and terror of absolute war voided through ellipses, indexical signs, and circumlocutions re-emerge with a vengeance in the novelistic form itself. They reappear as the psychological splitting and the dissolution of the characters' identity; the disruption of normative syntax (particularly present in Fichte's *Detlevs Imitationen "Grünspan"*); the abandonment of straightforward storytelling and linear chronology; the breaking up of the plot; narrative unreliability; and most interestingly, the fragmentation of literary discourse through the proliferation of embedded

---

[106] Sanford Budick and Wolfgang Iser, "Introduction," *Languages of the Unsayable: The Play of Negativity in Literature and Literary Theory*, ed. Sanford Budick and Wolfgang Iser (Stanford University Press, 1987), xvii, xix.

[107] "Horrorism" is a term developed by Adriana Cavarero in her book *Horrorism: Naming Contemporary Violence*, trans. William McCuaig (New York: Columbia University Press, 2009).

intertexts. In sum: the voided catastrophic event leads to the destruction of representation.

The void does not merely represent here, I would like to add, a pure negativity. Like the one inscribed in the traumatized mind, the narrative void embedded in the novels is indeed an empty space. Its boundaries, however, simultaneously separate *and* connect silence and language, forgetting and memory, traumatic absences and liberating presences. The novels considered in this section bring out this essential aspect of the void. By making the void conspicuous, the novelists highlight the unbearable violence and the unspeakable horror of absolute war as manifested in air raids, thereby directing our gaze straight to the core of the problem and forcing on us the production of an interpretation on the meaning of such a void. Thanks to their skillful voiding of the catastrophic traumatic event, the novels by Fichte and Vonnegut *reshape* our reading experience and demand from us the deployment of a patient hermeneutics of negativity. By so doing, they teach readers the language of silence, encouraging them to penetrate into the ostensible representation of the void. Readers are asked to fill in the gaps, to mentally add words in order to make up for those purposely left unsaid by the author – a readerly operation that has decisive consequences, for in the reader's reconstruction of the voided traumatic event one moves from an empty space, that is to say from the void of not-writing, to a space now populated with figures, actions, emotions, and words. In the same way that the narrative void mirrors the psychic void caused by a traumatic event, that crucial alteration in the order of the play between absences and presences (what was absent before is now partly present thanks to the reader's hermeneutic activity) is somewhat reminiscent of the "restorative power of truth-telling" in people suffering from a post-traumatic stress disorder:[108] for them, a narrative account of the traumatic event may recover the contents and emotions that up to then had been painfully inscribed in their minds as a negativity.[109] In other words: the articulation of a void within a narrative first, and the readers' filling in the gaps later, mirror the healing process, through the reconstruction of the story of the traumatic event, in traumatized people. Moreover, it signals a way for overcoming the epistemic, linguistic, and literary problems which often arise when someone attempts to represent multidimensional catastrophic events

---

[108] Judith Herman, *Trauma and Recovery: The Aftermath of Violence – From Domestic Abuse to Political Terror* (New York: Basic Books, 1997), 181.

[109] On the potentially therapeutic power of narrative for people suffering from trauma, see Herman, *Trauma and Recovery*, 176–95.

such as the massive aerial bombing of helpless civilians. The very act of embedding the void within a narrative contains the seeds of a liberating power. When it is articulated through a narrative, the language of silence may end up bringing understanding (as it may happen to readers who have applied a hermeneutics of silence in their reading of the novels analyzed above) and recovery (as it may be the case for traumatized patients under professional treatment). The extreme epistemic impasse and the trauma derived from absolute war do not necessarily have the last word, after all.

Atomic Bombing and the Imperative to Tell

To a certain extent, the bombings of Dresden, Hamburg, London, or Coventry were not unprecedented – their scale was. As already said, the first aerial bombardments were conducted by the Italians on enemy troops in the Italo-Ottoman War of 1911–12, while the bombing of civilians was first carried out during the First World War, and later in the 1920s in "low-intensity" colonial conflicts against local populations in the Middle East and Africa. The public familiarized itself with the potential horrors of strategic bombing with literary works produced from the 1910s onwards. As Paul K. Saint-Amour has demonstrated in *Tense Future*, between 1918 and 1939 in Europe many people lived with the fear that a new war would soon break out.[110] In the years between the two world wars Europeans became well aware of the dangers posed by military aviation on urban centers, and some governments even produced regulations on aerial defense and trained the population for possible massive air attacks. The air raids on Shanghai, Guernica, and Barcelona in the 1930s, as morally repulsive as they were, simply confirmed some of the predictions expressed by military strategists, politicians, journalists, and novelists, as well as the fears felt by many citizens at the time.[111]

Nothing of the sort can be said of the atomic bombings of Hiroshima and Nagasaki.[112] To be sure, some writers had already imagined the use of an atomic weapon. The term "atomic bomb" was coined by H. G. Wells

[110] Paul K. Saint-Amour, *Tense Future: Modernism, Total War, Encyclopedic Form* (New York: Oxford University Press, 2015).
[111] For a cultural approach to the social fears felt in Great Britain and the United States in that period, see Joanna Bourke, *Fear: A Cultural History* (Emeryville, CA: Shoemaker & Hoard, 2006), 167–88.
[112] For an excellent account, see Paul Ham, *Hiroshima Nagasaki: The Real Story of the Atomic Bombings and Their Aftermath* (New York: Picador, 2014). Robert Jay Lifton's *Death in Life* is still the best work on the psychological and physical effects of the atomic bomb on the *hibakusha* (literally "explosion-affected people"), or atomic-bomb surviving victims.

in his 1914 novel *The World Set Free*. Furthermore, before the Americans dropped the bomb many people in Hiroshima experienced the anticipatory thought that Hiroshima had been spared by the Americans because the enemy had planned something really sinister for that city. But nobody was prepared, with the exception perhaps of the scientists involved in the Manhattan Project, for the unspeakable horror unleashed on August 6 and 9 on those two Japanese cities. The completely unusual charge and functioning of the bombs, the magnitude of the destruction, the huge number of casualties, the fact that so many people died instantaneously, the uncanny events triggered by the blast (e.g., black rain), the scenes of sheer horror witnessed by the survivors, and the deadly effects of radiation on many *hibakusha* (survivors of the atomic bomb) still have, more than seventy years later, a haunting, arresting power. A clear instance of absolute war predicated on absolute enmity, an act of terrorism[113] that by November 1945 had killed 130,000 people in Hiroshima and between 60,000 and 70,000 people in Nagasaki,[114] the atomic bombing of those urban centers poses, as happens with other manifestations of absolute war, radical challenges to language, epistemology, and ethics. In addition to killing and injuring thousands of people, the blast of the atomic weapons was experienced by many *hibakusha* as an event that defied the ability of consciousness to understand, integrate, and express it.[115] A significant number of those who have attempted to write about it have felt the insufficiency of language to represent the catastrophic event. Writing about the atomic attack and its impact has been seen by some as what one may call *impossible writing*. From this angle, the conclusion would be that there are no words for describing an atomic bombing. At the same time, however, silence has not been considered an option. Strikingly, many people have experienced the need to write about the atomic bombing of Hiroshima and Nagasaki. Unlike the Germans, the French, or the Italians, most of whom preferred to forget altogether, for a variety of reasons, the bombing of their respective countries in 1940–45, a high number of victims of the atomic bomb as well as professional writers have felt the imperative to produce written testimonies or literary artifacts on the atomic bombing.[116] In this sense, writing on the atomic bomb is

[113] According to Joanna Bourke, "The Age of Terrorism was heralded by the explosions of 'Little Boy' and 'Fat Man' over the cities of Hiroshima and Nagasaki" (*Fear*, 363).

[114] See AtomicBombMuseum.org, www.atomicbombmuseum.org, 2006, accessed March 13, 2015.

[115] On this score, see Lifton, *Death in Life*.

[116] For a historical overview of *hibakusha* literature, see Stephanie Houston Grey, "Writing Redemption: Trauma and the Authentication of the Moral Order in Hibakusha Literature,"

imperative writing; the atomic holocaust must be put into writing, words must be found, one way or another, to express it. The tension existing within a discourse at once *impossible* and *imperative* articulates key works devoted to the atomic bombing of Hiroshima and Nagasaki.

Complaints about the difficulties inherent in expressing the completely novel events of August 6 and 9, 1945, can be easily spotted. Several *hibakusha* have mentioned their trouble in finding the right words to communicate their experiences. In a compelling testimony gathered in the anthology *Hibakusha: Survivors of Hiroshima and Nagasaki* (1986), Sachiko Masaki points out that "I always find myself in a quandary when I try to talk about my experiences as a victim of the atomic bomb. I want to tell what it was like, but I cannot find the words. How can I possibly make others understand? I tend to give up halfway. Yet now, after so many years have passed, I feel an urgent need to pass on to others what happened."[117] Similar words were expressed by two medical doctors who attended to the wounded after the bomb was dropped. In *The Bells of Nagasaki* (1949), Dr. Takashi Nagai observes that the force of the bomb dropped on Nagasaki was so terrible that "it cannot be expressed in words."[118] In his classic *Hiroshima Diary* (1955), Dr. Michihiko Hachiya gives a more elaborate explanation for the difficulty of expressing the experiences related to the atomic bomb. He starts by underscoring the senselessness of the whole event: "What kind of a bomb was it that had destroyed Hiroshima? What had my visitors told me earlier? Whatever it was, it did not make sense."[119] Moreover, Hachiya continues, the damage done by the bomb was beyond comprehension: "Damage of this order could have no explanation! All we

Text & Performance Quarterly 22.1 (2002), 1–23. On the cultural artifacts devoted to the bombing of Japan, see John Whittier Treat, *Writing Ground Zero: Japanese Literature and the Atomic Bomb* (University of Chicago Press, 1995); Reiko Tachibana, *Narrative as Counter-Memory: A Half-Century of Postwar Writing in Germany and Japan* (Albany, NY: State University of New York Press, 1998); and Akira Mizuta Lippit, *Atomic Light (Shadow Optics)* (Minneapolis, MN: University of Minnesota Press, 2005). See, also, Yoshikuni Igarashi's book *Bodies of Memory: Narratives of War in Postwar Japanese Culture, 1945–1970* (Princeton University Press, 2000) on the tension between remembrance and forgetting in Japanese society after the war. A succinct account of Japanese literature on the Second World War can be found in Reiko Tachibana, "The Japanese War," *The Cambridge Companion to the Literature of World War II*, ed. Marina MacKay (Cambridge University Press, 2009), 137–48.

[117] *Hibakusha: Survivors of Hiroshima and Nagasaki*, trans. Gaynor Sekimori (Tokyo: Kōsei Publishing Co., 1986), 146.

[118] Takashi Nagai, *The Bells of Nagasaki*, trans. William Johnston (Tokyo: Kodansha International, 1994), 64.

[119] Michihiko Hachiya, *Hiroshima Diary: The Journal of a Japanese Physician, August 6–September 30, 1945*, trans. and ed. Warner Wells (Chapel Hill, NC: University of North Carolina Press, 1995), 24.

had were stories no more substantial than the clouds from which we had reached to snatch them."[120] This accumulation of senselessness is at the root of Hachiya's problem with language. He finds himself lacking the proper words for describing the destruction he saw: "I had to revise my meaning of the word *destruction* or choose some other word to describe what I saw. Devastation may be a better word, but really, I know of no word or words to describe the view [of Hiroshima] from my twisted iron bed in the fire-gutted ward of the Communications Hospital."[121]

Novelists and poets who wrote on the atomic bomb faced the difficulties that are consubstantial to expressing an unprecedented extreme event. Theirs was a challenge not unlike the one that survivors of the Nazi genocide of the European Jews had to address when they attempted to put their experience into writing. The preface to the second edition of *City of Corpses*, a non-fictional novel by Yōko Ōta partially published in 1948 that appeared in an unabridged form in 1950, provides a thorough account of those difficulties.[122] She starts by stating that Hiroshima, the "city of death" as she calls it, "makes very difficult subject matter for literature."[123] This is so because "The new methods of description and expression necessary to write cannot be found in the repertoire of an established writer" (148). Without "creating a new terminology," Ōta perceptively writes, she is absolutely unable "to depict the truth" (148). As it is commonly understood and practiced, literature simply lacks the tools for capturing Hiroshima. "Using the writer's pre-existing concept of what constitutes literature," holds Ōta, "I found it difficult to communicate in writing the indescribable fright and terror, the gruesome misery, the numbers of victims and dead, the horrifying conditions of atomic bomb sickness" (148). This difficulty had a lot to do with the uniqueness and the magnitude of the event, as well as with its unspeakable horrors. Ōta again:

> I was a witness when for the first time ever, in one instant, a city of 400,000 people was wiped out by the fires of war ... it was also the first time that thousands, tens of thousands, hundreds of thousands of human beings died in one instant, and I was among the first to walk weeping among corpses lying about, so many that there was hardly place to set one's feet. I was also the first to see the gruesomeness of atomic bomb sickness. (149)

[120] Ibid., 25.   [121] Ibid., 31.
[122] Ōta's predicament vis-à-vis the difficulties concerning representation of the atomic bomb has been studied by John Whittier Treat in "Hiroshima and the Place of the Narrator," *Journal of Asian Studies* 48.1 (1989), 29–49.
[123] Yōko Ōta, *City of Corpses, Hiroshima: Three Witnesses*, trans. and ed. Richard H. Minear (Princeton University Press, 1990), 148. Further references in text.

Under those circumstances, therefore, "anything and everything I was forced to see was new under the sun" (149). Yōko Ōta affirms that remembering Hiroshima is something extremely painful, no doubt on account of the trauma she suffered from it. These are her words: "If I try to write about the Hiroshima of 1945, I am tormented, of course, by the accumulation of memories and of fragments of memories I have collected. I gaze fixedly at these events I have to call up from memory in order to write, and I become ill; I become nauseated" (150). Expressing worries similar to those stated by survivors of Nazi *Lager*, Ōta lived with the torturing fear that most of her readers would not believe her story (149). Furthermore, the atomic bombing of Hiroshima severely crippled her ability to produce literature on other matters. She tried to write books unrelated to the atomic bomb, "But the image of my hometown Hiroshima branded onto my mind drove away the vision of other works" (150).

The seeming impossibility of writing on the atomic bomb was counteracted and ultimately overcome by the imperative ethical drive of writers like Yōko Ōta herself. Simply put, writers felt a sense of responsibility towards the victims as well as the need, grounded on ethical and political imperatives, to tell the world what really happened in Hiroshima and Nagasaki. This is most certainly the case with the poet Tamiki Hara. After narrating his first impressions of the destruction brought on Hiroshima in his autobiographical novel *Summer Flowers* (1949), the narrator writes: "I thought to myself: I must set these things down in writing."[124] This sense of a literary *and* an ethical obligation is clearly addressed by Yōko Ōta in the aforementioned preface to the second edition of *City of Corpses*. Ōta believed that she had a moral responsibility to fulfill. The conditions under which she wrote made the process an agonizing one: "Death was breathing down my neck. If I was to die, I wanted first to fulfill my responsibility of getting the story written down" (147). Feeling that she could be suffering from a radiation-related illness, but led all the time by a simultaneous literary and ethical force, Ōta wrote around the clock in order to make sure that she would put everything in writing before she died. This imperative to write, this pressing urgency, at once literary and ethical, to write on the atomic bombing and its impact on ecology, urban space, and human life, made writing all the more difficult. Reflections on this sense of mission are interspersed throughout the book. In one scene from *City of Corpses* the narrator confirms her sister's observation that indeed she is

---

[124] Tamiki Hara, *Summer Flowers, Hiroshima: Three Witnesses*, trans. and ed. Richard H. Minear (Princeton University Press, 1990), 49.

gazing at the corpses lying on the streets of Hiroshima: "I'm looking with two sets of eyes – the eyes of a human being and the eyes of a writer" (205). Asked if she can write (in her sister's words) "about something like this," the narrator's answer condenses what Ōta wrote in the preface to the novel: "Someday I'll have to. That's the responsibility of a writer who's seen it" (205). In yet another passage the narrator spells out the political component of her ethical drive: "We have now reached a revolutionary moment in this human tragedy in which progress comes only through destruction. The only road to peace is to make progress without destruction. I hope this defeat contributes to making Japan truly peaceful. This is why, in the midst of all the suffering, I am writing this book" (254).

The tension between the *impossibility* of describing the power of the bomb and its effects on space and people on the one hand, and the *imperative* to write about it on the other, led writers to search for literary devices that could capture the two sides of the problem. An examination of the so-called A-bomb literature reveals that a significant number of authors came up with the same technical solution for conveying at once the impossibility of writing and the imperative to write: the iteration of the act of *talking about it.* This is generally achieved by two different means. One consists of the embedding of intradiegetic-homodiegetic narrators who talk about their experiences relating to the atomic bomb. The other is the use of what the theorists of narrative have called internal focalization. The almost obsessive iteration of the act of talking about the impact of the atomic bomb on people's bodies and lives refracts the literary, existential, and ethical imperative to tell what happened on August 6 and 9 in Hiroshima and Nagasaki, respectively.

Multiple or variable internal focalization on the one hand, and embedded intradiegetic-homodiegetic narrators on the other, are two pivotal literary techniques that criss-cross fictional and non-fictional accounts alike. Take, for instance, Dr. Michihiko Hachiya's *Hiroshima Diary.* Formally the journal kept by Hachiya from August 6 to September 30, 1945, this remarkable work includes not only information relating to the experiences of the author; it also contains reported and direct testimonies of other people. Thus, Hachiya reproduces or summarizes the accounts of other people on their experience of the atomic bombing. Dr. Nishimura, Dr. Tabuchi, Mr. Katsutani, and Mr. Hashimoto narrate stories about what they did and saw on August 6, 1945, thereby becoming occasional narrative voices of Hachiya's diary.[125] The insertion of these voices in

---

[125] Hachiya, *Hiroshima Diary*, 12–13, 13–15, 15–18, and 161–64, respectively.

Hiroshima Diary creates a fascinating kaleidoscopic effect. Hachiya's interest in other people's experiences partly stems from his wish to understand an event seemingly beyond understanding and representation. Listening to his patients' and colleagues' stories helps him to get a better picture of what Hiroshima is like, or, in Hachiya's own words, to see a "pattern."[126] Finding the "pattern," namely the structure of the event, is something connected, first of all, to Hachiya's job, that is, the cure of the wounded, and secondly, to his task as a writer. Hachiya strives to understand both the mysterious illnesses and wounds of his patients as of August 6 and the nature of the event itself. Thus, he pays close attention to patterns in the evolution of these illnesses and wounds, as well as in the phenomena that occurred as a result of the atomic blast and radiation. By so doing, he may be able to cure his patients *and* understand the event. Put differently: through careful observation and experimentation, by means of applying a clinical gaze, Hachiya aims to make sense of the situation. And the way he chooses to achieve understanding perpetuates the voices of people that otherwise might be lost forever. Comprehension and the gathering of testimonies go hand in hand.

Another medical doctor, Takashi Nagai, follows a similar track. In *The Bells of Nagasaki* Nagai narrates the bombing of that city through the eyes of five focalizers.[127] The immediate events that followed the blast are also told through multiple focalizers – nurses, medical students, and doctors who were working in university buildings at the time of the blast.[128] Thus, the atomic explosion and its effects are not told as experienced by the first-person narrator, Takashi Nagai, but through the narrative voice's reporting of the experiences of other people. In the first three chapters of Nagai's memoir, the main function of the extradiegetic narrator lies in connecting a number of focalizers. The extradiegetic narrator does not become the dominant voice and main character until chapter 4, when he and his team of collaborators begin their task of attending to the wounded, first in the buildings of the university, and later, after evacuating the buildings and moving to the outskirts of the city, in nearby towns. Takashi Nagai's other important book, *We of Nagasaki*, is built upon a similar literary technique. Again, this book on Nagasaki follows an ethical imperative. The author provides, in his own words, "one of the few discussions on the moral aftereffects of the bombings by any Japanese since the war."[129] But what

---

[126] Ibid., 20.   [127] Takashi Nagai, *The Bells of Nagasaki*, 6–10.   [128] Ibid., 11–27.
[129] Takashi Nagai, *We of Nagasaki: The Story of Survivors in an Atomic Wasteland*, trans. Ichiro Shirato and Herbert B. L. Silverman (New York: Duell, Sloan and Pearce, 1951), vii.

matters is the fact that Nagai expresses these "moral aftereffects" by lending his voice to nine different individuals. Instead of summarizing their experiences and drawing his own ethical conclusions, the author prefers to be a ghostwriter of sorts. Thus, *We of Nagasaki* has one extradiegetic narrator (Nagai himself) and eight intradiegetic voices. Nagai wanted those eight individuals to tell their story with their own voice, and to that effect he remains in the background for most of the narrative.

The iteration of the act of telling is even more evident in journalistic and novelistic accounts of the atomic bombing of Hiroshima and Nagasaki. I am thinking, for instance, of the famous book-length chronicle by John Hersey, *Hiroshima*, initially published in a single issue of *The New Yorker* in 1946 and shortly afterwards as a book.[130] Hersey's journalistic reportage on the impact of the atomic bomb on the population is not written by an omniscient narrator. Hersey chose to represent it by intertwining six different focalizers: Toshiko Sasaki, Reverend Mr. Tanimoto, Mrs. Hatsuyo Nakamura, Dr. Masakazu Fujii, Father Wilhelm Kleinsorge, and Dr. Terufumi Sasaki. Through this multiple perspective the author of *Hiroshima* creates an illusion of multitude, of a collective, of a shared experience. The catastrophe affected everybody. One way of conveying this fact lies in introducing a community of gazes as a formal element, thereby producing a kaleidoscopic effect that captures the perspectives of some survivors of the atomic explosion. The proliferation of discourse through intradiegetic narrators and/or internal multiple focalizers articulates several Japanese literary works on the atomic bomb. This is the case, for instance, of Hiroyuki Agawa's *Devil's Heritage*. Published in 1957, this novel tells the story of Sankichi Noguchi, a Tokyo-based writer who travels to Hiroshima to gather information in order to produce a chronicle titled "Hiroshima Eight Years After the Atomic Bomb." As part of his research, Sankichi meets with and interviews a number of members of an organization of *hibakusha*, The Willow Club. Instead of summarizing their stories, the narrator prefers to reproduce them verbatim, a choice that effectively interrupts the flow of his narrative: the different testimonies take up eighty pages of the novel.[131] Likewise, in Yōko Ōta's *City of Corpses* and Tamiki Hara's *Summer Flowers* the first-person narrator intersperses the testimony of several characters on the atomic bombing of their city. The first work, a hybrid of novel and memoir narrated by a first-person narrator who tells about her experiences on August 6 and the days that followed, includes

[130] John Hersey, *Hiroshima* (New York: Alfred A. Knopf, 1946).
[131] Hiroyuki Agawa, *Devil's Heritage*, trans. John Maki (Tokyo: Hokuseido Press, 1957), 113–93.

narratives of people who suffered from radiation-related sicknesses (244–48). Thus, in addition to the main narrative voice there are other voices and gazes that supplement the narrator's account of her own experiences in Hiroshima. As in the works previously commented on, using a multiple perspective is the main literary device – one that somehow harmonizes the impossibility to tell with the need to talk about it.

Makoto Oda's *H: A Hiroshima Novel* (1981) recounts the explosion of the atomic bomb twice. This novel's perspectivism consists of presenting two consecutive events (the blast and its immediate aftermath) through different focalizers. In the first instance, the blast is seen and experienced by medical personnel and patients from a hospital.[132] The second representation of the blast contains also a narrative about its aftermath, but it takes a very different point of view: an imprisoned American airman, who is taken blindfolded to the courtyard of the prison to exercise shortly before the bomb goes off. Unlike the nurse, her colleagues, and the patients from the hospital, this character does not *see* the explosion. In contrast to them, the American airman does experience the immediate aftermath. The force of the blast takes off the piece of cloth that covers his eyes. Thus, the bomb is paradoxically the condition of possibility for this character's freedom and perspective. By taking off the cloth that covers the airman's eyes, the bomb helps him to see and experience Hiroshima after being bombed. The narrator relates through a writing of cruelty what his character sees: "Beneath the flames the dark and silent earth lay exposed. Endless mounds of rubble were scattered over it. Here and there were black piles – scorched corpses. Some were white bones. As he struggled to take it all in, the flames roared up in a whirlwind, sweeping up the rubble, iron, glass and brick, the black piles and the white bones, into the black sky, then pelting them down mercilessly all around him."[133] In the end, the airman is lynched by Japanese survivors who, realizing that he is an American, move towards him and literally throw themselves upon him, thereby suffocating the enemy airman.[134]

The highpoint of this proliferation of discourse on the atomic bomb is Masuji Ibuse's novel *Black Rain* (1965).[135] The imperative to tell is the

[132] Makoto Oda, *H: A Hiroshima Novel*, trans. D. H. Whittaker (Tokyo: Kodansha International, 1990), 168.

[133] Ibid., 173.   [134] Ibid., 175–76.

[135] On *Black Rain*, see John T. Dorsey, "The Theme of Survival in John Hersey's *Hiroshima* and Ibuse Masuji's *Black Rain*," *Tamkang Review: A Quarterly of Comparative Studies between Chinese and Foreign Literatures* 14.1–4 (1983), 85–100; Antonín Líman, *Ibuse Masuji: A Century Remembered* (Prague: Karolinum, 2008), 349–408; Peter Messent, "Memoirs of a Survivor:

driving force of this masterpiece of A-bomb literature. A novel whose story
is told by several narrators, *Black Rain* is a deliberate reminder of the
atomic bombing, of its consequences, of its immorality. The imperative to
tell underpinning the entire novel is tacitly mentioned in an intervention
of a secondary character, Shōkichi, who complains about the fact that
"The people at Ikemoto's have forgotten that Hiroshima and Nagasaki
were atom-bombed. Everybody's forgotten! Forgotten the hellfires we
went through that day – forgotten them and everything else."[136] Ibuse
takes up his novel with the purpose of reminding everybody what happened on August 6, 1945, and the days that followed, and he does so by
elaborating a complex web of intertwining narratives.

Black Rain revolves around Shigematsu Shizuma – the owner of a small
hatchery business who during the war worked as an employee of the Japan
Textile Company – , his wife Shigeko, and their niece Yasuko Takamaru.
Its main story starts four years and nine months after the end of the war,
and it takes place in Kobatake, a village located 160 kilometers east of
Hiroshima. Aware that for several years "no suitable marriage was in sight"
for Yasuko due to the widely spread rumor that "she was a victim of
radiation sickness" (9), Shigematsu decides to set the record straight and
demonstrate in writing that Yasuko was safely far-away from ground zero
when the bomb went off. The first measure he takes is to copy "the
relevant parts" of Yasuko's own diary, starting with the entry for August
5, 1945. Shigematsu's goal is to pass on this edited version of Yasuko's
journal to the go-between, so that she and potential suitors will conclude
that indeed Yasuko was not exposed to radiation. But Shigematsu, who
copies selected passages until the entry of August 9, realizes that although
Yasuko was not in Hiroshima when the atomic bomb went off, she was
nonetheless exposed to black rain (34–35). This poses an editorial and
moral dilemma: whether to copy those passages or leave them out. Shigematsu's wife, Shigeko, is afraid that if they include the passages people
might get "the wrong idea" (33). Shigematsu puts off the final decision on
this possible editing, and while he thinks about how to proceed, he begins
to feel "like showing the go-between his own account of the same period,
from his own journal, so that they realize the difference" between Yasuko's
and Shigematsu's experiences on August 6 (35–36). The reason is simple:

Masuji Ibuse's *Black Rain*," *Foreign Literature Studies/Wai Guo Wen Xue Yan Jiu* 2.112 (2005),
128–32; John Whittier Treat, *Pools of Water, Pillars of Fire: The Literature of Ibuse Masuji* (Seattle,
WA: University of Washington Press, 1988), and his *Writing Ground Zero*, 261–99.
[136] Masuji Ibuse, *Black Rain*, trans. John Bester (New York: Kodansha International, 2012), 29–30.
Further references in text.

while Yasuko "must have been more than ten kilometers from the center of the blast" (35), Shigematsu was in Hiroshima when the bomb detonated. He immediately proceeds to rewrite his own account of the bombing with the idea not only of adding it, as an appendix, to Yasuko's diary, but also of giving it to the Primary School Library "for its reference" (36); he claims that "This diary of the bombing is my piece of history, to be preserved in the school library" (36). The imperative to tell is in essence a historical imperative: people must never forget what happened in Hiroshima. Later on, Shigematsu will tell his wife that the school's headmaster had actually asked him to present to the library his journal, and he insists that "It's my piece of history" (40). Shigematsu starts copying the entry from August 6 (36–39), interrupts his activity, and continues later (44–58). All these pages are devoted to the day of the bombing, and they establish a contrast with the text written by Yasuko on the same day. By putting the two journals together, Shigematsu means to demonstrate that he was far more exposed to radiation, and yet he is healthy – that is the implied message. Therefore, suitors should feel more at ease with his niece and take her as a bride. Talking with his wife, Shigematsu comes up with the following idea: that Shigeko should "jot down some notes about our family's meals during the war" (62), which would be included in his "Journal of the Bombing." Shigeko agrees, and she starts writing an account titled "Diet in Wartime Hiroshima" (63–71). This will be, therefore, an appendix to the appendix. After that, Shigematsu resumes the copying of his journal (76–84, 86–100, 101–25, 127–38, 139–219). Noticeably, there are embedded stories within the embedded text: Shigematsu recalls a scene in which he, his wife, and their niece were in a train that had to take them away from Hiroshima (113–16). At some point, other passengers began to tell their experiences of the atomic bomb. Shigematsu, the intradiegetic narrator, reproduces these stories (116–25).

Shigematsu modifies his tactics a bit when Yasuko starts to develop symptoms of radiation-related illness (219). Ongoing talks of marriage with the family of a young man are suddenly broken off. From now on Shigematsu and his wife's efforts will be addressed at curing their niece. Shigeko, who nurses her niece, decides, without telling her, to "keep a daily record of the progress of the disease" (224). Concerned for his niece's health, Shigematsu suggests to the doctor the reading of the diary on Yasuko's illness (225). The "Diary of the Illness of Yasuko Takamaru" (226–33) was written by her aunt Shigeko, and copied down by Shigematsu, "altering the style to suit his own taste wherever he felt like it" (226). The doctor reads this diary, thereby becoming a textual refraction of the reader of the novel. Later Shigematsu and his wife receive from Dr. Hosokawa a manuscript titled "Notes on the Bombing of Hiroshima by Hiroshi Iwakate, Medical Reserve." Iwakate is Hosokawa's brother-in-law. In the accompanying letter, Hosokawa writes that "One of my reasons for doing this is to escape the charge, as a doctor, of having refused to treat a patient. Another is the hope that you will perceive how essential for the patient is the determination to fight the sickness. It also shows, I might add, that one should never despair of a miraculous recovery even in the most gravely ill" (236–37). Here Shigematsu becomes a reader. He realizes that "Iwakate had been far more seriously hurt than Shigematsu. His body had shrunk to a mass of skin and bones, his fingers had fused together, and maggots had eaten away one of his earlobes. Yet he had come through. Plastic surgery had even restored his fingers to normal. Today, he was working as a general practitioner" (237). This text is reproduced on pages 237–55 and 268–70, but Ibuse alters here his technique: he alternates literal reproductions of the text (237–40, 242–45, 247–48, 252–55, 268–70) with summaries by the extradiegetic narrator focalized through Shigematsu (240–42, 245–47, 249–51). Along with Iwakate's account "came a record of Mrs. Iwakate's recollections of the same period" (255). This text is also reproduced (255–66), for "It promised to be useful for reference in treating Yasuko" (255). After these additional texts, Shigematsu returns to the transcription of his diary (273–300). It ends with the entry from August 15, that is, with the date of the Emperor's broadcast announcement of Japan's unconditional surrender.

The texts on the atomic bomb that I have examined in this section are driven by ethical concerns. For Hachiya, Nagai, Ōta, Hara, Ibuse, and other writers, showing the death and misery caused by the bomb was above all an ethical duty: they intimately sensed the need to bear witness for the sake of the victims and also for the benefit of the world, whose very existence has been endangered, as those authors point out or suggest, by the invention of the atomic bomb and the ensuing proliferation of nuclear weapons. In addition to this ethical drive, the multiple narration of the events and experiences determined by the atomic bomb may be seen as functioning as a coping mechanism to overcome trauma: as has been repeatedly noted by medical practitioners, telling the story of the traumatic event may be a therapeutic tool. Furthermore, the multiplication of voices and focalizers is a homage to the victims; it is a mourning of those who, due to their instantaneous death, could not be properly mourned. Finally, such a remarkable proliferation of discourse through the dissemination of voices and the overlapping of gazes seems to be meant to counteract the loss of life and the destruction of cultural memory. It is a celebration of something intrinsically human: language. The intertwining of stories builds up a community of voices, reflecting in the process the communal aspect of language.[137] In their ethical thrust and in their celebration of the human voice and gaze, the literary and journalistic works on the atomic bomb, as well as the memoirs, diaries, and testimonial texts written about it, make explicit something crucial that is implied in many narratives on strategic bombing explored earlier in this chapter. While they represent an extreme case of absolute war, their proliferation of discourse is life-affirming. Writing on the atomic bomb, as John T. Dorsey has under-scored, "is an affirmation in an age when man's destructive capacity ... threatens to exterminate the creature who imagines."[138] The imperative to tell represents a reparation of sorts. It brings back what had been obliterated by the bombs: all things human.

---

[137] In section 18 of his *Philosophical Investigations* (trans. G. E. M. Anscombe, 2nd ed. [Oxford: Blackwell Publishers, 1997]), Ludwig Wittgenstein famously compared language to the human community par excellence: the city.

[138] Dorsey, "The Theme of Survival in John Hersey's *Hiroshima* and Ibuse Masuji's *Black Rain*," 85.

CHAPTER THREE

Specters

A Hauntology of War

On April 11, 1945, a detachment of troops from the 6th Armored Division of General Patton's Third Army liberated Buchenwald. Among the 21,000 surviving camp inmates there was a young Spanish university student destined to become, years later, a prominent intellectual figure in France: Jorge Semprun. A member of the French Resistance who was deported to Buchenwald after being arrested and tortured by the Gestapo in 1943, Semprun evokes in *L'écriture ou la vie* (Literature or Life) (1994) his troubling encounter, the day the camp was liberated, with three Allied officers in British uniform. "They stand amazed before me," he recalls at the beginning of the book, "and suddenly, in that terror-stricken gaze, I see myself – in their horror."[1] Looking into the eyes of those officers, he realizes that their terrified gaze mirrors in fact the horror stamped on his own by the unspeakable life conditions at the *Lager*.[2] Semprun wonders, reflecting on this game of gazes mirroring each other, whether he had really survived Buchenwald; perhaps he had not, after all: "I am struck by the idea ... that I have not escaped death, but passed through it. That I have come back from it the way you return from a voyage that has transformed and – perhaps – transfigured you."[3] As he puts it elsewhere in the book, in Buchenwald he and the other camp inmates did not just escape death, they had "lived it."[4] Following the logic of these thoughts, Semprun concludes that he is a ghost;[5] likewise, the liberated inmates are not survivors, "but ghosts, revenants."[6] A belief deeply connected to that spectrality, Semprun was convinced that his being-in-the-world had been irrevocably transformed. After Buchenwald there would be no real homecoming because the notion of "home" had lost all meaning. A living dead, he

---

[1] Jorge Semprun, *Literature or Life*, trans. Linda Coverdale (New York: Penguin, 1997), 3.
[2] Ibid., 4.   [3] Ibid., 14–15.   [4] Ibid., 88.   [5] Ibid., 15.   [6] Ibid., 88.

writes: "Sometimes I felt certain that there hadn't really been any return, that I hadn't really come back, that an essential part of me would never come back, and this certainly upset my connection with the world, with my own life."[7]

Jorge Semprun memorably elaborated on a condition – the camp survivor's spectrality – that is also characteristic of many, if not all, war veterans. War is a life-changing event that routinely injures the body, the mind, and the moral sense of soldiers.[8] Troops die or are seriously wounded even in favorable circumstances. Soldiers are expected to perform what in civilian society is morally repugnant and legally prosecuted – wounding, killing, laying waste to conditions that make the world livable; their duties consist often of doing things that radically contravene their most profoundly seated ethical convictions. Furthermore, they may feel betrayed by their superiors, used by politicians, or misunderstood by civilians. Feelings of remorse, grief, shame, meaninglessness, and resentment, as well as self-loathing, loss of trust in people, and a general sense of alienation are the lot of many veterans. A high number of former combatants are haunted by the horrors they have lived through and by memories of the dead – of the men they have killed, of the comrades they have seen die. Once reintegrated into civilian society, veterans constitute haunting legacies; they are traces of political decisions that led to lethal action, traces of a world ruled by a logic of its own, traces of abjection, of horror. Spectrality is a traveling companion of combatants.

The "greatest man-made disaster in history," in Antony Beevor's authoritative words,[9] the Second World War set up the condition of possibility for the production of spectrality on an enormous scale. The horrific situations unleashed by absolute war on the eastern front, in Southeast Asia, and the Pacific; the absolute enmity that crucially determined, in some theaters of war, the treatment of civilians, partisans, and

---

[7] Ibid., 115.

[8] Like other scholars, I differentiate between "moral injury" and "psychological wound." While the latter is generally related, in the context of combatants, to a mental disorder, the former refers to "experiences of serious inner conflict arising from what one takes to be grievous moral transgressions that can overwhelm one's sense of goodness and humanity" (Nancy Sherman, *Afterwar: Healing the Moral Wounds of Our Soldiers* [New York: Oxford University Press, 2015], 8). For other approaches to the moral wounds of soldiers, see Rita Nakashima Brock and Gabriella Lettini, *Soul Repair: Recovering from Moral Injury after War* (Boston, MA: Beacon Press, 2012); Robert E. Meagher, *Killing from the Inside Out: Moral Injury and Just War* (Eugene, OR: Cascade Books, 2014); and David Wood, *What Have We Done: The Moral Injury of Our Longest Wars* (New York: Little, Brown and Company, 2016). On grieving after war, see Janis P. Stout, *Coming Out of War: Poetry, Grieving and the Culture of the World Wars* (Tuscaloosa, AL: University of Alabama Press, 2005).

[9] Antony Beevor, *The Second World War* (New York: Back Bay Books, 2012), 781.

wounded enemies; the indiscriminate aerial bombing of urban centers; the captivity endured by more than 30 million prisoners of war in Europe, the United States, and Asia;[10] the Nazi extermination of homosexuals, the Roma people, the mentally ill or handicapped, and the European Jews; in short, the witnessing and/or perpetration of all kinds of atrocities and war crimes – all this must have left an indelible mark on the psyche, behavior, and moral sense of countless veterans and survivors of the world war of 1939–45. More than ever in the history of warfare, the experience of war, absolute enmity, and death in the war zone was a transforming one. Many veterans, particularly those who had fought in an absolute war, had not really survived death: they had lived it, they had gone through it, they had internalized it as a paradoxical *modus vivendi*.[11] For this reason, these veterans ought to be considered as specters of sorts, as revenants returning from the kingdom of the dead. Veterans may display, in fact, what could be denominated as a *double spectrality*. First, many are haunted, as already said, by combat and the specters of those who died in battle or in war-related activities. Testimonies of former soldiers haunted by deaths and mutilation in the battlefield are legion. These veterans may be viewed as *possessed* by the ghosts of war. Second, haunted veterans may also be viewed as specters themselves, as ghostly entities whose experience of killing, wounding, and destruction is likely to haunt civilians in many different ways; as Rita Nakashima Brock and Gabriella Lettini put it, "War's lingering phantoms haunt every society. In the bodies and souls of those who experience combat, war always comes home to the rest of us."[12] The misgivings felt by some civilians in the wake of the Second World War towards returning soldiers on account of their training in

---

[10] Bob Moore, "Prisoners of War," *The Cambridge History of the Second World War*, ed. John Ferris and Evan Mawdsley, vol. 1/3 (Cambridge University Press, 2015), 664.

[11] On trauma in connection with the Second World War, see, among other works, Omer Bartov, "Trauma and Absence," *European Memories of the Second World War*, ed. Helmut Peitsch, Charles Burdett, and Claire Gorrara (New York: Berghahn Books, 1999), 258–71; Gerd Bayer, "World War II Fiction and the Ethics of Trauma," *Ethics and Trauma in Contemporary British Fiction*, ed. Susana Onega and Jean-Michel Ganteau (Amsterdam: Rodopi, 2011), 155–74; Mary Cosgrove, "Narrating German Suffering in the Shadow of Holocaust Victimology: W. G. Sebald, Contemporary Trauma Theory, and Dieter Forte's Air Raids Epic," *Germans as Victims in the Literary Fiction of the Berlin Republic*, ed. Stuart Taberner and Karina Berger (Rochester, NY: Camden House, 2009), 162–76; Yoshikuni Igarashi, *Bodies of Memory: Narratives of War in Postwar Japanese Culture, 1945–1970* (Princeton University Press, 2000); Helmut Schmitz and Annette Seidel-Arpaci, eds., *Narratives of Trauma: Discourses of German Wartime Suffering in National and International Perspective* (Amsterdam: Rodopi, 2011); and Lyndsey Stonebridge, "Theories of Trauma," *The Cambridge Companion to the Literature of World War II*, ed. Marina MacKay (Cambridge University Press, 2009), 194–206.

[12] Brock and Lettini, *Soul Repair*, xvii.

violence, their supposedly dissolute habits when on furlough, and their expertise at killing people bespeaks the civilians' intuitive perception of the potential perils lurking in the veterans' spectral condition.[13] By definition, revenants are threatening entities, for they return from the grave – so it is believed – to torment the living. It is only logical, therefore, that civilians perceived veterans with apprehension, if not with open hostility, once the initial welcoming enthusiasm waned.

Following in part a theoretical tradition that stems from Jacques Derrida's groundbreaking book on the specters of Marx, with the notion of specter I am referring to an unstable liminal entity that is neither alive nor dead, neither present nor absent, neither completely vocal nor totally silent.[14] Specters are social figures embedded in multifarious ways within the social fabric. They have a paradoxical phenomenality that distinguishes them from spirits. According to Derrida, with specters we have, on the one hand, "the furtive and ungraspable visibility of the invisible or an invisibility of a visible X," while on the other hand we have "the tangible intangibility of a proper body without flesh, but still the body of some*one* as some*one other*."[15] The definition of *specter* is, therefore, twofold: a specter is the phenomenal body of the spirit as well as "the impatient and nostalgic waiting for a redemption."[16] In Derrida's reading of spectrality, ghosts are the victims of history who come back in order to demand reparation and justice; they are the traces of those who have not been allowed to leave a trace. The 30,000 *desaparecidos* or "missing" in Argentina during the "dirty war" conducted by a military junta in 1976–83, the 120,000 people murdered by the Francoists during the Spanish Civil War (1936–39) and its immediate aftermath, and the almost half a million Germans who died as the result of the Allied aerial bombing of their country in 1940–45, all fall within the logic of the specter: killed and repressed from memory for a variety of reasons, they have returned in specific historical moments to haunt the living so as to demand their due.

[13] Alan Allport, *Demobbed: Coming Home after the Second World War* (New Haven, CT: Yale University Press, 2009), 6–7, 11–12; Thomas Childers, *Soldier from the War Returning: The Greatest Generation's Troubled Homecoming from World War II* (Boston, MA: Mariner Books, 2009), 129–32, 211, 215–16.

[14] On specters and spectrality, see Giorgio Agamben, *Nudities*, trans. David Kishik and Stefan Pedatella (Stanford University Press, 2011), 37–42; Jacques Derrida, *Specters of Marx: The State of the Debt, the Work of Mourning and the New International*, trans. Peggy Kamuf (London: Routledge, 1994); Avery F. Gordon, *Ghostly Matters: Haunting and the Sociological Imagination* (Minneapolis, MN: University of Minnesota Press, 2008); and Michael Sprinker, ed., *Ghostly Demarcations: A Symposium on Jacques Derrida's Specters of Marx* (London: Verso, 1999).

[15] Derrida, *Specters of Marx*, 6.   [16] Ibid., 169–70.

Derrida insists that ghosts are not psychic projections, but the persistent traces of a repressed past; the specter, therefore, refers to the ways in which what has been repressed lives on in our present.

Now, ghosts are not only a possible phenomenality of spirits. They can also arise out of the living. In this chapter I slightly depart from Derrida's theory in the sense that, while his notion of specter is predicated on someone's physical death, in the next sections I will also consider as specters individuals who have been decisively traversed and transfigured by the experience of death in an absolute war. Obviously, a specter always relates to a death, but this death is not necessarily the death of the body – it can perfectly well be the death of the soul. Take, for instance, Hans Werner Richter's 1949 novel *Die Geschlagenen* (The Defeated). Under intense American fire, the main character, Gühler, muses to himself: "We don't have any feeling left within ourselves, we are already dead, before we die."[17] Or take Philip Roth's *The Human Stain* (2000), a novel set in New England that depicts, among other characters, a Vietnam combat-crazed veteran, Lester Farley, as a man whose feelings are completely numbed because in some way he is already dead. He goes over "all the times I think I died. That's how I began to know that I can't die. Because I died already. Because I died already in Vietnam. Because I am a man who fucking *died*."[18] Or else think of Brian Castner's *The Long Walk* (2012), a novelized memoir based on the author's experience as the head of an Explosive Ordnance Disposal unit of the US Air Force in the Iraq War (2003–11). Haunted by his traumatic experiences in the war, the narrator and main character has no doubts as regards his hauntological structure: "I died in Iraq. The old me left for Iraq and never came back home. The man my wife married never came home. The father of my oldest three children never came home. If I didn't die, I don't know what else to call it."[19] In the last three quoted passages, Richter, Roth, and Castner describe the spectral nature of their respective characters. The experience of death in combat literally transfigured the three of them, and in the process, they became specters, living dead doomed to haunt the people who surround them back home.

Specters have a social, historical, and political import. Avery F. Gordon has demonstrated that a specter is not the invisible. "The ghost," she

[17] Hans Werner Richter, *Die Geschlagenen* (Munich: Deutscher Taschenbuch Verlag, 1969), 81.
[18] Philip Roth, *The American Trilogy, 1997–2000: American Pastoral, I Married a Communist, The Human Stain* (New York: Library of America, 2011), 772.
[19] Brian Castner, *The Long Walk: A Story of War and the Life That Follows* (New York: Anchor Books, 2013), 157.

writes, "is just the sign … that tells you a haunting is taking place."[20] For Gordon, a specter "is one form by which something lost, or barely visible, or seemingly not there to our supposedly well-trained eyes, makes itself known or apparent to us."[21] Ghosts coexist with the living in an unstable liminal space without exteriority. As Derrida rightly asserts, to possess a specter means necessarily to be possessed by it.[22] Insofar as veterans bring back to civilian life traces of the horrors perpetrated or suffered in war, they may be considered as belonging to the category of specter as defined by Derrida, Gordon, and other theorists. Their being haunted by trauma or moral injuries, as well as their ability to haunt civilians, constitutes the social manifestation of the specter. Haunting defamiliarizes ordinary life, it turns home into an ominous, threatening place, it disorients our movements and thoughts, it is a confounding force. In the specific case of veterans, former combatants are not necessarily the "repressed in history" that returns to haunt the present. More often, their homecoming projects onto civilian life the shadow of behaviors and drives that civilians have, or try, to repress, to put outside of daily social intercourse, namely, the systematic perpetration of destruction, extreme violence, and murder. Veterans may bring to the fore what is banned, contained, concealed. In the context of veterans, haunting is, to quote again from Gordon, a state "in which repressed or unresolved social violence is making itself known."[23] Through the specter's haunting, "we are notified that what has been concealed is very much alive and present."[24] In haunting, Gordon goes on, "organized forces and systemic structures that appear removed from us make their impact felt in everyday life in a way that confounds our analytic separations and confounds the social separations themselves."[25] This description of haunting perfectly captures the impact that the feelings, thoughts, and actions of veterans may have on civilian society.

The veterans' homecoming is the first phase of the intrusion, within the interstices of daily civilian life, of something seemingly alien and potentially threatening. Homecoming was not a smooth process for veterans of the Second World War, most particularly for those who had fought the absolute war waged on the eastern front or in the Pacific or who had been subjected to harsh captivity conditions.[26] For many demobilized soldiers, going home was fraught with problems. Some of those problems stemmed

---

[20] Gordon, *Ghostly Matters*, 8.   [21] Ibid., 8.   [22] Derrida, *Specters of Marx*, 165.
[23] Gordon, *Ghostly Matters*, xvi.   [24] Ibid., xvi.   [25] Ibid., 19.
[26] For Germany: Frank Biess, *Homecomings: Returning POWs and the Legacies of Defeat in Postwar Germany* (Princeton University Press, 2006). For Great Britain: Allport, *Demobbed*. For the United States: Childers, *Soldier from the War Returning*.

from the soldiers' transforming experience of violence and death, which
had turned some of them into specters; others, from structural changes
that had taken place on the home front during the conflict. Absolute war
and total war – which puts entire societies on a war footing – transform
soldiers and countryfolk alike. Away from home for many months on a
row, not always in regular contact with spouses, relatives, or friends, when
planning their return home many soldiers fantasized about and mentally
anticipated a reality that in fact no longer existed. Home would turn, for
the demobilized soldier, into a new, almost foreign place.[27] Marital life,
parenting, finding a job, and social intercourse in general were for many
veterans of the Second World War challenging experiences. Notwithstand-
ing the lack of comprehensive and comparative studies on the veterans'
homecoming after the Second World War, it is fair to assume that the out-
of-placeness felt by the veterans in their own country after having served
abroad was a generalized problem that affected soldiers from all the
countries involved in the world war of 1939–45.[28]

For instance, many of the returning 16 million Americans who served in
the US armed forces in 1941–45 encountered problems in readjusting to
civilian life – a readjustment far more complex and difficult than the
idealized narrative on the returning GIs, still current in the United States,
has made us believe. In a monograph devoted to this topic, Thomas
Childers has revealed the formidable challenges faced by American veterans
in their homeland in the wake of war. About 1.3 million GIs suffered from
psychological disorders, and more often than not they did not receive
proper medical treatment. Another problem was the lack of proper hous-
ing for those returning veterans, which had a negative impact on their
conjugal lives. In 1946, around 1.5 million veterans were living with the
family or friends. Cohabitation with spouses proved to be a difficult
experience, to say the least. Serious marital disputes abounded, and many
of them led to the dissolution of the marriage. In 1946, the United States
reached the highest divorce rate in its history, and also in the world.
Among veterans the divorce rate was twice as high as the divorce rate of

[27] See Willard Waller's summary, in *The Veteran Comes Back* (New York: Dryden Press, 1944), of the
usual changes in the homeland during a military conflict (82–90), as well as his detailed general
analysis of the sense of estrangement that veterans may feel upon returning home (92–191).
[28] This is, of course, a problem inherent in any war. In addition to Willard Waller's pioneering
sociological account of the veterans' homecoming (*The Veteran Comes Back*), see Jonathan Shay's
exploration, in his *Odysseus in America: Combat Trauma and the Trials of Homecoming* (New York:
Scribner, 2002), of combat trauma and the challenging homecoming of the Vietnam veterans; and
Nancy Sherman's sensitive study on the moral wounds – along with their healing – of homecoming
American veterans of the wars in Iraq and Afghanistan (*Afterwar*).

civilians. Moreover, for American veterans, particularly for those who had been physically disabled in the war, unemployment was endemic. At the beginning of 1946, around 52,000 disabled veterans applied for jobs, but only 6,000 of them were hired. In the summer of that year, no more than 20 percent of the veterans applying for jobs would be employed. The combination of all these different dimensions of homecoming led to increased resentment and disillusionment. A poll taken in 1947 indicated that about 30 percent of all American veterans felt alienated from civilian life, and another survey showed that 20 percent of veterans felt "completely hostile" towards civilians. Childers affirms that the sense of disenchantment was widespread amongst veterans, pointing out that in 1947 almost half of them "felt that the war had been a negative experience that had left them worse off than they had been before. They had lost the best years of their lives, and for many, even their homecoming was a letdown."[29]

Former prisoners of war constitute the group of veterans that seem to have borne the heaviest burden on their homecoming.[30] A study quoted by Childers suggests that more than two-thirds of the American former prisoners of war met the criteria for post-traumatic stress disorder.[31] Many of them were never treated or counseled. Adjusting to life back home was very hard for American ex-POWs. In Great Britain, the predicament of the former prisoners of war, particularly those who had been interned in Japanese concentration camps, was grueling. It has been calculated that the Japanese captured 132,134 British and American troops, out of which 35,756 never came back.[32] "The liberated [British] prisoner," Alan Allport points out, "would often bring these neuroses back to civilian life with him undetected and untreated."[33] He concludes that the reasons for the British ex-POWs' sense of alienation may lie in the fact that their experience of personal defeat and shame challenged the national narrative of victory.[34] Consider also the mental, physical, and moral condition of the more than 2 million Soviet POWs returning home from Nazi concentration and labor camps, or the 2 million German

---

[29] Ibid., 211. *The Best Years of Our Lives* is precisely the ambiguous title of William Wyler's 1946 classic film on the problems experienced by a group of homecoming American veterans.

[30] On the prisoners of war in the Second World War, see Bob Moore, "Prisoners of War," 664–89; and Iris Rachamimov, "Military Captivity in Two World Wars: Legal Frameworks and Camp Regimes," *The Cambridge History of War*, vol. 4: *War and the Modern World*, ed. Roger Chickering, Dennis Showalter, and Hans van de Ven (Cambridge University Press, 2012), 214–35.

[31] Childers, *Soldier from the War Returning*, 269–70.

[32] Rachamimov, "Military Captivity in Two World Wars," 224.   [33] Allport, *Demobbed*, 202.

[34] Ibid., 205–6.

POWs repatriated from Soviet captivity. First, those men had lived
through an absolute war in which the enemy was seen as an absolute
enemy; there had been no mercy for civilians, prisoners, captured partisans: anything went in the war of extermination conducted on the eastern
front; the troops had carried out unsoldierly, murderous acts, and everybody had seen or heard terrible things. Second, the soldiers' ordeal
acquired in captivity a new dimension. The captured soldiers of the Red
Army sent to Nazi concentration camps were treated with criminal
cruelty. Of the 5.7 million Soviet POWs taken by Germany and its allies,
at least 2.5 million died in captivity,[35] a figure all the more striking if
compared to the number of Allied prisoners of war who lost their lives in
German *Stammenlager* or in Italian camps (9,348 out of a total of
235,473, that is to say 4 percent).[36] In turn, although the Soviets had
no plan to exterminate their German POWs, they did treat them harshly,
and one-third of the 3.15 million Germans captured by the Red Army
died in transit or in Soviet camps.[37] The 2 million surviving German
POWs brought home the traces of absolute war and defeat to postwar
German society. As Frank Biess argues, "returning POWs represented one
of the most telling symbols of the Third Reich's failed ambitions ... they
were now streaming back ... as exhausted, undernourished, and sick
POWs. The reception and treatment of these returning POWs, then,
constituted one of the most important sites for processing and coming to
terms with the legacies of war and defeat."[38] Physically battered, psychologically injured, and morally ruined, many German returnees came back
with a mental illness.[39] While there are no precise figures for the number
of German veterans who suffered from a post-traumatic stress disorder, it
is fair to assume that many returned home traumatized by what they had
seen and done in an absolute war.

---

[35] Rachamimov, "Military Captivity in Two World Wars," 223.
[36] John W. Dower, *War without Mercy: Race and Power in the Pacific War* (New York: Pantheon Books, 1986), 48.
[37] Rachamimov, "Military Captivity in Two World Wars," 223.
[38] Biess, *Homecomings*, 43. Cf. the situation of the German POWs in American, British, and French camps; for an overview of this matter, see Giles MacDonogh, *After the Reich: The Brutal History of the Allied Occupation* (New York: Basic Books, 2007), 392–428; and Gregor Streim, "Germans in the *Lager*: Reports and Narratives About Imprisonments in Post-War Allied Internment Camps," *A Nation of Victims? Representations of German Wartime Suffering from 1945 to the Present*, ed. Helmut Schmitz (Amsterdam: Rodopi, 2007), 31–49.
[39] Biess (*Homecomings*, 70–94) offers a well-documented study of the trauma suffered by former German prisoners of war as well as their medical and psychological treatment in Germany in the postwar period.

The veterans' spectrality is an important family resemblance of the literature on absolute war.[40] By means of its articulation in literary texts, authors who have written on war veterans deploy what I suggest calling a *hauntology of war*. I use the notion of hauntology in the sense suggested by Derrida.[41] Jacques Derrida coined this neologism to describe an intellectual field that, instead of giving priority to "presence" and "being" (which are two main foci of ontology), centers on that which is neither present nor absent, neither alive nor dead – the specter. Consequently, a hauntology of war is not concerned with recovering the fullness of being, but rather with the dislocation that corrupts identity; it follows the traces of war stamped on the body, psyche, and moral sense of the veteran; it considers the veteran as a figure for the unsayability of war, as an image for the liminal status of absolute war (liminal because absolute warfare lies at the boundaries of significant language); it explores the defamiliarizing effect of the veterans' haunting of civilians; finally, a hauntology of war conjures up the specter so as to recover the repressed in history as well as what is banned and concealed in civilian society. In varying degrees, these constituents of the hauntology of war are present in literary works devoted to veterans, homecomings, and former prisoners of war. War writing on the specter attempts, more often than not, at setting the record straight. Its conjuring up of specters is a mourning of sorts, and to a certain extent, it is also a form of justice. As Avery F. Gordon underscores, "Perceiving the lost subjects of history makes all the difference to any project trying to find the address of the present ... To write a history of the present requires stretching toward the horizon of what cannot be seen with ordinary clarity yet."[42] Derrida views the conjuration of specters in similar terms. The French philosopher calls for an exorcism "not in order to chase away the ghosts," but so as to view them "as *arrivants* to whom a hospitable memory or promise must offer a welcome ... out of concern for *justice*."[43] Some of the works explored in this chapter undertake a hauntology of absolute war with a twofold ethical drive: their purpose is at once to vindicate and to restitute. Underlying these attempts at vindicating and setting the record straight one can find also a tacit ethical goal, namely to take the reader closer to the truth of war in order to make him or her aware of its

---

[40] On "literary veterans" and "veteran poetics," see Kate McLoughlin, *Veteran Poetics: British Literature in the Age of Mass Warfare, 1790–2015* (Cambridge University Press, 2018). For a study of "literary ghosts," see Luke Thurston, *Literary Ghosts from the Victorians to Modernism: The Haunting Interval* (London: Routledge, 2012).

[41] Derrida, *Specters of Marx*, 9, 63, 202.   [42] Gordon, *Ghostly Matters*, 195.

[43] Derrida, *Specters of Marx*, 220.

destructiveness. In addition to doing justice to the specter, these works also invoke ghosts so as to bring the reader to a more intimate and profound cognizance of the true nature of killing, absolute destruction, and war-related trauma and moral injury. Max Horkheimer and Theodor W. Adorno once observed that "Only the conscious horror of destruction creates the correct relationship with the dead: unity with them because we, like them, are the victims of the same condition and the same disappointed hope."[44] As specters, veterans may bring us into closer contact with the horrors of war, helping us to create that "correct relationship with the dead" mentioned by Horkheimer and Adorno.

The following sections of this chapter explore several hauntologies of war, placing particular emphasis on hauntologies of absolute war. With the purpose of laying out their main family resemblances, I deploy a spectral analysis of selected literary texts on specters of war.[45] The hauntologies of absolute war are grouped into four semantic clusters: (i) a hauntology of returnees from war, who are seen as both haunted and haunting entities; (ii) a hauntology of a specific kind of veteran and the traumatic nature of his or her specific haunting: the ex-combatant who is also a former prisoner of war; (iii) a hauntology of destroyed urban space, which is seen as a proper place for the specter; and (iv) a hauntology of the exorcism of the specter. As we will see, some works internalize, by means of formal hybridity, the liminal, unstable, and paradoxical nature of the ghost, themselves becoming spectral texts; such works build upon a *poetics of the specter*. Other works, namely those that proceed to exorcize the ghost in order to come to terms with it, usually choose a realist mode of writing. The decidability of the undecidable, the visibility of the invisible, as well as the instability and vanishing points of identity that define spectrality are brought into the open in the selected works. It may be argued that the specter is the perfect image for war writing and, especially, for writing on absolute war: it stands for the unsayability of war, but it also represents literature's stubborn persistence at *showing* it. And this is precisely what a hauntology of war ultimately reveals: that the truth of war and absolute war also needs to be looked for within the specter's interstitial field of action.[46]

[44] Max Horkheimer and Theodor W. Adorno, *Dialectic of Enlightenment*, trans. John Cumming (London: Verso, 1997), 215.
[45] Cf. my spectral approach to Elisabeth Bronfen's exploration of the haunting power of both warfare and its cinematic representation in her book *Specters of War: Hollywood's Engagement with Military Conflict* (New Brunswick, NJ: Rutgers University Press, 2012).
[46] While there is abundant scholarship on issues related to the ghosts of the First World War in the context of the remembrance and commemoration of those fallen in that conflict (see, for instance,

Revenants

The veterans' homecoming (*Heimkehr*) has been considered to be a central category of postwar Germany.[47] Omnipresent in the social landscape of Germany after the war, the *Heimkehrer* or returnee from war is a pervasive figure in the cultural representations produced in that country in the decade that followed the end of the military conflict. One can find the returnee, for instance, in *Trümmerfilme* (films of the rubble) such as Wolfgang Staunde's classic *Die Mörder sind unter uns* (The Murderers Are in Our Midst) (1946) and Gerhard Lamprecht's equally unforgettable *Irgendwo in Berlin* (Somewhere in Berlin) (1946).[48] The returnee is also present in the *Trümmerliteratur* (literature of the rubble) produced during that period.[49] Wolfgang Borchert's *Draußen vor der Tür* (The Man Outside) (1947), Walter Kolbenhoff's *Heimkehr in die Fremde* (Return to a Foreign Land) (1949), Josef Martin Bauer's *So weit die Füße tragen* (As Far as My Feet Will Carry Me) (1955), and Heinrich Böll's *Der Engel schwieg* (The Silent Angel) (1992, written 1949–50) have molded, together with other works, the figure of the returnee, thereby stamping the image of the *Heimkehrer* on the cultural memory of Germany. Historians and literary scholars have already explored a number of issues in relation to the *Heimkehrer*.[50] My purpose is not to rehearse their main arguments, but rather to reframe the debates on the returnee in German culture by

Sally Minogue and Andrew Palmer, *The Remembered Dead: Poetry, Memory and the First World War* [Cambridge University Press, 2018]; and Jay Winter, *Sites of Memory, Sites of Mourning: The Great War in European Cultural History* [Cambridge University Press, 1998]), most historians and cultural critics of the Second World War have ignored its specters. An exception to the norm is Monica Black's "The Ghosts of War," *The Cambridge History of the Second World War*, ed. Michael Geyer and Adam Tooze, vol. 3/3 (Cambridge University Press, 2015), 654–74.

47 See Elena Agazzi and Erhard Schütz, eds., *Heimkehr. Eine zentrale Kategorie der Nachkriegszeit* (Berlin: Duncker & Humblot, 2010).

48 For an introduction to the cinema of the rubble, see Robert R. Shandley's *Rubble Films: German Cinema in the Shadow of the Third Reich* (Philadelphia, PA: Temple University Press, 2001).

49 For a classic introduction to *Trümmerliteratur*, see Heinrich Böll's seminal essay "Bekenntnis zur Trümmerliteratur," *Werke. Essayistische Schriften und Reden*, by Heinrich Böll, ed. Bernd Balzer, vol. 1 (Cologne: Kiepenheuer & Witsch, 1979), 31–34. See, also, Darina Beloborodova, "Die Negativität in der Trümmerliteratur der Nachkriegszeit," *Triangulum. Germanistisches Jahrbuch für Estland, Lettland und Litauen* (2010), 11–29; Lisette Gebhardt, "Trümmerliteratur. Am Beispiel von Shiina Rinzō und Wolfgang Borchert," *Japanstudien. Jahrbuch des deutschen Instituts für Japanstudien* 8 (1996), 129–51; J. H. Reid, "From 'Bekenntnis zur Trümmerliteratur' to Frauen vor Flußlandschaft: Art, Power and the Aesthetics of Ruins," *University of Dayton Review* 24.3 (1997), 35–48; and Helena M. Tomko, "Böll's War: Catholic Inner Immigration, Apocalyptic Dystopia, and 'Stunde Null'," *German Life and Letters* 67.3 (2014), 358–77.

50 Biess, *Homecomings*; Bettina Clausen, "Der Heimkehrerroman," *Mittelweg 36* 5 (1992), 57–70; and Hans Hahn, "Intertextuelle Studien zur Kriegsheimkehr. Ein heuristischer Versuch," *German Life and Letters* 67.3 (2014), 341–57.

applying a new lens – the lens of a hauntology of war. My focus will be, in other words, the returnee's spectral condition. In order to sketch a sort of phenomenology of such a condition, I will analyze two literary representations of the returnee-as-a-specter that, produced in the wake of the war, are related to absolute warfare: Wolfgang Borchert's widely acclaimed drama *Draußen vor der Tür* and Heinrich Böll's posthumously published novel *Der Engel schwieg*.

Draußen vor der Tür was broadcast as a *Hörspiel* or audio drama on February 13, 1947, by the Nordwestdeutscher Rundfunk before its premiere at the Hamburg Kammerspiele on November 21, 1947.[51] The premiere was a huge overnight success. In addition to a new production of the play in Heidelberg that same year, *Draußen vor der Tür* was produced more than thirty times in theaters across Germany in 1948. The following year an adaptation of the play would be brought to the big screen as *Liebe 47* (Love '47), a film directed by Wolfgang Liebeneiner that met with little success. In Gordon Burgess's summary of the reception of *Draußen vor der Tür*, "The play clearly struck chords of shared experiences and empathy with the contemporary audiences of the immediate postwar period."[52] The prominence of Borchert's drama in German cultural life did not diminish, however, with the passing of time. *Draußen vor der Tür* has been a regular fixture in high-school reading lists as well as the German theater scene, being as it is one of the most represented dramas in contemporary Germany.

Divided into a short prologue written in prose poetry, a prelude, a scene titled "Der Traum" (The Dream), and five numbered scenes, Borchert's

[51] Much has been written on Borchert's drama. Among other scholarly works, see Bern Balzer, *Wolfgang Borchert. Draußen vor der Tür* (Frankfurt am Main: Diesterweg, 1983); Gordon J. A. Burgess, "The Failure of the Film of the Play: *Draußen vor der Tür* and *Liebe 47*," *German Life and Letters* 38.2 (1985), 155–64, and his *The Life and Works of Wolfgang Borchert* (Rochester, NY: Camden House, 2003), 151–73; Kurt J. Fickert, "The Christ-Figure in Borchert's *Draußen vor der Tür*," *Germanic Review* 54 (1979), 165–69; Robert F. Gross, "Figuring Guilt: Wolfgang Borchert's *Outside the Door* and Carl Zuckmayer's *The Song in the Fiery Furnace*," *Journal of Religion and Theatre* 5.1 (2006), 1–8; Donald F. Nelson, "To Live or Not to Live: Notes on Archetypes and the Absurd in Borchert's *Draußen vor der Tür*," *German Quarterly* 48.3 (1975), 343–54; Dirk Niefanger, "Die Dramatisierung der 'Stunde Null'. Die frühen Nachkriegsstücke von Borchert, Weisenborn und Zuckmayer," *Zwei Wendezeiten. Blicke auf die deutsche Literatur 1945 und 1989*, ed. Walter Erhart and Dirk Niefanger (Tübingen: Niemeyer, 1997), 51–56; J. H. Reid, "*Draußen vor der Tür* in Context," *Modern Languages: Journal of the Modern Language Association* 61 (1980), 184–90; and Gerhard Rupp, "Zweiter Weltkrieg im Drama. Literarhistorischer Kontext und schülerische Lebenswelt am Beispiel von Wolfgang Borchert, Günther Weisenborn und Carl Zuckmayer," *Deutsche Dramen. Interpretationen zu Werken von der Aufklärung bis zur Gegenwart*, vol. 2: *Von Hauptmann bis Botho Strauss*, ed. Harro Müller-Michaels (Königstein: Athenäum, 1981), 85–111.
[52] Burgess, "The Failure of the Film of the Play," 155.

drama centers on a twenty-five-year-old non-commissioned officer called Beckmann shortly after his homecoming from Soviet captivity. As the reader soon learns, Beckmann was captured by the Red Army in Stalingrad and sent away to internment camp, where he spent three years before his release and repatriation to Germany.[53] A survivor of absolute war and captivity, the father of a son who died in an air raid, upon his return home Beckmann finds his wife with another man. Deeply affected by his wife's infidelity, haunted by a trauma triggered by his war experience on the eastern front as well as his three years in the Gulag, and expecting from the future nothing but more pain, anguish, and disappointments, Beckmann tries unsuccessfully to kill himself at the beginning of the play. In all of his subsequent encounters with other characters (a mysterious character named The Other, a Girl, his former Colonel, a cabaret producer, and a lady who lodges in what used to be his parents' flat), for one reason or another Beckmann feels rejected. Embodying the fate of many returnees, Beckmann lacks a home in both the physical and metaphysical sense of the word; he has been expelled from his own house, and due to his war experience and the fact that he has been away for a long time, he has lost his own country forever; he will always remain an outsider – he simply doesn't belong.[54] Beckmann's last monologue in the play allows the audience to presume that he will attempt suicide once more.[55]

Wolfgang Borchert's drama is saturated with spectrality. *Draußen vor der Tür* may be considered as the spectral representation of the veteran-as-a-ghost par excellence.[56] In the literature on absolute war there is simply no other work that articulates the returnee's spectrality with the thoroughness and consistency displayed by Borchert in *Draußen vor der Tür*. This play may be read, in fact, as a ghost story. To begin with, Beckmann's physical aspect and attire give him a ghostly appearance that does not go unnoticed by the other characters. Beckmann's old uniform, camp haircut, and regulation army glasses (whose design had been adapted for wearing a gas mask) set him apart from the others, not only spatially, but also in a temporal sense, for his external appearance consists of a series of traces of

---

[53] On Beckmann as *Heimkehrer* within the drama's literary context, see Hahn, "Intertextuelle Studien zur Kriegsheimkehr," 353–57.

[54] Expand with McLoughlin's study of representations of the literary veteran as a *xenos* or stranger (*Veteran Poetics*, 63–102).

[55] Wolfgang Borchert, *Draußen vor der Tür und ausgewählte Erzählungen* (Hamburg: Rowohlt Taschenbuch, 2012), 53–54. Further references in text.

[56] On Beckmann's ghostliness, see Gebhardt, "Trümmerliteratur," 135–37; and Niefanger, "Die Dramatisierung der 'Stunde Null'," 54.

a past that many Germans wanted to forget – the war. By the sheer presence of Beckmann in the city (Hamburg), a repressed and embarrassing past returns to haunt the present. Beckmann himself is perfectly aware of his own ghostliness. About his bizarre glasses, he concedes that "perhaps they look odd," and also that they confer on him a "leaden robot's face" (16). The glasses are much more than a tool for improving his vision: they express Beckmann's ghostly nature. Without them, he feels "helplessly lost," "completely helpless" (16). The Girl perceptively notices that the glasses are not a mere exteriority, a simple functional device for seeing better, but rather an essential element of Beckmann's inner life: "I think that inwardly you also wear gas-mask glasses" (17). Since these glasses are traces of war, the Girl's shrewd remark seems to point out that Beckmann's soul is possessed by absolute war. Something similar could be said of Beckmann's haircut – the characteristic haircut of a prisoner of war, which naturally constitutes a dissonance at home. His former Colonel immediately notices Beckmann's ghostly appearance, particularly that "odd-looking haircut" (21). Perhaps aware that this ghostliness implies automatically a loss of his human condition, the Colonel tries to restitute Beckmann's humanity by offering him one of his own suits. Since external appearance is in fact the outward manifestation of an inner condition, changing clothes would convey a transfiguration of Beckmann's spectral nature, a remolding of his personality, a restitution of his human condition, in short, an exorcism of his spectrality, for "then, my boy, you will be a man again! Be first a man again!!!" (27). But this will never happen.

The other characters do not fail to notice and comment on Beckmann's ghostliness. The Girl is the first one to notice Beckmann's spectral appearance. Interestingly, this is foreshadowed by a comment that she makes after picking him up by the Elbe River: there, the Girl says, she often comes across dead men, "white like ghosts" (15). Soon the Girl realizes that Beckmann himself looks like one. First, she finds his way of talking "very strange" (15), and noticing Beckmann's odd-looking glasses, the Girl tells him that "with those glasses you look like a ghost" (17). Beckmann produces "such a desolate impression" only because "you have to wear those horrible gas-mask glasses" (17). Further on the Girl confirms her perception of Beckmann as a sad ghost: "you look so wonderfully sad, you, poor gloomy ghost . . . with the haircut and the stiff leg" (18). She also calls him "fish" several times, and upon his protests on this regard, she insists on Beckmann's spectrality: "Fish! You, fish! You gloomy repaired wet ghost" (18). Symptomatically, Beckmann agrees with the Girl's assessment. In Scene 1 he remarks that he is wet and cold "like a true corpse" (15). In the next scene, Beckmann acknowledges that "perhaps I am, too, a ghost," a ghost, he immediately adds, from a past that "today no one wants to see any longer" (17), remarking that he is a "ghost from the war, temporarily repaired for peace" (17). Such self-awareness of his spectral condition pervades the entire play. In the fourth scene, for instance, Beckmann calls himself, again, a "ghost" (29). In turn, the cabaret producer with whom he talks in Scene 4 immediately notices Beckmann's ghostliness. He comments on the ominous impression that Beckmann will produce on people. The intervention of this character on Beckmann's spectrality is important, for it captures his haunting power, and hence the dangerousness of his presence for people who want to forget the war: "my friend, the laughter will stick in their throats. At the sight of you, cold horror will creep up the nape of their necks. The damp horror before this ghost from the netherworld will take *possession* of them" (30; emphasis added). The public has no wish to see a ghost from the war on the stage, "People want exclusively to enjoy art, to feel uplifted, to edify themselves, and not to see a damp ghost" (30). Beckmann is a ghost from the war, and this is what makes him an unpleasant presence in Germany: "I am just a bad joke made by the war, a ghost from yesterday. And because I am only Beckmann and not Mozart all the doors are shut. Bang. The street stinks of blood because truth has been massacred and all the doors are shut" (34).

From the outset Beckmann is characterized as a revenant who returns from the experience of death on the battlefields of the eastern front and in captivity. A specter haunted by absolute war and captivity, Beckmann is a liminal entity between a precarious life and a powerful death-drive. Not only has he returned from the death of war and captivity; he also comes back to life from a failed suicide, which turns Beckmann into a revenant of sorts. To a degree, this attempted suicide mirrors the terrible war conditions on the eastern front and in the camp, situations and spaces in which the experience of death and pain made of him a revenant. In addition, and as happens with specters, Beckmann's identity is intrinsically unstable. Aside from representing the struggle between Beckmann's death drive and his pleasure principle, the duality of Beckmann/The Other splits Beckmann's personality, it fragments his psychic cohesiveness. At the end of the play Beckmann even feels already dead: "In any case I am dead. Everything is over, and I am dead, already dead" (45). Given that ghosts have nothing to do with ontology (the science of "being") and belong instead to hauntology (the science that centers on entities that are neither dead nor alive), it is only logical that Beckmann's being is represented as dissociated. This breaking up of a unified, integral identity may be seen as a result of the spectralization of Beckmann, and to a degree it reflects the rupture of all limits in absolute war.

Despite the lack of specific information on Beckmann's life as a soldier and as a camp inmate, the play underscores that he is haunted by his past. Thus we learn, in the dialogue between Beckmann and the Colonel, that the former is haunted in his dreams by the ghosts of eleven soldiers who died under his command. Non-commissioned officer Beckmann feels responsible – and guilty – for their deaths in a mission actually ordered by the Colonel. Beckmann refers to the "nightly ghosts" that haunt him in his nightmares every single night. He wakes up screaming (23). Beckmann tells his former Colonel about his nightmare in detail. It is a ghost story that encapsulates, as a *mise en abîme* of sorts, the spectral dimension of *Draußen vor der Tür*. At night, the dead men who died under his command in Stalingrad appear before him. They stand up from their mass graves, cross the steppes, the streets, the forests, living corpses with only one eye, with one arm, without legs, without hands, stinking, blind (24). Furthermore, Beckmann talks about the ghost-like apparition of relatives of these dead men. Once awake after having his nightmarish vision, as he lies in bed they appear to him demanding an explanation, asking where their son, brother, or fiancé is. "Non-commissioned officer Beckmann, where?, where?, where? This is what they whisper to me until the sun rises" (26). Beckmann lives in a world of specters – the specters of war. These nightmares and self-destructive daydreams are clear symptoms of a post-traumatic stress disorder. The way he talks, thinks, and feels, his alienating relationship with the other characters, as well as his suicidal ideation and behavior, clearly hint at a trauma likely caused by both the experience of absolute war and the life conditions at the camp. Surely aware of the potential effects of war on the soldiers' psyche, his former Colonel has no doubts about Beckmann's condition: "I have the strong impression that you are one of those whose perception and understanding have been obfuscated by a little bit of war" (22). In this context, Beckmann's stiff leg stands as an objective correlative, as a physical reminder of the effects of war and camp internment on his psyche. Beckmann himself is explicit about the meaning of his stiff leg: "I brought a stiff leg back with me. As a souvenir. Such souvenirs are good, you know, otherwise you forget the war too quickly. And I didn't want that" (13–14). On the other hand, as a ghost Beckmann is a haunting entity. This power of the specter can be seen in the third scene, when Beckmann visits his Colonel while he is about to have dinner with his wife, daughter, and son-in-law. With the exception of the Colonel, who out of professional experience knows what

Beckmann is going through, the other characters react with fear when they see Beckmann. The Mother asks her husband to tell him to take those glasses off: "I freeze when I see that" (21). The Colonel's daughter says that he is "deranged" (22), and the Colonel's son-in-law believes Beckmann to be "drunk" (22). The Mother insists: "Father, stay with us. I am afraid. I shudder before that man" (22). The Colonel's family feels threatened by Beckmann because he is clearly perceived as a revenant from the war – a war they want to forget about.

While the play does point out the main stations of Beckmann's war and camp experience (fighting on the eastern front, capture in Stalingrad, three years of captivity in the Gulag), Borchert omits giving more specific information on Beckmann's past as a Wehrmacht non-commissioned officer and a prisoner of war. By no means ideologically innocent, this omission is not uncommon in works on the *Heimkehrer*.[57] German authors who wrote on returnees repressed the memory of the atrocities committed by the Wehrmacht against enemy combatants, wounded soldiers, civilians, Jews, and all sorts of people on the eastern front. Tellingly, Beckmann feels guilty for the soldiers who died under his command, but does not seem particularly concerned or traumatized by the way the Wehrmacht treated captured Soviet soldiers, political commissars, and the Jewish population – a murderous treatment that Beckmann, like most if not all soldiers stationed on the eastern front (among them Wolfgang Borchert himself), must at least have witnessed or heard about. The lack of specific information, as well as the nonexistent concern for the enemy, helps to explain the enormous success of *Draußen vor der Tür*. By circumventing the unpalatable reality of the eastern front and by leaving out the dishonorable actions of the Wehrmacht, Borchert spared the public from being confronted with the criminal and genocidal behavior of the German armed forces.[58]

The play itself contains a spectral dimension. The realist language and the setting of Scenes 1–4 overlap with scenes such as the prologue, "Der Traum," the dialogue between Beckmann and God (41–43), and the

[57] See Clausen, "Der Heimkehrerroman," 57–70.
[58] On the morally and politically problematic points in this supposed indictment of war and the social hostility towards returnees, see Gross, "Figuring Guilt," 1–8; Joseph Mileck, "Wolfgang Borchert: 'Draußen vor der Tür': A Young Poet's Struggle with Guilt and Despair," *Monatshefte* 51 (1959), 328–36; and Reid, "*Draußen vor der Tür* in Context," 184–90. See, also, Friedemann Weidauer's important critical re-evaluation of Borchert's literary ambitions, political ideology, and poetics, in "Sollen wir ihn reinlassen? Wolfgang Borcherts *Draußen vor der Tür* in neuen Kontexten," *German Life and Letters* 59.1 (2006), 122–39.

dialogue between Beckmann and Death (represented as a road sweeper) (44), as well as the passage in which Beckmann dreams that he dies (41). These scenes are reminiscent of the expressionist tradition: abstract entities like Death, God, the Other, or the Elbe River are typical of Austro-German expressionism. In specialized scholarship it has been noted that Wolfgang Borchert follows, in *Draußen vor der Tür*, the expressionist *Stationen-drama*.[59] Indeed, one may argue for the existence of an intertextual dialogue between Borchert's play and expressionist dramas centered on the figure of the *Heimkehrer* from the First World War, such as *Die Wandlung* (The Transformation) (1919) and *Hinkemann* (1923), both by Ernst Toller. But Borchert's play contains also a realist dimension. The dialogues between Beckmann and other characters (the Girl, the Colonel and his family, the theater director, and Frau Kramer) are conducted in a straightforward, matter-of-fact language that is far removed from abstractions, and they take place in an urban setting. This generic hybridity sets *Draußen vor der Tür* within a liminal location, between realism and expressionism, between daily life on the one hand and the supernatural and abstractions on the other. Realistic language, settings, and situations mix with expressionistic and Gothic features that bring Borchert's work close to the orbit of the fantastic mode. Like Beckmann, *Draußen vor der Tür* is itself a liminal, spectral entity that introduces into mimetic representation elements that cannot be explained or that are manifestly unreal. As Rosemary Jackson claims in a statement that somehow describes Borchert's play, "Like the ghost which is neither dead nor alive, the fantastic is a spectral presence, suspended between being and nothingness."[60]

The second work that I would like to analyze in connection with the return of the specter has a publishing history that is not without interest given the topic of this chapter. Written in 1949–50, Heinrich Böll's *Der Engel schwieg* was not published until 1992, that is, seven years after the author's death in 1985.[61] Initially, the novel had been accepted for

[59] On the drama's expressionism, see Gross, "Figuring Guilt," 1; Bernd M. Kraske, "*Draußen vor der Tür*. Anmerkungen zur Hörspiel-Rezeption," *Wolfgang Borchert. Werk und Wirkung*, ed. Rudolf Wolff (Bonn: Bouvier, 1984), 44; Niefanger, "Die Dramatisierung der 'Stunde Null'," 51–52; and Reid, "*Draußen vor der Tür* in Context," 189.

[60] Rosemary Jackson, *Fantasy: The Literature of Subversion* (London: Routledge, 1988), 20.

[61] For more information on *Der Engel schwieg*, see Werner Bellmann, "Nachwort," *Der Engel schwieg*, by Heinrich Böll, 6th ed. (Munich: Deutscher Taschenbuch Verlag, 2009), 193–211; Enza Gini, "'Nachdenklich und hungrig' – Heinrich Böll kehrt aus dem Krieg heim," *Heimkehr. Eine zentrale Kategorie der Nachkriegszeit*, ed. Elena Agazzi and Erhard Schütz (Berlin: Duncker & Humblot, 2010), 129–41; Kálmán Kovács, "*Der Engel schwieg*. Heinrich Bölls Roman aus dem Nachlaß," *University of Dayton Review* 23.2 (1995), 15–27; and Reinhard Renger, "'Der Engel schwieg': Heinrich Bölls erster Roman," *Kultur-Chronik* 10.6 (1992), 18–21.

publication, and its appearance had been announced for early 1951, but the editor Friedrich Middelhauve called off all publication plans because it was believed that German readers would not welcome yet another bleak portrait of daily life amidst the rubble of a bombed-out city. A member of Gruppe 47 and one of the most respected literary and moral voices of postwar Germany, Böll did not attempt to publish the novel again, using instead several episodes and characters from that work for short stories and novels that he would write later. History was somehow repeating itself: *Kreuz ohne Liebe* (Cross without Love), written by Böll in 1946–47, had been rejected by the editor Johann Wilhelm Naumann, this time on account of the author's treatment of the Wehrmacht and National Socialism; what was in fact Böll's first novel would not be published until 2002. Both novels are closely connected. *Kreuz ohne Liebe* is devoted to narrating the life of two brothers from 1933 until the end of the war, while *Der Engel schweig*, as it were continuing the chronicle started in that first novel, relates the life of a German deserter from the day Germany capitulated until the fall of 1945. Given their publishing history, *Kreuz ohne Liebe* and *Der Engel schwieg* may be read as the spectral return of the repressed, as traces of a past thought to be dead that reappeared in a period in the history of Germany – the post-reunification years – in which scholars and the public at large began to examine in earnest the war years by focusing on topics that prior to then had been mostly left in the margins, as for instance the victims of the air war against Germany and the *Flüchtlinge* or refugees from the eastern regions of the Reich who in the winter of 1945 fled in panic from the advancing Red Army.

 Der Engel schwieg is a novel devoted to the figure of the *Heimkehrer*. It unveils with the utmost clarity the spectral dimension of the returnee as well as the ghostliness of the devastated space in which he settles in order to adjust to a new civilian life.[62] Divided into nineteen chapters, spectrality articulates the story, plot, and discourse of *Der Engel schwieg*, particularly in chapters 1 to 12. Böll deploys a hauntology of war from the first chapter, in fact from the very first page. On the night of May 8, 1945 (the date of Germany's capitulation), the deserter Hans Schnitzler arrives in his hometown (an unnamed city by the Rhine that stands for Cologne) and goes immediately to the Hospital of the Sisters of Charity of Saint Vincent de Paul. In figurative terms, Hans is a ghost: a few days earlier he had been condemned to death for *Fahnenflucht* or desertion, and he evaded his fate

---

[62] For a partial approach to the so-called *Heimkehrerroman* (novel of the returnee), see Clausen, "Der Heimkehrerroman," 57–70.

because a non-commissioned officer named Willy Gompertz, who was tired of living, suggested to Hans that they switch identities. Therefore, and not unlike Beckmann in *Draußen vor der Tür*, Hans makes his first appearance in the novel as someone who figuratively comes back, as a revenant of sorts, from his grave. To underscore the main character's ghostliness, the narrator explicitly likens Hans to a ghost by portraying him as a "weak specter with tottering arms."[63] The place where Hans goes to in the city could hardly be more fitting for this condition, for the hospital, seriously damaged presumably by the bombs dropped by Allied squadrons, is itself a specter – a still functional place, yet one that is partly dead due to the extreme destruction that it has sustained. The severely damaged sign with the name of the hospital by the main entrance emblematizes such a spectral condition: thanks to the glow of the fire raging on the northern boroughs of the city, Hans can decipher what is left of the hospital's name on the sign: "cent-Haus" (5), that is to say – as we learn later – *"Krankenhaus der Vinzentinnerinen"* (74). Hans Schnitzler's ghostliness, the fires in the city, the destruction brought onto the hospital, the damaged sign, and the fact that the scene takes place at night on the day of Germany's capitulation (that is, at the end or "death" of war in Europe) are the main pillars of the spectral and Gothic dimension of this first chapter of *Der Engel schwieg*.

The first thing that Hans encounters in the hospital contains a spectral side. With hesitation and apprehension, Hans goes into the building, "his own shadow in front of him, which rose above, on an undamaged wall, and became bigger and wider" (5). Walking over rubble and broken glass, he sees on his right, in a niche, a figure: the dusty statue of an angel. First Schnitzler moves nearer the statue, and he "recognized under the dim light a stone-like angel" (6). He leans forward and looks intently for a long time, "with a strange delight, at this face, the first face that he saw in the city: the stony countenance of an angel, gently and sadly smiling" (5–6). Hans cleans up the dust covering this figure that seems to be smiling at him. But soon he realizes that the smile is made of plaster – and hence it is "inauthentic." A welcoming figure that had initially triggered in him a bit of joy, the angel has in fact a sinister aspect: "The joy that he had felt upon seeing the smiling stony face disappeared . . . the atrocious varnish of the devoutness industry, the gilded brim on the garments – and the smile on the face seemed to him, suddenly, as dead as the excessively curly

[63] Heinrich Böll, *Der Engel schwieg*, 6th ed. (Munich: Deutscher Taschenbuch Verlag, 2009), 5. Further references in text.

hair ... His heart had ceased to beat" (6). Thus, the angel turns out to be yet another specter, thereby foreshadowing what is in stock for Hans in the city. If we take exception of chapter 19 – the last of the novel – , which to a great extent functions as an epilogue, Böll structures his novel in a circular fashion, for the end of chapter 18 portrays Hans Schnitzler coming across, for a second time, "the smiling angel that back then had welcomed him" (185). The contrast between the two sides that make up the spectral dimension of the angel reappear in this second and last encounter, but with one significant variation. First, the statue "seemed to him to wave or from the side to smile," but then Hans realizes that "the staring eyes looked past him" (185); even more: "he saw that the smile of the angel was a sad smile" (185). That gaze staring at the infinite, as well as the angel's doleful smile, relate in a supplementary fashion to the angel's dead aspect at the outset of the novel. The silence kept by the angel alluded to in the title of the novel refers precisely to this sad, ominous, ultimately dead side of the statue. In both scenes, the first and the last of the novel if we do not take into account, as just said, chapter 19, the angel symbolizes the empty, alienating, and harsh reality of the ruined world where Hans and the other inhabitants of the city must beat on. Thus, one could argue that the angel's spectrality, in fact a projection of Hans's own ghostliness, functions at once as a core symbol and as a frame for the entire novel – hence its importance.

Like Hans Schnitzler and the angel, the hospital is depicted in ghostly terms. Böll achieves this effect through a mimetic description of the ruins, as well as by the skillful handling of light effects, most prominently by the use of the technique of the chiaroscuro. Focalizing his gaze through Hans Schnitzler, the narrator renders in detail the ruinous state of the hospital. "Fallen-off stucco, chunks of stone, and ... filth laid everywhere ... the doors had been torn apart ... Everything smelled of cold smoke and wet mud" (6–7). Chairs and sofas have been whirled towards each other, while cabinets are completely flattened (6–7). The whole chapter abounds in descriptions of the immense destruction brought about by the "attack" (6) (most likely aerial, which makes that destruction a result of absolute war waged against civilians) on the hospital. Along with the ruinous state of the building, a lack of proper illumination transforms this hospital administered by nuns into a Gothic place. The chiaroscuro that predominates in chapter 1 greatly contributes to producing such a Gothic atmosphere. In general, characters cannot see things clearly in this hospital. During a conversation with a medical doctor – for instance – Hans could barely see his face (14). The changing room where Hans goes is almost completely in darkness (15), and when he opens the door to leave that room "everything was dark" (16). In a corridor of the hospital the light comes only from one window (17). Hans looks through "a slit" and sees a scene equally portrayed in a chiaroscuro: "between four big lit-up candles on candelabra . . . stood a stretcher like a catafalque. On the stretcher there seemed to lay an old woman, he saw only the back of her head: soft white abundant hair that shimmered under the candles' light" (17). Of the doctor he could only see his "red forehead" (18). In another scene from this chapter the only source of light for the entire room are the embers of the doctor's cigarette (19). All through the chapter this chiaroscuro (by definition the proper illumination for the specter, for it refracts the ghost's unstable nature and liminality) enhances the destruction brought by the bombs to the hospital, making certain objects and people barely visible, while others stay invisible due to lack of illumination.

A constitutive dimension of his spectrality, Hans Schnitzler's identity is unstable and multiple. To begin with, he goes to the hospital with a false name. As previously mentioned, in order to escape death by a firing squad he switched identities with non-commissioned officer Willy Gompertz. He goes to the hospital precisely to persuade one of the doctors to sell him the identity of a dead patient. Hans Schnitzler enters the hospital as "Willy Gompertz," and leaves that place as "Erich Keller" (21). Significantly, in his encounter with Frau Gompertz he characterizes himself as someone who lacks both name and identity. When she asks him about his name, Hans gives a puzzling answer: "I don't know . . . really, I don't know what name I have at this moment, really, I don't know; the last I had was Hungretz. What my name is now, I don't know, the piece of paper [where the name is written] is somewhere in my pocket" (50). Schnitzler's reaction might be explained as simple forgetfulness (after all, he received his new identity in a poorly illuminated place shortly before this encounter), by the effects on memory of pressing hunger ("Hungretz," his false last name before being "Willy Gompertz," is a play on words with the German adjective *hungrig* or "hungry"), or simply because he has had so many false identities in the past that now he cannot remember the most recent one. During the war Hans Schnitzler constantly switched identities. In the army he was in possession of an official seal and forms which let him create fake identities at will (51). In the years he served in the Wehrmacht up to the end of the war, Hans Schnitzler was, at least, Private Schnorr, Private Waldow, Lance-Corporal Hermann Wilke, non-commissioned officer Hungretz, and non-commissioned officer Willy Gompertz. "He chose the names at random," the narrator writes, ". . . He created lives that could not have been real, and that were not in fact real, but that were given the appearance of life by means of a stamp on a piece of paper . . . and these variants of his self lived on in lists and ledgers without ever having really lived" (51–52). Throughout the novel Hans Schnitzler will try to get identification papers, but not the real ones, that is, those that would identify him as "Hans Schnitzler," for if he did so he might be taken by the occupying forces into an internment camp given the fact that Schnitzler is a deserter of the German army; the goal will be to procure for himself identification papers that seem perfectly legal. Hans Schnitzler has been at once many people and no one in particular, having many identities – none his own. Schnitzler is somewhat aware of the meaning and consequences of his unstable identity. He believes, for instance, that by exchanging his fate with Willy Gompertz's, the latter "had stolen my own death" (47). He was supposed to die, but someone else died on his behalf. Hans has gone through the vicarious experience of his own death. Like someone who has not been properly buried, Hans is a ghost on account of that death that factually was not his real death. As he tells Frau Gompertz, he wanted to live, and Willy Gompertz meant to offer him his own life as a gift; but now he has realized that whoever donates his own life to someone, is also stealing his death (47–48). These words do not reflect, as Kálmán Kovács seems to suggest, a wish to be dead born out of the realization that life will be from now on a daunting struggle.[64] Rather, they belong to Hans's vague understanding of his own spectral dimension. Schnitzler has become a specter. As "Hans Schnitzler," he died the moment he replaced his true identity with a false one. He is condemned to always be *someone else*; his personal documents will bear the name of an *other*, his identity never stable, always in the process of shifting from one name to the next. Already dead, Hans Schnitzler is destined to die as someone else. He has died many deaths – the deaths of all his identities – yet he has survived each of them as another man.

Hans Schnitzler is haunted by war. Although the narrator does not address this issue explicitly, Hans's behavior in the three weeks following his arrival in the city is clearly that of someone who has been traumatized by his war experience. This haunting by the ghosts of war is part and parcel of Hans Schnitzler's spectrality. Far from being a sign of "boredom" – as Kovács has claimed – [65] his acute apathy needs to be read as a symptom of trauma. Hans spends twenty-one days in bed. The understated description offered by the narrator presents the protagonist of *Der Engel schwieg* as an

---

[64] Kovács, "*Der Engel schwieg*," 17. [65] Ibid., 17.

emotionally numbed war veteran: "He lay down in bed all the time, he didn't know what he thought of. He was mostly tired, but at times he could not sleep" (70). During those three weeks, he hardly got up of bed. Despite the fact that he was hungry most of the time, "hunger was not strong enough to take him out of bed. He left it only to go to the bathroom" (71). In this turpitude, in this total lack of energy and motivation he feels half asleep and half awake (that is, half dead and half alive), sensing the slow passing of time. When he realizes that he has spent three weeks, almost inert, in bed, "he was petrified," thinking that "he had his whole life in bed" (71–72). Schnitzler has lost all sense of time; the weeks spent in bed "seemed to him longer than one year" (78).

In *Der Engel schwieg*, Hans Schnitzler is not the only spectral figure. Other characters from the novel display a spectral dimension as well. They seamlessly fit in with the devastated city where they live. In chapter 3, for instance, on his way to Frau Gompertz's, Schnitzler comes across a woman whose face is "lethargic" (44); in fact, her face "seemed for a second to be dead" (44). The narrator describes how Hans saw "the yellowish thick lower lip hanging down, which gave to her face the expression of a repulsive grin" (45). Frau Gompertz herself looks ghostly: "The woman was wearing a dark high-necked jacket, and her face appeared paler as he got nearer; the hair was very light, almost colorless, it reminded him . . . of the wig of a pale doll" (45–46); from up close, "her face looked even paler" (48). Likewise, Hans's first impression of Regina Unger serves to characterize her as an almost spectral figure: "Her hair was light, almost white; the face was round and pale" (56). While walking in the city, Hans Schnitzler meets people who look and behave like ghostly figures: "Later, he arrived at a borough where buildings still stood – inhabited buildings. Between two damp piles of ashes a woman with dirty blond hair stood up, a featureless face with dead eyes" (52). Shortly afterwards Hans sees a lady described as a "doll" (53). A tramway-stop – to give one last example – is slowly crowded with silent ghostly looking people; the narrator even uses the word "ghosts" to characterize them: "it was not clear where they came from, they seemed to sprout from the hills, invisibly, inaudibly, they seemed to revive from that plain of nothingness, ghosts whose path and goals could not be discerned: figures with packages and sacks, cartons and boxes" (55).

All these spectral characters inhabit a city that may be described as a ghost. Like other coeval novelists and journalists (think, for instance, of the poignant chronicles produced by Stig Dagerman on German cities shortly after the war, later gathered in his book *German Autumn* [1947], or of

Victor Gollancz's compelling book *In Darkest Germany* [1947]), Heinrich
Böll describes in detail a bleak, destroyed urban space. Ruins, the perfect
setting for a ghost, must be considered as the spectral residues of a space
that, once alive, is now neither alive nor dead. Traces of the past, ruins bear
the marks of violence and death. They are reminders of an act of destruction, but also of something that is no more. The rubble left of a destroyed
street or a building signifies at once sudden death and the precarious
persistence of produced space. Urban ruins exist at the intersection of life
and death, they are placed in a temporal frame in which the past is barely
visible and the future looks grim, for sooner or later the rubble is going to
be cleared away: at some point, *nothing* will be left of that past signaled by
the urban ruin. Phantoms, therefore, of human ecology, urban ruins have a
precarious future. The result of absolute war manifested through the terror
of strategic bombing, the ghostliness of urban space projects the spectrality
of survivors still numbed by the catastrophic event.[66]

In Böll's *Der Engel schwieg*, the three itineraries followed by Hans
Schnitzler after leaving the hospital are itineraries of destruction. First,
he goes to his mother's house. The place is barely recognizable: "The front
door had been blown off by the air pressure … A section of the staircase
still remained there, too … He stepped over a pile of masonry and, at the
end of the entrance way, scraped a white, undamaged marble step at
the edge of a large mound of rubble … The pile of accumulated debris
collapsed under his weight as soon as he stepped on it" (23). The second
itinerary, namely Hans's visit to Frau Gompertz, follows a devastated,
spectral urban space: "As he continued, he didn't come across anyone for
a long time. Most of the streets were not walkable. Debris and rubble piled
up to the first floor of the burned-up façades" (43). To cover the distance
from the Gürtel to the Rubenstraße he needs almost an hour, while before
the war he covered it in ten minutes (43). Absolutely everything has been
destroyed: "In the Rubensstraße itself there wasn't a single building left
standing. The great public baths at the beginning of the street had
collapsed" (43). Hans's third itinerary is to Regina Unger's flat. That area
of the city has acquired a ghostly appearance as well. Next to the ruins of
buildings little trees and weeds (signs of life reborn) have started to grow
(54), a foreshadowing of Hans and Regina's love relationship related
further on in the novel. The narrator adds: "Hans sat … and saw in the
far distance beyond the hill the silhouettes of burned-out buildings and the
ugly stumps of churches in ruins" (55). Once at Regina Unger's

---

[66] See Robert Ginsberg, *The Aesthetics of Ruins* (Amsterdam: Rodopi, 2004).

apartment, Hans has a wider view of the ruins of the city: "In the distance . . . he saw the charred ruins of the city, a dark, ragged silhouette – he felt a profound, penetrating sadness and closed the window again" (68–69). Observing the mounds of rubble and the destruction of the city, Hans notes that "there wasn't a blade of grass to be seen . . . here there was just naked destruction, desolately and terribly empty, as if the breath of the bomb still hung in the air" (90–91). As in the first chapter, Böll sometimes describes the destruction with the technique of the chiaroscuro, thereby emphasizing the spectral condition of the city (e.g., 57, 61, 82–83).

Heinrich Böll's novel is as much a work on ghosts as it is about the overcoming of spectrality. In the last third of *Der Engel schwieg* (chapters 13–19) the narrator characterizes Hans Schnitzler as someone with a life-affirming attitude driven by his reciprocated love for Regina Unger as well as his renewed Christian faith. Indeed, the victory of cynicism and avidity in the last chapter, symbolized by the collapsing of the sculpture of an angel in a bombed-out church under the weight of two men doing a dubious business transaction, prefigures a German society dominated by material interests and money. But in addition to this reality, the narrator depicts his protagonist, in the last chapters of the novel, as someone who is trying to give cohesiveness, meaning, and purpose to his life through love and faith. Both love and religion exorcize, as it were, Hans's spectral condition. *Der Engel schwieg* makes the point that religious faith and human love may help the returnee from war to shed his spectral condition. The ghosts of absolute war that haunt the homecoming veteran may be exorcized. This new existence of Hans Schnitzler's is one of meaning and purpose despite the strenuous circumstances. Heinrich Böll thus depicts something that will be explored in the last section of this chapter: an act of exorcism, out of which a new man emerges – a man who has found his humanity again, who has adjusted to civilian life after a difficult homecoming, and who is ready to fight for his happiness.

The Trauma of the Specter

In contrast to former combatants who were never captured by the enemy, ex-prisoners of war had a harder time to exorcize their ghosts of war. Like anyone who has been subjected to captivity (e.g., in prisons, concentration and labor camps, but also religious cults, brothels, and families), former prisoners of war are prone to prolonged, repeated trauma; they are likely to develop, as Judith Herman puts it, "an insidious, progressive form of post-traumatic stress disorder that invades and erodes the personality."[67] When that is the case, ex-prisoners of war will feel themselves to be changed forever or believe that they have no self at all.[68] Typical symptoms of trauma produced by captivity are the fear that the moment of horror will recur, the loss or lack of a baseline state of physical calm or comfort, the avoidance or constriction of personal relations, the difficulty of establishing emotional connections, the ability to alter consciousness and perceptions, a constriction in initiative and planning, oscillations between intense attachment and withdrawal, as well as fundamental alterations in the victim's identity and sense of time.[69] Unlike the symptoms of single acute trauma, whose intensity tends to decrease in a matter of weeks or months, those of trauma derived from captivity "may persist with little change for many years after liberation from prolonged captivity."[70] Several studies on former POWs of the Second World War have demonstrated that these men still had all sorts of symptoms of a post-traumatic stress disorder many years after being released.[71] Moreover, their symptoms were more severe than those of coetaneous veterans who had not been captured by the enemy and sent to a camp for prisoners of war.

The predicament and psychological trauma of prisoners of war who returned home in the wake of the Second World War has been portrayed in several literary works. We have already examined the case of Beckmann, the protagonist of Wolfgang Borchert's drama *Draußen vor der Tür*. As mentioned earlier, the play starts shortly after Beckmann comes home from a Soviet camp, where he has spent three years. In *Draußen vor der Tür* Wolfgang Borchert confronts us with the profound and long-lasting effects of absolute war and captivity on the body, psyche, and moral sense of the victim. One more literary treatment of post-traumatic stress disorder can be found in the anti-climactic epilogue to Josef Martin Bauer's highly successful novel *So weit die Füße tragen* (1955). After narrating at length the years spent by Clemens Forell – a German veteran – in the Gulag, as well as his harrowing escape from Siberia all the way to Turkey, the narrator succinctly addresses the trauma of this veteran and former

[67] Judith Herman, *Trauma and Recovery: The Aftermath of Violence – From Domestic Abuse to Political Terror* (New York: Basic Books, 1997), 86.
[68] Ibid., 86. [69] On trauma derived from captivity, see ibid., 74–95. [70] Ibid., 87.
[71] On the post-traumatic stress disorder suffered by POWs of the Second World War, see A. Favaro et al., "Full and Partial Post-Traumatic Stress Disorder among World War II Prisoners of War," *Psychopathology* 39.4 (2006), 187–91; Jules Rosen, "The Persistence of Traumatic Memories in World War II Prisoners of War," *Journal of the American Geriatrics Society* 57.12 (2009), 2346–47; and N. Speed, B. Engdahl, B. Schwartz, and R. Eberly, "Post-Traumatic Stress Disorder as a Consequence of the POW Experience," *Journal of Nervous and Mental Disease* 117.3 (1989), 147–53.

prisoner of war – a trauma that will hinder Forell's readjustment to an otherwise much-longed-for life in Germany. First of all, we are told that Forell cannot hear his own voice any longer; according to the narrator, the "boundless loneliness" that he endured in Siberia has taken away from him "the cry for help, the curse, and the moan."[72] As if that were not enough of a problem, Forell has also lost "the sense of colors."[73] The doctors tell him that because of all the time spent in captivity and the three years during which he lived like an animal amongst animals, he came back as a different person from the one who had earlier left for the front. Among other serious impairments, Forell cannot remember the specific contents of his experiences; his memory only has access to the general circumstances of past actions. Clemens Forell, the veteran, former prisoner of war, and escapee from Siberia, is a wreck of a man whose physical war scars reflect the psychic wounds characteristic of severe trauma. The narrator writes: "the scars have remained in both his body and soul ... especially the signs of that fright that for three years he had tried to deny to himself."[74] The epilogue to *So weit die Füße tragen* is, therefore, a psychological and structural vanishing point of the novel: Clemens Forell has come back indeed, but as a broken man, as a ghostly figure who has brought home the violence and the wounds of both absolute war and harsh captivity. Therefore, Forell's war trauma constitutes a haunting presence; it inserts within the present a past thought – and wished – to be gone for good by many fellow Germans. Bauer's novel ends with Clemens Forell's symbolic end. The protagonist of the novel is simply someone else – a shadow of himself, a living dead, a ghost. His past as a soldier and prisoner of war has radically transfigured his body and mind. Thus, the epilogue may be seen as the beginning of another potential novel, one devoted to narrating the vicissitudes of this new self back in civilian society. *So weit die Füße tragen* opens up, thanks to its epilogue, a new field of action. This field of action, which Bauer left unexplored, had been fully elaborated a few years earlier in two very different yet complementary novels written by two of the most eminent English writers of their time: Henry Green's *Back* (1946) and Rose Macaulay's *The World My Wilderness* (1950).

When he published *Back* in 1946,[75] Henry Green had already written two novels whose main action unfolds against the backdrop of the war:

---

[72] Josef Martin Bauer, *So weit die Füße tragen* (Frankfurt am Main: Fischer, 1963), 361.
[73] Ibid., 361.   [74] Ibid., 362.
[75] On *Back*, see, for instance, Gerard Barrett, "Souvenirs from France: Textual Traumatism in Henry Green's *Back*," *The Fiction of the 1940s: Stories of Survival*, ed. Rod Mengham and N. H. Reeve (Basingstoke: Palgrave, 2001), 169–84; David Copeland, "Reading and Translating Romance in

Caught (1943), devoted, as we saw in Chapter 2, to the activities of the Auxiliary Fire Service in the early months of the Blitz, and *Loving* (1945), which narrates daily life in an Irish big house during the war. While *Back* shares with these two works its focus on the home front, Green addresses in this novel an entirely different issue. In this new novel on the war, the writer zooms in on the vicissitudes of a British veteran and former prisoner of war, Charley Summers, from his return to England in June 1944 after five years of German captivity to the "trial night" with Nancy Whitmore during the Christmas holiday of that year.⁷⁶ The detailed attention paid to Charley Summers's personality, thoughts, and behavior makes *Back* one of the most thorough narrative accounts of the trauma caused by captivity to prisoners of war. Most of the novel is devoted to relating the evolution of Charley's delusional belief that Nancy is, in truth, Rose, a former lover who actually died the same week Charley was wounded (he would lose one leg as a result of the injuries) and captured. The resemblance of the two young women (they are in fact half-sisters) facilitates the delusion in Charley's traumatized psyche.

In *Back* trauma is at once omnipresent and elusive. It is omnipresent because the narrative voice represents, through Summers's behavior, many of the symptoms of trauma caused by captivity: delusions, psychic numbing, hyperarousal, avoidance or constriction of personal relations, the difficulty of establishing emotional connections, the ability to alter consciousness and perceptions, a lack of initiative, and a number of psychosomatic reactions.⁷⁷ At the same time, the trauma is elusive because the narrator does not explain the symptoms or spell out its etiology; rather, he *shows* them through the behavior of his character. Moreover, he omits the narration of his character's war experience and captivity. Had the narrator

Henry Green's *Back*," *Studies in the Novel* 32.1 (2000), 49–69; Marius Hentea, "Fictional Doubles in Henry Green's *Back*," *Review of English Studies* 61.251 (2010), 614–26, and his *Henry Green at the Limits of Modernism* (Brighton: Sussex Academic Press, 2014), 32–36, 85–88, 102–5; Marina MacKay, *Modernism and World War II* (Cambridge University Press, 2007), 109–12; McLoughlin, *Veteran Poetics*, 175–84; Rod Mengham, *The Idiom of the Time: The Writings of Henry Green* (Cambridge University Press, 1982), 157–80; Michael North, *Henry Green and the Writing of His Generation* (Charlottesville, VA: University Press of Virginia, 1984), 101–37; Keith C. Odom, *Henry Green* (Boston, MA: Twayne, 1978), 101–10; Stephen A. Shapiro, "Henry Green's *Back*: The Presence of the Past," *Critique: Studies in Contemporary Fiction* 7 (1964), 87–96; and Nick Shepley, *Henry Green: Class, Style, and the Everyday* (Oxford University Press, 2016), 106–37.
⁷⁶ For other British novels on veterans, see Helen Ashton's *The Captain Comes Home* (1947), Nigel Balchin's *Mine Own Executioner* (1945), Betty Miller's *On the Side of the Angels* (1945), and J. B. Priestley's *Three Men in New Suits* (1945).
⁷⁷ On Charley Summers's psychology and post-traumatic stress disorder, see, for instance, Barrett, "Souvenirs from France," 169–84; and Shapiro, "Henry Green's *Back*," 87–96.

followed that track, he might have helped the reader to better understand Charley's trauma. But as things stand, readers are on their own to figure out the specific circumstances in which Charley's trauma emerged. Likewise, Charley consistently refuses to think or talk about it. Several characters try to make Charley talk about his experiences in war and in the camp for prisoners of war, but they always receive the same response: an open refusal to answer the question, an awkward silence, or an evasive curt sentence while Charley does his best to hide a growing feeling of distress and psychosomatic reactions.[78] On occasion, the narrative voice shows him actively repressing memories of war and captivity. For instance, hearing from the living-room the cries of Mrs. Grant and Nancy upstairs, which denote that Mr. Grant has just died, reminds Summers of something related to war that he wants to forget. His attitude clearly points out the spectral condition of Charley, namely his transfiguring experience of death: "and the culmination of all this was about to remind Summers of something in France which he knew, as he valued his reason, that he must always shut out. He clapped his hands down tight over his ears. He concentrated on not ever remembering. On keeping himself dead empty."[79] Immediately afterwards, he sees a cat in the room, and "at the idea that this animal could ignore crude animal cries above, which he had shut out with his wet palms, he nearly let the horror get him, for the feelings he must never have again were summoned once more when he realized the cat, they came rumbling back, as though at a signal, from a moment at night in France" (183). He succeeds in repressing those memories, "he won free. He mastered it" (183). The only occasion on which Charley gives away specific information is a conversation with Nancy almost at the end of *Back*:

> "I had a mouse out there," he said.
> She had a quick inkling of this. "And the guards took it away from you?" she asked, as if to a child. But he did not notice.
> "No, I had it in a cage I made," he said. (197)

But this is all he says about his captivity in the entire novel. In the mouse motif we can make out one of the symptoms of the deep, prolonged trauma in former captives: their identification with their master. The narrator never offers supplementary information, thereby reinforcing the haunting force and the uncanniness of Summers's silence on his past.

---

[78] David Copeland has interpreted these silences as representing "war's incommunicability" ("Reading and Translating Romance in Henry Green's *Back*," 53).

[79] Henry Green, *Back* (Champaign, IL: Dalkey Archive Press, 2009), 183. Further references in text.

The silence of the former prisoner of war on his captivity is a typical symptom of his repeated, prolonged trauma. As Judith Herman puts it, "In an attempt to reenter ordinary life, former prisoners may consciously suppress or avoid the memories of their captivity, bringing to bear all the powers of thought control that they have acquired";[80] repressing those memories perpetuates trauma, for "the chronic trauma of captivity cannot be integrated into the person's ongoing life story."[81] Specialized literature has demonstrated that prisoners of war rarely discuss their experiences. But "The more the period of captivity is disavowed, however, the more this disconnected fragment of the past remains fully alive, with the immediate and present characteristics of traumatic memory,"[82] which is exactly what happens in *Back*. This is most interesting because it produces a void in the novel. Summers's refusal to discuss or think about this issue translates into his lack of a past. The reader knows practically nothing about Summers's biography. And yet, the past – the past of war and captivity – functions in the novel as an everlasting present. Summers's past as a prisoner of war is not over: it works within his psyche, overlapping with and conditioning the present. The past of captivity and war are haunting presences. This peculiar temporality of the former captive has been studied, among others, by Judith Herman. She argues that "Alterations in time sense begin with the obliteration of the future but eventually progress to the obliteration of the past ... The past, like the future, becomes too painful to bear, for memory, like hope, brings back the yearning for all that has been lost. Thus, prisoners are eventually reduced to living in an endless present."[83] The narrator does not provide information about the past of his protagonist. The reader learns nothing about his family, his childhood, his adolescence, his war service. Trauma is a narrative void: we do not know much about the specific origin of Charley's trauma. The narrative voice does not even fill in the gaps left by his character: he could narrate Charley's past experiences in war, or in captivity, but instead he refracts Summers's refusal to revisit those times, thereby contributing to produce that void I just mentioned. All this makes Charley a ghost.

The novel refracts at the formal level Charley's fractured psyche. First, through the thematization of fragmentation in other characters (e.g., Mrs. Grant's amnesia caused by trauma [11–12, 154]) or texts (e.g., Charley's collage of a letter made by pasting together passages from letters that he received from Rose [115–18]); and second, through the embedding of a translation of a fake version of the *Souvenirs* of Madame de Créquy

---

[80] Herman, *Trauma and Recovery*, 89.   [81] Ibid., 89.   [82] Ibid., 89.   [83] Ibid., 89.

(87–99), which tells a story that duplicates, as a *mise en abîme*, the triangle of Charley/Rose/Nancy. The extract of a passage from the *Souvenirs* of Madame de Créquy has been interpreted by Gerard Barrett as a textual amputee that duplicates Charley's peg leg and parallels his "mental disorientation."[84] And third, the novel formally refracts the protagonist's traumatized mind by means of interweaving in the narrative a remarkable number of intertexts from very diverse works, such as Thomas Hardy's *The Well-Beloved*, the *Romance of the Rose*, T. S. Eliot's *Four Quartets*, and John Keats's "Ode on Melancholy."[85] The novel is "littered with fragmented bodies and texts."[86] As Barrett puts it, "The text, like its hero, exists in a state of traumatism; his disorder is mirrored by the morbid condition of the narrative system."[87] The intertextualities in *Back* are the "aesthetic equivalent of the trauma that afflicts it central character. Green has written the novel in such a way that it can be perceived as a 'double' of other texts, as Nancy, in Charley's traumatized consciousness, is the 'living image' of Rose."[88] In contrast to Borchert's drama, Green's *Back* is not a hybrid literary work; the fantastic element is altogether missing in this novel. However, *Back* does reproduce formally the ghostliness of the character by means of the practice of catastrophic modernism.

Like much of the novel, the title is polysemous. "Back" refers, of course, to the former POW's homecoming, but it also alludes to the presentness of Charley's past captivity in the form of post-traumatic stress disorder. In a sense, Charley Summers is never truly back. First, because British society has dramatically changed as a result of the war. Unlike other novelists of the period (most memorably Elizabeth Bowen in her 1948 novel *The Heat of the Day*), Green does not directly address these changes. The narrator focuses on his main character's psychology and actions, favoring the use of a concatenation of scenes over the embedding of descriptive pauses. We learn generalities about those changes indirectly through another war veteran, Arthur Middlewitch. In a conversation with Charley, Middlewitch says: "Yes . . . we all of us came back to what we didn't expect" (24); he adds: "When we were over in Hunland, thinking of home, didn't you and I imagine summer evenings and roses and all that guff . . . And what happened when we did get back? Why, we got stinking tight, old lad, and catted it all up" (25). In sum: "we found everything different to what we expected" (25). The second reason that explains the impossibility of going

[84] Barrett, "Souvenirs from France," 180.   [85] Ibid., 177.
[86] Copeland, "Reading and Translating Romance in Henry Green's *Back*," 55.
[87] Barrett, "Souvenirs from France," 171.   [88] Ibid., 178.

"back" home is Charley's post-traumatic stress disorder, which makes the past captivity, as we have seen, a present matter that interferes in daily life. To some extent, Charley has not returned from captivity. His peg leg, described as a "souvenir he had brought back from France" (7), will be an insidious reminder of this presentness of the past.

The first chapter portrays this presence of past death and violence that haunts Charley. The very beginning of the novel is loaded with the ghosts of war. The limits between the war zone and the home front are diluted. The scene narrates Charley's visit to the church graveyard where his former lover, Rose, lies buried. Everything seems normal in the description of his arrival at the cemetery. But as happens with the main character of Borchert's *Draußen vor der Tür*, Charley views reality through the lens of war, or to be more precise, through the lens of his haunting war trauma: "As he looked up he noted well those slits, built for defense, in the blood colored brick. Then he ran his eye with caution over cypresses and between gravestones. He might have been watching for a trap, who had lost his leg in France for not noticing the gun beneath a rose" (3). This is a clear instance of hypervigilance, a symptom of post-traumatic stress disorder; often, the purpose of hypervigilance is the detection of potential threats. Shortly afterwards, while climbing the path leading to the graves, "came a sudden upthrusting cackle of geese in panic, the sound of which brought home to him a sack of faggots he had seen blown high by a grenade" (4). Summers transfers the trauma born in war and captivity to a different context: love. The same week he was wounded and captured his lover Rose died. The name "Rose" must evoke in him the source of his injury and – we may assume – of his captivity; after all, the enemy sniper who shot him was hidden amidst roses. Summers has an analogical mind: the name "Rose" surely evokes in him the source of his misfortune (a bunch of "roses"). The association "roses/Rose" explains the transferring of his war and captivity trauma to a different kind of loss – the loss of his lover. It is in this context that the ambiguous last scene needs to be interpreted. Nancy Whitmore has asked Charley to marry her but with one condition: to have a "trial night" before the wedding. "She was lying stark naked on the bed, a lamp with a pink shade at her side," Charley knelt by the bed, "and because the lamp was lit, the pink shade seemed to spill a light of roses over her in all their summer colors, her hands that lay along her legs were red, her stomach gold, her breasts the colour of cream roses, and her neck white roses for the bride" (207). Charley reacts in a quite ambiguous way: "She had shut her eyes to let him have his fill, but it was too much, for he burst into tears again, he buried his face in her side just below the ribs, and bawled like a child. 'Rose,' he called out, not knowing he did so, 'Rose'" (207). The ambiguity of this scene cannot be solved. Charley's reaction may mean an overcoming of his trauma or else be one of its symptoms.

The trauma of the former combatant and the haunting power of the ghosts of war take center stage in a coeval novel by the noted British writer Dame Rose Macaulay, *The World My Wilderness*, published in 1950.[89] Properly speaking, this is not a novel about a prisoner of war, even if its main character, a seventeen-year-old girl named Barbary Deniston, who fought with the maquis (guerrilla units that operated in southern France during the Second World War), was once arrested by the Germans. And yet *The World My Wilderness* perfectly captures the spectrality and haunting force that are characteristic of many former combatants and prisoners of war, as well as their trauma. Despite her youth, Barbary needs to be considered as a veteran – not of a regular army, like the veterans we have seen so far, but of an irregular unit whose essence is, precisely, spectrality: the French maquis. Reading Macaulay's novel helps us to understand the main issues that are present in narratives produced by, or centered on, veterans and former POWs. The narrator of *The World My Wilderness* addresses the psychological legacies of war by placing the main character, Barbary, against the backdrop of postwar London. The main action, set in France and Great Britain between April and October 1946, focuses on a veteran guerrilla fighter who has been deeply affected by the war. Stranded in France with her divorced mother when the Germans invaded the country, Barbary spent the entire war living with his mother and stepfather in the outskirts of Collioure, or else in the hideouts of the maquis. Somewhat neglected by her mother, a lack of proper education fed into

---

[89] Rose Macaulay, *The World My Wilderness* (London: Collins, 1950). All references in text. For other analyses of this novel, see K. L. Anderson, "A Horrid, Malicious, Bloody Flame: Elegy, Irony and Rose Macaulay's Blitzed London," *Literary London: Interdisciplinary Studies in the Representation of London* 5.2 (2007), 14 www.literarylondon.org, accessed September 14, 2016; Sarah Beckwith, "Preserving, Conserving, Deserving the Past: A Meditation on Ruin as Relic in Postwar Britain in Five Fragments," *A Place to Believe In: Locating Medieval Landscapes*, ed. Clare A. Lees and Gillian R. Overing (University Park, PA: Pennsylvania State University Press, 2006), 191–210; D. A. Boxwell, "Recalling Forgotten, Neglected, Underrated, or Unjustly Out-of-Print Works," *War, Literature, and the Arts* 11.2 (1999), 207–16; Lara Feigel, *The Love-Charm of Bombs: Restless Lives in the Second World War* (New York: Bloomsbury, 2013), 435–37, 438–40, 441–42, 444–45; Ben Highmore, "Playgrounds and Bombsites: Postwar Britain's Ruined Landscapes," *Cultural Politics* 9.3 (2013), 323–36; Phyllis Lassner, "Reimagining the Arts of War: Language & History in Elizabeth Bowen's *The Heat of the Day* & Rose Macaulay's *The World My Wilderness*," *Perspectives on Contemporary Literature* 14 (1988), 30–38; and Beryl Pong, "The Archaeology of Postwar Childhood in Rose Macaulay's *The World My Wilderness*," *Journal of Modern Literature* 37.3 (2014), 92–110.

Barbary's predisposition for rebellious behavior, which, together with an inclination for adventure, made her join the local *maquisards*.

In order to understand the connection between trauma and ghostliness in this novel, it is important to bear in mind the spectrality intrinsic to the maquis. Like any guerrilla group, the maquis were a ghostly conglomerate of irregular units. Guerrilla fighters are the masters of silence and disguise, they adopt fake names, favor nightly missions, plan attacks for when and where they are least expected, hide in remote, sometimes inaccessible, areas, are always on the move. They avoid open confrontations with large regular armies; they favor surprises, preferring the sudden, swift, unexpected attack, followed by a quick withdrawal to the rearguard. The guerrilla is an armed ghost. Stealth, secrecy, and invisibility lie at the core of his or her activities. Guerrillas are ghostly units that have adapted to combat the ways of the specter; they follow the tactics of the phantom. It is no coincidence that Joseph Kessel's 1943 classic novel on the French Resistance bears the title *L'armée des ombres* (Army of Shadows). This title beautifully captures the spectrality of the Resistance – and of any guerrilla or partisan group for that matter – , for like any irregular clandestine unit, the French Resistance was indeed an army of "shadows," of silent "ghosts" who materialized suddenly for lethal action only to become invisible again once the mission had been accomplished.[90] In addition, the guerrilla fighter can expect no mercy from a regular army. Regulated now by international law and treaties, the usual, if by no means universal, respect that the regular armies have for captured enemy soldiers is rarely present before guerrillas or partisans. Irregular troops are seen in terms of absolute enmity. That was true of the Peninsular War (1808–14), the Franco-Prussian War (1870–71), and most particularly, the Second World War and the Vietnam War. The war waged by regular armies against the guerrilla is, to a great extent, an absolute war: the extermination of the enemy is the only outcome that counts. In several of his writings, Clausewitz had already noted that guerrilla warfare is an intensification of war, establishing a connection between that kind of military conflict and the breakup of limits that is consubstantial to war in the absolute degree.[91]

---

[90] Years later, Vietnam veteran Philip Caputo would underscore throughout his war memoir *A Rumor of War* (1977; 2nd ed. [New York: Picador, 2017]) the spectrality of the Viet Cong's guerrillas. "Phantoms," he thinks shortly after arriving in Vietnam, "we're fighting phantoms" (58).

[91] Carl von Clausewitz's pioneering reflections on *"den kleinen Krieg"* or guerrilla warfare can be found in *On War* (trans. And ed. Michael Howard and Peter Paret [Princeton University Press, 1984]), book 6, ch. 26; and in *Schriften – Aufsätze – Studien – Briefe. Dokumente aus dem Clausewitz-, Scharnhorst- und Gneisenau-Nachlass sowie aus öffentlichen und privaten Sammlungen*, ed. Werner Hahlweg, vol. 1 (Göttingen: Vandenhoeck & Ruprecht, 1966), 226–558, 604–11, 661–69, 681–751.

Barbary's experience in guerrilla activities against the Germans has had a traumatic effect on her. In particular, the novel singles out three war-related events that triggered her trauma: she was caught, interrogated, and tortured by the Germans (76–77), she was raped by the interrogating officer (76–77), and she did nothing to stop the maquis from killing her stepfather (a suave, good-natured French businessman who occasionally collaborated with the Germans more out of bonhomie than out of malice or opportunism) shortly after the war (230–31, 237). This last event left a deep mark on Barbary, to the extent that she refuses to talk about him. Barbary, the narrator points out, "did not care for their stepfather as a topic, and never pursued it . . . It was as if Maurice, that genial collaborator . . . had slipped out of [her] memories when he was drowned in Collioure bay" (38). Significantly, the memory of Maurice has left a "haunting phantom" in his place (38). In a conversation with her biological father, Barbary reacts very emotionally to this topic: "'He's dead, he's dead, he's dead,' she cried, and her voice fell to a whisper" (139). Later in the novel, Barbary runs away from Scotland back to London because their host in Arshaig, a medical doctor, wanted to have a therapeutic conversation with her. Since Barbary refuses to face her ghosts, she flees the place and goes back to London, in particular to its ruined neighborhoods, which is where she really belongs. Once in the city, she will tell the housekeeper that Sir Angus (the medical doctor) wanted her to talk about her mother, "and about the maquis, and the Germans, and what we did. Lots of things. I didn't want to talk about it. I won't.' Her voice rose shrilly. 'I *won't* talk, I won't, I won't'" (132–33). The protagonist of *The World My Wilderness* does not want to revisit the sources of her trauma, and only at the end of the novel does she open up to her mother about Maurice's death (230–31). Several characters insist on the traumatic mark left by the war on combatants (e.g., 120).

The maquis did not dissolve immediately, and they continued their activities even against local Frenchmen or institutions. In the case of Barbary, her unruly behavior continues in the civilized place par excellence – London. Her mother has sent her there to live with her father and be "civilized." Once in London, Barbary is supposed to attend a drawing school, but she spends most of the time amidst the rubble and ruins of the city. In London, both Barbary and her brother Raoul feel out of place. These first impressions alter as soon as they wander into the ruins of London (51–59).[92] "They got off in Cheapside," the narrator writes, "and

---

[92] On the treatment and meaning of ruins in *The World My Wilderness*, see Beckwith, "Preserving, Conserving, Deserving the Past," 191–210; Boxwell, "Recalling Forgotten, Neglected, Underrated,

walked up Foster Lane. Having crossed Gresham Street, the road became a lane across a wrecked and flowering wilderness, and was called Noble Street. Beyond Silver Street, it was a still smaller path, leading over still wilder ruins and thicker jungles of greenery, till it came out by the shell of a large church" (51–52). Neither Barbary nor her brother "was surprised, or even greatly interested; these broken habitations, this stony rubbish, seemed natural to them" (52). In his descriptions of this area of London, the narrator talks about the "broken city" (52), the "wrecked city" (53), or the "fantastic ruined city" (59). The narrator describes at length the ruin of this area of London (e.g., 52–59, 65–67, 252–54). It is in this ruined urban landscape, similar to the warscapes they were used to during the war, where they will feel at home. Barbary takes up residence, so to speak, in Somerset Chambers, between a ruined café and an equally ruined church. This London in rubble is a correlative objective of Barbary. She spends most of her days with her brother in the ruins, painting them, roaming through them, or conversing with marginal characters who trade on the black market. The ruins of London are the perfect setting for a traumatized guerrilla veteran. The ruins themselves are the mark of a wound, and the narrator describes them all in detail, usually pointing out the specters of their previous inhabitants, now gone or dead. Haunted by the scars of war, Barbary feels at home in the ruins, surrounded by specters. As her brother Raoul puts it, the ruins are *"chez nous"* (181).

Barbary, who was a specter during the war given her status of *maquisarde*, and is a specter now due to the trauma that she suffers, lives in the ruins amongst specters.[93] Like the hospital and the city in *Der Engel schwieg*, the bombed areas of London are inhabited by ghosts. Barbary is a specter, someone haunted by violence and death, and the narrator underscores repeatedly that the ruins are inhabited by the ghosts of those who lived there earlier. The ruins are described as "the maze of little streets threading through the wilderness," as a "scarred and haunted green and stone and . . . wilderness" (128). Or even more clearly: "the ghosts of the centuries-old merchant cunning crept and murmured among weeds and

---

or Unjustly out-of-Print Works," 209–11; Highmore, "Playgrounds and Bombsites," 323–36; and Pong, "The Archaeology of Postwar Childhood in Rose Macaulay's *The World My Wilderness*," 92–110. On the ruins of London as portrayed in British literature, see Marina MacKay, *Modernism, War, and Violence* (London: Bloomsbury, 2017), 124–30; and Leo Mellor, *Reading the Ruins: Modernism, Bombsites and British Culture* (Cambridge University Press, 2011). See, also, Sara Wasson's monograph on the British "urban Gothic" of bombed-out London, *Urban Gothic of the Second World War: Dark London* (New York: Palgrave Macmillan, 2010).

[93] On the "street haunting" novelized in *The World My Wilderness*, see Pong, "The Archaeology of Postwar Childhood in Rose Macaulay's *The World My Wilderness*," 99–104.

broken stones" (159; see also 158). In his description of the former inhabitants of that area of London, the narrator intones the motif of the *ubi sunt?* (181–83). While Barbary and Raoul are being pursued by the police, the ghosts of the ruins go about their business or look at what is going on (193). "Barbary" means the return to civilization of what had been repressed and sent to the margins. She is the equivalent of the uncanny in the sense given by Freud to the word in his classic essay *Das Unheimliche* (The Uncanny) (1919). According to Freud, "The uncanny is that class of the frightening that leads back to what is known of old and long familiar."[94] In *The World My Wilderness* the intimate, familiar, home-like (*heimlich*) London metamorphoses into an eerie, strange, "un-homely" (*unheimlich*) space as soon as it brings back to conscious life what once had been repressed and pushed out to the periphery (the performance of violence in guerrilla warfare in southern France, in this case), thus remaining "secret," "hidden," and therefore potentially "dangerous" (Barbary). A former member of the maquis, this young woman is the ghost of violence haunting civilization, breeding *within* civilization. Barbary's return to her own country has to be read, consequently, as the return of the *Unheimliche*, of that class of frightening which is familiar yet which had been pushed to the margins for a long time, and now comes back to the center with threatening force. Insofar as she undermines or contradicts the ordered life of her father, which in the novel stands for civilization and orderliness, Barbary constitutes a haunting presence.

In the end, her mother takes her back to France. And in the same way that Barbary's threat is taken care of by sending her back to the margins of civilization, bulldozers clear away ruins so as to make anew the destroyed areas of the city (253). It will be a precarious order, however, for the disorder and the wilderness will threaten to break out again. The narrator points out: "So men's will to recovery strove against the drifting wilderness to halt and tame it; but the wilderness might slip from their hands, from their spades and trowels and measuring rods, slip darkly away from them, seeking the primeval chaos and old night which had been before Londinium was, which would be when cities were ghosts haunting the ancestral dreams of memory" (253). Rose Macaulay novelizes the threatening presence of the ghosts of war and trauma, namely the double spectrality of the veteran, by pointing out that the return and the trauma of the specter

[94] Sigmund Freud, *The Uncanny*, *The Standard Edition of the Complete Psychological Works of Sigmund Freud*, trans. James Strachey, ed. James Strachey, Anna Freud, Alix Strachey, and Alan Tyson, vol. 17/24 (London: Hogarth/Institute of Psycho-Analysis, 1953–74), 220.

meant no less than the return of what civilization had tried to repress. As the last scene suggests, repression will never be completely successful, for spectrality and trauma are consubstantial to human life. The right attitude, the implied author seems to remark, is not to deny the existence of the specter, or to send it back to the margins, but rather to welcome it, to make a habitation for it, not only to placate the danger that it may posit, but also, and especially, out of a sense of justice.

The City of the Specter

Ghosts thrive in wars. Military conflicts produce, nurture, and mold specters. Thus far we have seen, in specific literary works, the double spectrality of veterans, of former combatants at once haunted by the ghosts of absolute war and haunting the people who surround them. But modern absolute wars, as we know, are not the exclusive affair of armies; they also target civilians. The line separating combatants from non-combatants has slowly dissolved ever since the Peninsular War of 1808–14, and in conditions of absolute war everyone becomes fair game. This is most true of the Second World War. For the first time in the history of warfare, civilians died in a much higher proportion than military personnel: according to some sources, between 21 and 25 million troops died in the Second World War, whereas civilian deaths totaled around 50–55 million people. Those who survived the ravages of absolute war had to live with memories of war and sometimes of unspeakable atrocities. Some surviving civilians would develop the double spectrality we have seen in combatants – the spectrality of someone who, possessed by the ghosts of war, haunts those around him or her.

In the context of the Second World War, the production of specters out of civilians is most noticeable in bombed-out urban spaces. The devastating bombings and ensuing firestorms of Hamburg and Dresden, as well as the atomic bombings of Hiroshima and Nagasaki, were of such a terrible, almost unimaginable intensity, that they generated spectrality on a vast scale. In testimonial literature and literary works devoted to the obliteration of these and other cities we can see an overwhelming presence of specters. The destroyed cities, themselves spectral entities, became cities of specters. Take, for instance, the cases of Hiroshima and Nagasaki. A striking leitmotif in testimonial literature on the atomic bombings of these two Japanese cities is the description of large groups of badly injured survivors in rags and tatters walking together in silence, their faces burned, their gazes vacant, their peeled skin hanging off, their minds completely numbed; their slow movements, like everything else about them, were reminiscent of those usually attributed to the living dead. Kosaky Okabe, a survivor of the atomic-bombing of Hiroshima, remembers that on August 6, 1945,

> Hundreds of those still alive were wandering around vacantly. Some were half-dead, writhing in their misery. Others were shuffling along like forlorn ghosts, terrible burns covering more than half the body, the skin of the face and arms peeling off and flapping around them. Some were roaming around lost, crying out for water; but when someone called out to them, they seemed not to hear ... They were no more than living corpses.[95]

Teiichi Teramura notes likewise that on the day after the bombing survivors "were walking around stupefied" through roads and streets that "were strewn with the fire-blackened corpses of people, horses, and dogs."[96] In turn, Tadaomi Furuishi points out that in Hiroshima he "met streams of people walking around ... Their hair was burned and frizzled. The skin had peeled from their faces and was hanging in strips. Their mouths were contorted. White bones protruded from their faces. Their clothes were in shreds ... They held their arms out in front of them like ghosts ... They wandered around dazed and uncertain, like sleepwalkers."[97] Descriptions of sinister parades of specters can also be read in the autobiographic accounts of Hiroshi Shibayama, Masae Kawai, and Hiroshi Sawachika.[98] A classic work on Hiroshima written by a survivor, Dr. Michihiko Hachiya's *Hiroshima Diary* (1955), contains, too, parades of the living dead.[99] Literature offers an equally ample spectrum of such descriptions of walking specters. In his 1949 autobiographic novel on the atomic bombing of Hiroshima, *Summer Flowers*, Tamiki Hara narrates a procession of ghosts,[100] and so do Makoto Oda in his 1981 novel *H: A Hiroshima Novel*,[101] John Hersey in his 1946 book-length chronicle *Hiroshima*,[102] and Yōko Ōta in *City of Corpses*, published

[95] *Hibakusha: Survivors of Hiroshima and Nagasaki*, trans. Gaynor Sekimori (Tokyo: Kōsei Publishing Co., 1986), 38.
[96] Ibid., 49.   [97] Ibid., 161–62.   [98] Ibid., 98–99, 108–9, and 170, respectively.
[99] Michihiko Hachiya, *Hiroshima Diary: The Journal of a Japanese Physician, August 6–September 30, 1945*, trans. and ed. Warner Wells (Chapel Hill, NC: University of North Carolina Press, 1995), 14, 21, 54–55.
[100] Tamiki Hara, *Summer Flowers, Hiroshima: Three Witnesses*, trans. and ed. Richard H. Minear (Princeton University Press, 1990), 51–52.
[101] Makoto Oda, *H: A Hiroshima Novel*, trans. D. H. Whittaker (Tokyo: Kodansha International, 1990), 174–76.
[102] John Hersey, *Hiroshima* (New York: Alfred A. Knopf, 1946), 9–10, 39–40.

first in an incomplete edition in 1948; the unabridged version of the book would see the light of day two years later.[103]

Narratives on the bombings of German cities contain similar descriptions of specters. We can find them, for instance, in Hans Erich Nossack's account of the bombing of Hamburg, *Der Untergang* (The End) (1948). At the time of the bombing, Nossack was in Horst bei Maschen, a town 15 kilometers south of Hamburg. Awoken by the sound of the sirens, Nossack stepped out of the cottage where he and his wife were lodging, and from there he saw the squadrons of Lancasters and Halifaxes flying en route to their target as well as the bombing of the city. Sometime after the bombing, a stream of people fleeing Hamburg came towards the town "almost silently."[104] The description of the silent, numbed people fleeing Hamburg is reminiscent of the above-quoted descriptions of parading specters in Hiroshima. Nossack relates that the refugees from Hamburg brought with themselves "an ominous silence. Nobody dared to question them as they sat mute on the wayside."[105] When Nossack and his wife visited the city after one of the several attacks undertaken by the British bombers, they walked through its streets "like dead people ... who have no share in the little worries of the living."[106] In like fashion, Hiltgunt Zassenhaus, in an autobiographic narrative of the bombing of Hamburg and its aftermath, remembers seeing from the window of her flat a mass of people walking, like the living dead, out of the city: "they trudged on the pavement. No voice emerged from the crowd ... They wandered away from the city," adding shortly afterwards that "Any trace of life had disappeared from their faces."[107] Identical images pervade several accounts of the bombing of Dresden. In Walter Kempowski's montage of testimonies on the aerial attack against that city, *Der rote Hahn* (2001), there are texts that portray streams of people walking together in silence, half-alive, half-dead. For instance, in a passage written by Aleida Montijn, we read that the people streaming out of the city were "broken and apathetic."[108] Christian Just recalls the long procession of people leaving the destroyed city,[109] while Gisela Neuhaus writes: "An endless column of

[103] Yōko Ōta, *City of Corpses, Hiroshima: Three Witnesses*, trans. and ed. Richard H. Minear (Princeton University Press, 1990), 199, 204, 205, 217, 232, 233.
[104] Hans Erich Nossack, *Der Untergang* (Frankfurt am Main: Suhrkamp, 1976), 20–21.
[105] Ibid., 24.   [106] Ibid., 51.
[107] In Volker Hage, ed., *Hamburg 1943. Literarische Zeugnisse zum Feuersturm* (Frankfurt am Main: Fischer, 2003), 160.
[108] Walter Kempowski, *Der rote Hahn. Dresden im Februar 1945* (Munich: btb, 2001), 179.
[109] Ibid., 192.

men, women, and children trudged slowly and silently" out of the city, adding that "only the scuff of their feet, and occasionally a sob or a yell, were to be heard."[110] In a similar way does the narrator of Dieter Forte's 1999 trilogy, *Das Haus auf meinen Schultern* (The House on My Shoulders), depict the stream of disoriented, numbed, silent people who moved in columns, half-dazed, like sleepwalkers, after a heavy bombing of their city (Düsseldorf).[111]

Of all the literary works that portray, one way or another, specters in destroyed, ghostly cities, there are two, both written in the fantastic mode, that stand out: *Nekyia. Bericht eines Überlebenden* (Nekyia: A Report by a Survivor), a novella by Hans Erich Nossack published in 1947, and Hermann Kasack's *Die Stadt hinter dem Strom* (The City beyond the River) (1947). Written within a tradition decisively marked, in the German literary field, by Alfred Kubin's *Die andere Seite* (The Other Side) (1909) and Franz Kafka's *Das Schloß* (The Castle) (1926), these works by Nossack and Kasack capture, thanks to the fantastic mode, the spectralization of civilians derived from the obliteration of their cities. Also by their use of that literary mode, *Nekyia* and *Die Stadt hinter dem Strom* internalize the spectrality that they portray; in other words, on account of their constitutive hybridity and use of the fantastic mode (whose chief family resemblance consists of the introduction within reality of what altogether lacks a rational explanation), they deploy what could be termed as *spectral writing*. In this sense, *Nekyia* and *Die Stadt hinter dem Strom* have much in common with another hybrid work: Wolfgang Borchert's *Draußen vor der Tür*. Since these works by Nossack and Kasack address an important aspect of warfare, namely the production of specters through violent action, they may be considered as instances of war writing despite the fact that neither narrates war – their concern is war's aftermath.

As Julia Hell has already noted, *Nekyia* is intertextually connected to Nossack's *Der Untergang*.[112] Both works constitute a diptych on the destruction of Hamburg in the summer of 1943. They are organized in

---

[110] Ibid., 162.

[111] Dieter Forte, *Das Haus auf meinen Schultern* (Frankfurt am Main: Fischer, 2002), 638–39. Cf. Curzio Malaparte, *Kaputt*, trans. Dan Hofstadter (New York Review Books, 2005), 412–13, 415–22, a haunting variant to the *topos* of the procession of people walking, numbed by bombing, like living dead after an Allied aerial attack on Naples.

[112] Julia Hell, "Ruins Travel: Orphic Journeys through 1940s Germany," *Writing Travel: The Poetics and Politics of the Modern Journey*, ed. John Zilcosky (University of Toronto Press, 2008), 132. On *Nekyia*, see W. G. Sebald's remarks in *Luftkrieg und Literatur. Mit einem essay zu Alfred Andersch*, 5th ed. (Frankfurt am Main: Fischer, 2005), 56–59.

the same way: once the attack against the city is over, the narrator and main character goes back to the city. *Der Untergang* is a realistic, documentary portrayal of the destruction wrought on Hamburg; in this text Nossack centers on the rubble, on the ruins, on what is left, as well as on what is gone forever. *Der Untergang* describes a field of presences and visibilities. In contrast, *Nekyia* depicts through fantasy and imagination absences as well as what cannot be seen by the eye, a reality that is considered as lacking reality; put differently, it addresses what cannot be grasped by mimetic language: dead people, ghosts, the city's new spectrality, which is much more than rubble and ruins. As Rosemary Jackson reminds us, "literary fantasies have appeared to be 'free' from many of the conventions and restraints of more realistic texts," namely the unities of time, space, and character, chronology, as well as rigid distinctions between animate and inanimate objects, self and other, and life and death.[113] Because of its overlapping of the inexplicable and the empiric world, the fantastic seems to be better equipped than realism for capturing the sense of non-reality derived from the bombing itself, the destruction of human habitation, and the death of so many people. Let us not forget that fantastic literature is a mode of writing "which seeks that which is experienced as absence and loss."[114] Therefore, *Nekyia* may be viewed as the negative – in the photographic sense of the word – of the world represented in *Der Untergang*. For this reason, the two works complement each other, they form a whole destined to capture all the dimensions involved in the almost complete destruction of a city. Following this logic, to fully understand the destruction of Hamburg one needs to read *both* texts, and not only one of them.

The title of Nossack's novella, *Nekyia*, condenses both its contents and purpose. In ancient Greece, a *nekyia* was a rite by which ghosts were invoked and questioned about the future. *Nekyia* generally included the meaning of *katabasis*, a word that specifically referred to the journey to the netherworld (as for instance Odysseus's visit to Hades, where he meets with and talks to the dead, in book 11 of the *Odyssey*). As in a *nekyia* that encompasses the meaning of *katabasis*, Nossack's novella narrates the unnamed autodiegetic narrator's return to a city where, as he will discover, everything and everybody is dead as a result, so we are told later in the book, of war.[115] The novella even subtly suggests that the city has

---

[113] Jackson, *Fantasy*, 1–2.   [114] Ibid., 3.
[115] Hans Erich Nossack, *Nekyia. Bericht eines Überlebenden* (Frankfurt am Main: Suhrkamp, 1961), 95, 137. Further references in text.

undergone aerial attacks (95). Nossack is not concerned, however, with destruction – which is one of the main motifs in *Der Untergang* – but rather with the spectrality produced by the war. In fact, the city described in *Nekyia* is not in ruins. The intact state of the city makes the death of everyone even more ominous and disturbing. At the same time, the impeccable aspect of buildings and streets needs to be seen, as said earlier, as the "negative" of a destroyed city. Although the buildings are in place, they are, like everything else, *dead*. What the narrator faces is the over-lapping of the past physical aspect of the city and its present deadness. The entire city is a ghost of itself. *Nekyia* uncovers the unsaid and the unseen derived from absolute war. A spectral atmosphere surrounds the narrator from the very beginning. The people to whom he announces his plan to return to the city do not seem to be alive; they give no reply to the narrator, they lie around "like clods of clay," and have "lost all sense of direction" (8). Likewise, once in the city the narrator encounters people who possibly have not noticed his absence because, he says, "they lie there all the time, and seem to be sleeping" (8). But after this initial encounter, the narrator finds himself in a city without people, with no sign of life whatsoever. A rarified, *unheimliche* atmosphere surrounds a city described as a specter, as an entity that is neither dead nor alive. Thus, stores are open, and from the windows hang pieces of clothing, but "from the chimneys came out no smoke" (12). Flowers do not look real, and there is something bizarre about the trees as well (13). Later, as he enters a building and goes to the kitchen of an apartment, we learn why: there are no smells in this city. "Nowhere was there a smell. Not of food, not of unaired clothes, not of cellars. There was absolutely no smell. Not even of rain or of myself" (13). Something similar happens to colors, light, and darkness: they are notions that have lost their usual meaning. The narrator writes: "there was no obscurity in the staircases in the buildings over there, where it should have been dark. To speak of colors is hard . . . There was no darkness and there was no light" (13). Food also looks different. Inspecting the food on a stove, the narrator has the impression that it is not cold and yet it lacks all flavor (20). Objects are equally dead. Mirrors, for instance, do not reflect images (25, 28).

On occasion, the narrator suddenly finds himself in the presence of specters, among "nameless, exhausted sleepers" that one could not prop-erly call human beings (12). In a long dream he has while sleeping in one of the houses which he enters, the narrator encounters people who seem to be sleeping or dead: "I looked at the sleepers around me; they could have lain there since eternity, for no shepherd woke them up. I was the only one standing up next to them" (35). Such is the nature of what he sees or dreams about that at some point he wonders whether he is really alive (25–26), a doubt that places the narrator himself within a gray zone, between the living and the dead, thereby turning him into a specter of sorts. His conclusion that he is alive does not completely eliminate the narrator's spectrality: "If I had been dead, why was I alone in the city? Where were the other countless dead who had died at the same time that I did? ... No, I could not be dead, for only a living being could be as lonely as I was" (26). This is a poor demonstration to say the least. At any rate, and mostly through his dreaming, the narrator meets and converses with the specters of friends, relatives, and acquaintances. Interestingly, the specters seem to have lost a sense of time: "their faces are completely expressionless, they seem to have no past" (46). Perhaps as a result of the death of the city, the narrator also feels as if lacking a time and a past. "I feel timeless" (110), he writes. Or as he affirms shortly afterwards: "In no time my past was irrevocably sunk buried. The houses, cities, countries in which I had lived, through the whirl of my fall, had been blown into nothingness" (110).

Representing specters, that is representing the visibility of the invisible as well as the invisible within the visible, is not an easy task. The use of the fantastic in *Nekyia* has to do with the author's intention of capturing something as elusive as ghosts are. But language, regardless of the mode and literary genre that one chooses for the narration of specters, lacks the right tools for expressing spectrality. On several occasions the narrator underscores the difficulty of representing through language the spectral reality in which he is immersed. Language cannot depict with accuracy the reality of an entirely dead city. Transformed into something else, the things the narrator talks about have lost all validity (11). Referring to them is even "dangerous" (11). One "can think about many matters. One can think about them, one can experience them. But when you use words to refer to all this, all being [*Dasein*] becomes inauthentic" (11). Elsewhere in the text the narrator insists on the fact that not only is "there ... nothing here"; in addition, "words do not have any validity any longer" (35). The world of specters demands its own language. Nossack treats the unrepresentability of strategic bombing in terms that are characteristic of fantastic literature. For fantastic literature is the realm of non-signification. Rosemary Jackson writes: "The fantastic ... pushes towards an area of non-signification. It does this either by attempting to articulate 'the unnameable', the 'nameless things' of horror fiction, attempting to visual-ize the unseen, or by establishing a disjunction of word and meaning

through a play upon 'thingless names'."[116] At the same time, in a space
that has been destroyed language is the only company for those who
manage to survive: amidst the destruction, "I will live together with my
words" (48). Even more: it could very well be, according to the narrator,
that "suddenly something shows itself under the words, something that
cannot be forgotten, and when this is expressed, it starts to live" (12).

Nossack's novella ends with an afterword (152–54) that hints at renewal
and a new beginning in such a way that one is tempted to see in these
pages a reference to Germany's *Wiederaufbau* (reconstruction). For
instance, the narrator exhorts the people who lie around him in this
fashion to: "go out and look for a river. There wash yourselves so that
you can recognize each other. Then, when your face is visible again, you
will give each other a name. And when the names ring out, the Earth
will . . . awaken and think" (152). The narrator also reflects on the birth of
a child – a birth that will initiate new life and therefore will return the past
to men who have lost it amidst the rubble (153). *Nekyia*, a journey to the
netherworld, a visit to a city of specters, ends with the hope in that new
beginning (154).

Received with much applause by critics and readers alike, and justly
considered as one of the most important novels published in the immediate postwar period in Germany, *Die Stadt hinter dem Strom* is a novel on
spectrality.[117] In a very literal sense, it may be read as a ghost story. The
overwhelming presence of the ghost and spectrality correlates with the
literary mode chosen by Kasack for his novel: the fantastic. As in Nossack's
Nekyia, there is here a logical connection between the literary practice

[116] Jackson, *Fantasy*, 41.
[117] Cf. Volker C. Dörr, *Mythomimesis. Mythische Geschichtsbilder in der westdeutschen (Erzähl-)
Literatur der frühen Nachkriegszeit (1945–1952)* (Berlin: Schmidt, 2004), and his "Mythos als
diskursive und narrative Kategorie in der frühen Nachkriegsliteratur Westdeutschlands,"
Komparatistik als Arbeit am Mythos, ed. Monika Schmitz-Emans and Uwe Lindemann
(Heidelberg: Synchron, 2004), 305–18; Hubert Roland and Judith Schneiberg, "Hermann
Kasacks Nachkriegsroman *Die Stadt hinter dem Strom* (1947). Versuch einer ethischen
Deutung," *Literarische Mikrokosmen. Begrenzung und Entgrenzung/Les microcosmes littéraires:
Limites et ouvertures*, ed. Christian Drösch, Hubert Roland, and Stephanie Vanasten (Brussels:
Presses Interuniversitaires Européennes (P.I.E.)/Peter Lang, 2006), 123–46; Annette
Schmollinger, "Leben im Angesicht des Todes. Anmerkungen zu Hermann Kasacks Roman *Die
Stadt hinter dem Strom*," *Die totalitäre Erfahrung. Deutsche Literatur und Drittes Reich*, ed. Frank-
Lothar Kroll (Berlin: Duncker & Humblot, 2003), 235–66; W. G. Sebald, "Zwischen Geschichte
und Naturgeschichte. Versuch über die literarische Beschreibung totaler Zerstörung mit
Anmerkungen zu Kasack, Nossack und Kluge," *Orbis Litterarum: International Review of
Literary Studies* 37.4 (1982), 345–66, and his *Luftkrieg und Literatur*, 53–56; and Herbert
Schütz, *Hermann Kasack: The Role of the Critical Intellect in the Creative Writer's Work*
(Frankfurt am Main: Peter Lang, 1972).

chosen to narrate the story and the death and destruction portrayed in *Die Stadt hinter dem Strom*. Kasack's novel is a work that refracts, with the language of the fantastic mode, the spectralization of cities and people resulting from aerial bombing. W. G. Sebald has sharply criticized Kasack's presumed ignorance "of the appalling reality of collective catastrophe" by taking refuge in a fantastic world;[118] the horrors of the time disappear under the pretense of metaphysical reflections and the artifice of abstraction. But the truth is that Kasack is able to capture and narrate life in a spectral city precisely thanks to his use of the fantastic. Spectrality, death, and complete destruction lay beyond reason and the language of realism; their representation requires other linguistic and rhetorical tools. Kasack understood that in many senses bombing is a multilayered phenomenon that resists language and representation. And he acted accordingly, writing a novel of fantasy that stands as one of the most disturbing representations of absolute war's spectralization of life and space produced in Europe in the wake of the Second World War.

The entire novel is narrated through the eyes of Robert Lindhoff, an expert in Oriental languages hired by the administration of a mysterious city located "beyond the stream" as its main archivist and chronicler.[119] Upon his arrival Lindhoff encounters people he thought to be dead, or who had mysteriously disappeared: his father, his former lover Anna, and Kastell. Furthermore, the inhabitants of the city all have a bizarre aspect and behave strangely. Thus, in a large public dining-room Lindhoff sees people who "in their inexpressive way looked like tailor's dummies" (12). Similarly, in the expression of the employees who work in the Prefecture there is "an empty earnestness" (20). One of the people in charge of the hostel where Lindhoff lodges moves in a way reminiscent of "a marionette" (39), while the pedestrians he comes across in the street pass by "lethargic," "as if they did not sense any longer the dreariness of the surroundings" (152); they seem to exist, as Lindhoff will later think, "in a dollhouse of time" (217). In sum: "he could not help any longer having the impression that everything he saw was the continuation of scenes from a theatrical piece in which each character had a role to play" (49). Only much later will Lindhoff realize what the reader has suspected all along: the city where he works is a city of specters. His epiphany comes in a failed love scene with Anna. When he embraces her, he realizes that she is only "a ghost," "a

[118] Sebald, *Luftkrieg und Literatur*, 56.
[119] Hermann Kasack, *Die Stadt hinter dem Strom* (Frankfurt am Main: Suhrkamp, 1996), 24–25. Further references in text.

woman who wasn't alive" (257). Lindhoff understands that he has always been "surrounded by phantoms" (257), that he lives "in the city of the dead" (257), that his father, Kastell, Anna, and everybody he has met since his arrival are "only specters" (257). Interestingly, he is the exception to the norm. To the specters, Robert has a spectral quality, for he is a living being who resides in a city where he does not belong. As Anna tells him, he is "not one of us" (257), Robert is "a stranger ... a guest amidst larvae" (259), "an emissary from life" (300). He lives, in sum, in a *Zwischenreich* or "realm in-between" (as the city is repeatedly referred to), whose main mission is to gather everybody who dies in order to eliminate from them any residue of individuality and consciousness that may still be left in them; as soon as they are purified from themselves, they are sent to their final, definitive death. The river that flows next to the city separates, therefore, the realm of the living from that of the specter. The inhabitants of the city are literally the living dead. For this reason, it would be inaccurate to call that place "the city of the dead." It is, instead, "the city of the specter."

The *Zwischenreich*, with its implication of liminality, functions as a trope for the spectrality that permeates all levels of the reality described in *Die Stadt hinter dem Strom*. Kasack has perfectly captured in his novel the spectral dimension produced by absolute war on buildings and people. It could be argued that *Die Stadt hinter dem Strom* is a novel on absolute war's production of ghosts. The city itself, for instance, has a spectral aspect that derives from absolute war; it is as spectral as its inhabitants. Many of its streets and buildings have been destroyed, most likely by indiscriminate air raids given the kind of destruction that they have sustained. In one of his first impressions of the city, Lindhoff realizes suddenly that "From the buildings of the surrounding rows of streets only the façades loomed ... through the bare windows one could see the sky" (10); there is nothing behind the walls of many buildings; the few of them that still have a more or less intact roof look like "strange parts" that do not seem to belong to the "image of ruins of the urban landscape" (10). The narrator describes in great detail the destroyed areas and buildings of the city (e.g., 19–20, 31–34, 93–100, 150–51). The destruction, according to Lindhoff, is typical of an earthquake or a war (17). The city itself is spectral, namely it is neither entirely alive nor completely destroyed. The narrator talks about the "lifeless appearance of the buildings" (34) and the streets that "lie extinct" (87), he depicts the "prosaic ruins of the rows of streets" and "the empty façades" (88). The city is an "annihilated world" (151); something evil breathed "out of the exposed stone structures whose half-destroyed façades stood ghostly against the glaring blue of the sky" (151). In the narrator's rendering of destruction, "from time to time a face leaned out of the window's cavity of a dead building" (153).

One of the climactic moments of the connection between specters, spectral city, and war comes in chapter 15.[120] A character named Berthelet has taken Lindhoff to a barracks where "veterans" from many wars lodge – that is to say, soldiers who died and are waiting for the extinction of what is left of their individuality. At some point during his visit Lindhoff addresses the specters of these soldiers, and encourages them *to haunt the living* – a haunting that makes people realize the horrors involved in war. Lindhoff says, "cross back over the river! . . . Go as ghosts of [the living's] dreams, take possession of their sleep . . . ! Appear like admonishing voices, like warning and demanding voices . . . Compel the living!" (299). The specters of war have, therefore, an ethical task: to haunt the living so as to make them realize that war must always be resisted. This is exactly what the novelist has undertaken in writing *Die Stadt hinter dem Strom*, and this is ultimately what the novel attempts to do: to haunt readers by telling a fantastic story on the destructive power of absolute war as well as the specters born out of it.

Lindhoff himself becomes a haunting presence among the living when he returns to his country back from the *Zwischenreich*. In the wake of war, the country has been devastated, and many people are on the move because they have lost everything. The chapter represents Lindhoff on a train in almost constant movement. There he meets all sorts of people (refugees, homeless, and so on), to whom he delivers the lesson learnt in the "city beyond the stream": "Transformation is the law. Transformation from one condition to another: what is solid into liquid, joy into sorrow and sorrow into joy, stone into dust and dust into stone, matter into spirit and spirit into matter. Death transforms into life and life into death" (434). Lindhoff is now a specter, a revenant who comes back from the kingdom of the specters to haunt the living with a message of hope. In a passage vaguely reminiscent of the last scene of Émile Zola's *La bête humaine* (The Human Beast) (1890), the train in permanent movement is, in Kasack's novel, an image of the new nomadism produced by war, as well as a representation of life itself. At the end, the train takes Lindhoff back to the *Zwischenreich*, this time not as a living being, but as someone who has just died.

---

[120] Cf. Roland and Schneiberg, "Hermann Kasacks Nachkriegsroman *Die Stadt hinter dem Strom* (1947)," 130–32.

Exorcisms

According to Jo Labanyi, there are several ways of dealing with specters.[121] One may deny their existence, refuse to see them, shut them out. This attitude has been predominant in state structures and discourses of power. One may also obsessively cling to them through "melancholia" as defined by Sigmund Freud. Or one can offer them habitation and acknowledge their presence through the healing process known, again in the sense given to the term by Freud, as "mourning"; this third way of relating to specters may lead to setting oneself free from them. Indeed, the spectrality of war survivors explored thus far is not necessarily a permanent condition. Under certain circumstances, it is possible to exorcize the ghosts of war that haunt veterans, war survivors, and those who surround them. As mentioned earlier in this chapter, Heinrich Böll relates such an occurrence in the last third of his novel *Der Engel schwieg*: its protagonist, the war veteran and deserter Hans Schnitzler, conjures up his ghosts and overcomes war trauma after falling in love with Regina Unger and rekindling his Christian faith through his acquaintanceship with a local priest. Slowly but surely readjusting to his regained civilian life, Schnitzler prepares himself to fight for his happiness beyond melancholia and mourning. Two important novels, in addition to Böll's, are predicated upon the exorcism of the ghosts of war: Sloan Wilson's hugely popular *The Man in the Gray Flannel Suit* (1955), and Walter Kolbenhoff's *Heimkehr in die Fremde* (Return to a Foreign Land) (1949). Interestingly, in these two cases the exorcism of the specter correlates with the use of the realist mode. The formal or generic hybridity, the catastrophic modernism, and the fantastic mode that we have seen associated, in varying degrees, with the representation of ghostly possession and haunting in several of the previously analyzed works is replaced, in the novels by Wilson and Kolbenhoff, with realism. Although it is hard to establish a rule for all cases, one could argue, after examining the literary treatment of specters produced by absolute war, that the overcoming of spectrality tends to correlate, on the one hand, with the avoidance of generic hybridity, modernism, and the fantastic mode, and on the other, with the use of a straightforward, mimetic, representational mode of writing.

---

[121] Jo Labanyi, "History and Hauntology; or, What Does One Do with the Ghosts of the Past? Reflections on Spanish Film and Fiction of the Post-Franco Period," *Disremembering the Dictatorship: The Politics of Memory in the Spanish Transition to Democracy*, ed. Joan Ramon Resina (Amsterdam: Rodopi, 2000), 65–66.

The Man in the Gray Flannel Suit (Sloan Wilson's sensitive portrayal of the search for existential meaning and personal purpose by a veteran in a world dominated by corporate business) was immensely successful at the time of its publication.[122] An eponymous cinematic adaptation of the novel, directed by Nunnally Johnson, would be released in 1956. *The Man in the Gray Flannel Suit* is a *tranche de vie* that centers on Thomas R. Rath, a thirty-three-year-old veteran married to a lovely, beautiful, devoted wife, and the father of three children. With the exception of flashbacks that narrate key moments of Tom's war service during the Second World War, the narrator follows a linear temporality that runs from the early summer to the fall of 1953. Initially, Tom works for a charitable foundation and lives with his family in Westport, Connecticut, but he accepts a better-paid position in public relations at the United Broadcasting Corporation in New York City. Shortly afterwards, he and his family move to a house in South Bay inherited from Tom's recently deceased grandmother. Despite appearances to the contrary, Tom feels alienated in the corporate world. His life is fragmented and somewhat unsatisfactory. He lives in four separate worlds: the "ghost-ridden world of his grandmother and his dead parents"; the "isolated, best-not-remembered world in which he had been a paratrooper"; his workplace; and the world formed by his family, "the only one of the four worlds worth a damn."[123]

A former captain of the US Army, Tom is haunted by his past as a paratrooper in the war, particularly by several pivotal dramatic events: his killing of a total of seventeen men, and most poignantly, his brutal, savage murder of a very young German soldier and his accidental killing of a friend and comrade-in-arms during combat in the Pacific. Since the end of the war, Tom has done his best to repress all memories of the war. The remembrance of war events, he seems to think, destabilizes the psyche and

---

[122] More information on *The Man in the Gray Flannel Suit* in Malcolm Gladwell, "Getting over It: *The Man in the Gray Flannel Suit* Put the War Behind Him. What's Changed?," *The New Yorker* 80.34 (2004), 75–79; Catherine Jurca, "The Sanctimonious Suburbanite: Sloan Wilson's *The Man in the Gray Flannel Suit*," *American Literary History* 11.1 (1999), 82–106; Christian Long, "Mapping Suburban Fiction," *Journal of Language, Literature and Culture* 60.3 (2013), 193–213; Jürgen Martschukat, "Men in Gray Flannel Suits: Troubling Masculinities in 1950s America," *Gender Forum* 32 (2011), 1–9; Stefanie Mueller, "Corporate Power and the Public Good in Sloan Wilson's *The Man in the Gray Flannel Suit*," *COPAS: Current Objectives of Postgraduate American Studies* 14.1 (2013), 1–12; and Joseph Colin McNicholas, "Corporate Culture and the American Novel: Producers, Persuaders, and Communicators," Ph.D. dissertation (University of Texas at Austin, 1999), 205–46.

[123] Sloan Wilson, *The Man in the Gray Flannel Suit* (New York: Thunder's Mouth Press, 2002), 22. Further references in text.

empties the world of all meaning. Family precedents advise caution: Tom's father, a veteran of the First World War, had suffered from a post-traumatic stress disorder and ended up killing himself (19–20, 52–53). In a telling passage, Tom believes that there should be a clear line separating war and peace. The past of war "is something best forgotten," after all it is a "wildly unrelated dream," a "chamber of horrors" (97). He is not willing to "brood" about a past that is gone and disconnected to the present: "I have to be tough" (97), he tells himself. Besides, "This is a time of peace, and I will forget about the war" (97). Tom thinks that they should begin wars "with a course in basic training and end them with a course in basic forgetting" (173). War is "a disconnected" and "lunatic" world (98) that has its own truths – truths that are only valid in the battlefield; for instance: the commandment "Thou Shalt Not Kill and the fact that one has killed a great many men means nothing, absolutely nothing" (98). By contrast, now, back in civilian life, "is the time to raise legitimate children, and make money, and dress properly, and be kind to one's wife, and admire one's boss, and learn not to worry" (98). Later in the novel he will refuse to tell his wife Betsy about the war (173). As he will explain to her on another occasion, "It's not that I want to and can't – it's just that I'd rather think about the future" (272).

But the past intrudes into Tom's life once and again. It re-emerges, for instance, during his job interview with the United Broadcasting Company. As part of the interview process, he is asked to produce a short autobiography that highlights the most significant facts in his life. And the one significant fact that first comes to his mind is his having killed seventeen men in the war: "It wasn't a thing he had deliberately tried to forget – he simply hadn't thought about it for quite a few years. It was the unreal-sounding, probably irrelevant, but quite accurate fact that he had killed seventeen men" (12). In a draft of that text, Tom writes: "The most significant fact about me is that for four and a half years my profession was jumping out of airplanes with a gun, and now I want to go into public relations" (13). He does not turn in this statement to his future employers, but what matters is the fact that he wrote on his war experience in the *first* drafts. The ghosts of the past reappear when in the commuter train Tom sees a young man wearing a leather jacket; this triggers Tom's memory of his killing of a young German soldier just in order to take from him his jacket. Initially, his consciousness is not aware of the contents of the remembrance, a remembrance that has been clearly repressed. This is how the narrator puts it: "Somehow the jacket nagged at Tom's mind – he had seen one like it somewhere a long time ago. It was ridiculous to have one's mind keep returning to a leather jacket when there was work to be done. The memory of the leather jacket was like a riddle, the answer to which had been half forgotten, obscurely important, as though someone had told him a secret he was never to repeat, a secret with some hidden meaning, but now he couldn't remember it" (70). Later in the day, however, Tom will remember the most significant episodes of his war service in Europe and the Pacific, including his extramarital affair with an Italian young woman, Maria (70–96). In its activation of involuntary memory, the leather jacket functions, therefore, as a sort of Proustian motif.

Although Tom tried to put them aside, these events could not be easily forgotten. They are threatening, for in their everlasting presentness they make the world and Tom himself seem absurd. This is what Tom thinks apropos of his war actions and his affair during the war with Maria: "How curious it was," Tom reflects, "to find that apparently nothing was ever really forgotten, that the past was never really gone, that it was always lurking, ready to destroy the present, or at least to make the present seem absurd, or if not that, to make Tom himself seem absurd" (77). In Tom's view, the war needed to be forgotten at all costs mostly because it was incomprehensible. The fact that he accidentally killed his friend Mahoney, or that several sailors had wanted Japanese skulls for souvenirs, among other horrible facts from his war experience, "were simply incomprehensible and had to be forgotten" (95). Decisively, according to Tom, this incomprehensibility "was the final truth of the war" (95–96). War is unfathomable and destroys meaning. Because of the war, the world has become insane, absurd. "Maybe we are all, the killers and the killed, equally damned," Tom thinks, "not guilty, not somehow made wise by war, not heroes, just men who are either dead or convinced that the world is insane" (164). In a crucial dialogue with his wife Betsy, he will insist on the absurdity of the world as a result of the sense-destroying nature of war: ever since it happened, "it's been as though I were trying to figure something out. I've never been able to get it quite clear in my mind, but I keep feeling just the way I did when I was about to make a jump and knew a lot of us were going to get killed. I keep having the same feeling I had when I killed Hank Mahoney, the feeling that the world is nuts, that the whole world is absolutely insane" (266).

Tom's exorcism of his ghosts occurs when he takes full responsibility for his own destiny. This happens through the combination of two actions. First, after realizing that he lacks professional ambition and that he wants a job that does not hinder family life (240–41), Tom tells his boss, the powerful Ralph Hopkins, that he does not have a strong professional ambition, that he is in fact an 8-to-5-man who wants to spend time with his family (251–52). Second, he confesses to Betsy his love affair with Maria, with whom he has a son (262–72). Tom wants to help Maria and their son by sending money on a regular basis (262). By making these two moves, he overcomes his being haunted by the ghosts of war. As Tom himself says, "I can't do anything about the state of the world, but I can put my own life in order" (266). And this is exactly what he does at the end of the novel: he tells his boss the kind of job he wants, and he tells the whole truth to his wife, thereby taking control over his life.

The Man in the Gray Flannel Suit is a novel, on the one hand, about the ghosts of war haunting the present, and on the other, about the exorcism of those specters through personal honesty and decisive self-assertive action. Tom assumes the presence of the ghosts, and takes responsibility for his actions in wartime by confessing them to his wife. Redemption comes not through rewarded professional ambition, but rather through the acknowledgement that a potential professional reward would be insufficient, meaningless in fact. The real purpose in life lies, for Tom Rath, in accepting a middle-class aurea mediocritas, in living in American suburbia, in enjoying a cozy self-enclosed family life. As strange as this may sound to a contemporary reader, in Wilson's novel these are the sources for personal fulfillment and existential authenticity. The assumption of purpose and meaning is reached as soon as Tom gives a proper habitation to his ghosts of war. He welcomes them, makes them part of the family (Betsy will agree to the payment of a monthly allowance to Maria in order to cover the expenses related to the education of Tom's illegitimate son), thereby undermining their force on the present. Tom has learnt to live with his ghosts; he has finally accepted them. Those ghosts must not be forgotten or repressed – as he had done earlier – but rather be granted proper recognition, which is a way of giving them a proper burial. In a sort of Albert Camus-like argument, the novel claims that war may have made the world absurd, but every human being is responsible for making the right choices – that is part of their radical freedom. One needs to face the ghosts of war that have made the world absurd, measure one's strengths and limitations, and act accordingly.

The kind of exorcism performed in The Man in the Gray Flannel Suit makes sense in a stable and advanced individualistic society moving fast towards a post-industrial articulation of the economy. In contrast, the one carried out in Heimkehr in die Fremde belongs to a physically devastated and morally ruined world in need of material reconstruction and spiritual healing.[124] *Heimkehr in die Fremde* was written by the novelist and journalist Walter Kolbenhoff, a member of the German Communist Party, a veteran of the Wehrmacht, and a prisoner of war who, after being released from internment in the United States, went back to Germany, joined the editorial board of *Die neue Zeitung*, worked for the magazine *Der Ruf – unabhängige Blätter der jungen Generation*, and participated in the founding meeting of Gruppe 47.[125] In *Heimkehr in die Fremde* he presents a *writerly* exorcism, one entirely different from Tom Rath's in *The Man in the Gray Flannel Suit*. Unlike Sloan Wilson, Walter Kolbenhoff does not suggest an exorcism through accommodation (to social class, to family life, to one's own limitations), but rather through rebellion against, and criticism of, the pervasive climate of despondency, demoralization, and defeat in Germany in the immediate postwar period. The tool chosen to express such a rebellion is writing itself. Put differently: in *Heimkehr in die Fremde* exorcism is carried out by means of a mimetic literary writing predicated on a critical attitude.

Kolbenhoff's novel is told by an autodiegetic narrator. A reflection of the author himself (like the novelist, the unnamed narrator and main character is a writer born to a working-class family, who in the 1930s emigrated abroad and worked in different countries before fighting in the war, where he was captured by the Americans and sent to internment camps in the United States), the narrator came back from captivity a few months before the beginning of the action told in the novel, which takes place in the spring of 1946. Using a straightforward, mater-of-fact language underpinned by the poetics of realism, he focuses on several subplots and motifs, such as the daily lives of Steffi and Molly – two of his neighbors who prostitute themselves in order to survive – , his feelings of solitude and alienation in the unnamed German city where he has taken up residence, the grim reality of Germany in the immediate postwar period, and most important, his mission as a writer as well as the

[124] An introduction to Walter Kolbenhoff and *Heimkehr in die Fremde* can be found in Eva Banchelli, "Heimkehr als Gründungsmythos: Walter Kolbenhoff," *Heimkehr. Eine zentrale Kategorie der Nachkriegszeit*, ed. Elena Agazzi and Erhard Schütz (Berlin: Duncker & Humblot, 2010), 117–28. See, also, Helmut Peitsch, "Vom 'Realismus' eines Kriegsromans – 'Unmittelbar', 'Magisch', oder 'Tendenziös'? Walter Kolbenhoff: *Von unserem Fleisch und Blut* (1947)," *Von Böll bis Buchheim. Deutsche Kriegsprosa nach 1945*, ed. Hans Wagener (Amsterdam: Rodopi, 1997), 63–90.
[125] William Cloonan (*The Writing of War: French and German Fiction and World War II* [Gainsville, FL: University Press of Florida, 1999], 40–46) provides a useful overview of Gruppe 47 in relation to the literary challenges posed by the Second World War.

contents, form, and socio-political purpose of the novel that he is writing, an activity that reflects, in a *mise en abîme*, Kolbenhoff's own writing of *Heimkehr in die Fremde*. While it is true that the novel does not openly depict ghostly possession, the writing of both the author and his narrator performs a kind of double exorcism: on the one hand, it conjures up their own demons, born, the reader is left to suppose, out of the war; on the other, it attempts to exorcize those Germans – the vast majority, if we are to believe the novel – who carried on haunted by memories of absolute war.

The title of this novel represents the feeling of alienation experienced by the narrator in his own country after so many years of living abroad. As happens to other veterans, the narrator has returned to a country that feels foreign to him. Consequently, at times he is overtaken by feelings of loneliness and alienation. When that occurs, the narrator has the almost unbearable impression that he does not belong to the city at all. He feels oppressed by the city, while acknowledging that perhaps the problem lies in himself: "I have been away for too long and now I cannot feel myself at home any longer [in the city]."[126] But in congruence with his stated plan to regenerate his country through literature, the narrator uses his writing to address those feelings of solitude and alienation:

> I have to write, I have to tell how it is for whoever comes back home … I start to write. I write … on how loneliness began to devour me, and on how the evening came threatening to choke me with melancholy. I wrote for a long time, but writing did not alleviate me. I stood up again and looked out into the night, over the broken roofs of this city, which had chained my destiny and which was so alien to me. (13–14)

Ever since his arrival in the city, the narrator has been observing very closely the grim reality in which Germans have to live, the bleakness and pessimism of most people, their ruined soul. "This country has such a dismal aspect when you look at it," he writes, "but even more desolate seemed to be the destruction in the souls of the people" (49). After all, a house can be rebuilt, one needs only the proper materials, but "How should they [the Germans] expel the oppressiveness that choked their souls?" (49). At the beginning of chapter 21 the narrator provides a detailed description of the desolate aspect of the city and its inhabitants (153–55). His purpose, declared earlier in the novel, is to change that reality and those people: "The faces next to me and before me were worse

---

[126] Walter Kolbenhoff, *Heimkehr in die Fremde* (Frankfurt am Main: Suhrkamp, 1988), 14. Further references in text.

than the ruins ... I wanted to see another face and hear a voice different from the voice of quarrel and desperation" (92), or as he says elsewhere, "We should forget these sad times and try to find new paths" (98). The narrator will deal with these issues throughout the novel, and his answer to his own questions will be that one way of lifting that pressure from the people's souls is precisely to describe *mimetically* that bleak reality. In *Heimkehr in die Fremde*, realistic writing is understood as leading to collective catharsis, as an exorcism of the coeval readers' ghosts.

The novel argues for the need to find new paths for German society. The reconstruction of the country is the main task of the narrator's generation, according to the implied author. *Heimkehr in die Fremde* contains a message of reconstruction, of hope after the catastrophe. His generation, the narrator says, is the most prepared for undertaking the molding of a new society. "We know life before the catastrophe, and then we became soldiers," the narrator states, "and now we are still young enough to start again from the point where we left it" (65). This new generation has no confidence in the older one because "its world has disappeared" (65), whereas the younger people lack experience and knowledge. "We must do something" (65), concludes the narrator. Before them lies "the most daunting revolution of our history," and this breathtaking realization makes "my heart beat faster" (91). Occasionally, he is tortured with doubts, and there are moments in which he feels threatened by loneliness. His times mix like no other period in history "desperation and the feeling of going with optimism and joy," but the mission is clear: "we want to be completely bare and completely honest, so that we can really start again, completely afresh. The disaster lies behind us ... Have no fear ... It will be just fine" (91). As the narrator affirms further on in the novel, his generation fought in the war, and the survivors who returned home only knew that "they don't believe in anything and that all must be done differently" (101). They face a completely new beginning. Their first task consists of "finding the right path" (102).

This wish to reform society can be seen in other coeval novels about war veterans produced in countries other than Germany. I am thinking, for instance, of Flannery O'Connor's novel *Wise Blood* (1952), whose main character, a disturbing American veteran named Hazel Motes, means to regenerate people by preaching, on the streets of a sinister town in the southern United States, the anti-religious, atheistic gospel of his "Church without Christ." Another case in point is *Three Men in New Suits* (1945), a novel by J. B. Priestley. In the last scene, war veteran Alan Strete delivers the authorial message of the novel. "Modern man is essentially a co-operative and communal man," he says to two former comrades-in-arms.[127] "Our problem, which we must solve . . . is how to use this power of working together for the benefit of the largest possible common human denominator."[128] They must make the entire world "our home," they must have "faith" and "compassion" for everybody regardless of their race. "This hope of a home on earth, this faith and this compassion are now at the very center of our lives."[129] Should they ignore such a task, "then we cheat ourselves into cruelty and murder, sink into madness, turn into stone."[130] Alan Strete concludes that "Either the earth must soon be the miserable grave of our species or it must be at last our home, where men can live at peace and can work for other men's happiness."[131] Priestley does not specify in *Three Men in New Suits* how to articulate and carry out this rather vague socialist program of universal brotherhood after catastrophe, as if he took for granted that the reader would understand what his character meant without further elaboration. In contrast to this lack of specificity, Kolbenhoff does offer an answer: the regeneration of society will come through the material reconstruction of cities and infrastructures *as well as* the spiritual healing of the German soul. Writing will be one way of contributing to the latter dimension of Germany's *Wiederaufbau*.

Writing has an exorcizing function. As we saw earlier, according to the narrator Germans will realize what needs to be done as soon as they face, head-on, their grim reality. Literature can put in front of them a bleak world, thereby helping people to exorcize their war ghosts. As he explicitly says, "I want to hold before the reader, as if it were a mirror, his current life. He should see into it and be appalled. He should say: that's no good. It is unworthy of men to live like this, we must have the strength to live differently" (101–2). The narrator's writing is led by a political and social program: "I must tell them about it. I must tell them how Steffi lives and how I live, and how Germany looks to someone who has been so long away . . . Perhaps others find our country equally as strange as I find it and get as terrified as I was" (17). In an important passage, he spells out the contents and representational outlook of his own novel, his social mission as a writer, and the message of hope and reconstruction contained in it (27).

The autodiegetic narrator acknowledges that he could have applied for a job, but he felt the peremptory need to write: "I would rather suffer from hunger and write the book" (90). Taking as a point of reference the

[127] J. B. Priestley, *Three Men in New Suits* (New York: Harper & Brothers Publishers, 1945), 215.
[128] Ibid., 215.   [129] Ibid., 216.   [130] Ibid., 216.   [131] Ibid., 216.

German literary field from 1933 to 1945, the kind of mimetic and simple writing that he is proposing is new; nobody has attempted the kind of novel he is writing (90). The narrator himself spells out the style and mode of his writing: "Be honest ... write honestly, narrate with complete simplicity, try to narrate as simply as possible" (192). These sorts of comments introduce a modernist self-referential dimension to Kolbenhoff's *Heimkehr in die Fremde*. This is a novel about its own making; it is also a novel that proposes what the author considers to be the right poetics for the spiritual reconstruction of the country. As Christopher Prendergast has shown, realism establishes common frames of reference for the shared understanding of reality.[132] Realist narratives may help readers to create a sense of belonging to a specific society. It is not by chance that nation building in Europe and the Americas in the nineteenth century was shaped by realist historical novels. A country devastated by the war whose cultural memory had been partly wiped out by the Allied bombers, Germany had to be rebuilt. The simultaneous exorcism of the ghosts of war and the symbolic reconstruction of the country found in realism a most adequate tool. Furthermore, in Kolbenhoff's novel realist writing regenerates literature itself, it exorcizes literary activity from the demons that had possessed it during Nazism. As Victor Klemperer and George Steiner have demonstrated in two important works, National Socialism had a very noxious, corrupting effect on the German language.[133] Like other members of the generation of young authors that emerged in the early postwar period (e.g., Wolfgang Borchert, Hans Werner Richter, Heinrich Böll, Siegfried Lenz), Walter Kolbenhoff realized that linguistic and literary regeneration could only be accomplished by the use of a straightforward language and the practice of a realist poetics. When speech "has been injected with falsehoods," wrote Steiner apropos of the Nazi corruption of the German language, "only the most drastic truth can cleanse it."[134] This is precisely one of the objectives undertaken by Kolbenhoff and his narrator in *Heimkehr in die Fremde*.

The closing scene of the novel is crucial, for it highlights the two pending reconstructions in Germany. One, the physical reconstruction

---

[132] Christopher Prendergast, *The Order of Mimesis: Balzac, Stendhal, Nerval, Flaubert* (Cambridge University Press, 1986).

[133] Victor Klemperer, *The Language of the Third Reich: LTI – Lingua Tertii Imperii. A Philologist's Notebook*, trans. Martin Brady (London: Continuum, 2002); George Steiner, *Language & Silence: Essays on Language, Literature, and the Inhuman* (New Haven, CT: Yale University Press, 1998), 95–109.

[134] Steiner, *Language & Silence*, 108.

of cities, is represented by Steffi's husband, Hannes, who was taken prisoner in Stalingrad and returns from Soviet captivity at the end of *Heimkehr in die Fremde*. Hannes does not understand the people's lack of resolve in rebuilding their city, finding outrageous the presence of rubble in the streets one year after the war's end. What needs to be done, he categorically states, is to take out the rubble (220–21). After conversing with Hannes, the narrator goes back to his flat and starts working on his novel: "I left them both and went through the long corridor to my room ... I looked into the drawer but there was no more bread there. Then I sat down and began to write" (224). The ending underscores, therefore, the interdependence of the two kinds of *Wiederaufbau*. The one undertaken by the narrator had already been spelled out earlier: "Up until now no one has said what I want to say, I must do it. I should show them what they perhaps don't see; maybe they had become too lazy, too apathetic, to see it. Excuse me, I thought, clear the rubble for a while yourself, I have another kind of work, a work that is no less important [than clearing the rubble]" (90). By so doing, Kolbenhoff refers metatextually to his own novel. The novel that the narrator is writing has the same content, style, mode, and mission as *Heimkehr in die Fremde*. Kolbenhoff's work performs the only kind of exorcism available at the time to a German author: his own realist writing. In this specific case, the basic purpose of the novel lies in exorcizing the ghosts of war that haunt at once the postwar readers and German literature.

Kolbenhoff attempts in his novel the ultimate hauntology of war, namely the exorcism of ghosts through writing. In this sense, it could be argued that *Heimkehr in die Fremde* constitutes a metaliterary commentary on the hauntologies of absolute war articulated in the other works analyzed in this chapter. Writing is an excellent tool not only for representing spectrality, but also for exorcizing the specters of war. In addressing the haunting power of the ghost, literature may give a proper habitation to the specter. In the final analysis, this is the lesson taught not only by Walter Kolbenhoff's novel *Heimkehr in die Fremde*, but by all the texts explored here. The examined works by Borchert, Böll, Bauer, Green, Macaulay, Nossack, Kasack, Wilson, and Kolbenhoff do not deny or reject the ghost; they embrace it, they set out to understand it on its own terms, bringing the reader closer to its predicament and its claims. To an extent, their function is cathartic. While none of those works justify or condone the warrior's violent, lethal action, they do show empathy for those war survivors whose psyche is haunted by the extreme violence of absolute war. As medical practitioners know well, empathy and narrative are two fine tools for exorcizing the ghosts of war in the often tortuous, difficult path followed to attain the social, psychological, and moral rehabilitation of the veteran and the war survivor. In the words of Sidonie Smith and Julia Watson, "speaking or writing about trauma becomes a process through which the narrator finds words to give voice to what was previously unspeakable. And that process can be, though it is not necessarily, cathartic."[135] Therefore, by means of both the representation and the exorcism of the specter literary writing on war's spectrality may constitute a useful instrument for bringing about the rehabilitation of veterans and war survivors.

Except perhaps for Henry Green's *Back*, all the texts studied in this chapter depict specters that were either born out of the horror experienced in the battlefields of absolute war – and, in some cases, of an ensuing period of captivity – or of the terror brought about by aerial bombing. Veterans, former prisoners of war, survivors of the air war, and the cities devastated by air raids or atomic weapons make up a rich canvas of the spectrality derived from the absolute war as it was waged in the world war of 1939–45. All of them are haunting forces that, together with the horror and terror examined in Chapters 1 and 2 respectively, constitute crucial semantic clusters of the language of absolute war. A sobering truth speaks to us through these spectral presences: the truth of extreme cruelty and ruthless violence, absolute animus, shameful decisions, unspeakable acts, dishonorable deeds, devastated urban landscapes, frozen corpses and mangled bodies, damaged minds, men and women burned alive in melting asphalt, people buried in the cellars of their own apartment buildings. In 1939–45, perpetrators and victims of absolute war gazed into the abyss of nothingness – an extreme experience that turned many of them into specters doomed to haunt future generations. "He who fights with monsters," Nietzsche once wrote, "should be careful lest he thereby become a monster. And if you gaze long into an abyss, the abyss will also gaze into you."[136] Because of this close encounter with death and total destruction, many people came back from absolute war forever transfigured. These remains of destruction bore in themselves the traces of absolute war, the almost indelible mark of that which resists language and representation. Witnesses of an altogether unprecedented carnage,

[135] Sidonie Smith and Julia Watson, *Reading Autobiography: A Guide for Interpreting Life Narratives* (Minneapolis, MN: University of Minnesota Press, 2001), 22.

[136] Friedrich Nietzsche, *Jenseits von Gut und Böse, Sämtliche Werke*, ed. Giorgio Colli and Mazzino Montinari, vol. 5/15 (Munich: Deutscher Taschenbuch Verlag, 1999), ch. 4, section 146.

the specters of the Second World War stage a play of visibilities and invisibilities, of presences and absences, of speech and silence. These living dead emblematize the boundaries that separate what can be told from what cannot be said. This is precisely yet another crucial truth unveiled by the deployment of a hauntology of war to analyze absolute war writing, a truth that reveals not only the composite hauntology of ghosts, but also the constitutive liminality of the very event that has created them in the first place – absolute war.

Coda
Remains

Hibakusha resting in a local hospital. Scorched metal. Twisted metal. Charred stones. Shattered stones. Bottle caps inextricably fused into a single mass. Human flesh exhibited in flasks. Piles of hair from women who lost it due to exposure to the radiation delivered by the bomb. Photographs of burned bodies. A film that reconstructs the events of August 6, 1945. Newsreels showing the complete destruction of the city and scars stamped on scalps and necks, on backs and shoulders, on arms and legs. Newsreels on infant survivors with all sorts of injuries and bodily deformities. Newsreels on daily life in the city after the war, its inhabitants trying to rebuild their lives as best they can.

Such are the remains of Hiroshima seen by the unnamed female protagonist of Alain Resnais's acclaimed motion picture *Hiroshima mon amour* (1959).[1] A French actress (Emmanuelle Riva) who has traveled to Hiroshima to perform in a movie shot on location, *She* knows no more – nor no less – about the atomic bombing of that city and its aftermath than what those haunting remains poignantly tell her. Her lover, an unnamed architect (Eiji Okada) born in Hiroshima, holds that none of those remains has any cognitive value. In the sixteen-minute-long first scene of *Hiroshima mon amour*, during which *She* tells *Him* all she has learnt about Hiroshima while they lie naked on her bed, *He* occasionally interrupts her narrative to point out in curt sentences that in truth she knows nothing – nothing at all: "You saw nothing in Hiroshima. Nothing" (0:03:53), "You didn't see the hospital at Hiroshima" (0:04:33), "You made it all up" (0:09:41), "You know nothing, nothing" (0:16:00) – these are his categoric words. At the very outset of his film, Alain Resnais sets off in counterpoint

---

[1] Alain Resnais, director, *Hiroshima mon amour* (Neuilly sur Seine: Argos Films, 1959), www.amazon.com/Hiroshima-mon-amour-English-Subtitled/dp/BooZRCAG3M/ref=sr_1_1?keywords=hiroshima+mon+amour&qid=1558516754&s=instant-video&sr=8-1, accessed September 1, 2018. All references in text.

two central views on the radical epistemological challenges posed by Hiroshima to language and understanding. On the one hand, *She* believes in the mind's power to draw conclusions from the close observation of empirical reality and in the capacity of language to communicate it, no matter how extreme that reality may be. On the other, *He* denies the validity of that attitude as regards the atomic bombing of his hometown: there is simply no possible knowledge of Hiroshima. No narrative can truly capture an event as unique as the atomic bombing of that Japanese city. The gap between language and the reality of absolute destruction is unbridgeable.

Hiroshima mon amour shares the male protagonist's point of view. Certainly, the film does embed documentary footage on Hiroshima. The tragedy is thus represented, but through the somewhat naive eyes of the French actress. Resnais does not re-enact what happened on August 6, 1945, in that Japanese city or in the immediate aftermath. Instead, his complete attention focuses on a thirty-six-hour-long love affair between two complete strangers in Hiroshima one decade after the atomic holocaust. Following the French filmmaker's implied standpoint, the motion picture's cognitive value on Hiroshima lies in the fact that Resnais emphatically leaves the event out of the film's visual field. In *Hiroshima mon amour* the atomic bombing is thought to be beyond language. While he probably felt an ethical imperative to shoot a movie related to the atomic bombing of Hiroshima, similar to the ethical drive that moved (as we saw in the last section of Chapter 2) important Japanese writers to produce works on the bombing, Resnais opted for not representing it. Memory, forgetting, trauma, the love affair of two people damaged by the world war of 1939–45: these are the themes to which he devotes all his attention. Resnais's decision to leave Hiroshima out of the representational field of his film is, at the same time, a consistent move in the context of the representation of modern warfare in general. A number of writers, filmmakers, artists, and scholars have investigated the difficulties involved in the representation of war. This is a well-trodden path. Without denying the importance within the film of the non-representability of Hiroshima, I would like to underscore two additional interrelated claims that Resnais seems to be making. First, there is the claim that representation needs to be considered as one of the casualties of the atomic bomb. In the same way that the weapon destroyed life, ecology, and human habitation in a completely unprecedented way, it also had an extremely negative effect on language and existing conceptual frameworks. The catastrophic event has hindered the human capacity for understanding and communicating it. Insofar as violence has a detrimental impact on the linguistic, narrative, and rhetorical tools used to symbolize the extralinguistic world, representation itself ought to be viewed as one of its casualties. For that reason (and this would be the second claim subtly made by Alain Resnais), narratives on the bombing, like the newsreels embedded in the film, are aftereffects of the atomic blast as well as its *remains* – remains that may haunt those who approach them, as happens to the French actress. One must logically conclude that *Hiroshima mon amour*, a movie about the remains of war, is itself one of these remains.

By placing emphasis on the remains of Hiroshima, Resnais underscores their capacity to haunt. In *Hiroshima mon amour* the remains of war have a ghostly dimension. From the very first scene, the atomic bombing of Hiroshima haunts the love affair of the two protagonists. It is no coincidence that the very first shot of the film shows two naked bodies in an amorous embrace covered by what seems to be ashes; shortly afterwards, in a different shot, the bodies appear young, muscular, sweaty, alive. This montage of mutually reflecting shots obviously connects the love-making of the French actress and the Japanese architect to the embracing of a couple incinerated in the midst of the atomic holocaust. The overlapping of shots seems to convey the message that the French actress and the Japanese architect are, themselves, protracted victims, and therefore remains, of the bombing. Indeed, the effects of Hiroshima are felt in the present of the love affair as a haunting traumatic memory, which in the case of the French actress is closely related to her own traumatic experiences suffered at the end of the war in her hometown of Nevers. The last scene of the movie underlines the haunting power of Hiroshima through a symbolically charged dialogue in which *She* tells *Him*: "Hiroshima: that's your name" (1:30:02). Thus, the ghostliness and haunting force of Hiroshima and its remains are transferred to the Japanese lover. More than the unknowability of Hiroshima, the ghostly character of Hiroshima and the haunting power of its remains are, precisely, the two main driving forces of *Hiroshima mon amour*.

Resnais's choice to articulate his movie through spectrality and haunting sheds light on an important feature of many cultural products on war. Like corpses, survivors, ruins, debris, human detritus, and ghosts, texts on war (e.g., personal diaries, memoirs, fictional accounts, photographs, documentaries, motion pictures, and so on) are remains of warfare. Texts devoted to represent war constitute a peculiar kind of remains due to their special relation to liminality. In the specific case of written cultural objects, war writing tries to bridge the awareness of the impossibility of capturing warfare in all its complexity and the need to understand military confrontation. As happens with ghosts, war writing stands between the visible and the invisible, the sayable and the unsayable, memory and forgetfulness. Also like ghosts, and in contrast to remains of war marked by their ephemeral nature (e.g., corpses, rubble, urban ruins), war writing brings to the present actions from the past, thereby projecting past (oftentimes remote) military conflicts onto present affairs, a phenomenon that impels readers to reflect on literary decisions, historical accounts, and ethical issues that *still* matter. Indeed, war literature has a powerful capacity to project to the present past events. Although this ability to project the past to the future is intrinsic to writing itself, war writing brings this characteristic of any written work to an extreme. The textual remains of warfare always bring past violence to our minds, leaving on them a mark, perhaps even a "scar."

The written texts explored in this monograph relate to *Hiroshima mon amour* in the sense that they may be understood, too, as haunting remains of absolute war. Except for Jonathan Littell, who was born two decades after the war, the authors whose work I have studied in this book lived through the world war of 1939–45. Their narratives on absolute war are personal responses to a reality surely experienced with great emotional intensity. Furthermore, war in its absolute degree challenged their language and conditioned their literary choices. This is most evident in traumatic realist works and catastrophic modernist texts. In these two literary practices, literature internalizes the extremes of absolute war at the formal level. Literary works may even project onto the reader the depicted violence (as we saw in Chapters 1 and 2) through the deployment of a writing of cruelty. It could be argued that absolute war's unbridled violence interpellates authors, who in turn haunt readers by means of their literary, historical, and ethical choices for representing sheer violence, military force almost beyond the control of policy, absolute animus, the drive to annihilate the enemy, the targeting of civilians, the dissolution of all boundaries; in sum: war in itself, carried out without the usual external factors that hinder it from reaching its absolute degree.

Being themselves remains, then, of the war that they narrate, literary artifacts on absolute war may be interpreted as the epitome of modern representations of warfare. Narratives on absolute war display very openly essential aspects of all kinds of war literature. They do so in a particular manner: literature on absolute war as fought in the battlefield or against urban centers unveils situations and problems that in literary works centered on non-absolute military conflicts somehow have less intensity, or are merely latent. Theodor Plievier's *Stalingrad* (1945), Otto Erich Kiesel's *Die unverzagte Stadt* (The Undaunted City) (1949), Gert Ledig's *Vergeltung* (Payback) (1956), Vasily Grossman's *Life and Fate* (1980), or Yōko Ōta's *City of Corpses* (1950) – to mention just a few – present unparalleled levels of violence, animosity, and destruction that books on conventional military conflicts rarely match. It is the very nature of absolute war that engenders such uniqueness. Works on the Iraq War such as David Finkel's *The Good Soldiers* (2009), Kevin Powers's *The Yellow Birds* (2012), Phil Klay's *Redeployment* (2014), and Roy Scranton's *War Porn* (2016) portray a violent reality that, as harsh and unforgiving as it is in itself, does not compare to the one described in many fictional and non-fictional narratives on the Second World War. The differences between written works on absolute war and narratives on conventional conflicts lie not, therefore, in the substance; rather, they are a matter of degree. By definition, all wars contain within themselves, let it not be forgotten, the seeds of absolute war. The Vietnam War is an example of how a war that began as a conventional, limited military conflict, can quickly escalate and approach its absolute character as soon as all limits hindering the complete discharge of war's energy break up.[2]

The extremes of absolute war are refracted in literature through a heightened intensity in the verbal representation of war's constitutive elements. To put it otherwise, in addition to taking war's violence, enmity, and hatred to extremes, war in its absolute degree also has an impact on its written representation, often shaping literary works after its own nature. This explains the relevance, in important works on the Second World War, of literary practices that somehow undermine our trust in the representability of nonlinguistic reality. Thus, the homology between the nature of absolute war and catastrophic modernism is of the utmost importance: the study of that literary practice reveals crucial aspects of absolute war. Exploring absolute war writing may be a productive way, therefore, for learning about war in its absolute degree. The grammar and logic of absolute war can be approached not only by examining descriptions of and stories on

---

[2] In *A Rumor of War* (1977; 2nd ed. [New York: Picador, 2010]), Philip Caputo has emphasized the transformation of a supposedly easy, quick, and victorious campaign in Vietnam into an intense, vicious, merciless war of attrition. Cf. Michael Herr's 1977 war memoir *Dispatches: 1967–1975* (*Reporting Vietnam: American Journalism 1959–1975*, vol. 2/2 [New York: Library of America, 1998], 592–95, 629–30). See Nick Turse's book on the deliberate, pervasive, and systematic targeting of Vietnamese civilians by the US armed forces – a targeting that resulted in millions of noncombatants being killed or wounded (*Kill Anything That Moves: The Real American War in Vietnam* [New York: Metropolitan Books, 2013]).

absolute war, but also through the analysis of the images, tropes, formal devices, narrative conventions, and means of expression deployed by the writing on absolute warfare. Furthermore, in the same way that the exploration of absolute war is a necessary analytic move for refining our understanding of any war, studying the characteristics of the literature and language of absolute war sheds new light on most kinds of war writing. Literature on absolute war highlights what in literary works on limited military conflicts usually remains attenuated, understated, concealed, or in the background, or simply plays a secondary role. The motifs, themes, rhetoric, tone, and formal devices of literature on absolute war may be present in war writing on limited military conflicts, but bearing a distinct imprint. For all these reasons, I am tempted to conclude that the texts studied in this book make up, in their representation of absolute warfare, the kernel of many, if not all, instances of war writing. If absolute war is a concept – as Clausewitz suggests in *Vom Kriege* – required by theory for a philosophical approach to war, we could equally argue that the literature of absolute war constitutes an essential point of reference for the analysis and understanding of war writing in general.

Catastrophic modernism, traumatic realism, traditional realism, and the fantastic are the four main literary practices underlying the textual remains of absolute war. Indeed, none of them are peculiar to the writing on war in its absolute degree; they also underpin works on themes that have nothing to do with military violence, absolute or otherwise. However, the respective family resemblances of these four literary practices do combine in ways that are specific to the representation of absolute war. Many of the family resemblances – for example – of catastrophic modernism are present in countless modernist works unrelated to catastrophe, but when used to articulate a narrative on absolute war they become functions of essential constituents of absolute war writing, such as kaput, the abject, the absurd, useless suffering, the writing of cruelty, polyphony, montage, variable or multiple internal focalization, narrative unreliability, extreme violence, radical evil, and spectrality. Catastrophic modernism on absolute war has its own specificity. The hallmark of the catastrophic modernism that underlies key representations of the Second World War consists of the criss-crossing of the usual family resemblances of modernism, the set of five core features mentioned in the Introduction, and (crucially) a radicalization in literary experimentation partly developed so as to capture the extreme reality of absolute warfare.

Cultural artifacts on absolute war – and not only those of a catastrophic modernist nature – are often passionate utterances addressed at having consequential effects on the readers' affects, emotions, thinking, and actions. One of their chief goals is to haunt readers with the representation of extreme, unbracketed military violence. This is an ambiguous haunting, though, for while some literary works and motion pictures contain warnings against war, they may be paradoxically read or viewed as gratifying the readers' senses and violent instincts. War narratives with a pacifist subtext have the potential for being interpreted in the opposite political direction, namely as praises to courage and bravery in combat and calls to military violence and the armed forces. Stanley Kubrick's movie *Full Metal Jacket* (1987) is a case in point: despite its unforgiving antimilitaristic subtext, American young men have enlisted in the US Marine Corps moved precisely by the film's depiction of military life.[3] A former marine himself, Anthony Swofford argues in his bestselling Gulf War memoir *Jarhead* (2003) that Vietnam War films taken to be antiwar are, in fact, pro-war regardless of the message intended by the filmmakers. To be sure, civilians who watch these films may conclude that war is "inhumane and terrible," but military men and women "watch the same films and are excited by them, because the magic brutality of the films celebrates the terrible and despicable beauty of their fighting skills. Fight, rape, war, pillage, burn. Filmic images of death and carnage are pornography for the military man."[4] This brings us to the ethics of reading. Readers need to be actively vigilant and to decode the ethical claims made by war narratives by trying to reconstruct what Umberto Eco has called the "*intentio operis*" or the text's intention.[5] The literary, historical, and moral *Bildung* that we can attain by reading books on absolute war is, in the last analysis, up to us. Attentiveness to the texts' ethical claims and literary nuances is one of our chief moral responsibilities as readers of war writing. The narrative remains of war often propound historical and moral lessons that for their proper understanding require from readers the rigorous deployment of a literary competence, historical knowledge, and an ethical engagement with the text. This is precisely what *Hiroshima mon amour* and the works studied in

---

[3] Anthony Swofford, "*Full Metal Jacket* Seduced My Generation and Sent Us to War," *The New York Times Magazine* (August 18, 2018), www.nytimes.com/2018/04/18/magazine/full-metal-jacket-ermey-marine-corps.html, accessed October 8, 2018.

[4] Anthony Swofford, *Jarhead: A Marine's Chronicle of the Gulf War and Other Battles* (New York: Scribner, 2003), 6–7. That peculiar reading by military personnel of antiwar movies partly derives from the aesthetization of war, which has been a constant in the history of culture. Philip D. Beidler has studied the fascination exerted by war on art and literature in *Beautiful War: Studies in a Dreadful Fascination* (Tuscaloosa, AL: University of Alabama Press, 2016).

[5] Umberto Eco, *The Limits of Interpretation* (Bloomington, IN: Indiana University Press, 1990), 58–59.

The Literature of Absolute War try to tell us: the haunting textual remains of absolute war will talk to us *only* if we know how to listen.

The horror, terror, specters, remains – this is the stuff the Gothic is made of. I was unaware of the Gothic dimension of my book until after I drafted the final version of the table of contents. Upon remarking its Gothic outlook, I began to suspect that perhaps there is indeed a nexus between absolute war and the Gothic – a nexus that I had somehow overlooked. I was not only thinking of the spectral condition of many veterans and their haunting power, both explored in the third chapter; I also had in mind the historical manifestation and literary representation of human drives that are usually repressed in regular social intercourse, such as the acting-out of absolute animosity, murder, torture, cruelty, the relentless persecution of the innocent, the destruction of the world, as well as utter abjection, the cannibalization of the "other," and the omnipresence of the *Unheimliche*. This last element is, I suspect, the most important of them all. Both absolute war and the Gothic have a profound, intimate association with the uncanny – and this association constitutes, in turn, an essential link between these two phenomena. War in the absolute degree and the Gothic bring to the fore extremely powerful destructive forces that for some time had remained concealed, cast out to the remotest corners of the psyche or social life, their renewed prominence threatening to upset the stability of the ego, the integrity of the body, social relations, the status quo, even – as happened in 1939–45 – the entire world. Ending a book can bring all sorts of surprises. Secondary statements, unremarked connections, invisible undercurrents, or hidden patterns may unexpectedly creep to the surface, as if demanding attention. To finish a monograph, only to start it anew. In the end there is a beginning: the beginning of writing.

Bibliography

Abraham, Nicolas, and Mária Török, *The Shell and the Kernel: Renewals of Psychoanalysis*, trans. and ed. Nicholas T. Rand (University of Chicago Press, 1994).

Adams, Robert Martin, *Nil: Episodes in the Literary Conquest of Void during the Nineteenth Century* (Oxford University Press, 1966).

Adkins, Joan F., "Sacrifice and Dehumanization in Plievier's *Stalingrad*," *War, Literature, and the Arts* 2.1 (1990), 1–22.

Agamben, Giorgio, *Nudities*, trans. David Kishik and Stefan Pedatella (Stanford University Press, 2011).

Remnants of Auschwitz: The Witness and the Archive, trans. Daniel Heller-Roazen (New York: Zone Books, 1999).

Agawa, Hiroyuki, *Devil's Heritage*, trans. John Maki (Tokyo: Hokuseido Press, 1957).

Agazzi, Elena, and Erhard Schütz, eds., *Heimkehr. Eine zentrale Kategorie der Nachkriegszeit* (Berlin: Duncker & Humblot, 2010).

Aglan, Alya, and Robert Frank, eds., *1937–1947: La guerre-monde*, 2 vols. (Paris: Gallimard, 2015).

Ahrens, Jörn, "Macht der Gewalt. Hannah Arendt, Theodor W. Adorno und die Prosa Gert Ledigs," *Literatur für Leser* 24.3 (2001), 165–78.

Allport, Alan, *Demobbed: Coming Home after the Second World War* (New Haven, CT: Yale University Press, 2009).

Alt, Peter-André, "Der Schelm und die Nazis. Ordnungsstörung als pikareskes Prinzip im Erzählen über das Dritte Reich: Malaparte, Grass und Littell," *Wilde Lektüren. Literatur und Leidenschaft*, ed. Wiebke Amthor, Almut Hille, and Susanne Scharnowski (Bielefeld: Aisthesis, 2012), 383–407.

Améry, Jean, *At the Mind's Limits: Contemplations by a Survivor on Auschwitz and Its Realities*, trans. Sidney Rosenfeld and Stella P. Rosenfeld (Bloomington, IN: Indiana University Press, 1980).

Anderson, K. L., "A Horrid, Malicious, Bloody Flame: Elegy, Irony and Rose Macaulay's Blitzed London," *Literary London: Interdisciplinary Studies in the Representation of London* 5.2 (2007), www.literarylondon.org, accessed September 14, 2016.

Andrews, Colman, "Eating Malaparte," *Malaparte: A House Like Me*, ed. Michael McDonough and Tom Wolfe (New York: Clarkson Potter, 1999), 150–55.

Arendt, Hannah, *Eichmann in Jerusalem: A Report on the Banality of Evil*, revised and expanded ed. (New York: Penguin, 1994).
  The Origins of Totalitarianism, new ed. (New York: Harcourt Brace and Company, 1979).
Arnold, Jörg, *The Allied Air War and Urban Memory: The Legacy of Strategic Bombing in Germany* (Cambridge University Press, 2011).
Aron, Raymond, *The Century of Total War* (New York: Doubleday & Company, 1954).
  Penser la guerre, Clausewitz (Paris: Gallimard, 1976).
Assmann, Aleida, *Der lange Schatten der Vergangenheit. Erinnerungskultur und Geschichtspolitik* (Munich: C. H. Beck, 2006).
AtomicBombMuseum.org, www.atomicbombmuseum.org, 2006, accessed March 13, 2015.
Baldoli, Claudia, and Andrew Knapp, *Forgotten Blitzes: France and Italy under Allied Air Attack, 1940–1945* (London: Continuum, 2012).
Baldoli, Claudia, Andrew Knapp, and Richard Overy, eds., *Bombing, States and Peoples in Western Europe, 1940–1945* (London: Continuum, 2011).
Balzer, Bernd, *Wolfgang Borchert. Draußen vor der Tür* (Frankfurt am Main: Diesterweg, 1983).
Bance, Alan F., "The Brutalization of Warfare on the Eastern Front: History and Fiction," *The Second World War in Literature: Eight Essays*, ed. Ian Higgins (Edinburgh: Scottish Academic Press, 1986), 97–114.
Banchelli, Eva, "Heimkehr als Gründungsmythos: Walter Kolbenhoff," *Heimkehr. Eine zentrale Kategorie der Nachkriegszeit*, ed. Elena Agazzi and Erhard Schütz (Berlin: Duncker & Humblot, 2010), 117–28.
Barjonet, Aurélie, and Liran Razinsky, eds., *Writing the Holocaust Today: Critical Perspectives on Jonathan Littell's The Kindly Ones* (Amsterdam: Rodopi, 2012).
Barnhart, Michael A., *Japan Prepares for Total War: The Search for Economic Security, 1919–1941* (Ithaca, NY: Cornell University Press, 1987).
Barnouw, Dagmar, *Germany 1945: Views of War and Violence* (Bloomington, IN: Indiana University Press, 1996).
  The War in the Empty Air: Victims, Perpetrators, and Postwar Germans (Bloomington, IN: Indiana University Press, 2005).
Barrett, Gerard, "Souvenirs from France: Textual Traumatism in Henry Green's *Back*," *The Fiction of the 1940s: Stories of Survival*, ed. Rod Mengham and N. H. Reeve (Basingstoke: Palgrave, 2001), 169–84.
Barthes, Roland, *The Pleasure of the Text*, trans. Richard Miller (New York: Farrar, Strauss and Giroux, 1975).
Bartov, Omer, *Hitler's Army: Soldiers, Nazis, and War in the Third Reich* (New York: Oxford University Press, 1991).
  "Trauma and Absence," *European Memories of the Second World War*, ed. Helmut Peitsch, Charles Burdett, and Claire Gorrara (New York: Berghahn Books, 1999), 258–71.
Bataille, Georges, *La littérature et le mal* (Paris: Gallimard, 1957).

Bauer, Josef Martin, *So weit die Füße tragen* (Frankfurt am Main: Fischer, 1963).

Bayer, Gerd, "World War II Fiction and the Ethics of Trauma," *Ethics and Trauma in Contemporary British Fiction*, ed. Susana Onega and Jean-Michel Ganteau (Amsterdam: Rodopi, 2011), 155–74.

Beckwith, Sarah, "Preserving, Conserving, Deserving the Past: A Meditation on Ruin as Relic in Postwar Britain in Five Fragments," *A Place to Believe In: Locating Medieval Landscapes*, ed. Clare A. Lees and Gillian R. Overing (University Park, PA: Pennsylvania State University Press, 2006), 191–210.

Beevor, Antony, *The Second World War* (New York: Back Bay Books, 2012).

Beidler, Philip D., *Beautiful War: Studies in a Dreadful Fascination* (Tuscaloosa, AL: University of Alabama Press, 2016).

Bell, David A., *The First Total War* (Boston, MA: Houghton Mifflin Company, 2007).

Bellamy, Chris, *Absolute War: Soviet Russia in the Second World War* (New York: Alfred A. Knopf, 2007).

Bellmann, Werner, "Nachwort," *Der Engel schwieg*, by Heinrich Böll, 6th ed. (Munich: Deutscher Taschenbuch Verlag, 2009), 193–211.

Bellosta, Marie-Christine, "*Féerie pour une autre fois* I et II: Un spectacle et un prologue," *La Revue des Lettres Modernes* 543–546 (1978), 31–62.

Beloborodova, Darina, "Die Negativität in der Trümmerliteratur der Nachkriegs-zeit," *Triangulum. Germanistisches Jahrbuch für Estland, Lettland und Litauen* (2010), 11–29.

Bergen, Doris L., *War & Genocide: A Concise History of the Holocaust*, 2nd ed. (Lanham, MD: Rowman & Littlefield Publishers, 2009).

Berlemann, Dominic, "Das soziale Gedächtnis und der Nebencode des Litera-tursystems am Beispiel von Gert Ledigs Luftkriegsroman *Vergeltung*," *Kanon, Wertung und Vermittlung. Literatur in der Wissensgesellschaft*, ed. Matthias Beilein, Claudia Stockinger, and Simone Winko (Berlin: De Gruyter, 2012), 77–92.

Bernstein, Richard J., *Radical Evil: A Philosophical Interrogation* (Cambridge: Polity, 2002).

Bevan, David, ed., *Literature and War* (Amsterdam: Rodopi, 1990).

Bevan, Robert, *The Destruction of Memory: Architecture at War*, 2nd expanded ed. (London: Reaktion Books, 2016).

Biddle, Tami Davis, "Air Power," *The Laws of War: Constraints on Warfare in the Western World*, ed. Michael Howard, George J. Andreopoulos, and Mark R. Shulman (New Haven, CT: Yale University Press, 1994), 140–59.

Biess, Frank, *Homecomings: Returning POWs and the Legacies of Defeat in Postwar Germany* (Princeton University Press, 2006).

Black, Jeremy, *The Age of Total War, 1860–1945* (Lanham, MD: Rowan & Littlefield Publishers, 2006).

Black, Monica, "The Ghosts of War," *The Cambridge History of the Second World War*, ed. Michael Geyer and Adam Tooze, vol. 3/3 (Cambridge University Press, 2015), 654–74.

Blanchot, Maurice, *L'écriture du désastre* (Paris: Gallimard, 1980).

Boemeke, Manfred, Roger Chickering, and Stig Förster, eds., *Anticipating Total War: The German and American Experiences, 1871–1914* (Cambridge University Press, 1999).

Böhme, Hartmut, *Hubert Fichte. Riten des Autors und Leben der Literatur* (Stuttgart: J. B. Metzlersche Verlagsbuchhandlung, 1992).

Bohrer, Karl Heinz, "Der Skandal einer Imagination des Bösen. Im Rückblick auf *Die Wohlgesinnten* von Jonathan Littell," *Merkur. Deutsche Zeitschrift für europäisches Denken* 65.2 (2011), 129–46.

Böll, Heinrich, "Bekenntnis zur Trümmerliteratur," *Werke. Essayistische Schriften und Reden*, by Heinrich Böll, ed. Bernd Balzer, vol. 1 (Cologne: Kiepenheuer & Witsch, 1979), 31–34.

Der Engel schwieg, 6th ed. (Munich: Deutscher Taschenbuch Verlag, 2009).

Booth, Wayne C., *The Rhetoric of Fiction*, 2nd ed. (University of Chicago Press, 1983).

Borchert, Wolfgang, *Draußen vor der Tür und ausgewählte Erzählungen* (Hamburg: Rowohlt Taschenbuch, 2012).

Bourke, Joanna, *Fear: A Cultural History* (Emeryville, CA: Shoemaker & Hoard, 2006).

Bowen, Elizabeth, *The Heat of the Day* (New York: Anchor Books, 2002).

Boxwell, D. A., "Recalling Forgotten, Neglected, Underrated, or Unjustly Out-of-Print Works," *War, Literature, and the Arts* 11.2 (1999), 207–16.

Braudel, Fernand, *Écrits sur l'histoire* (Paris: Flammarion, 1969).

Brock, Rita Nakashima, and Gabriella Lettini, *Soul Repair: Recovering from Moral Injury after War* (Boston, MA: Beacon Press, 2012).

Bronfen, Elisabeth, *Specters of War: Hollywood's Engagement with Military Conflict* (New Brunswick, NJ: Rutgers University Press, 2012).

Brown, Kevin, "The Psychiatrists Were Right: Anomic Alienation in Kurt Vonnegut's *Slaughterhouse-Five*," *South Central Review: The Journal of the South Central Modern Language Association* 28.2 (2011), 101–9.

Brown, Llewellyn, "L'esthétique du cataclysme: *Féerie pour une autre fois* II de L.-F. Céline," *Littératures* 42 (2000), 115–25.

Browning, Christopher R., *Ordinary Men: Reserve Police Battalion 101 and the Final Solution in Poland*, revised ed. (New York: Harper Perennial, 2017).

Budick, Sanford, and Wolfgang Iser, "Introduction," *Languages of the Unsayable: The Play of Negativity in Literature and Literary Theory*, ed. Sanford Budick and Wolfgang Iser (Stanford University Press, 1987), xi–xxi.

eds., *Languages of the Unsayable: The Play of Negativity in Literature and Literary Theory* (Stanford University Press, 1987).

Budge, Kent G., "The Pacific War Online Encyclopedia," 2007–13, www.pwen cycl.kgbudge.com, accessed September 12, 2017.

Buelens, Gert, Sam Durrant, and Robert Eaglestone, eds., *The Future of Trauma Theory: Contemporary Literary and Cultural Criticism* (London: Routledge, 2014).

Burdett, Charles, "Changing Identities through Memory: Malaparte's Self-Figurations in *Kaputt*," *European Memories of the Second World War*, ed.

Helmut Peitsch, Charles Burdett, and Claire Gorrara (New York: Berghahn Books, 1999), 110–19.

Burgess, Gordon J. A., "The Failure of the Film of the Play: *Draußen vor der Tür* and *Liebe 47*," *German Life and Letters* 38.2 (1985), 155–64.

The Life and Works of Wolfgang Borchert (Rochester, NY: Camden House, 2003).

Cacicedo, Alberto, "'You Must Remember This': Trauma and Memory in *Catch-22* and *Slaughterhouse-Five*," *Critique: Studies in Contemporary Fiction* 46.4 (2005), 357–68.

Calder, Angus, *The Myth of the Blitz* (London: Pimlico, 1991).

Calvocoressi, Peter, Guy Wint, and John Pritchard, *Total War: The Causes and Courses of the Second World War*, 2nd ed. (New York: Pantheon Books, 1989).

Calzoni, Raul, "Chasms of Silence: The *Luftkrieg* in German Literature from a Reunification Perspective," *Memories and Representations of War: The Case of World War I and World War II*, ed. Elena Lamberti and Vita Fortunati (Amsterdam: Rodopi, 2009), 255–72.

"Vielstimmigkeit der Zeitgeschichte in Walter Kempowskis *Das Echolot*," *Keiner kommt davon. Zeitgeschichte in der Literatur nach 1945*, ed. Erhard Schütz and Wolfgang Hardtwig (Göttingen: Vandenhoeck & Ruprecht, 2008), 130–50.

Caputo, Philip, *A Rumor of War*, 2nd ed. (New York: Picador, 2017).

Carp, Stefanie, "Schlachtbeschreibungen. Ein Blick auf Walter Kempowski und Alexander Kluge," *Vernichtungskrieg. Verbrechen der Wehrmacht, 1941–1944*, ed. Hannes Heer and Klaus Naumann (Hamburg: Hamburger Edition, 1995), 664–79.

Caruth, Cathy, "Introduction," *Trauma: Explorations in Memory*, ed. Cathy Caruth (Baltimore, MD: Johns Hopkins University Press, 1995), 3–12.

Unclaimed Experience: Trauma, Narrative, and History (Baltimore, MD: Johns Hopkins University Press, 1996).

Caruth, Cathy, ed., *Trauma: Explorations in Memory* (Baltimore, MD: Johns Hopkins University Press, 1995).

Caserio, Robert L., "*The Heat of the Day*: Modernism and Narrative in Paul de Man and Elizabeth Bowen," *Modern Language Quarterly: A Journal of Literary History* 54.2 (1993), 263–84.

Castner, Brian, *The Long Walk: A Story of War and the Life That Follows* (New York: Anchor Books, 2013).

Cavarero, Adriana, *Horrorism: Naming Contemporary Violence*, trans. William McCuaig (New York: Columbia University Press, 2009).

Cavell, Stanley, *Philosophy the Day after Tomorrow* (Cambridge, MA: The Belknap Press of Harvard University Press, 2005).

Céline, Louis-Ferdinand, *Féerie pour une autre fois* (Paris: Gallimard, 1995).

Cerovic, Masha, "Le front Germano-Soviétique (1941–1945): Une apocalypse européenne," *1937–1947: La guerre-monde*, ed. Alya Aglan and Robert Frank, vol. 1/2 (Paris: Gallimard, 2015), 913–62.

Chatman, Seymour, *Story and Discourse: Narrative Structure in Fiction and Film* (Ithaca, NY: Cornell University Press, 1978).

Chickering, Roger, "Are We There Yet? World War II and the Theory of Total War," *A World at Total War: Global Conflict and the Politics of Destruction, 1937–1945*, ed. Roger Chickering and Stig Förster (Cambridge University Press, 2005), 1–18.

"Introduction to Part II," *The Cambridge History of War*, vol. 4: *War and the Modern World*, ed. Roger Chickering, Dennis Showalter, and Hans van de Ven (Cambridge University Press, 2012), 183–91.

"Total War: The Use and Abuse of a Concept," *Anticipating Total War: The German and American Experiences, 1871–1914*, ed. Manfred F. Boemeke, Roger Chickering, and Stig Förster (Cambridge University Press, 1999), 13–28.

Chickering, Roger, and Stig Förster, eds., *Great War, Total War: Combat and Mobilization on the Western Front, 1914–1918* (Cambridge University Press, 2000).

The Shadows of Total War: Europe, East Asia, and the United States, 1919–1939 (Cambridge University Press, 2003).

Chickering, Roger, Dennis Showalter, and Hans van de Ven, eds., *The Cambridge History of War*, vol. 4: *War and the Modern World* (Cambridge University Press, 2012).

Childers, Thomas, *Soldier from the War Returning: The Greatest Generation's Troubled Homecoming from World War II* (Boston, MA: Mariner Books, 2009).

Childs, Peter, *Modernism* (London: Routledge, 2000).

Clausen, Bettina, "Der Heimkehrerroman," *Mittelweg 36* 5 (1992), 57–70.

Clausewitz, Carl von, *On War*, trans. and ed. Michael Howard and Peter Paret (Princeton University Press, 1984).

Schriften – Aufsätze – Studien – Briefe. Dokumente aus dem Clausewitz-, Scharnhorst- und Gneisenau-Nachlass sowie aus öffentlichen und privaten Sammlungen, ed. Werner Hahlweg, vol. 1 (Göttingen: Vandenhoeck & Ruprecht, 1966).

Vom Kriege, ed. Werner Hahlweg (Bonn: Ferdinand Dümmlers, 1973).

Clément, Murielle Lucie, ed., *Les Bienveillantes de Jonathan Littell* (Cambridge: Open Book, 2010).

Cliche, Anne Élaine, "Féerie pour un temps sans mesure: Louis-Ferdinand Céline chroniqueur du désastre," *Des fins et des temps: Les limites de l'imaginaire*, ed. Jean-François Chassay, Anne Élaine Cliché, and Bertrand Gervais (Les Presses de l'Université de Montréal, 2005), 59–113.

Cloonan, William, *The Writing of War: French and German Fiction and World War II* (Gainesville, FL: University Press of Florida, 1999).

Coady, C. A. J., "Bombing and the Morality of War," *Bombing Civilians: A Twentieth-Century History*, ed. Yuki Tanaka and Marilyn B. Young (New York: New Press, 2009), 191–214.

Compagnon, Antoine, "Nazism, History, and Fantasy: Revisiting *Les Bienveillantes*," *Yale French Studies* 121 (2012), 113–27.

Connelly, Mark, *We Can Take It! Britain and the Memory of the Second World War* (Harlow: Pearson Education Limited, 2004).

Conrad, Joseph, *Heart of Darkness. The Congo Diary* (London: Penguin, 2007).

Copeland, David, "Reading and Translating Romance in Henry Green's *Back*," *Studies in the Novel* 32.1 (2000), 49–69.

Copjec, Joan, ed., *Radical Evil* (London: Verso, 1996).

Cosgrove, Mary, "Narrating German Suffering in the Shadow of Holocaust Victimology: W. G. Sebald, Contemporary Trauma Theory, and Dieter Forte's Air Raids Epic," *Germans as Victims in the Literary Fiction of the Berlin Republic*, ed. Stuart Taberner and Karina Berger (Rochester, NY: Camden House, 2009), 162–76.

Costello, John, *The Pacific War, 1941–1945* (New York: Harper Perennial, 2009).

Craps, Stef, "Beyond Eurocentrism: Trauma Theory in the Global Age," *The Future of Trauma Theory: Contemporary Literary and Cultural Criticism*, ed. Gert Buelens, Sam Durrant, and Robert Eaglestone (London: Routledge, 2014), 45–61.

Crosthwaite, Paul, *Trauma, Postmodernism and the Aftermath of World War II* (Basingstoke: Palgrave Macmillan, 2009).

Damiano, Carla A., *Walter Kempowski's Das Echolot: Sifting and Exposing the Evidence via Montage* (Heidelberg: Universitätsverlag Carl Winter, 2005).

Daudet, Léon, *La guerre totale* (Paris: Nouvelle Librairie Nationale, 1918).

Dawes, James, *The Language of War: Literature and Culture in the U.S. from the Civil War through World War II* (Cambridge, MA: Harvard University Press, 2002).

Dawidowicz, Lucy S., *The War against the Jews, 1933–1945* (New York: Holt, Rinehart and Winston, 1975).

de Certeau, Michel, *The Practice of Everyday Life*, trans. Steven Rendall (Berkeley, CA: University of California Press, 1984).

DeCoste, Damon Marcel, "Modernism's Shell-Shocked History: Amnesia, Repetition, and the War in Graham Greene's *The Ministry of Fear*," *Twentieth Century Literature* 45.4 (1999), 428–52.

Deer, Patrick, *Culture in Camouflage: War, Empire, and Modern British Literature* (Oxford University Press, 2009).

Derrida, Jacques, *Specters of Marx: The State of the Debt, the Work of Mourning and the New International*, trans. Peggy Kamuf (London: Routledge, 1994).

Dörr, Volker C., *Mythomimesis. Mythische Geschichtsbilder in der westdeutschen (Erzähl-) Literatur der frühen Nachkriegszeit (1945–1952)* (Berlin: Schmidt, 2004).

"Mythos als diskursive und narrative Kategorie in der frühen Nachkriegsliteratur Westdeutschlands," *Komparatistik als Arbeit am Mythos*, ed. Monika Schmitz-Emans and Uwe Lindemann (Heidelberg: Synchron, 2004), 305–18.

Dorsey, John T., "The Theme of Survival in John Hersey's *Hiroshima* and Ibuse Masuji's *Black Rain*," *Tamkang Review: A Quarterly of Comparative Studies between Chinese and Foreign Literatures* 14.1–4 (1983), 85–100.

Douhet, Giulio, *The Command of the Air*, trans. Dino Ferrari (Washington, DC: Office of Air Force History, 1983).

Dower, John W., *War without Mercy: Race and Power in the Pacific War* (New York: Pantheon Books, 1986).

Downes, Alexander B., *Targeting Civilians in War* (Ithaca, NY: Cornell University Press, 2008).

Drews, Jörg, "Die Toten sind nicht wirklich tot. Zu Walter Kempowskis literarischen Memorial *Das Echolot*," *Vergangene Gegenwart – gegenwärtige Vergangenheit. Studien, Polemiken und Laudationes zur deutschsprachigen Literatur, 1960–1994*, ed. Jörg Drews (Bielefeld: Aisthesis, 1994), 225–38.

Dukes, Thomas, "Desire Satisfied: War and Love in *The Heat of the Day* and *Moon Tiger*," *War, Literature, and the Arts* 3.1 (1991), 75–97.

Echevarria II, Antulio J., *Military Strategy: A Very Short Introduction* (New York: Oxford University Press, 2017).

Echternkamp, Jörg, and Stefan Martens, eds., *Experience and Memory: The Second World War in Europe* (New York: Berghahn Books, 2010).

"The Meanings of the Second World War in Contemporary European History," *Experience and Memory: The Second World War in Europe*, ed. Jörg Echternkamp and Stefan Martens (London: Berghahn Books, 2010), 245–69.

Eco, Umberto, *The Limits of Interpretation* (Bloomington, IN: Indiana University Press, 1990).

Eksteins, Modris, *Rites of Spring: The Great War and the Birth of the Modern Age* (Boston, MA: Mariner Books, 2000).

Ellis, Steve, *British Writers and the Approach of World War II* (Cambridge University Press, 2015).

Engberg-Pedersen, Anders, *Empire of Chance: The Napoleonic Wars and the Disorder of Things* (Cambridge, MA: Harvard University Press, 2015).

Engberg-Pedersen, Anders, and Kathrin Maurer, eds., *Visualizing War: Emotions, Technologies, Communities* (London: Routledge, 2018).

English, Richard, *Modern War: A Very Short Introduction* (Oxford University Press, 2013).

Enzensberger, Hans Magnus, *Europa in Ruinen. Augenzeugenberichte aus den Jahren 1944–1948* (Munich: Deutscher Taschenbuch Verlag, 1995).

Eysteinsson, Astradur, *The Concept of Modernism* (Ithaca, NY: Cornell University Press, 1990).

Favaro, A., et al., "Full and Partial Post-Traumatic Stress Disorder among World War II Prisoners of War," *Psychopathology* 39.4 (2006), 187–91.

Favret, Mary A., *War at a Distance: Romanticism and the Making of Modern Wartime* (Princeton University Press, 2010).

"Féerie," *Le Grand Robert de la langue française*, ed. Alain Rey (Paris: Dictionnaires Le Robert, 2001).

Feigel, Lara, *The Love-Charm of Bombs: Restless Lives in the Second World War* (New York: Bloomsbury, 2013).

Ferdjani, Youssef, "*Les Bienveillantes*: Le National-Socialisme comme mal méta-physique," *Les Bienveillantes de Jonathan Littell*, ed. Murielle Lucie Clément (Cambridge: Open Book, 2010), 263–76.

Ferguson, Rex, "Blind Noise and Deaf Visions: Henry Green's *Caught*, Synaesthesia and the Blitz," *Journal of Modern Literature* 33.1 (2009), 102–16.

Ferris, John R., et al., eds., *The Cambridge History of the Second World War*, 3 vols. (Cambridge University Press, 2015).

Fichte, Hubert, *Detlevs Imitationen "Grünspan"* (Frankfurt am Main: Fischer, 2005).

Fickert, Kurt J., "The Christ-Figure in Borchert's *Draußen vor der Tür*," *Germanic Review* 54 (1979), 165–69.

Florentin, Eddy, (with the collaboration of Claude Archambault), *Quand les Alliés bombardaient la France, 1940–1945* (N.p.: Perrin, 1997).

Förster, Alice, and Birgit Beck, "Post-Traumatic Stress Disorder and World War II: Can a Psychiatric Concept Help Us Understand Postwar Society?," *Life after Death: Approaches to a Cultural and Social History of Europe during the 1940s and 1950s*, ed. Richard Bessel and Dirk Schumann (Cambridge University Press, 2003), 15–35.

Förster, Stig, "Introduction," *Great War, Total War: Combat and Mobilization on the Western Front, 1914–1918*, ed. Roger Chickering and Stig Förster (Cambridge University Press, 2000), 1–16.

"Das Zeitalter des totalen Krieges," *Mittelweg 36* 8 (1999), 19–29.

Förster, Stig, ed., *An der Schwelle zum totalen Krieg. Die militärische Debatte über den Krieg der Zukunft, 1919–1939* (Paderborn: Ferdinand Schöningh, 2002).

Förster, Stig, and Jörg Nagler, eds., *On the Road to Total War: The American Civil War and the German Wars of Unification, 1861–1871* (Cambridge University Press, 1997).

Forte, Dieter, *Das Haus auf meinen Schultern* (Frankfurt am Main: Fischer, 2002).

Fox, Thomas C., "East Germany and the Bombing War," *Bombs Away! Representing the Air War over Europe and Japan*, ed. Wilfried Wilms and William Rasch (Amsterdam: Rodopi, 2006), 113–30.

Frank, Joseph, *The Idea of Spatial Form* (New Brunswick, NJ: Rutgers University Press, 1991).

Freese, Peter, "Kurt Vonnegut's *Slaughterhouse-Five*: Or, How to Storify an Atrocity," *Historiographic Metafiction in Modern American and Canadian Literature*, ed. Bernd Engler and Kurt Müller (Paderborn: Ferdinand Schöningh, 1994), 209–22.

Freud, Sigmund, *The Standard Edition of the Complete Psychological Works of Sigmund Freud*, trans. James Strachey, ed. James Strachey, Anna Freud, Alix Strachey, and Alan Tyson, 24 vols. (London: Hogarth/Institute of Psycho-Analysis, 1953–74).

The Uncanny, The Standard Edition of the Complete Psychological Works of Sigmund Freud, trans. James Strachey, ed. James Strachey, Anna Freud, Alix Strachey, and Alan Tyson, vol. 17/24 (London: Hogarth/Institute of Psycho-Analysis, 1953–74).

Friedländer, Saul, *Nazi Germany and the Jews, 1939–1945: The Years of Extermination* (New York: Harper Perennial, 2008).

Friedrich, Jörg, *Der Brand. Deutschland im Bombenkrieg, 1940–1945* (Munich: Propyläen, 2002).

Fritz, Stephen G., *Ostkrieg: Hitler's War of Extermination in the East* (Lexington, KY: University Press of Kentucky, 2011).

Fuchs, Anne, *After the Dresden Bombing: Pathways of Memory, 1945 to the Present* (New York: Palgrave Macmillan, 2012).

Fussell, Paul, *The Great War and Modern Memory* (Oxford University Press, 1975).

Gallie, W. B., *Philosophers of Peace and War: Kant, Clausewitz, Marx, Engels and Tolstoy* (Cambridge University Press, 1978).

Ganteau, Jean-Michel, "'A Conflict between an Image and a Man': The Visual Diction of Romance in Graham Greene's *The End of the Affair*," *Etudes Britanniques Contemporaines: Revue de la Société d'Etudes Anglaises Contemporaines* 31 (2006), 69–81.

Gardiner, Juliet, *The Blitz: The British under Attack* (London: Harper Press, 2010).

Garrard, John, and Carrol Garrard, *The Life and Fate of Vasily Grossman*, 2nd ed. (Barnsley: Pen & Sword, 2012).

Gebhardt, Lisette, "Trümmerliteratur. Am Beispiel von Shiina Rinzō und Wolfgang Borchert," *Japanstudien. Jahrbuch des deutschen Instituts für Japanstudien* 8 (1996), 129–51.

Gesing, Fritz, "Sterben im Bombenhagel: Hans Erich Nossacks *Der Untergang* und Gert Ledigs *Vergeltung*," *Deutschunterricht. Beiträge zu seiner Praxis und wissenschaftlichen Grundlegung* 54.1 (2002), 48–58.

Gillian, Annie, "*Féerie pour une autre fois* et le cinéma," *La Revue des Lettres Modernes* 543–546 (1978), 83–106.

Gini, Enza, "'Nachdenklich und hungrig' – Heinrich Böll kehrt aus dem Krieg heim," *Heimkehr. Eine zentrale Kategorie der Nachkriegszeit*, ed. Elena Agazzi and Erhard Schütz (Berlin: Duncker & Humblot, 2010), 129–41.

Ginsberg, Robert, *The Aesthetics of Ruins* (Amsterdam: Rodopi, 2004).

Gladwell, Malcolm, "Getting over It: *The Man in the Gray Flannel Suit* Put the War behind Him. What's Changed?," *The New Yorker* 80.34 (2004), 75–79.

Gordon, Avery F., *Ghostly Matters: Haunting and the Sociological Imagination* (Minneapolis, MN: University of Minnesota Press, 2008).

Grana, Gianni, *Curzio Malaparte* (Milan: Marzorati editore, 1961).

Grayling, A. C., *Among the Dead Cities: The History and Moral Legacy of the World War II Bombing of Civilians in Germany and Japan* (New York: Bloomsbury, 2006).

Grayzel, Susan R., *At Home and Under Fire: Air Raids and Culture in Britain from the Great War to the Blitz* (Cambridge University Press, 2012).

Green, Henry, *Back* (Champaign, IL: Dalkey Archive Press, 2009).
Caught (New York Review Books, 2016).

Greene, Graham, *The End of the Affair* (New York: Penguin, 2004).

The Ministry of Fear (New York: Penguin, 2005).

Gross, Robert F., "Figuring Guilt: Wolfgang Borchert's *Outside the Door* and Carl Zuckmayer's *The Song in the Fiery Furnace*," *Journal of Religion and Theatre* 5.1 (2006), 1–8.

Grossman, Vasily, *Life and Fate*, trans. Robert Chandler (New York Review Books, 2006).

A Writer at War: A Soviet Journalist with the Red Army, 1941–1945, trans. and ed. Antony Beevor and Luba Vinogradova (New York: Vintage Books, 2005).

Guest, Kristen, ed., *Eating Their Words: Cannibalism and the Boundaries of Cultural Identity* (Albany, NY: State University of New York Press, 2001).

Guillemard, Julien, *L'enfer du Havre, 1940–1944: Témoignage* (Paris: Les Éditions Médicis, 1945).

Gumpert, Matthew, *The End of Meaning: Studies in Catastrophe* (Newcastle upon Tyne: Cambridge Scholars Publishing, 2012).

Hachiya, Michihiko, *Hiroshima Diary: The Journal of a Japanese Physician, August 6–September 30, 1945*, trans. and ed. Warner Wells (Chapel Hill, NC: University of North Carolina Press, 1995).

Hage, Volker, *Zeugen der Zerstörung. Die Literaten und der Luftkrieg* (Frankfurt am Main: Fischer, 2003).

ed., *Hamburg 1943: Literarische Zeugnisse zum Feuersturm* (Frankfurt am Main: Fischer, 2003).

Hagen, Jerome T., *War in the Pacific*, 5 vols. (Honolulu, HI: Hawaii Pacific University, 1998–2010).

Hahn, Hans, "Intertextuelle Studien zur Kriegsheimkehr. Ein heuristischer Versuch," *German Life and Letters* 67.3 (2014), 341–57.

Ham, Paul, *Hiroshima Nagasaki: The Real Story of the Atomic Bombings and Their Aftermath* (New York: Picador, 2014).

Hamilton, Patrick, *The Slaves of Solitude* (New York Review Books, 2007).

Handel, Michael I., ed., *Clausewitz and Modern Strategy* (Totowa, NJ: Frank Cass and Company Limited, 1986).

Hanley, James, *No Directions* (London: André Deutsch, 1990).

Hanson, Victor Davis, *The Second World Wars: How the First Global Conflict Was Fought and Won* (New York: Basic Books, 2017).

Hara, Tamiki, *Summer Flowers, Hiroshima: Three Witnesses*, trans. and ed. Richard H. Minear (Princeton University Press, 1990).

Harris, Frederick, *Encounters with Darkness: French and German Writers on World War II* (New York: Oxford University Press, 1983).

Harrisson, Tom, *Living through the Blitz* (New York: Schocken Books, 1976).

Hasegawa, Tsuyoshi, "Were the Atomic Bombings of Hiroshima and Nagasaki Justified?," *Bombing Civilians: A Twentieth-Century History*, ed. Yuki Tanaka and Marilyn B. Young (New York: New Press, 2009), 97–134.

Hastings, Max, *Inferno: The World at War, 1939–1945* (New York: Alfred A. Knopf, 2011).

Heer, Hannes, and Klaus Naumann, eds., *Vernichtungskrieg. Verbrechen der Wehrmacht, 1941–1944* (Hamburg: Hamburger Edition, 1995).

Hell, Julia, "Ruins Travel: Orphic Journeys through 1940s Germany," *Writing Travel: The Poetics and Politics of the Modern Journey*, ed. John Zilcosky (University of Toronto Press, 2008), 123–62.

Hempel, Dirk, *Walter Kempowski. Eine bürgerliche Biographie* (Munich: btb, 2004).

Hentea, Marius, "Fictional Doubles in Henry Green's *Back*," *Review of English Studies* 61.251 (2010), 614–26.

Henry Green at the Limits of Modernism (Brighton: Sussex Academic Press, 2014).

Herbert, Ulrich, "Zwischen Beschaulichkeit und Massenmord. Die Kriegswende 1943 aus der Perspektive des Alltags," *Neue politische Literatur* 40.2 (1995), 185–89.

Herman, Judith, *Trauma and Recovery: The Aftermath of Violence – From Domestic Abuse to Political Terror* (New York: Basic Books, 1997).

Herr, Michael, *Dispatches: 1967–1975, Reporting Vietnam: American Journalism 1959–1975*, vol. 2/2 (New York: Library of America, 1998).

Hersey, John, *Hiroshima* (New York: Alfred A. Knopf, 1946).

Hibakusha: Survivors of Hiroshima and Nagasaki, trans. Gaynor Sekimori (Tokyo: Kōsei Publishing Co., 1986).

Hicks, Jim, *Lessons from Sarajevo: A War Stories Primer* (Amherst, MA: University of Massachusetts Press, 2013).

Higgins, Ian, ed., *The Second World War in Literature: Eight Essays* (Edinburgh: Scottish Academic Press, 1986).

Highmore, Ben, "Playgrounds and Bombsites: Postwar Britain's Ruined Landscapes," *Cultural Politics* 9.3 (2013), 323–36.

Hilberg, Raul, *The Destruction of the European Jews* (New York: Holmes & Meier, 1985).

Hippler, Thomas, *Bombing the People: Giulio Douhet and the Foundations of Air-Power Strategy, 1884–1939* (Cambridge University Press, 2013).

Hodgson, Katharine, "The Soviet War," *The Cambridge Companion to the Literature of World War II*, ed. Marina MacKay (Cambridge University Press, 2009), 111–22.

Hoefert, Sigfrid, "Zur Darstellung von Kampfhandlungen mit technischen Mitteln – Anhand von Werken von Gert Ledig und Stefan Heym," *Wahrheitsmaschinen. Der Einfluss technischer Innovationen auf die Darstellung und das Bild des Krieges in den Medien und Künsten*, ed. Claudia Glunz and Thomas F. Schneider (Göttingen: Vandenhoeck & Ruprecht, 2010), 253–62.

Hope, William, *Curzio Malaparte* (Market Harborough: Troubador, 2000).

"The Narrative Contract Strained: The Problems of Narratorial Neutrality in Malaparte's *Kaputt*," *Italianist: Journal of the Department of Italian Studies, University of Reading* 19 (1999), 178–92.

Horkheimer, Max, and Theodor W. Adorno, *Dialectic of Enlightenment*, trans. John Cumming (London: Verso, 1997).

Horn, Maren, and Christina Möller, "'Sie erzählen, und ich werfe die Geschichten mit dem Bildwerfer an die Wand'. Der Schriftsteller Walter Kempowski als Archivar – Der Archivar Walter Kempowski als Schriftsteller," *Aktenkundig? Literatur, Zeitgeschichte und Archiv*, ed. Marcel Atze et al. (Vienna: Praesens, 2007), 316–37.

Horowitz, Sara R., *Voicing the Void: Muteness and Memory in Holocaust Fiction* (Albany, NY: State University of New York Press, 1997).

Horta Fernandes, António, *Livro dos contrastes: Guerra & política* (Porto: Fronteira do Caos Editores, 2017).

Houston Grey, Stephanie, "Writing Redemption: Trauma and the Authentication of the Moral Order in *Hibakusha* Literature," *Text & Performance Quarterly* 22.1 (2002), 1–23.

Howard, Michael, *Clausewitz* (Oxford University Press, 1983).

Höyng, Peter, "From Darkness to Visibility: Walter Kempowski's *Das Echolot* [Sonar] and Günter Grass' *Im Krebsgang* [Crab Walk] as Two Overdue Narratives Facing World War II in Germany," *Reconstructing Societies in the Aftermath of War: Memory, Identity, and Reconciliation*, ed. Flavia Brizio-Skov and Susanna Delfino (Boca Raton, FL: Bordighera, 2004), 169–87.

Hull, Isabel V., *Absolute Destruction: Military Culture and the Practices of War in Imperial Germany* (Ithaca, NY: Cornell University Press, 2005).

Hundrieser, Gabriele, "Die Leerstelle der Leerstelle? Das Phänomen Gert Ledig, die Ästhetik der Gewalt und die Literaturgeschichtsschreibung," *Weimarer Beiträge. Zeitschrift für Literaturwissenschaft, Ästhetik und Kulturwissenschaften* 49.3 (2003), 361–79.

Husson, Édouard, and Michel Terestchenko, *Les complaisantes: Jonathan Littell et l'écriture du Mal* (Paris: François-Xavier de Guibert, 2007).

Hutchinson, George, *Facing the Abyss: American Literature and Culture in the 1940s* (New York: Columbia University Press, 2018).

Hutton, Margaret-Anne, "Jonathan Littell's *Les Bienveillantes*: Ethics, Aesthetics and the Subject of Judgment," *Modern & Contemporary France* 18.1 (2010), 1–15.

Hynes, Samuel, *The Soldiers' Tale: Bearing Witness to Modern War* (London: Penguin, 1997).

Ibuse, Masuji, *Black Rain*, trans. John Bester (New York: Kodansha International, 2012).

Igarashi, Yoshikuni, *Bodies of Memory: Narratives of War in Postwar Japanese Culture, 1945–1970* (Princeton University Press, 2000).

Indiana, Gary, "A Million Little Theses: Curzio Malaparte Became the Proust of the Abattoir of Europe's Upheaval. Does It Matter That He Made It Up?," *BookForum: The Review for Art, Fiction, & Culture* 13.2 (2006), 8–10.

Jackson, Rosemary, *Fantasy: The Literature of Subversion* (London: Routledge, 1988).

Jameson, Fredric, *The Antinomies of Realism* (London: Verso, 2013).

Jones, James, *The Thin Red Line* (New York: Dial Press Trade Paperbacks, 2012).

Jünger, Ernst, "Total Mobilization," trans. Joel Golb and Richard Wolin, *The Heidegger Controversy: A Critical Reader*, ed. Richard Wolin (New York: Columbia University Press, 1991), 119–39.

Jurca, Catherine, "The Sanctimonious Suburbanite: Sloan Wilson's *The Man in the Gray Flannel Suit*," *American Literary History* 11.1 (1999), 82–106.

Kant, Immanuel, *The Metaphysics of Morals*, trans. and ed. Mary Gregor (Cambridge University Press, 1996).

Religion within the Boundaries of Mere Reason and Other Writings, trans. and ed. Allen Wood and George di Giovanni (Cambridge University Press, 1998).

Kapoor, S., "Chaos and Order in Elizabeth Bowen's *The Heat of the Day*," *Panjab University Research Bulletin (Arts)* 22.2 (1991), 119–23.

Kasack, Hermann, *Die Stadt hinter dem Strom* (Frankfurt am Main: Suhrkamp, 1996).

Kasperl, Claudio, "'Nun ist alles anders'. Zur narrativen Gestaltung einer Grenzsituation in Hubert Fichtes Roman *Detlevs Imitationen 'Grünspan'*," *Grenzsituationen. Wahrnehmung, Bedeutung und Gestaltung in der neueren Literatur*, ed. Dorothea Lauterbach, Uwe Spörl, and Uli Wunderlich (Göttingen: Vandenhoeck & Ruprecht, 2002), 303–30.

Keegan, John, *A History of Warfare* (New York: Vintage Books, 1994).

The Second World War (New York: Penguin, 1989).

Kempowski, Walter, *Culpa. Notizen zum "Echolot"* (Munich: btb, 2007).

Das Echolot. Abgesang'45. Ein kollektives Tagebuch, 4th ed. (Munich: btb, 2007).

Das Echolot. Barbarossa'41. Ein kollektives Tagebuch, 5th ed. (Munich: btb, 2004).

Das Echolot. Fuga furiosa. Ein kollektives Tagebuch, Winter 1945, 2nd ed., 4 vols. (Munich: btb, 2004).

Das Echolot. Ein kollektives Tagebuch. Januar und Februar 1943, 2nd ed., 4 vols. (Munich: btb, 1997).

Der rote Hahn. Dresden im Februar 1945 (Munich: btb, 2001).

Kershaw, Ian, *Hitler, the Germans, and the Final Solution* (New Haven, CT: Yale University Press, 2008).

Kiesel, Otto Erich, *Die unverzagte Stadt* (Hamburg: Volksbücherei-Verlag Goslar, 1949).

Kilgour, Maggie, *From Communion to Cannibalism: An Anatomy of Metaphors of Incorporation* (Princeton University Press, 1990).

Kita, Morio, *The House of Nire*, trans. Dennis Keene (Tokyo: Kodansha International, 1990).

Klein, Holger, with John Flower and Eric Homberger, eds., *The Second World War in Fiction* (London: Macmillan Press, 1984).

Klein, Thoralf, and Frank Schumacher, eds., *Kolonialkriege. Militärische Gewalt im Zeichen des Imperialismus* (Hamburg: Hamburger Edition, 2006).

Klemperer, Victor, *The Language of the Third Reich: LTI – Lingua Tertii Imperii: A Philologist's Notebook*, trans. Martin Brady (London: Continuum, 2002).

Kluge, Alexander, *Der Luftangriff auf Halberstadt am 8. April 1945* (Frankfurt am Main: Suhrkamp, 2008).

Knoll, Samson B., *"Moskau–Stalingrad–Berlin*: Theodor Plievier's War Trilogy Revisited," *Literatur und Geschichte*, ed. Karl Menges, Michael Winkler, and Jörg Thunecke (Amsterdam: Rodopi, 1998), 171–203.

Kolbenhoff, Walter, *Heimkehr in die Fremde* (Frankfurt am Main: Suhrkamp, 1988).

Kovács, Kálmán, *"Der Engel schwieg*. Heinrich Bölls Roman aus dem Nachlaß," *University of Dayton Review* 23.2 (1995), 15–27.

Kraske, Bernd M., *"Draußen vor der Tür*. Anmerkungen zur Hörspiel-Rezeption," *Wolfgang Borchert. Werk und Wirkung*, ed. Rudolf Wolff (Bonn: Bouvier, 1984), 38–55.

Krellner, Ulrich, "'Aber im Keller die Leichen sind immer noch da'. Die Opfer-Debatte in der deutschen Literatur nach 1989," *Moderna Språk* 99.2 (2005), 155–68.

Krimmer, Elisabeth, *The Representation of War in German Literature* (Cambridge University Press, 2010).

Kristeva, Julia, *Powers of Horror: An Essay on Abjection*, trans. Leon S. Roudiez (New York: Columbia University Press, 1982).

"A propos des *Bienveillantes* (De l'abjection à la banalité du mal)," *Infini* 99 (2007), 22–35.

Krystal, Henry, "Integration and Self-Healing in Post-Traumatic States: A Ten-Year Retrospective," *American Imago* 48 (1991), 93–118.

Kuehn, John T., "The War in the Pacific, 1941–1945," *The Cambridge History of the Second World War*, ed. John Ferris and Evan Mawdsley, vol. 1/3 (Cambridge University Press, 2015), 420–54.

Kuß, Susanne, "Kriegführung ohne hemmende Kulturschranke. Die deutschen Kolonialkriege in Südwestafrika (1904–1907) und Ostafrika (1905–1908)," *Kolonialkriege. Militärische Gewalt im Zeichen des Imperialismus*, ed. Thoralf Klein and Frank Schumacher (Hamburg: Hamburger Edition, 2006), 208–47.

Kuznetsov, A. Anatoli, *Babi Yar: A Document in the Form of a Novel*, trans. David Floyd (New York: Farrar, Straus and Giroux, 1970).

Labanyi, Jo, "History and Hauntology; or, What Does One Do with the Ghosts of the Past? Reflections on Spanish Film and Fiction of the Post-Franco Period," *Disremembering the Dictatorship: The Politics of Memory in the Spanish Transition to Democracy*, ed. Joan Ramon Resina (Amsterdam: Rodopi, 2000), 65–82.

LaCapra, Dominick, *Writing History, Writing Trauma*, 2nd ed. (Baltimore, MD: Johns Hopkins University Press, 2014).

Lakoff, Robin Tolmach, *The Language War* (Berkeley, CA: University of California Press, 2000).

Lamberti, Elena, and Vita Fortunati, eds., *Memories and Representations of War: The Case of World War I and World War II* (Amsterdam: Rodopi, 2009).

Lamy-Rested, Élise, *Parole vraie, parole vide: Des Bienveillantes aux exécuteurs* (Paris: Garnier, 2014).

Lanzmann, Claude, *Shoah* (Paris: Gallimard, 1997).

Lassner, Phyllis, "Reimagining the Arts of War: Language & History in Elizabeth Bowen's *The Heat of the Day* & Rose Macaulay's *The World My Wilderness*," *Perspectives on Contemporary Literature* 14 (1988), 30–38.

Laub, Dori, "Bearing Witness, or the Vicissitudes of Listening," *Testimony: Crises of Witnessing in Literature, Psychoanalysis, and History*, by Shoshana Felman and Dori Laub (London: Routledge, 1992), 57–74.

Lawson, Colette, "The Natural History of Destruction: W. G. Sebald, Gert Ledig, and the Allied Bombings," *Germans as Victims in the Literary Fiction of the Berlin Republic*, ed. Stuart Taberner and Karina Berger (Rochester, NY: Camden House, 2009), 29–41.

Ledig, Gert, *Die Stalinorgel* (Frankfurt am Main: Suhrkamp, 2000).

Vergeltung (Frankfurt am Main: Suhrkamp, 2001).

Ledwidge, Frank, *Aerial Warfare: The Battle for the Skies* (New York: Oxford University Press, 2018).

Lehmann, Rosamond, *The Echoing Grove* (London: Virago, 2000).

Lethen, Helmut, "Das Echolot des Geschichtszeichens Stalingrad," *Walter Kempowski. Bürgerliche Repräsentanz, Erinnerungskultur, Gegenwartsbewältigung*, ed. Lutz Hagestedt (Berlin: De Gruyter, 2010), 319–31.

Levenson, Michael, ed., *The Cambridge Companion to Modernism* (Cambridge University Press, 1999).

Levinas, Emmanuel, "Useless Suffering," *The Provocation of Levinas: Rethinking the Other*, ed. Robert Bernasconi and David Wood, trans. Richard Cohen (London: Routledge, 1988), 156–65.

Lifton, Robert Jay, *Death in Life: Survivors of Hiroshima* (New York: Random House, 1967).

Líman, Antonín, *Ibuse Masuji: A Century Remembered* (Prague: Karolinum, 2008).

Limon, John, *Writing after War: American War Fiction from Realism to Postmodernism* (Oxford University Press, 1994).

Lindqvist, Sven, *A History of Bombing*, trans. Linda Haverty Rugg (New York: New Press, 2001).

Link-Heer, Ursula, "Versuch über das Makabre. Zu Curzio Malapartes *Kaputt*," *LiLi. Zeitschrift fur Literaturwissenschaft und Linguistik* 19.75 (1989), 96–116.

Lippit, Akira Mizuta, *Atomic Light (Shadow Optics)* (Minneapolis, MN: University of Minnesota Press, 2005).

Littell, Jonathan, *Les Bienveillantes* (Paris: Gallimard, 2006).

Long, Christian, "Mapping Suburban Fiction," *Journal of Language, Literature and Culture* 60.3 (2013), 193–213.

Lothe, Jakob, "Authority, Reliability, and the Challenge of Reading: The Narrative Ethics of Jonathan Littell's *The Kindly Ones*," *Narrative Ethics*, ed. Jakob

Lothe, Jeremy Hawthorn, and Leonidas Donskis (Amsterdam: Rodopi, 2013), 103–18.

Louar, Nadia, "Is Kindly Just Kinky? Irony and Evil in Jonathan Littell's *The Kindly Ones*," *Evil in Contemporary French and Francophone Literature*, ed. Scott M. Powers (Newcastle upon Tyne: Cambridge Scholars Publishing, 2011), 136–58.

Luckhurst, Roger, *The Trauma Question* (London: Routledge, 2008).

Ludendorff, Erich, *Der totale Krieg* (Munich: Ludendorffs Verlag, 1935).

Macaulay, Rose, *The World My Wilderness* (London: Collins, 1950).

MacDonogh, Giles, *After the Reich: The Brutal History of the Allied Occupation* (New York: Basic Books, 2007).

MacKay, Marina, *Modernism, War, and Violence* (London: Bloomsbury, 2017).
  Modernism and World War II (Cambridge University Press, 2007).

MacKay, Marina, ed., *The Cambridge Companion to the Literature of World War II* (Cambridge University Press, 2009).

Magot, Céline, "Elizabeth Bowen's London in *The Heat of the Day*: An Impression of the City in the Territory of War," *Literary London: Interdisciplinary Studies in the Representation of London* 3.1 (2005), www.literarylondon.org/, accessed August 9, 2016.

Mailer, Norman, *The Naked and the Dead* (New York: Picador, 1998).

Malaparte, Curzio, *Kaputt*, trans. Dan Hofstadter (New York Review Books, 2005).

Markusen, Eric, and David Kopf, *The Holocaust and Strategic Bombing: Genocide and Total War in the Twentieth Century* (Boulder, CO: Westview Press, 1995).

Martelli, Giampaolo, *Curzio Malaparte* (Turin: Borla, 1968).

Martschukat, Jürgen, "Men in Gray Flannel Suits: Troubling Masculinities in 1950s America," *Gender Forum* 32 (2011), 1–9.

Matthews, J. H., *The Inner Dream: Céline as a Novelist* (Syracuse, NY: Syracuse University Press, 1978).

Mayer, Arno J., *Why Did the Heavens Not Darken? The "Final Solution" in History* (New York: Pantheon Books, 1988).

McCarthy, Patrick, "La multiplicité des narrateurs dans *Féerie pour une autre fois*," *Céline: Actes du Colloque International de Paris (27–30 Juillet 1976)* (Paris: Société d'Etudes Céliniennes, 1978), 231–46.

McLoughlin, Kate, *Authoring War: The Literary Representation of War from the Iliad to Iraq* (Cambridge University Press, 2011).
  Veteran Poetics: British Literature in the Age of Mass Warfare, 1790–2015 (Cambridge University Press, 2018).
  "War and Words," *The Cambridge Companion to War Writing*, ed. Kate McLoughlin (Cambridge University Press, 2009), 15–24.

McLoughlin, Kate, ed., *The Cambridge Companion to War Writing* (Cambridge University Press, 2009).

McMillin, Arnold, "The Second World War in Official and Unofficial Russian Prose," *The Second World War in Literature: Eight Essays*, ed. Ian Higgins (Edinburgh: Scottish Academic Press, 1986), 19–31.

McNicholas, Joseph Colin, "Corporate Culture and the American Novel: Producers, Persuaders, and Communicators," Ph.D. dissertation (University of Texas at Austin, 1999).

Meagher, Robert E., *Killing from the Inside Out: Moral Injury and Just War* (Eugene, OR: Cascade Books, 2014).

Melfi, Mary Ann, "The Landscape of Grief: Graham Greene's *The Ministry of Fear*," *South Atlantic Review* 69.2 (2004), 54–73.

Mellor, Leo, *Reading the Ruins: Modernism, Bombsites and British Culture* (Cambridge University Press, 2011).

Mengham, Rod, "Broken Glass," *The Fiction of the 1940s: Stories of Survival*, ed. Rod Mengham and N. H. Reeve (Basingstoke: Palgrave, 2001), 124–33.

The Idiom of the Time: The Writings of Henry Green (Cambridge University Press, 1982).

Messent, Peter, "Memoirs of a Survivor: Masuji Ibuse's *Black Rain*," *Foreign Literature Studies/Wai Guo Wen Xue Yan Jiu* 2.112 (2005), 128–32.

Meyer-Minnemann, Klaus, "Die (Un)Sagbarkeit des Schreckens: Alexander Kluge, Hans Erich Nossack und Ralph Giordano über Bombentod und Zerstörung," *Etudes Germaniques* 67.2 (2012), 351–76.

Mieszkowski, Jan, *Watching War* (Stanford University Press, 2012).

Mileck, Joseph, "Wolfgang Borchert: 'Draußen vor der Tür': A Young Poet's Struggle with Guilt and Despair," *Monatshefte* 51 (1959), 328–36.

Miller, Kristine A., *British Literature of the Blitz: Fighting the People's War* (New York: Palgrave Macmillan, 2009).

"'Even a Shelter's Not Safe': The Blitz on Homes in Elizabeth Bowen's Wartime Writing," *Twentieth Century Literature* 45.2 (1999), 138–58.

"'The World Has Been Remade': Gender, Genre, and the Blitz in Graham Greene's *The Ministry of Fear*," *Genre: Forms of Discourse and Culture* 36.1–2 (2003), 131–50.

Minogue, Sally, and Andrew Palmer, *The Remembered Dead: Poetry, Memory and the First World War* (Cambridge University Press, 2018).

Moore, Bob, "Prisoners of War," *The Cambridge History of the Second World War*, ed. John Ferris and Evan Mawdsley, vol. 1/3 (Cambridge University Press, 2015), 664–89.

Morlang, Thomas, "'Die Wahehe haben ihre Vernichtung gewollt.' Der Krieg der 'kaiserlichen Schutztruppe' gegen die Hehe in deutsch-Ostafrika (1890–1898)," *Kolonialkriege. Militärische Gewalt im Zeichen des Imperialismus*, ed. Thoralf Klein and Frank Schumacher (Hamburg: Hamburger Edition, 2006), 80–108.

Mueller, Stefanie, "Corporate Power and the Public Good in Sloan Wilson's *The Man in the Gray Flannel Suit*," *COPAS: Current Objectives of Postgraduate American Studies* 14.1 (2013), 1–12.

Müller, Hans-Harald, "Nachwort. *Stalingrad*. Zur Geschichte und Aktualität von Theodor Plieviers Roman," *Stalingrad*, by Theodor Plievier, 2nd ed. (Cologne: Kiepenheuer & Witsch, 2011), 443–63.

Munton, Alan, *English Fiction of the Second World War* (London: Faber and Faber, 1989).

Murat, Jean-Christophe, "City of Wars: The Representation of Wartime London in Two Novels of the 1940s: James Hanley's *No Directions* and Patrick Hamilton's *The Slaves of Solitude*," *Anglophonia: French Journal of English Studies* 25 (2009), 329–40.

Murphy, Richard, "History, Fiction, and the Avant-Garde: Narrativisation and the Event," *Phrasis: Studies in Language and Literature* 48.1 (2007), 83–103.

Nagai, Takashi, *The Bells of Nagasaki*, trans. William Johnston (Tokyo: Kodansha International, 1994).

    We of Nagasaki: The Story of Survivors in an Atomic Wasteland, trans. Ichiro Shirato and Herbert B. L. Silverman (New York: Duell, Sloan and Pearce, 1951).

Nekrasov, Victor, *Front-Line Stalingrad*, trans. David Floyd (Barnsley: Pen & Sword Military, 2012).

Nelson, Donald F., "To Live or Not to Live: Notes on Archetypes and the Absurd in Borchert's *Draußen vor der Tür*," *German Quarterly* 48.3 (1975), 343–54.

Nettelbeck, Colin W., "Temps et espaces dans *Féerie pour une autre fois*," *La Revue des Lettres Modernes* 543–546 (1978), 63–81.

Nickel, Gunther, "Faction: Theodor Plievier: *Stalingrad* (1945)," *Von Böll bis Buchheim. Deutsche Kriegsprosa nach 1945*, ed. Hans Wagener (Amsterdam: Rodopi, 1997), 49–62.

Niefanger, Dirk, "Die Dramatisierung der 'Stunde Null'. Die frühen Nachkriegsstücke von Borchert, Weisenborn und Zuckmayer," *Zwei Wendezeiten. Blicke auf die deutsche Literatur 1945 und 1989*, ed. Walter Erhart and Dirk Niefanger (Tübingen: Niemeyer, 1997), 47–70.

Nietzsche, Friedrich, *Jenseits von Gut und Böse, Sämtliche Werke*, ed. Giorgio Colli and Mazzino Montinari, vol. 5/15 (Munich: Deutscher Taschenbuch Verlag, 1999).

Niven, Bill, ed., *Germans as Victims: Remembering the Past in Contemporary Germany* (New York: Palgrave Macmillan, 2006).

Norris, Margot, *Writing War in the Twentieth Century* (Charlottesville, VA: University Press of Virginia, 2000).

North, Michael, *Henry Green and the Writing of His Generation* (Charlottesville, VA: University Press of Virginia, 1984).

Nossack, Hans Erich, *Nekyia. Bericht eines Überlebenden* (Frankfurt am Main: Suhrkamp, 1961).

    Der Untergang (Frankfurt am Main: Suhrkamp, 1976).

Oda, Makoto, *H: A Hiroshima Novel*, trans. D. H. Whittaker (Tokyo: Kodansha International, 1990).

Odom, Keith C., *Henry Green* (Boston, MA: Twayne, 1978).

Ōta, Yōko, *City of Corpses, Hiroshima: Three Witnesses*, trans. and ed. Richard H. Minear (Princeton University Press, 1990).

Overy, Richard, *The Bombing War: Europe, 1939–1945* (London: Allen Lane, 2013).

Russia's War: A History of the Soviet War Effort, 1941–1945 (New York: Penguin Books, 1998).

Pake, Lucy S., "Courtly Love in Our Own Time: Graham Greene's *The End of the Affair*," *Lamar Journal of the Humanities* 8.2 (1982), 36–43.

Panitz, Eberhard, *Die Feuer sinken. Roman der Dresdner Februartage 1945* (Schkeuditz: Schkeudizer Buchverlag, 2000).

Leben für Leben. Roman einer Familie (Halle: Mitteldeutscher Verlag, 1987).

Pape, Walter, "'Mich für mein ganzes Leben verletzendes Geschehen als Erlebnis'. Die Luftangriffe auf Salzburg (1944) in Thomas Bernhards *Die Ursache* und Alexander Kluges *Der Luftangriff auf Halberstadt am 8. April 1945*," *Bombs Away! Representing the Air War over Europe and Japan*, ed. Wilfried Wilms and William Rasch (Amsterdam: Rodopi, 2006), 181–97.

Paret, Peter, *Clausewitz and the State* (Oxford University Press, 1976).

The Cognitive Challenge of War: Prussia 1806 (Princeton University Press, 2009).

Paris, Michael, "The First Air Wars – North Africa and the Balkans, 1911–13," *Journal of Contemporary History* 26.1 (1991), 97–109.

Peitsch, Helmut, "Theodor Pliviers *Stalingrad*," *Faschismuskritik und Deutschlandbild*, ed. Christian Fritsch and Lutz Winckler (Berlin: Argument, 1981), 83–102.

"Vom 'Realismus' eines Kriegsromans – 'Unmittelbar', 'Magisch', oder 'Tendenziös'? Walter Kolbenhoff: *Von unserem Fleisch und Blut* (1947)," *Von Böll bis Buchheim. Deutsche Kriegsprosa nach 1945*, ed. Hans Wagener (Amsterdam: Rodopi, 1997), 63–90.

Peitsch, Helmut, Charles Burdett, and Claire Gorrara, eds., *European Memories of the Second World War* (New York: Berghahn Books, 1999).

Phelan, James, *Living to Tell about It: A Rhetoric and Ethics of Character Narration* (Ithaca, NY: Cornell University Press, 2005).

Piette, Adam, *Imagination at War: British Fiction and Poetry, 1939–1945* (London: Papermac, 1995).

Piper, Don, "Soviet Union," *The Second World War in Fiction*, ed. Holger Klein, John Flower, and Eric Homberger (London: Macmillan Press, 1984), 131–72.

Piper, Ernst, *Nacht über Europa. Kulturgeschichte des Ersten Weltkriegs* (Berlin: List Taschenbuch, 2014).

Plievier, Theodor, *Stalingrad*, 2nd ed. (Cologne: Kiepenheuer & Witsch, 2011).

Pöhlman, Markus, "Zur Etymologie des totalen Krieges," *An der Schwelle zum totalen Krieg. Die militärische Debatte über den Krieg der Zukunft, 1939–1939*, ed. Stig Förster (Paderborn: Ferdinand Schöningh, 2002), 346–51.

Pong, Beryl, "The Archaeology of Postwar Childhood in Rose Macaulay's *The World My Wilderness*," *Journal of Modern Literature* 37.3 (2014), 92–110.

"Space and Time in the Bombed City: Graham Greene's *The Ministry of Fear* and Elizabeth Bowen's *The Heat of the Day*," *Literary London: Interdisciplinary Studies in the Representation of London* 7.1 (2009), www.literarylondon.org, accessed June 4, 2016.

Powers, Scott M., "Jonathan Littell's *The Kindly Ones*: Evil and the Ethical Limits of the Post-Modern Narrative," *Evil in Contemporary French and Francophone Literature*, ed. Scott M. Powers (Newcastle upon Tyne: Cambridge Scholars Publishing, 2011), 159–202.

Pratt, Mary Louise, "Harm's Way: Language and the Contemporary Arts of War," *PMLA* 124.5 (2009), 1515–31.

Prendergast, Christopher, *The Order of Mimesis: Balzac, Stendhal, Nerval, Flaubert* (Cambridge University Press, 1986).

Preußer, Heinz-Peter, "Regarding and Imagining: Contrived Immediacy of the Allied Bombing Campaign in Photography, Novel and Historiography," *A Nation of Victims? Representations of German Wartime Suffering from 1945 to the Present*, ed. Helmut Schmitz (Amsterdam: Rodopi, 2007), 141–59.

Priestley, J. B., *Three Men in New Suits* (New York: Harper & Brothers Publishers, 1945).

Rachamimov, Iris, "Military Captivity in Two World Wars: Legal Frameworks and Camp Regimes," *The Cambridge History of War*, vol. 4: *War and the Modern World*, ed. Roger Chickering, Dennis Showalter, and Hans van de Ven (Cambridge University Press, 2012), 214–35.

Radvan, Florian, "Nachwort," *Die Stalinorgel*, by Gert Ledig (Frankfurt am Main: Suhrkamp, 2003), 203–29.

Rapoport, Anatol, "Introduction," *On War*, by Carl von Clausewitz, ed. Anatol Rapoport (London: Penguin, 1982), 11–80.

Rasson, Luc, "How Nazis Undermine Their Own Point of View," *Writing the Holocaust Today: Critical Perspectives on Jonathan Littell's The Kindly Ones*, ed. Aurélie Barjonet and Liran Razinsky (Amsterdam: Rodopi, 2012), 97–110.

"Le narrateur SS a-t-il lu Sade?," *Paroles de salauds: Max Aue et cie*, ed. Luc Rasson (Amsterdam: Rodopi, 2013), 103–13.

Rau, Petra, "The Common Frontier: Fictions of Alterity in Elizabeth Bowen's *The Heat of the Day* and Graham Greene's *The Ministry of Fear*," *Literature and History* 14.1 (2005), 31–55.

Rawlinson, Mark, *British Writing of the Second World War* (New York University Press, 2000).

Razinsky, Liran, "We Are All the Same: Max Aue, Interpreter of Evil," *Yale French Studies* 121 (2012), 140–54.

Rehfeldt, Martin, "Archiv und Inszenierung. Zur Bedeutung der Autorinszenierung für Walter Kempowskis *Das Echolot* und Benjamin von Stuckrad-Barres *Soloalbum*," *Walter Kempowski. Bürgerliche Repräsentanz, Erinnerungskultur, Gegenwartsbewältigung*, ed. Lutz Hagestedt (Berlin: De Gruyter, 2010), 369–90.

Reid, J. H., "From 'Bekenntnis zur Trümmerliteratur' to Frauen vor Flußlandschaft: Art, Power and the Aesthetics of Ruins," *University of Dayton Review* 24.3 (1997), 35–48.

"*Draußen vor der Tür* in Context," *Modern Languages: Journal of the Modern Language Association* 61 (1980), 184–90.

Renger, Reinhard, "'Der Engel schwieg': Heinrich Bölls erster Roman," *Kultur-Chronik* 10.6 (1992), 18–21.

Resnais, Alain, director, *Hiroshima mon amour* (Neuilly sur Seine: Argos Films, 1959), www.amazon.com/Hiroshima-mon-amour-English-Subtitled/dp/B00 ZRCAG3M/ref=sr_1_1?keywords=hiroshima+mon+amour&qid=15585167 54&s=instant-video&sr=8-1, accessed September 1, 2018.

Rhodes, Richard, *Masters of Death: The SS-Einsatzgruppen and the Invention of the Holocaust* (New York: Vintage Books, 2003).

Richter, Hans Werner, *Die Geschlagenen* (Munich: Deutscher Taschenbuch Verlag, 1969).

Riggan, William, *Pícaros, Madmen, Naïfs, and Clowns: The Unreliable First-Person Narrator* (Norman, OK: University of Oklahoma Press, 1981).

Rigney, Ann, "All This Happened, More or Less: What a Novelist Made of the Bombing of Dresden," *History and Theory* 48.2 (2009), 5–24.

Rohrwasser, Michael, "Theodor Plieviers Kriegsbilder," *Schuld und Sühne? Kriegserlebnis und Kriegsdeutung in deutschen Medien der Nachkriegszeit (1945–1961)*, ed. Ursula Heukenkamp (Amsterdam: Rodopi, 2001), 139–53.

Roland, Hubert, and Judith Schneiberg, "Hermann Kasacks Nachkriegsroman *Die Stadt hinter dem Strom* (1947). Versuch einer ethischen Deutung," *Literarische Mikrokosmen. Begrenzung und Entgrenzung/Les microcosmes littéraires: Limites et ouvertures*, ed. Christian Drösch, Hubert Roland, and Stephanie Vanasten (Brussels: Presses Interuniversitaires Européennes (P.I.E.)/Peter Lang, 2006), 123–46.

Rosen, Jules, "The Persistence of Traumatic Memories in World War II Prisoners of War," *Journal of the American Geriatrics Society* 57.12 (2009), 2346–47.

Roth, Philip, *The American Trilogy, 1997–2000: American Pastoral, I Married a Communist, The Human Stain* (New York: Library of America, 2011).

Rothberg, Michael, *Traumatic Realism: The Demands of Holocaust Representation* (Minneapolis, MN: University of Minnesota Press, 2000).

Rupp, Gerhard, "Zweiter Weltkrieg im Drama. Literarhistorischer Kontext und schülerische Lebenswelt am Beispiel von Wolfgang Borchert, Günther Weisenborn und Carl Zuckmayer," *Deutsche Dramen. Interpretationen zu Werken von der Aufklärung bis zur Gegenwart*, vol. 2: *Von Hauptmann bis Botho Strauss*, ed. Harro Müller-Michaels (Königstein: Athenäum, 1981), 85–111.

Ryan, Judith, *The Uncompleted Past: Postwar German Novels and the Third Reich* (Detroit, MI: Wayne State University Press, 1983).

Saint-Amour, Paul K., *Tense Future: Modernism, Total War, Encyclopedic Form* (New York: Oxford University Press, 2015).

Santiáñez, Nil, *Investigaciones literarias: Modernidad, historia de la literatura y modernismos* (Barcelona: Crítica, 2002).

Sauer, Fritz Joachim, "Der Luftkrieg der Literatur," *Sprache – Literatur – Kultur. Text im Kontext*, ed. Bo Andersson, Gernot Müller, and Dessislava Stoeva-Holm (Uppsala University, 2010), 263–77.

Scarry, Elaine, *The Body in Pain: The Making and Unmaking of the World* (Oxford University Press, 1985).

Schaffer, Ronald, "The Bombing Campaigns in World War II: The European Theater," *Bombing Civilians: A Twentieth-Century History*, ed. Yuki Tanaka and Marilyn B. Young (New York: New Press, 2009), 8–29.

Schmitt, Carl, *The Concept of the Political*, trans. George Schwab, expanded ed. (University of Chicago Press, 2007).

The Nomos of the Earth in the International Law of the Jus Publicum Europaeum, trans. G. L. Ulmen (New York: Telos, 2003).

Theory of the Partisan: Intermediate Commentary on the Concept of the Political, trans. G. L. Ulmen (New York: Telos, 2007).

Writings on War, trans. and ed. Timothy Nunan (Cambridge: Polity, 2011).

Schmitz, Helmut, ed., *A Nation of Victims? Representations of German Wartime Suffering from 1945 to the Present* (Amsterdam: Rodopi, 2007).

Schmitz, Helmut, and Annette Seidel-Arpaci, eds., *Narratives of Trauma: Discourses of German Wartime Suffering in National and International Perspective* (Amsterdam: Rodopi, 2011).

Schmollinger, Annette, "Leben im Angesicht des Todes. Anmerkungen zu Hermann Kasacks Roman *Die Stadt hinter dem Strom*," *Die totalitäre Erfahrung. Deutsche Literatur und Drittes Reich*, ed. Frank-Lothar Kroll (Berlin: Duncker & Humblot, 2003), 235–66.

Schumacher, Frank, "'Niederbrennen, plündern und töten sollt ihr.' Der Kolonialkrieg der USA auf den Philippinen (1899–1913)," *Kolonialkriege. Militärische Gewalt im Zeichen des Imperialismus*, ed. Thoralf Klein and Frank Schumacher (Hamburg: Hamburger Edition, 2006), 109–44.

Schütz, Herbert, *Hermann Kasack: The Role of the Critical Intellect in the Creative Writer's Work* (Frankfurt am Main: Peter Lang, 1972).

Schwab, Gabriele, *Haunting Legacies: Violent Histories and Transgenerational Trauma* (New York: Columbia University Press, 2010).

Scullion, Rosemarie, "Writing and Resistance in Louis-Ferdinand Céline's *Féerie pour une autre fois* I," *Esprit créateur* 38.3 (1998), 28–39.

Sebald, W. G., *Luftkrieg und Literatur. Mit einem Essay zu Alfred Andersch*, 5th ed. (Frankfurt am Main: Fischer, 2005).

"Zwischen Geschichte und Naturgeschichte. Versuch über die literarische Beschreibung totaler Zerstörung mit Anmerkungen zu Kasack, Nossack und Kluge," *Orbis Litterarum: International Review of Literary Studies* 37.4 (1982), 345–66.

Seidel Arpaci, Annette, "Lost in Translations? The Discourse of 'German Suffering' and W. G. Sebald's *Luftkrieg und Literatur*," *A Nation of Victims? Representations of German Wartime Suffering from 1945 to the Present*, ed. Helmut Schmitz (Amsterdam: Rodopi, 2007), 161–79.

Selden, Mark, "A Forgotten Holocaust: U.S. Bombing Strategy, the Destruction of Japanese Cities, and the American Way of War from the Pacific War to Iraq," *Bombing Civilians: A Twentieth-Century History*, ed. Yuki Tanaka and Marilyn B. Young (New York: New Press, 2009), 77–96.

Semprun, Jorge, *Literature or Life*, trans. Linda Coverdale (New York: Penguin, 1997).

Sevin, Dieter H., *Individuum und Staat. Das Bild des Soldaten in der Romantrilogie Theodor Plieviers* (Bonn: Bouvier, 1972).

Shahan, Cyrus, "Less than Bodies: Cellular Knowledge and Alexander Kluge's 'The Air Raid on Halberstadt on 8 April 1945'," *Germanic Review* 85.4 (2010), 340–58.

Shandley, Robert R., *Rubble Films: German Cinema in the Shadow of the Third Reich* (Philadelphia, PA: Temple University Press, 2001).

Shankman, S., "God, Ethics, and the Novel: Dostoevsky and Vasily Grossman," *Neohelicon* 42.2 (2015), 371–87.

Shapiro, Stephen A., "Henry Green's *Back*: The Presence of the Past," *Critique: Studies in Contemporary Fiction* 7 (1964), 87–96.

Shay, Jonathan, *Odysseus in America: Combat Trauma and the Trials of Homecoming* (New York: Scribner, 2002).

Shepley, Nick, *Henry Green: Class, Style, and the Everyday* (Oxford University Press, 2016).

Sherman, Kenneth, "Vasily Grossman's Treblinka," *Brick* 82 (2009), 138–46.

Sherman, Nancy, *Afterwar: Healing the Moral Wounds of Our Soldiers* (New York: Oxford University Press, 2015).

Sherry, Vincent, *The Great War and the Language of Modernism* (New York: Oxford University Press, 2006).

Sherry, Vincent, ed., *The Cambridge History of Modernism* (Cambridge University Press, 2017).

Sloterdijk, Peter, *Terror from the Air*, trans. Amy Patton and Steve Corcoran (Los Angeles: Semiotext(e), 2009).

Smith, Sidonie, and Julia Watson, *Reading Autobiography: A Guide for Interpreting Life Narratives* (Minneapolis, MN: University of Minnesota Press, 2001).

Snape, Ray, "Plaster Saints, Flesh and Blood Sinners: Graham Greene's *The End of the Affair*," *Durham University Journal* 74.2 (1982), 241–50.

Snyder, Timothy, *Bloodlands: Europe between Hitler and Stalin* (New York: Basic Books, 2010).

Sontag, Susan, *Regarding the Pain of Others* (New York: Picador, 2003).

Speed, N., B. Engdahl, B. Schwartz, and R. Eberly, "Post-Traumatic Stress Disorder as a Consequence of the POW Experience," *Journal of Nervous and Mental Disease* 117.3 (1989), 147–53.

Speier, Hans, "The Social Types of War," *American Journal of Sociology* 46.4 (1941), 445–54.

Sprinker, Michael, ed., *Ghostly Demarcations: A Symposium on Jacques Derrida's Specters of Marx* (London: Verso, 1999).

Stašková, Alice, "Transfigurations d'un procès: Les narrataires céliniens dans *Féerie pour une autre fois* I," *Classicisme de Céline*, ed. André Derval (Paris: Société d'Etudes Céliniennes, 1999), 339–54.

Steiner, George, *Language & Silence: Essays on Language, Literature, and the Inhuman* (New Haven, CT: Yale University Press, 1998).

Stevenson, Randall, *Literature and the Great War, 1914–1918* (Oxford University Press, 2013).

Stewart, Victoria, "The Auditory Uncanny in Wartime London: Graham Greene's *The Ministry of Fear*," *Textual Practice* 18.1 (2004), 65–81.

Narratives of Memory: British Writing of the 1940s (New York: Palgrave Macmillan, 2006).

Stone, David R., "Operations on the Eastern Front, 1941–1945," *The Cambridge History of the Second World War*, ed. John Ferris and Evan Mawdsley, vol. 1/3 (Cambridge University Press, 2015), 331–57.

Stonebridge, Lyndsey, "Bombs and Roses: The Writing of Anxiety in Henry Green's *Caught*," *Diacritics: A Review of Contemporary Criticism* 28.4 (1998), 25–43.

"Theories of Trauma," *The Cambridge Companion to the Literature of World War II*, ed. Marina MacKay (Cambridge University Press, 2009), 194–206.

The Writing of Anxiety: Imagining Wartime in Mid-Century British Culture (New York: Palgrave Macmillan, 2007).

Stotesbury, John A., "A Postcolonial Reading of Metropolitan Space in Graham Greene's *The End of the Affair*," *London in Literature: Visionary Mappings of the Metropolis*, ed. Susana Onega and John A. Stotesbury (Heidelberg: Universitätsverlag Carl Winter, 2002), 107–21.

Stout, Janis P., *Coming Out of War: Poetry, Grieving, and the Culture of the World Wars* (Tuscaloosa, AL: University of Alabama Press, 2005).

Strachan, Hew, *Carl von Clausewitz's On War: A Biography* (New York: Atlantic Monthly Press, 2006).

Streim, Gregor, "Der Bombenkrieg als Sensation und als Dokumentation. Gert Ledigs Roman *Vergeltung* und die Debatte um W. G. Sebalds *Luftkrieg und Literatur*," *Krieg in den Medien*, ed. Heinz-Peter Preußer (Amsterdam: Rodopi, 2005), 293–312.

"Germans in the *Lager*. Reports and Narratives About Imprisonments in Post-War Allied Internment Camps," *A Nation of Victims? Representations of German Wartime Suffering from 1945 to the Present*, ed. Helmut Schmitz (Amsterdam: Rodopi, 2007), 31–49.

Suleiman, Susan Rubin, "Performing a Perpetrator as Witness: Jonathan Littell's *Les Bienveillantes*," *After Testimony: The Ethics and Aesthetics of Holocaust Narrative for the Future*, ed. Jakob Lothe, Susan Rubin Suleiman, and James Phelan (Columbus, OH: Ohio State University Press, 2012), 99–119.

"When the Perpetrator Becomes a Reliable Witness of the Holocaust: On Jonathan Littell's *Les Bienveillantes*," *New German Critique: An Interdisciplinary Journal of German Studies* 106 (2009), 1–19.

Swofford, Anthony, "*Full Metal Jacket* Seduced My Generation and Sent Us to War," *The New York Times Magazine* (August 18, 2018), www.nytimes.com/2018/04/18/magazine/full-metal-jacket-ermey-marine-corps.html, accessed October 8, 2018.

Jarhead: A Marine's Chronicle of the Gulf War and Other Battles (New York: Scribner, 2003).

Tachibana, Reiko, "The Japanese War," *The Cambridge Companion to the Literature of World War II*, ed. Marina MacKay (Cambridge University Press, 2009), 137–48.

Narrative as Counter-Memory: A Half-Century of Postwar Writing in Germany and Japan (Albany, NY: State University of New York Press, 1998).

Takayoshi, Ichiro, *American Writers and the Approach of World War II, 1935–1941: A Literary History* (Cambridge University Press, 2015).

Tanaka, Yuki, and Marilyn B. Young, eds., *Bombing Civilians: A Twentieth-Century History* (New York: New Press, 2009).

Teekell, Anna, "Elizabeth Bowen and Language at War," *New Hibernia Review/ Iris Éireannach Nua: A Quarterly Record of Irish Studies* 15.3 (2011), 61–79.

Thiher, Allen, *Céline: The Novel as Delirium* (New Brunswick, NJ: Rutgers University Press, 1972).

"*Féerie pour une autre fois*: Mythe et modernisme," *La Revue des Lettres Modernes* 560–564 (1979), 107–21.

Thurston, Luke, *Literary Ghosts from the Victorians to Modernism: The Haunting Interval* (London: Routledge, 2012).

Tillman, Barrett, *Whirlwind: The Air War against Japan, 1942–1945* (New York: Simon & Schuster, 2010).

Timm, Uwe, *Am Beispiel meines Bruders*, 4th ed. (Munich: Deutscher Taschenbuch Verlag, 2007).

Tomko, Helena M., "Böll's War: Catholic Inner Immigration, Apocalyptic Dystopia, and 'Stunde Null'," *German Life and Letters* 67.3 (2014), 358–77.

Traverso, Enzo, "Prologue. 1914–1945: Le monde au prisme de la guerre," *1937–1947: La guerre-monde*, ed. Alya Aglan and Robert Frank, vol. 1/2 (Paris: Gallimard, 2015), 23–58.

Treat, John Whittier, "Hiroshima and the Place of the Narrator," *Journal of Asian Studies* 48.1 (1989), 29–49.

Pools of Water, Pillars of Fire: The Literature of Ibuse Masuji (Seattle, WA: University of Washington Press, 1988).

Writing Ground Zero: Japanese Literature and the Atomic Bomb (University of Chicago Press, 1995).

Truman, Harry S., "Statement by the President Announcing the Use of the A-Bomb at Hiroshima," The American Presidency Project, 1999–2017, www.presidency.ucsb.edu/ws/?pid=1216, accessed August 6, 2017.

Turse, Nick, *Kill Anything That Moves: The Real American War in Vietnam* (New York: Metropolitan Books, 2013).

Valla, Jean-Claude, *La France sous les bombes américaines, 1942–1945* (Paris: Éditions de la Librairie Nationale, 2001).

van Creveld, Martin, *The Changing Face of War: Combat from the Marne to Iraq* (New York: Presidio Press, 2008).

Vandervort, Bruce, *Wars of Imperial Conquest in Africa, 1830–1914* (Bloomington, IN: Indiana University Press, 1998).

Vees-Gulani, Susanne, "Diagnosing Billy Pilgrim: A Psychiatric Approach to Kurt Vonnegut's *Slaughterhouse-Five*," *Critique: Studies in Contemporary Fiction* 44.2 (2003), 175–84.

Trauma and Guilt: Literature of Wartime Bombing in Germany (Berlin: De Gruyter, 2003).

Voinovich, Vladimir, "The Life and Fate of Vasily Grossman and His Novel," *Survey: A Journal of East & West Studies* 29.1 (1985), 186–89.

Vonnegut, Kurt, *Slaughterhouse-Five, or, The Children's Crusade: A Duty-Dance with Death* (New York: Dell Publishing, 1991).

Waldmeir, Joseph J., *American Novels of the Second World War* (The Hague: Mouton & Co., 1969).

Waller, Willard, *The Veteran Comes Back* (New York: Dryden Press, 1944).

Walsh, Jeffrey, *American War Literature, 1914 to Vietnam* (New York: St. Martin's Press, 1982).

Wasson, Sara, *Urban Gothic of the Second World War: Dark London* (New York: Palgrave Macmillan, 2010).

Watson, Barbara Bellow, "Variations on an Enigma: Elizabeth Bowen's War Novel," *Southern Humanities Review* 15.2 (1981), 131–51.

Watts, Philip, "An Introduction to Céline," *Fiction* 12.1 (1994), 35–54.

Waugh, Evelyn, *Sword of Honor* (New York: Back Bay Books, 2012).

Wehler, Hans-Ulrich, "'Absoluter' und 'totaler' Krieg. Von Clausewitz zu Ludendorff," *Politische Vierteljahresschrift* 19 (1969), 220–48.

Weidauer, Friedemann, "Sollen wir ihn reinlassen? Wolfgang Borcherts *Draußen vor der Tür* in neuen Kontexten," *German Life and Letters* 59.1 (2006), 122–39.

White, Hayden, *The Content of the Form: Narrative Discourse and Historical Representation* (Baltimore, MD: Johns Hopkins University Press, 1987).

Wilms, Wilfried, and William Rasch, eds., *Bombs Away! Representing the Air War over Europe and Japan* (Amsterdam: Rodopi, 2006).

Wilson, Sloan, *The Man in the Gray Flannel Suit* (New York: Thunder's Mouth Press, 2002).

Winn, James Anderson, *The Poetry of War* (Cambridge University Press, 2008).

Winter, Jay, *Sites of Memory, Sites of Mourning: The Great War in European Cultural History* (Cambridge University Press, 1998).

Wittgenstein, Ludwig, *Philosophical Investigations*, trans. G. E. M. Anscombe, 2nd ed. (Oxford: Blackwell Publishers, 1997).

Tractatus Logico-Philosophicus, trans. D. F. Pears and B. F. McGuinness (London: Routledge, 2001).

Wood, David, *What Have We Done: The Moral Injury of Our Longest Wars* (New York: Little, Brown and Company, 2016).

Wright, Gordon, *The Ordeal of Total War, 1939–1945* (New York: Harper & Row, 1968).

Zimmerer, Jürgen, "Krieg, KZ und Völkermord in Südwestafrika. Der erste deutsche Genozid," *Völkermord in Deutsch-Südwestafrika. Der Kolonialkrieg (1904–1908) in Namibia und seine Folgen*, ed. Joachim Zeller and Jürgen Zimmerer (Berlin: Ch. Links, 2003), 45–63.

Zimmering, Max, *Phosphor und Flieder. Vom Untergang und Wiederaufstieg der Stadt Dresden* (Berlin: Dietz, 1954).

Zimmermann-Thiel, Gisela, "'Echolot': A Warning," *Kultur-Chronik* 12.4 (1994), 4–8.

Žižek, Slavoj, *Tarrying with the Negative: Kant, Hegel, and the Critique of Ideology* (Durham, NC: Duke University Press, 1993).

Index

For EU product safety concerns, contact us at Calle de José Abascal, 56–1°,
28003 Madrid, Spain or eugpsr@cambridge.org.

www.ingramcontent.com/pod-product-compliance
Ingram Content Group UK Ltd.
Pitfield, Milton Keynes, MK11 3LW, UK
UKHW010250140625
459647UK00013BA/1767